Best wishes of

Stephen Morrow Wilson

The Commoner

William Jennings Bryan

BY CHARLES MORROW WILSON

The Commoner William Jennings Bryan

DOUBLEDAY & COMPANY, INC.

GARDEN CITY, NEW YORK

1970

Contents

List of Illustrations

All photographs, unless otherwise credited, are courtesy of the Nebraska State Historical Society, with special thanks to Mrs. Louise Small, Librarian

DEDICATION

TO WILLIAM JENNINGS BRYAN, JR.

Acknowledgments

I am deeply and lastingly appreciative of the help and encouragement provided by Samuel S. Vaughan, Marc Haefele, Karen Van Westering and other friends at Doubleday. I am also grateful for the many courtesies of the staff of the New York Public Library, including permission to make use of the Frederick Lewis Allen Authors' Room.

1. The Fence Breaker

During the summer of 1861 Judge Silas Bryan and his wife Mariah of Salem, Illinois, gave a great deal of time and thought to keeping their first son from breaking through or crawling under the yardway fence and communing with the world beyond.

By the calendar, William Jennings Bryan was a toddler; as the first summer of the Civil War began, Willy (as his mother usually spelled the name) was fifteen months old. By sprinting standards, as a one-to-five-yard dasher the child was already prodigiously impressive. His mother confided to her sister that the big-headed, blockily built boy could already move like a storm wind and that his effectiveness at breaking through or under picket fences was almost unique. And when anyone left a gate open, Willy was through it like a shot cat.

For at least two reasons, this gift was not good. Although Salem was the county seat of Marion County, it remained a farmers' village and an open-range or free-grazing municipality with an estimated one thousand people and, according to the going estimate, at least two thousand freely roaming cattle, horses, hogs, and other livestock. Included were less than docile stallions, boars, and prolific sows, the last frequently trailing litters of pigs which they would defend aggressively against meddlers or competitors of whatever species. Also, Silas and Mariah Bryan were well aware that their son exhibited, along with excessive curiosity, an irrepressible fondness for practically all forms of animal life, including people.

The Bryans were expecting again. About four years earlier, Mariah had lost her first child, a daughter, at birth, and although their second daughter, Frances, twenty-seven months older than Willy, had lived and was even then helping to keep her younger brother within the fence, Mariah was in no condition to have the living daylights scared out of her. Nor was Silas disposed to endure the risk of having his first begotten son gored by a strolling bull or bitten by an officious, pig-leading sow, or stepped on by a footloose horse.

Silas Bryan took his young son's fence breaking as a personal challenge. Less than five years before he had built that yardway fence with his own hands, to keep livestock out and children in. And none who knew Silas Bryan well could doubt either his competence as a fence builder or as a doer of what he believed to be right.

Back on the old Bryan "homestead" near Sperryville, in Culpeper, now Rappahannock County, Virginia, some forty miles across the mountains from Edom (homeland of the first Abraham Lincoln, grandfather of the newly elected President of the United States), Silas Bryan had begun building fences at an exceptionally early age. When he was fourteen, following the death of both his parents, the slender, frail-looking youngster had set forth to make his own way west. In the beginning, the west turned out to be northeastern Missouri, where Silas first found shelter as what he later called a "helpful boy on farms." Later, in southern Illinois, the grim-looking young Virginian found regular employment as a farm hand.

There he came to excel as a fence builder, rail splitter, and what he termed a rough carpenter. "Before I was twenty," Silas recounted, "I had felled, split, and set up more fencing rails than the grandson of *the* Abraham Lincoln ever got close to." Long before he reached man's age, Willy Bryan's father had mastered the multiple techniques and strategies of building fences—with stones, rails, boards, pickets, and eventually, wire. He had also, rather literally, fenced his way through college.

At twenty-three, after having managed a very few terms of country schooling, the young and never hardy emigrant from Virginia tramped on to Lebanon, Illinois, where he entered and worked his way through the five years of McKendrie Baptist College.

McKendrie was a poor and believing school, typical of the frontier church-sponsored "colleges" of its era. While there Silas Bryan became a duly converted Baptist and had his sins washed away by total immersion. He remained a devout Baptist for the rest of his life; a friend of the poor, a determined temperance worker, a legislator, judge, and church leader, and an irrepressible moralist. His world was one of good and bad; his chosen mission was that of differentiating between the right and the wrong, serving the right and preventing the wrong.

Following graduation, the serious and frail young man set out afoot to find work. The quest led him into the lower fringe of Illinois, then known as Little Egypt. At the village of Walnut Grove he met a friendly farmer, school board member, and Methodist singing master named Charles Jennings, who told him that the local school was in need of a teacher.

When Silas pointed out that there was nothing wrongful about earning one's living by the "sweat of one's face," Charlie Jennings, as a hard working, freely sweating farmer agreed, but he added that there was nothing wrong and much right about taking over a teacherless school when one had the qualifications to do so. Jennings said that the one-room "all-grades" district school was of special interest to him because, quite aside from being a board member, he was the father of six girls and two boys who were or would be presently enrolled in the school. A board meeting was scheduled at the local Methodist Church; he suggested that Silas come along and show his face. The "right" teacher would be well paid— four dollars a week plus keep—and board and room "rotated" among local residents.

From the first, so he later admitted, Silas liked the idea. He knew that his health was probably not adequate for sustained farm labor. But there were considerations of righteousness to be heeded, as well. "I'm a Baptist," he explained. "If I should teach, I'd feel faith bound to open each school day with prayer."

Jennings saw no grounds for objection. He and his people happened to be Methodists, though certainly this was also Baptist country, and nobody stood against Christian prayer and principles. Charlie Jennings added that his grandfather, Israel Jennings, who had pioneered from Kentucky, was an old-style country missionary and church founder who also had served in the state legislature. People had called this Illinois first settler "the Christian statesman."

Silas Bryan explained that he, too, would like to be a Christian statesman. He was already a Democrat. Jennings could and did point out that the Jenningses had been an unbroken line of Democrats since the time of Thomas Jefferson. Jennings added that he would feel honored to keep Silas in his home for the first term of school, and that as choir leader for the local Methodist Church, a specialist in hymns, and a singing teacher by hobby, he offered *gratis* singing lessons to anyone wishing them, not excepting Baptists.

That was how Silas Bryan became a country schoolteacher and how he eventually made his entry into politics. He tried hard to be a good teacher, but poor health turned out to be a dogging impediment to his beginning career. After several sieges of illness that he described as bilious colic, Silas was, as he put it, blessed by a saving grace. She was Mr. Jennings' fourth, and some said prettiest, daughter, Mariah, who was then fifteen and newly admitted to the top class—by contemporary equivalents, the sixth grade—of the district school. Mariah was also the best cook in the Jennings household. Without coaxing, she undertook to prepare a health-restoring diet for the new schoolmaster.

Silas Bryan began to recover from his violent seizures of indigestion, to excel as a schoolteacher, and to love his bright and attractive pupil and cook.

After the close of his second year of teaching, Bryan also managed to pass the Illinois State Bar examination. Almost immediately he announced his candidacy for the State Senate.

Charlie Jennings was amused when his No. 4 daughter explained what Silas Bryan's platform would be. Silas would stand for the poor rent-farmers of the area; he would sponsor a law to set up state-supported libraries in all towns, and he would advocate the lawful closing of saloons. Charlie Jennings personally favored the proposed planks, but he doubted that his favorite schoolmaster had any real chance of winning the election. Marion and adjoining counties usually went Whig; certainly no Democrat had ever dared stand simultaneously against the landowners and mortgage handlers, the salon keepers, and in favor of free public libraries, which many voters still regarded as sinful.

But Silas Bryan believed in his causes. In patched clothes and with a customarily thin purse, the tall and serious schoolmaster set out afoot along the country roads to visit the farm people, leaving both his Whig opponents free to campaign in the towns. When voting day came, Bryan won the State Senate seat by three votes, to the surprise of many. Four years later he won re-election by eight votes.

Between sessions of the legislature Silas completed another two terms of teaching, then set up a law office over a livery stable in Salem. Next he made a down payment on, and as his free time allowed, began rebuilding the little frame house with the neat picket fence—exactly halfway between the box-shaped county courthouse and the newly built railroad depot one mile down the road. He celebrated his thirtieth birthday by marrying Mariah Jennings who, by then, was eighteen. Neighbors agreed that the newlyweds didn't have any great show of a dwelling; the well-built and neatly whitewashed paling fence was probably its most impressive facility.

Many of the Salem neighbors did not see comparable merit in Silas' work in the State Senate. On first taking his seat at Vandalia, the new senator from Marion County assured his fellow senators that he was a peace lover, that he deplored the arising ill feelings between the North and the South, and held that such feelings comprised sacrilege in the sight of God.

In southern Illinois of the 1850s practically nobody remained neutral on the questions that would soon bring war. There were still at least a hundred slaveowners scattered throughout Little Egypt, and there were thousands of voters who believed that anybody who could afford them had the right to own slaves; after all, George Washington had owned slaves, as had Thomas Jefferson. Southern Illinois settlers were divided between comers from the old-line slavery states, particularly Virginia, Kentucky, Maryland, and the Carolinas, and abolitionists or "anti-slaveryites" from New England, Ohio, Michigan, and elsewhere in the newer Midwest.

Young Senator Bryan stated only that he regarded slavery as morally wrong. He also insisted that all war is sinful, and that no armed victory can be morally tenable. His accompanying stands were hardly less unorthodox in terms of political expedience. Silas sought to hold down or reduce all public salaries, including his own. He strongly opposed any form of public indebtedness. During both his Senate terms he failed utterly in his repeated efforts to enact state support of public libraries. His one successful move during his first term consisted of writing and steering to passage a law requiring all members of the Illinois legislature to attend morning prayer services. In his second, he helped effectively with the enactment of a "poor debtor's law" to alleviate the threat of imprisonment for indebtedness.

He puzzled friends and foes alike by his steadfast refusal to remove himself from the Democratic Party, which continued to fare badly throughout his adopted state. In one of his more emotional speeches on the Senate floor, Silas Bryan recounted that he was a born Democrat; a son, grandson, and great-grandson of Democrats; he would live and die a Democrat. There were many who doubted the grim young legislator's real understanding of living. None could reasonably doubt the extensiveness of his acquaintance with dying. Before his fourteenth birthday Silas had been present at the death of two of his elder brothers, three of his grandparents, and both his parents. He had barely won re-election when his first child, Lucinda, died at birth.

Two years later the Bryans' second child, Frances, had been born well and strong. As their way of expressing thanks, both parents had gone even more deeply into church work. Silas had taken the post of deacon for the Salem Baptist Church, while Mariah with her father's expert help had taken over as choir leader for the Salem Methodist Church.

If some of the neighbors thought it odd for a husband and wife to belong to different churches, almost all regarded Silas' next political move as even more odd. During 1859, as the "war fever" grew hotter, the senator for Marion County announced that he would gamble his upcoming campaign for re-election on a plea for peace; that he would "preach" peace throughout his district, his state, and, as opportunity permitted, the nation. His faith and his concept of right held that America could gain allies and friends abroad and earn favor in the sight of God only by stifling and wiping away the terrible image of an approaching civil war. That would call for harder work, more humility, much greater devotion to the will of God. For only in that way could America be saved.

As he began to attract audiences in his one-man crusade for peace, Silas Bryan abruptly dropped his campaign for re-election to the State Senate. He explained matter-of-factly that his "home people" had invited him to serve as judge of the circuit court in his judiciary district; the presiding judge had died lately in office. He would fill out the term and seek regular election to the judgeship the following November. He may have been influenced by the fact that his young wife was again with child so that he felt it was his duty to be with her.

In any case, March 1, 1860 found the determined, early-graying young ex-senator back in Salem. On March 19 (St. Vincent's Day), his first son was born. The delighted parents named him William Jennings Bryan— William for the first Bryan to come to America; Jennings for the mother's "people." "Little did we guess what a terrible fence breaker we were producing," the father soon noted.

Silas Bryan had dropped out of his campaign at a good time. In the 1860 election not one Democrat was returned to the Illinois Senate. As the nominee of the new Republican Party, Abraham Lincoln squeezed into the Presidency of the United States with approximately 1.8 million of the popular vote of about 4.6 million. Silas Bryan, an early veteran of close election counts, was deeply impressed by Lincoln's minority victory. Although the electoral college vote had given Lincoln 180 votes to 123 for his three opponents combined, the tall man from Vandalia and Springfield had not proved impressive as a popular vote winner and, as his downstate Democratic acquaintance saw it, he had not spoken out openly on any principal issue.

By contrast, Silas Bryan waged his campaign for the circuit court judgeship in a region of strong war sentiments as the "Democrat for peace" candidate; he opened every campaign speech with a prayer for peace while his principal opponent trumpeted that the Union must be saved, as need be, by war. Even more remarkably, Silas Bryan again won his campaign, this time with a majority of about fifty votes from about eight thousand cast.

His opponent, possibly foreseeing defeat, had bowed out by enlisting in the Union Army, but there was reason to believe that Judge Bryan had chosen the harder course. The outbreak of the Civil War found southern Illinois torn, full of outrageous and sad paradoxes as brothers set forth to fight brothers, as sons and fathers enlisted in opposing armies. A wave of lawlessness swept over the countryside, making it bristle with robberies, gang fights, and other violence.

In spite of this, the peace-favoring Democrat succeeded in maintaining an impressive objectiveness in judgments. For example, one morning when he discovered that his own smokehouse had been ransacked and all his home-cured hams, shoulders, and bacon sides stolen, Silas declined to prosecute; his court dockets were already crowded with more serious cases.

Judge Bryan differentiated between the judicial obligation to reform and the mere wreaking of vengeance by punishment. He began each court session with prayer and adjourned for prayer before passing sentence. At a time when most American courts were handing down brutally severe sentences, Silas Bryan usually kept with the mildest sentences then permitted by law. Even so, he was frequently seen weeping when announcing them.

Sometimes after his opening prayer Judge Bryan would criticize himself. One entry was a direct apology for his inability to effect enough improvement in the moral rectitude of his fellows, including those close to him. "The sad truth is," he once confessed in open court, "that I do not even appear to be able to keep my fifteen-month-old son from breaking out of the fence that I built myself, and I have thought of myself as a pretty good fence builder."

Throughout the long, war-plagued summer of 1861 Willy kept on breaking through the yardway fence. His parents hoped for normal improvement and encouraged Willy's well-behaved sister, Frances, to aid the cause. But the parents soon had more urgent worries. Early that September when their second son, "little Harry," was born, the judge received a heartbreaking verdict from the doctor, who stated that only a miracle could save the baby, even for a month.

"Then we will pray for a miracle," Silas Bryan replied. He began building an altar in the front room of the little home. Next he bought a small, foot-pumped organ on which Mariah was presently able to "chord" several hymns she had learned from her musically illiterate father. Each morning and evening the Bryans and their two healthy children prayed together for the recovery of the sickly baby.

When Mariah expressed sorrow that Willy could not have a healthy brother as his playmate, Silas answered that their strong son had also to learn that a Bryan's duty was to cherish and care for those weaker than he. In due time Willy would record this with considerable eloquence.

But no miracle occurred. Little Harry did not live through his first month. The neighbors noted that the Bryans expressed their grief in a most unusual way. They began giving a series of dinners to which they invited all the pastors of Salem and other ministers of the entire county.

Next summer—it was Willy's third—saw the youngest Bryan further increasing his fence-bursting prowess. "Any space that's big enough for Willy to get his head through," Mariah wrote her elder sister Margaret Antwerps, "guarantees that he is as good as gone. . . . Willy is good natured but very headstrong and stubborn. . . ."

Silas took the position that their Willy was getting old enough to know better. Having set baseboards around the entire length of the fence, he decreed that Willy would refrain or be rightfully punished. Baseboards or no, Willy kept breaking out. The resulting spankings seemed to have no effect. Judge Bryan next tried tying his young son to a bedpost. That didn't stop him either.

When Silas reflected that the boy would simply not be fenced in, he could not refrain from castigating himself for failure to maintain discipline in his own home. Yet he presently noted, probably with a grim smile, that with Willy by then grown almost the size of his sister, and each wearing similar dark homespun, it was easy at least to tell his offspring apart: Willy was the one to be found on the wrong side of the fence.

During the season that was bloodied by the Battle of Gettysburg, Willy's talents had much greater effect. By then he could break through or over the yardway fence. Despite the vigilance of his sharp-eyed sister, Willy would break free and trot happily through the village, investigating the wandering livestock and, as his mother noted, inspecting backyards and chatting pleasantly with neighbors.

One morning an alarmed housewife interrupted a trial to inform the judge that she had just seen Willy frolicking in her husband's bull pasture. Silas recessed the court and hurried to the rescue. But Willy by then was back home innocently placing stovewood on the back porch. Seconds later Willy was getting what he long remembered as the spanking of his life. But it, too, was less than reformatory.

William Jennings Bryan would later reminisce about these episodes. Well before he was five, he had found the world beyond home fences unendingly alluring.

When word of Lee's surrender came, Silas Bryan, as first deacon of the First Baptist Church, helped to improvise and conduct a succession of interdenominational prayer services. His wife was not able to join him. She was confined, and later that April she bore a stillborn baby, John, her fifth child—the third to die within hours or days of birth.

For the first time he could remember, Willy was deeply grieved. "But it must be right," he told his father, "because God let it be, didn't He?"

"God knows best," his father told him.

Willy was not to suffer loneliness. There soon materialized a near-deluge of incoming cousins and other blood kin. Two of Mariah's elder sisters (Mrs. Antwerps and Mrs. Smith) and two of Silas' younger brothers (John and Russell), all except John with large and growing families, were moving to Salem. John Bryan, the judge's youngest brother, had come to study law. Russell, already the father of seven, was taking over as resident manager of the railway livestock yards directly beyond the new depot. By his sixth birthday Willy had thirty-eight cousins, ranging in age from a few weeks to fourteen or fifteen years, all within ready visiting distance. One undeniable result was that Willy soon bade farewell to privacy. Inevitably, as a robust young male he would be challenged to lead; he would also encounter the instructive experience of being pushed along by the crowd.

Silas Bryan announced that he was obliged to acquire a larger dwelling; his little white house halfway between the courthouse and the depot was no longer big enough to provide his multiplying kin room to sit, much less to sleep. But this was not an abrupt decision. Several years earlier Silas had discreetly begun the purchase of contiguous plots of land near Salem; by 1866 he owned or held option on 501 acres, beginning within a mile of the village limits. At the time his salary was barely one hundred dollars a month, but land was cheap and Silas' credit was excellent. The fact that he double-tithed, 10 percent to his church and 10 percent to his wife's, had not impaired it at all.

The dutiful judge had already shaped plans for building

what he called a Virginia Corinthian mansion near the
center of his newly acquired land holdings. Willy had listened in wide-eyed approval to his father's planning. The
new mansion, to be built of brick, would have ten large
rooms, each with at least four windows. A frontal line of
huge white columns would sentinel two oversize and ban-
istered porches, one above the other. The roof was to be
of dark blue slate, not unlike the color of Willy's eyes.
There would be impressive iron latticework and orna-
mental gingerbreading without.

Within, floors and woodwork of native walnut; silver-
ware of real silver; the chinaware, real procelain. Five of
the rooms were to have fireplaces—with marble hearths
and walnut mantelboards. The guest room would be about
the size of the local Knights of Pythias hall and heated
with an oversize Franklin stove.

The "estate" included at least three renters' farms; Bryan
planned to dignify it with a mile of special roads and
driveways, an impressively large barn, and a hunting preserve, early Virginia style, to include eighty acres of
fenced woodlands stocked with an entire herd of native
deer, specifically no fewer than fourteen.

One may reflect that Silas Bryan was building a long-
classic American paradox. He had unfalteringly represented his political philosophy as being of the "plain"
Jacksonian Democratic orientation. But his grandiose building plans were not easily correlated with the virtues of
plain living. Quite probably, Silas Bryan was looking back
into the mirror of his moderately impoverished boyhood.
The first American Bryans, William and John, had owned
a small farm back in Ireland. They sold the farm in 1765,
emigrated to the Virginia Tidewater, worked briefly as
plantation foremen, and probably in 1768 or 1769 traveled to Sperryville. Near that community the Bryan brothers bought small farms and built themselves log cabins.
Directly thereafter they merged their plots and joined in
building a modest two-family farm home.

Subsequently the Bryans bought additional farm lands and developed what Silas Bryan termed a respectable homestead. The American-born Bryans who followed were hard-working and of medium prosperity. This writer finds no records of any of the lineage having been slave owners. Silas Bryan, one of a third generation of the Virginia-born Bryans, was the eldest surviving son of one of the poorer branches of the family. At the time of his birth, 1822, the Sperryville countryside was preponderantly populated by yeomen of modest means or land owners who practiced family and subsistence-style farming. At the time there were, however, at least three plantation mansions within walking distance of the home of the second William Bryan.

Silas probably remembered these; almost certainly he remembered clearly the McCollister mansion of Sperryville. The country home he planned for himself and his own family showed distinct but not flattering similarities to the early-nineteenth-century McCollister place in his native countryside. There was *ipso facto* evidence that Silas Bryan continued to regard the country mansion or gentleman's estate as a hallmark of success and eminence, indeed, that at least in private he looked on a man's home not only as his castle but also as his earthly monument. There was broader evidence that he was also following in the somewhat paradoxical wake of his two Democratic heroes, Thomas Jefferson and Andrew Jackson, both men with mansions—and intermittent personal poverty, as well as compassion for the poor.

As it took form, the Bryan mansion grew big but less than beautiful. Long before completion, its architectural imitativeness became a parody. Showplace or no, the Bryan "estate" looked like a much-vented shoebox built of brick. Even so, from his first sight of it Willy believed the unusual structure to be imposing and prestigious; in time he, too, would be a builder of large, cockeyed residential monuments.

About three weeks before Willy's sixth birthday another and more conventional blessing came to the Bryans—the birth of a sixth child, another son. Russell was a small, frail baby who required special care. Even so, the new arrival survived.

By late May 1866, the big country house was ready for occupancy. As a gracious preliminary, Silas and Mariah joined in deeding the little frame house and its furnishings to John Bryan, the Judge's neediest brother, who had helped manfully with building and outfitting the new mansion. The actual moving therefore required little more than a twenty-minute walk from the cottage to the mansion.

Having effected the generous gift to his youngest brother, Silas Bryan set out on what would be an unending marathon of frugality. He had borrowed most of the money for building and furnishing the mansion; further loose spending simply could not be tolerated.

What a local history would term "the showplace of the greater Salem community" was almost as devoid of conveniences as a hastily raised pioneer's cabin. Water for household and barnyard uses had to be drawn and toted from newly dug wells. There were no servants; Mariah planned to do all the housekeeping, cooking, and laundry. Her father, by then a widower, had agreed to live in the big "grandparents' room" upstairs and help with the chores, including the huge task of chopping and fetching in wood for the Franklin stove, the cook stove, and the five fireplaces.

Charlie Jennings hoped that he would be able to carry on until Willy grew big enough to take over. Certainly Silas would not be available for attending to the daily chores. As the circuit judge he could not expect to spend more than two or, at most, three nights a week at home; his judiciary circuit included five county seats besides Salem. He proposed to be as helpful as possible in and about his own home but conceded that his official duties held first lien on his working time. He believed in hard, dedicated work. Accepting that there can be no excellence without great labor, Silas Bryan righteously sought excellence.

2. The Boy Believer

Willy Bryan was plunged virtuously and progressively into an unrelenting grind of household and farm work. His initial light chores, such as feeding the chickens, cleaning and refilling the oil lamps, fetching in water, and helping with the weekly all-day washing, were rapidly expanded to include feeding and watering the horses, hogs, cattle, and miscellaneous livestock, not excepting the obese penned deer—which turned out to be his most precarious duty.

Within another year he was taking an increasing part in the back-straining task of helping to chop, stack, and carry in firewood. Before he was nine, Willy took over the duty of building and keeping fires in the Franklin stove in the big front room. Silas Bryan viewed his son's progress at woodcutting with approval. "Willy can't sing. He's not worth a whoop on any musical instrument. But with an ax or crosscut saw that boy is learning to make real music!"

Clearly, Willy was learning much besides that. He was learning to like animals; his warm affection for chickens, hogs, cattle, and horses was to be a lifelong attribute. He did not like housework. Though he was given a room of his own on condition that he keep it swept and tidy, he apparently grew into a lifelong disdain for the conventions of neatness. When not in use, his clothing usually reclined dissolutely on the floor; his papers, books, and toys were in disorderly piles. This enjoyment of spontaneous and self-perpetuating disorder was also to endure for life.

The same held true of his feeling for the producing earth. During his seventh and eighth summers, Willy planted and tended a pumpkin bed directly beyond the new barnyard; its yields resulted in his first recorded ambition—to be a grower of pumpkins so magnificent that they would win prizes at the Marion County fair. As far back as he could remember, the Bryan boy was profoundly confident that the same Almighty God who had made him would permit, encourage, and reward the growing of grand-champion pumpkins.

"That Willy is already a true, deep believer," his mother noted thoughtfully. His father agreed that the hard work was strengthening his son's faith as well as his body and, quite reasonably, his mind. As a moralist, Silas Bryan believed wholeheartedly in the virtues of hard work as the only, sure way to salvation. Silas' first son agreed, at least in retrospect. Yet from the fragmentary diversity of early records, one gathers that William Jennings Bryan agreed not so much as a student or teacher of morals as a fundamentalist, an unquestioning believer in an absolute, diligence-advocating God.

Along with this vigorous and placid God-belief, Willy was developing a no less impressive physical strength. By his eighth birthday, an apparent correlation between strength of body and of faith was materializing. Willy's propensities for hard work and intense beliefs appeared for a time to match Silas Bryan's devoutness as a Baptist. Yet when the youngster went with his father to a baptismal service being held at nearby Bois d'Arc Creek, he was terrified at the sight of the penitents being dunked bodily in the chilly, muddy water. When he asked if a Baptist preacher would have to be so vehemently dipped under, his father said yes, explaining that baptism was an obligation of the creed, symbolizing the washing away of sin and rebirth as a cleansed child of God. Abruptly and permanently, Willy's interest in becoming a Baptist preacher faded. From that time on (circa 1869–70), although his religious environment was still strong, one can note a distinct dimming of sectarian interest. Willy Bryan was showing a strengthening disposition to believe in God, a dramatically powerful, never-waning God, rather than in specific creeds of His real or purported worshipers.

Silas Bryan sought still greater stature as a moralist and, to rationalize his existence as a crusader, in Christian righteousness. In this Silas could not and did not argue that Jesus the Christ had either practiced or advocated dwelling in a mansion, but he contended fervently that he and his wife were at least using their earthly palace in a self-sustaining Christian spirit. He added that the Silas Bryans continued to labor mightily, live frugally, and bear their own burdens.

On like moral principles, which he termed "Christian doctrines," Silas, his "devoted companion" assenting, also determined to bear the responsibility of their children's schooling. He did not regard the education of one's offspring as a responsibility for relegation to taxpayers. He would therefore provide home schooling, old Virginia style. Democratic principles or no, this distinctly formidable enterprise fell on the less-than-robust shoulders of Mariah Bryan, since the judge was absent from home most of the time on official duties. Accordingly, and within a few weeks after moving into their new country home, Mariah set up what she called her kitchen corner school.

Each morning, as soon as the breakfast dishes were cleared away, Frances and Willy reported for schooling. Their father provided them with the basic textbooks he and Mariah had used during their premarital years in and

about the district public school at Walnut Grove. The texts
included McGuffey's *Readers,* Webster's *Speller,* Nolan's
Arithmetic, and James' *Geography.* In the course of her
morning work, Mariah would have the children take turns
at standing on a low table and reciting the lessons they had
studied the previous afternoon.

Quite correctly, she called this "orating." It began with
reading, memorizing, and presently reciting each successive morsel of learning, beginning with the ABC's the multiplication tables, and other primary "exercises" in arithmetic; then followed the word lists from the speller; then
the primer and subsequent "exercises" from the reader.
During the afternoon, prior to chores, the children were
required to spend time—at least two hours—studying
their lessons for the following morning.

During the first year the kitchen corner pupils also began memorizing and reciting poems. Included were the
words of Silas' favorite church song, "Kind Words Can
Never Die," and what would remain Willy's favorite
poem, William Cullen Bryant's "To a Waterfowl," with
Willy's favorite stanza:

He who from zone to zone
Guides through the boundless sky thy certain flight,
In the long way that I must tread alone
Will guide my steps aright.

Mariah's home school was firmly kept; Mariah was also
the family disciplinarian. She and Silas, agreed that sparing
the rod spoiled the child, spared nothing and spoiled no
one.

As the second year of home schooling began, Charlie
Jennings, up in the grandparents' room, suffered a fatal
apoplectic stroke. Within the same month another son was
born to the Bryans. He was named Charles, for the recently departed grandfather. Little Charlie was also a

frail baby; throughout the ten ensuing years Willy was to
have two fragile younger brothers to help care for.

"I was grateful for that opportunity; no less grateful
because my mother and father taught me industry and
obedience and they gave me exercise which no gymnasium
can supply," the strong son later recorded piously.

Busy as he was, Willy's boyhood gradually began assuming normal patterns. He formed a close and enduring
friendship with Jackie Chance, the son of a poor widow
who lived directly down the road. During the summer of
1869 the two joined as a near-champion marbles-playing
team. Significantly, they played for keeps.

Beginning in their tenth summer, Willy and Jackie were
moving spirits for a rather engaging make-believe "U. S.
Senate." That development began on a June Saturday
morning when the widow Chance asked in five of her son's
friends for a breakfast of buckwheat cakes with homemade sorghum molasses and sausage cakes. The second-
breakfasters included Willy, Judd Glens, Freddy Wendt,
Gran Huett, and Junior McDonald. In the course of the
early feast, the youngsters decided to organize what presently took form as a feeble play-acting concept of a Senate
gathering.

In common with his young companions at the Chance
breakfast table, Willy was deeply interested in national
politics. As a home-school reciter, too, he was already
prone to political speaking. This predisposition was also
encouraged by his environment. Marion County, Illinois,
was "oratin' country." At the original state capital, Vandalia, Abraham Lincoln had found himself in wrestling
or scuffling country. Fortunately for his future career,
Lincoln was a competent wrestler. By contrast, in Marion
County and the Little Egypt sweep of Illinois the saying
was that "oratin' came in the air and drinking water."
The public schools took pride in their traditional Friday
afternoon speaking contests. Almost every weekend found
the country courthouses the scenes of public debates, dis-

cussion, or forums on subjects ranging from "What is the World Coming To, Anyhow?" to the pros and cons of public whippings and the merits of temperance—a subject on which Judge Bryan spoke frequently and with deep conviction. Willy had attended many of these sessions to hear his father and others speak.

After breakfast the prepuberal, self-elected senators convened in a vacant nearby store building. There Willy opened the show by mounting a vacant counter, announcing himself as Senator Whoever, and reciting, with more fervor than skill, "Ode to a Waterfowl," or whatever else came to mind. In due course his fellow daydreamers joined in. The group voted to "reconvene" at the same time and place every Saturday morning.

Ed McDonald, Jr., recalled that the ensuing "Senate" session was adjourned quite abruptly when his own and another father interrupted, razor strops in hand, to advise their offspring that if they didn't get back to work on their woodpiles they wouldn't be able to sit in the Senate or anywhere else.

But Silas Bryan took a more tolerant view of the enterprise. He permitted the mock Senate to reconvene, first in the Bryan barn and presently in the front parlor. McDonald recalled that at one of the parlor meetings Willy Bryan favored everyone with an improvised pronouncement that politics is a godly institution because, as the voice of the people, the children of God, it is necessarily the voice of God. In other ways the Bryan boy exhibited a fundamental conviction that the prototype Senators Webster or Clay or whoever else were durably noble, untarnished, and for all practical purposes, infallible.

The same did not hold of Willy's responses to his father's efforts to teach him the ways of an oncoming country gentleman, especially the sporting quality. This involved the use of an oversize muzzle-loading musket, and learning to mold lead bullets and measure and tamp powder charges. Such preparations attended to, Silas Bryan repeatedly led his son to the hunting preserve and helped scare out rabbits. Willy recalled that in one instance, after he had fired several rounds without visible results, an unfortunate rabbit skipped directly in front of the lowered musket. Willy pulled the trigger, and the rabbit was instantly reduced to a gory pulp.

Though his spirit remained willing and his marksmanship deplorable, nobody could deny that Willy's struggles to become a hunter were on occasion dramatic. He recalled a time when he slipped while climbing a rail fence and accidentally pulled the trigger with the musket's muzzle placed squarely against his chest. He suggested later that God had directed that the gun not fire; a skeptic might surmise that Willy had forgotten to set the firing cap.

Silas next introduced his son to the sport of hunting with dogs. Willy recruited two odd-looking mongrels that he named Carlo and Dixie. They led him an interesting chase, and gave him a new lease on rabbit hunting. Though they rarely overtook any, Carlo and Dixie served to warn the rabbits of approaching peril and to make Willy a lifelong lover of dogs—with special fondness for mongrels, which, he noted, are the most lovable and least expensive kind.

As his twelfth year began, Willy, again with his father leading, made his enduring choice of what would presently materialize as his truly favorite sport, the quest of public office. During 1871, Judge Bryan had helped draft a new constitution for Illinois; it was destined to win voters' acceptance and endure as a model for many other state constitutions. An unanticipated dividend was Silas' decision to seek election to the highest national office then available to direct election—the post of representative in the Congress of the United States. (U.S. senators were still being elected by state legislatures.)

With renewed confidence in his competence as a lawmaker, Silas Bryan announced early in 1872 his decision to bow out of his judgeship and seek election as representative for the Illinois Fourteenth Congressional District. As usual, the decision to seek a higher office involved personal considerations. Early in 1871, the Bryans had produced still another mouth to feed, a daughter, "Little Connie," sometimes called Nancy. This third Bryan daughter and ninth child was born strong and well. Before the year ended Mariah was again pregnant.

On the practical side, Bryan farming was not working as well as Bryan family formation; a principal cause was their inability to find competent rent farmers. In his farewell address to the court, Judge Bryan confined himself to an optimistic appraisal: ". . . I have not grown rich from the spoils of office. . . . I have received no more than a living. . . . [My] reasonable competence . . . has been the result of rigid economy, long and patient professional labor, and the sweat of my face in agricultural pursuits, aided and supported by heaven's greatest endowment— an affectionate, confiding, and prudential companion. . . ." Even so, the need for a growing income for a persistently growing family was self-evident.

Evident, too, was the surging enthusiasm of the congressional candidate's eldest son, who had instantly begun picturing himself in great Washington, his father's diligent helper. Willy was arduously confident that his father could and would win.

There was also evidence that Silas Bryan shared in that confidence—but also evidence that the "prayin' judge" had taken too much for granted. His congressional district included twelve counties in which Silas had never campaigned, since they were not in his judiciary district. The larger part of the Illinois Fourteenth Congressional was Republican country.

Though Silas had gained the Democratic nomination without contest, his only rational hope for winning the election was to effect fusion with other anti-Republicans. These were principally present as the vigorously reawakened Greenback Party, which stood for helping "poor folks" by drastically increasing currency issues, a tenet strongly opposed by both the "wholehearted" Republicans and the so-called Wall Street and/or Tammany-controlled Democrats.

Though Silas approved of the general position of the Greenbackers, he made clear his intentions to "swim or sink as a Democrat." His likelihood of sinking increased markedly when, without convincing cause, he openly praised Horace Greeley, who had received the so-called Liberal Republican nomination for the Presidency. When local Greenbackers and more than a few Democrats expressed disapproval, the outgoing judge followed with an even less discreet move. He distributed with his personal blessings the proceedings of the Tammany-steered Democratic National Convention of 1872. Many Greenbackers regarded that as a willful insult to the honest and ill-used citizens of Illinois; more than a few western Democrats were no less annoyed.

As a next step into deepening trouble, Silas Bryan bluntly refused the request from the State Central Democratic Committee for a donation or "party contribution" of five hundred dollars. He explained that he sought no donations to his own campaign, that good Democrats work and pay their own ways into office, and that his refusal to be shaken down was substantially a moral issue. With that sentiment off his slender chest, the bold but unrobust candidate opened his campaign on the courthouse steps of Salem Village. Listeners were respectful, but they seemed able to control their enthusiasm.

The campaign took another turn for the worse with the emergence of a most vexing and paradoxical opponent. A gangling and bellicose come-lately, John Martin, who called himself General Martin of the Unconquerable Confederate Army, had belatedly acquired the Republican nomination. Some suspected that Soldier Martin was probably unconquerable, doubting that he had even been near the Confederate Army. By 1872 there was apparently no documentation to prove or disprove the claim. One could wonder, too, as some did, why an ex-Confederate general should be seeking office in Illinois as a Republican. But John Martin's appeal was to dissatisfied Republican voters and the rather numerous Greenbackers. To that end he described himself as a "red-blooded fighting American who would lay down his life for his fellow underdogs— the little, big and noble, poor people." Whereas, he maintained, Silas Bryan, the "praying peace-preacher," defended the poor mostly by slapping them into jail or the state penitentiary.

Willy was astonished and deeply hurt by his first exposure to mud-slinging rabble-rousing. As the hot and ugly campaign moved along, "General" Martin's tirades grew even more abusive. When the Bryans' final child, Mary Elizabeth, was born, Martin spoke derisively of the "prayin' judge's" competence in the bed rather than in the battlefield.

"He just can't say such awful things and win!" Willy repeated. But John Martin did win—by a margin of 271 of the 31,881 votes counted. Willy simply could not believe it. Neither could other Silas Bryan followers. Several urged him to contest the count. Silas shook his head, reiterating that he had no lawful cause for contesting the balloting—"And there is no sense to beating the log after the coon has gone . . ."

Willy's disappointment moldered as a profound and spirit-crushing grief. Why had God permitted such an outrageous malfeasance? There had to be a reason; just as there was a God. But why had God abandoned Silas Lillard Bryan? As an alert listener, Willy overheard the summaries of the local pundits; old Silas' political goose was cooked. He could give temperance lectures, preside at Baptist prayer meetings, and entertain preachers until hell froze over. But politically he was finished. A capable Republican had taken over as circuit judge; the Democrats, certainly in Illinois, were surely crushed by the presidential triumph of General U. S. ("Sam") Grant, the "regular" Republican nominee.

Silas Bryan's situation was truly grim by other standards. He was still heavily in debt; he was no longer able as he put it, to earn a living by the sweat of his face. He had six young—at least two of them invalids—to raise and educate. His health was failing. The only way out was to begin all over again at practicing law in Salem, where already there were nearly as many lawyers as cows in the streets.

In his weighing grief, Willy Bryan resolved to help redeem his father. But to attain this, he was convinced that he would have to "find" God again. The young God-seeker sought advisers. One was his elder sister Frances. Another was the Reverend Mr. John Hendrick, newly graduated from New York's already renowned Union Theological Seminary and just arrived in Salem for his first charge as pastor of the new Cumberland Presbyterian Church.

John Hendrick, at twenty-seven, was particularly interested in young people and in winning them to his congregation. One gathers that he was astutely responsive to the adolescent urge to find—or lose—God. Primarily to serve this end, the young pastor set up a series of Progressive Sequences, or revival services, inviting "open questioning" by prospective members of his church and, perhaps, others. He invited the entire Bryan family to attend. Frances and Willy responded. They enjoyed the first service; both agreed that they felt "nearness"—if not to a sectarian creed, then more certainly to a living, ever-mighty God.

Following the third sequence Frances and Willy made their decisions together. They joined the Cumberland Presbyterian Church. A student of Bryan has reason to doubt that his was entirely a sectarian decision. One has cause to believe that the youth had sought and succeeded in attaining an affirmation of his own fundamental faith. Significantly, as a Baptist pillar, Silas Bryan noted dryly that his children were duty-bound to make this serious decision for themselves. And Mariah Bryan, determined Methodist that she had been, was showing an allegiance to her husband's church, the First Baptist.

3. Wells of Learning

Though both his health and earnings were declining, Silas Bryan kept his resolve to help his offspring on to an education. By the end of 1874, Frances and her eldest brother (who by then had made clear his preference for being called Will), were approaching the pedagogical limits of their mother's kitchen corner school. Mariah had no schooling higher than the "public grades," and her tutorial talents, such as they were, had to be refocused on the needs of the younger children.

In Salem two additional grades of public schooling were available. There the two-room, two-teacher school was housed in the ugly one-time home of the defunct Salem Female Academy. The reins of the four upper grades were held firmly by the reigning queen, oversize and overwhelming Mrs. Mary Putnam Reed Lemen, commonly known as Mountaineeous Mary. Like practically all the Salem youth then and during the prior generation, Frances and Will were foredoomed to take their turns at yielding to the Lemen tutelage.

It wasn't easy. The first tenet of Mrs. Lemen's pedagogy was that superlatively good behavior is all that really counts. Mountaineeous Mary was a whipping teacher, and a Lemen whipping—local pronunciation "whuppin' "— was an epochal event that auditors long remembered and recipients never forgot. Mary Lemen whipped without favor or discrimination in sex or size, and for offenses no more culpable than "slouching in the seat" or answering "I don't know" as if one really didn't care. She was bigger and more muscular than her largest backwoods pupils; none was too big or too small to feel the sting of her choice of a suitably sized cane or switch.

The behavior of the two Bryan children must have been exemplary, since neither received a flogging during their two five-month "upper terms." Certainly their capacity to endure tyranny was proven, and both would remember Mary Lemen as a giant economy-size personification of omnipotent wrath and vengeance. Will Bryan recalled that the experience of seeing and hearing others receiving appallingly severe whippings afflicted him with an intense nausea that recurred in moments of tension throughout most of his life. The daily intermixing of prayers and floggings opened the gates of imagination to vivid comprehension of such Biblical phrases as the "wrath of God," and the "vengeance of Jehovah."

Quite possibly the sheer violence of Mary Lemen's teaching may have goaded Silas into effecting college plans for his two older children. He had located a respectable Baptist seminary for girls (Lebanon "college") to which Frances could gain admission, at least for the one-year teaching course. Will's case was different. He still lacked at least two years of being prepared for admission to any reasonable facsimile of a men's college, even including the distinctly marginal Jewell Baptist College of Liberty, Missouri.

Understandably, Silas held back. The fact that he was obliged to make an almost microscopically small income

stretch and stretch did not subdue his conviction that Will
was the family's best bet for a professional education. The
boy was not only an exceptionally serious and well-behaved student, he was advanced for his age. Nearing
fifteen, he was already interested in fifteen-year-old Mollie
Smith, a cousin-once-removed on his mother's side. He and
Mollie had been seen studying together; in that pursuit
they had been known to wander as far away as Picnic
Bluff or nearby Mauvais Terre Creek (the native pro-
nunciation still sounds a great deal like "Movie Star").
Some forty years later, the durability of this affection would
be confirmed when William Jennings Bryan, while U. S.
Secretary of State, managed to secure for unwed Mollie
Smith an appointment as postmistress fourth class. Silas
Bryan had nothing against pretty, vivacious Mollie Smith.
He simply did not favor premature marriage.

One senses, too, that the former judge was less than
satisfied with the chances for his son's advancement in persistently rustic Salem, Illinois. By contrast to its lavish
abundance of dusty and muddy streets, Salem had a
marked shortage of avenues of opportunity for promising
young men. Gran Huett, Don Kagy, and Junior McDonald, all fellow lawyers' sons, had already completed plans
to go away to college. Will's stay-at-home companions,
such as Judd Glens, Freddie Wendt, and Erastus Hallie,
were good boys, but anyone could see that they really
weren't going to get anywhere beyond the status of farm
hands, well diggers, or at best, store clerks.

Another local development that troubled Silas Bryan was
the fact that Salem was becoming a kind of subcapital for
the Granger or Farm Grange movement, of which he had
never approved. Throughout the countryside Grange chap-
ters were springing up like bitterweeds in a desirable cow
pasture and, as Silas saw it, these self-glorified farmers'
clubs with their silly rituals were working the political hay
fields with shameless audacity. Furthermore, since the
Granges were wide open to female members, it was com-

monly agreed that a foremost object of the Grangerettes was husband chasing. Silas Bryan did not want his eldest and most eligible son ensnared.

At about this point, early in 1875, Silas took his ailments and his problems to his friend and family physician, who was also his cousin.

Hiram Kenneth Jones, M.D., practiced medicine with outstanding success and served without salary as professor of health sciences for Illinois College in Jacksonville, about a hundred miles from Salem. Cousin Hiram pointed out that his adopted town was practically overflowing with education. Its roster of five "private" schools included the respected Illinois College for men and a poor but adequate preparatory academy, Whipple's, that was associated with the college. Since he served as physician and trustee for both institutions, Hiram Jones knew whereof he spoke. Moreover, as Silas Bryan remembered, Dr. Jones and his wife Mattie had no children of their own; they had a big and empty house on College Hill. They would be very happy to take Will into their home while he attended school, first at Whipple's, which he might be able to push through in two years, then the four-year college. There would be no point to having Will work for his board and room—the Joneses already had a competent hired man, and Will would need all his free time for studying, which would be rigorous. The generous and thoughtful offer was accepted.

As the new boy shortly learned, the academy's enrollment of about eighty teen-age youngsters regularly exceeded that of the college itself—which rarely had more than sixty-five. Whipple's, as the preparatory associate of Illinois College, was a plain-living school that stressed the three R's, plus an introduction to the classics; also hard work, plain fare, and compulsory attendance at daily chapel services. There was immediate use of Silas Bryan's cherished and extremely heavy Greek and Latin lexicons, which had been given to Will as a going-away present.

The academy kept six full days per week, with Sunday church services in town the one occasion for leaving the campus. Students were required to do "grounds duty," which ranged from lawn mowing, window washing, and general laundry service to feeding and milking the school's dairy herd and working the gardens. Whipple's was a poor school for poor boys; self-subsistence, though never literally attained, was a standing goal.

Although he lodged and took his meals at Cousin Hiram's, Will joined wholeheartedly in the life of the academy. He was accustomed to work and had no difficulty in adapting to the Whipple tradition of frugality. His father granted him an allowance of forty cents a week, and required that it be accounted for. On one occasion when Will spent thirty-five cents for his own purposes and contributed only a nickel to the church offering, Silas wrote to protest. When Will requested funds to buy a new pair of pants ("I am growing taller but my pants aren't growing . . ."), Silas replied that the means at hand would have to suffice until the end of the school year.

Although the Bryan boy's schooling was not polluted by affluence, it was influenced by an unusual outside environment—unusual at least for the Midwest of the 1870s and 1880s. The town of Jacksonville bore a remarkable resemblance to earlier New England towns. The streets were grass-fringed and wide, there were grassy commons and many Cape Cod-style cottages; also town houses of New England saltbox style, and red brick mansions that looked a great deal like those known in New England as wool merchants' palaces.

From his first day in Jacksonville, Will was deeply impressed by the town and its people. But his most ardent interest was in the college that he was resolved to enter. The minimal two years at Whipple's were essentially a matter of working and waiting in line for admission to Illinois College.

Both the town and college were of historic confluence.

Jacksonville had been a meeting place of two formative currents of immigration to the Midwest, one from New England, the other from the border South. By Bryan's time the two were at least partially integrated but there were still a small Negro community and scatterings of German and Irish settlers and even remnants of a one-time colony of Portuguese from Madeira. Thus Jacksonville had remained a point of significant comings-together; it was a rather astonishing sociological showcase.

Illinois College was itself termed a "daughter" or, for the more literal, "son" of Yale. The oldest college in Illinois, it had been founded in 1829 by "private subscription," for the most part local; but Julian Monson Sturtevant, a Yale graduate and Connecticut native, had opened it.

After thirty-two years as president of the college, Julian Sturtevant continued to serve as professor of economics and social sciences. His remained the school's best-known name; his textbook on economics, first published in 1877 and widely used throughout the college world, taught and defended the principles of free trade and bimetallism. Perhaps more than any other faculty member, Sturtevant personified his college. To a degree his "line of thinking" had influenced the town as well as the college; it was also perceptible in the arduous study at Whipple's Academy. And for good measure, Sturtevant was a man of deep faith—a revered spokesman for the Congregational Church. Even before he met him, Will Bryan was among Sturtevant's admirers.

Whipple's Academy took due heed of the New England tendencies of the Illinois College curriculum, which included a compulsory three years of Latin and four of Greek. The freshman Latin included readings from Horace, Tacitus, and the Tuscan Disputations, while the Greek courses were weighted with Thucydides and Demosthenes. A three-month course in rhetoric was compulsory, but the remainder of the training in English consisted of "rhetoricals" devoted to reading original writings and to the delivery of orations or declamations. The college was strongly in favor of oratory, a fact that appealed to young Bryan.*

Since Whipple's was essentially a "younger brother" of the college, and because the academy's meager staff of three full-time combination teachers and proctors was supplemented on a catch-as-catch-can basis with faculty men of the college, Will became acquainted with the goals and functioning of the college. He had cause to note its tradition for tolerating "free thinking."

As the newcomer from Salem learned, the foremost local proponent of free thinking was none other than his own generous host and sponsor, Hiram Kenneth Jones, who possessed an M.A. as well as an M.D. degree. On many fronts, or sides, Will's engaging cousin-once-removed was the leader of Jacksonville and its cultural structure. Hiram Jones attended and helped cure the sick, without heed to creed, race, color, or ability to pay bills. His prescriptions sometimes included secret donations of groceries or payment of lapsed grocery bills. Even so, his medical practice was the largest and most lucrative in the area; he had recently made Illinois College an outright gift of the very impressive sum of ten thousand dollars.

In addition, as Will Bryan discovered, Dr. Jones generously encouraged all the schools in the area, serving at

* Three years of mathematics, including advanced algebra and trigonometry, were required of all students, with calculus elective for the senior year. The second- and third-year curricula featured a three-month basic course in physics, chemistry, astronomy, geology, and mechanics. The senior year was devoted largely to economics, logic, psychology ("mental philosophy"), and political science, each occupying what the catalogue described as an intensive six-week course. The final term was largely devoted to a course entitled "Evidence of Christianity," after Butler's then-revered text of the same title. This course, apparently, was a sort of bonus from and for the believers. The college held daily and compulsory chapel services, but except for the "Evidence," there were no courses in theology as such.

least three as *gratis* physician. Even more extraordinary were the discussion or lecture "bees" he sponsored and hosted at his own home. He described this enterprise as a hopeful effort to serve as a cultural link between the learned East and the new West.

Living in Cousin Hiram's home was itself a many-phased educational experience. From the windows of his room, Will could look out on a vista of brave green grass and the elm-shaded walks of the Presbyterian Female Academy directly beyond. Here each afternoon, weather permitting, the young inmates took their constitutionals, walking sedately in twos with ladylike deliberation and the certain knowledge that their principal, Erastus Franklin Bullard, was never far away.

As a newly arrived "prep" boy (an instructor characterized him as a "typical farmer lad with all the crudities that are characteristic of the species"), Will saw the parading young ladies as a denominator of a new and baffling discipline. Here, surely, was a contrast to what he had known back in Salem Village, which a few of the vulgar persisted in calling Pig Town. There the young women, however repressed, did not parade like well-dressed, spring-wound mannequins. In Salem, older girls usually went sauntering with boys.

In Jacksonville there were no real children, only young grown-ups. There were no towering Mary Lemens to overwhelm with switches that cut into young flesh. Yet, as Will sensed, there were disciplines, and these had at least one point in common with those of his home community: they were directly related to religion. Whipple's Academy, like Illinois College, supplemented its own daily and compulsory chapel services with the "required privilege" of attending Sunday morning church services in town.

The usual procedure was for the respective student bodies, with one or more faculty members acting as bellwethers, to tramp forth to a given service, rotating the visits to include all principal denominations. Students who preferred to attend their own churches or to "shop around" individually were permitted to do so, with the understanding that playing hookey would nullify the privilege. Will Bryan attended Catholic and Jewish services and even made bold to visit the local Negro church. Though he had a letter of transfer from his own church to the Cumberland Presbyterian at Jacksonville, he did not effect the transfer during his two busy years at Whipple's Academy. His liking for church hopping began early.

Meanwhile, Will continued to find Dr. Jones an oddly engaging combination of counseling skills. Cousin Hiram had studied at Harvard, where he had acquired both his degrees. During the somewhat giddy 1840s, the wispy little man had there become deeply involved in the vagaries of New England transcendentalism. He had listened to and become a friend of Ralph Waldo Emerson, had gotten to know William T. Harris, the principal organizer and teacher of the Concord School of Philosophy, and Bronson Alcott, who was predestined to be best remembered as the father of Louisa M. Alcott. Subsequently, by the doctor's contrivances, New England intellectuals and educators had appeared in Jacksonville as public lecturers; Emerson had twice visited and lectured in the "Little Athens of the Middle West," as Dr. Jones' house guest.

At fortnightly intervals the Joneses hosted "conversational at-homes." These were informal discussions as a rule, and were often pegged to aspects of Greek and western European philosophy, including American adaptations thereof. From time to time educators and miscellaneous pundits who happened to be traveling in the area were invited to lead the discussions. The reticent young roomer, Will Bryan, held a standing invitation to attend these gatherings. (As his host explained, "standing invitations" were inevitable; the Joneses rarely had enough chairs to go around.) Will sometimes put in an appearance as a respectful listener. Apparently his reactions were of almost sphinxlike silence.

But there were indirect reactions. Toward the end of his first year at Whipple's Academy, Will managed to hear at least part of a series of lectures on "Fallacies Regarding the Bible," as spilled forth by B. F. Underwood, a widely publicized "free thinker and materialist." In a theme that Bryan developed during the next school year, he summarized the Underwood tenets in thoughtful detail and recounted that they had exercised a disquieting influence on his "trend of religious thought."

During his second year at Whipple's, Will answered an advertisement extolling the brilliance of Robert Ingersoll, the "Great Agnostic" of the era, and in return received a brochure of Ingersoll lectures that he seems to have read with great care. When he wrote to ask Ingersoll's views on God and immortality, he received a printed waiver in which the Great Agnostic stated:

I do not say there is no God. I simply say I do not know. I do not say there is no life beyond the grave, I simply do not know.

Bryan's reaction was frustration and some degree of disgust. Certainly it was to jell as a durable antipathy for occupational agnosticism. Many years later he wrote:

From that day to this, I have asked myself the question and have been unable to answer it to my own satisfaction, how could anyone find pleasure in taking from a human heart a living faith and substituting therefor the cold and cheerless doctrine, "I do not know."

The youth studied hard and worked hard at the daily four-to-six-hour stint of grounds duty. When vacation came, he went home to a laborious summer on the farm. He was, as he had written, growing rapidly—three inches during his first year at Whipple's. During the summer of 1876, and for the first time, he worked directly with the thresher crew, pitched hay, and worked the heavy turning plow, as his father and grandfather had done before him.

The vacationing scholar regained a place in the family life. When time permitted, he joined his two younger brothers and his two younger sisters in play. Frances had acquired her first beau. Brother Russell was seriously ill part of the summer. Charlie, who at eight objected vehemently to being called Little Charlie, became abruptly his eldest brother's devoted admirer—an admiration that would endure.

Will's second year at the academy appears to have been virtually a repetition of the first. In the course of the year he grew another two inches, to five feet eleven, and aided by the excellent meals at the Jones home, his weight mounted to 176 pounds. It was during this period that one of Bryan's favorite anecdotes materialized. His father at the time weighed 180 pounds. "Dad," Will exclaimed, "I'm as tall as you and weigh only four pounds less. In practically no time I'll be as big as you are."

With an audible sigh Silas Bryan said: "Yes, son, when you have gained four pounds, all of them of brains, you will be my size."

At fifteen and sixteen, two years is a long time to wait for admission to college; but Will rather enjoyed the wait and the work. He was busy, he was making friends, he was living comfortably, and Cousin Mattie's cookies were superior.

In Jacksonville, Illinois, college opening in 1877 followed the usual pattern. Illinois College began with a day-long convocation, at which administrators and faculty took turns at giving admonitions and orientation. Classes were introduced, first collectively, and then by individual members. The freshman class, with eleven students, was officially formed. William J. Bryan (as his registration read) found himself elected its vice president. There was no hazing, boisterous conduct, or group snobbery. The college began its twenty-seventh consecutive school year with sixty-three students enrolled. Of the freshmen, seven, including Bryan, were registered for the "classics" course, the other four for the science course. Their ages ranged from seventeen to thirty-one; Bryan and his fellow townsman, Gran Huett, were both seventeen; Sam Eveland, the oldest member and soon to be Bryan's closest college friend, was thirty-one.

For the first time in Gran Huett's recollection, Will was neatly dressed. He was wearing a trim black suit; his normally unruly black hair was now neatly combed, parted on the right, and shiny as silk. Although he continued to room with the Joneses, he turned collegian with intensity. He had no choice of courses; all were prescribed. He had no choice of fraternities; it was the custom for the two available "literary" fraternities to bid for the incoming freshmen, and Bryan was taken into Sigma Phi. He did have the choice of companions. In the opinion of one of the younger faculty members, George R. Poague, who had been named adviser to the freshman class, Bryan chose well. Poague wrote:

> It is significant that his [Bryan's] chosen companions were not the crude and roistering element among the students but those of quiet, studious tastes and refined manners. Yet he was in no way exclusive or snobbish. His friends were not among his fellow students alone. There were young men he met in the business houses of the town in whom his generous nature and magnetic personality inspired friendships which persisted.

Bryan gave a somewhat different version of his choice of college friends. He insisted that he chose to like the whole lot, but concentrated on special friends who usually chose him first. Sam Eveland, though fourteen years his senior, was first.

Sam had come in from rural Michigan, where he had worked several years in a lumber camp and intermittently tramped the country in search of other jobs, which usually failed to materialize. In the course of one of his pedestrian job hunts Eveland had stopped by a church, found conversion, and resolved to preach the Gospel. Bryan later recorded with somewhat awe-stricken respect:

> . . . I have never know a man more completely consecrated to the service of God and to the life patterned after the example of Christ.

At Illinois College grading was "by 10"; 10 was the highest attainable mark, 7 the lowest passing mark. As his college career began, Bryan showed an aptitude for mathematics and made his lowest grade (7.3) in German, though with apparently prodigious study he soon raised the mark to 9.3. A testimony of faculty—or student—competence was provided by the close balancing of the class's grades. In time Bryan was to emerge as valedictorian, with a four-year grade average of 8.95; the lowest in the class was 8.01.

During his freshman year he set the pace for what many were to designate as a pattern of consistent inconsistency. His grades zigzagged unpredictably from the highest to the lowest in his class. During all his first three years of college, the tall and easy-smiling young man from Salem Village ranked first in only three courses. Then during his senior year, he changed pace, and held first place in five of the eight courses.

Quite early it became apparent that Bryan's college career could not be measured adequately by grades or percentages. The entire town was his school and campus. Even during his preliminary stay at Whipple's Academy, the amiable and usually shabbily dressed youngster was deeply interested in the comings and goings and doings of the town. These had included a strongly controversial and quickly abandoned effort to have enacted saloon closing by local option. Bryan only looked on, but his recorded comment was that the "liquor issue" was moral, not legal.

The next local event evoked a deeper and more aggressive reaction. The officious free thinker, B. F. Underwood, again invaded Jacksonville, this time to deliver a series of three lectures at a local lodge hall. Illinois College took a neutral stand, but did not prohibit students from attending, and some, including Bryan, did. The Underwood lectures were: "The Positive Side of Modern Free Thought"; "Popular Assumptions and Fallacies Regarding the Bible and Christianity"; and "Origin and Evolution of Religion."

Bryan, now eighteen, took issue boldly. In a classroom essay and in several oratorical essays, he quoted the arguments of the addresses and sternly branded them as evasive and impudent. He expressed particular disappointment in the fact that Underwood would destroy or seriously weaken faith in the Bible without suggesting any replacement for that faith. Furthermore, Underwood was not a "free" or any other kind of thinker. He would repress thought. He did cite science when convenient. Will devised phrases for refuting him. One was: "I'd rather trust the Rock of Ages than know the ages of the rocks."

The Underwood broadsides seem to have helped to precipitate a long-delayed decision by William Jennings Bryan; it moved him to present his letter of transference of membership to the Cumberland Presbyterian Church of Jacksonville. As long as he remained in Jacksonville, his name would never again be missing from the membership roster of that church. Furthermore, faculty and fellow students began noticing that he carried his Bible along with the rest of his armload of books. In his rhetoric course he began writing essays or addresses on Biblical subjects; he usually chose topics from the Old Testament, particularly the Book of Proverbs and the lives of the earlier prophets. His recurring theme was of the sovereignty and might of God.

Simultaneously, his campus activities began extending into politics. One of his more serious addresses to his literary fraternity was on "God and Politics." On the more interpretable side, the student from Salem began using his fraternity as a doorway to campus politics. For the first 2½ years these efforts were not especially telling. During that time all but one of the fraternity offices he took over were appointive—chaplain, critic, and sergeant-at-arms. As usual, the surest way to latch onto an appointive post was to aid in the election of a president favorably disposed to the aspirant.

Bryan did not excel as a prospect for direct election. One conspicuous reason was his insistence on remaining a Democrat. Most of the Illinois College students listed themselves as Republicans, obviously by family background or preference. Bryan repeated with more emphasis than discretion that he, for one, was truly a Democrat and, as such, a defender of the underdog. This proved to be expensive, at least in the strange world of campus politics.

The rather dreary Sigma Phi meeting room, and the no less somber general convocation hall, were to reveal and stimulate other interests in Bryan, the Bible-steered politician. The general outlook of the college was eastern, but listeners were emphatically reminded that Will Bryan opposed what he saw or felt was ravaging his West. By then the age of the covered wagon had yielded to the era of the steel rail. The first transcontinental railroad system had been in operation for five years, but Bryan felt that the principal gainers were the promoters, not the "people." Emotionally, and not always logically, he stood against the railroads. Some of his classmates were sons of railroad employees. Such facts of life seemed to have no influence on the boy politician.

During his freshman year Bryan showed evidence of

what may have been an intuitive awareness of social injustice. According to the fraternity record book, he was called on to participate in an impromptu debate on the subject, "Resolved that the Indian has more cause to complain of his treatment by the white than the Negro." With an onrush of Irish impulsiveness, possibly reinforced by a firsthand look at Jacksonville's Negrotown, Bryan joined the negative and opened with a loud, clear pronouncement: "I would rather be an Indian than a Negro subject to the white man's hate."

He lost the judges' decision, but he won the vehement approval of his audience. There was already precedent for this. As a little-noted middler in Whipple's Academy, he had entered the declamation contest with a brisk rendition of Patrick Henry's "There Is No Peace" ("Give me liberty or give me death!"). The judges had not been favorably impressed, but the student audience, in spontaneous violation of the rules, clapped and cheered.

Bryan spent his entire clothing allowance for his second college year on special elocution lessons with a Professor Mueller, a temporary faculty member. The would-be orator had hoped to earn back the money by working Saturday afternoons in Hofra's Hat Store, but this plan was temporarily frustrated when the college designated Saturday afternoons a compulsory study period. His hopes for an immediate place on the newly founded student newspaper, *The Rambler,* were also frustrated temporarily when he failed to win election as editor.

But his serious labors at elocution were rewarded. As a sophomore he won second place in an oratorical contest, and in fraternity meetings he began to shine as a speaker. Here he apparently began a practice of delivering the same or substantially the same speech again and again, but seeking to make each delivery more effective than the one before. Among his favorites were Henry Clay's "Ambition of a Statesman" and a heart-throbber entitled, "The Burning of Chicago."

Bryan continued as a "serious debater"—strongly predisposed to taking the negative side and applying the techniques thereof. As a result he succeeded far better in swaying or otherwise winning audiences than in winning judges' decisions or campus offices. Of twelve debates recorded during his first two years, Bryan was on the winning side in six. During the same period he lost three campus elections and won only one. His most notable exhibition was in a debate: "Resolved that intemperance is more detrimental to mankind than war." The youthful disdainer of intemperance again took the negative, and in his text the observant teacher, George R. Poague, recognized the beginnings of what were to become the Bryan tenets for developing arbitration devices to maintain peace among nations.

Still a sophomore, he began to center his writing efforts on prevailing political measures, concentrating on a fair deal for farmers. In this development he was probing what was substantially a personal problem. The Bryan homestead was not thriving. The renters were not doing well by the soil, and the sharecroppers were failing to deliver. Crop prices were seriously under par. As an independent law practitioner, Silas Bryan was meeting extremely hard times, while his health grew less and less dependable. Both his younger sons remained sickly. Will again sought and this time received permission to begin working Saturday afternoons at Hofra's Hat Store in downtown Jacksonville. There he formed a lifelong preference for broad-brimmed, gray or black planter-style sombreros.

The eldest Bryan boy now resolved to put in the following summer (1879) at restoring his father's deteriorating farm to productiveness. He opened with a strong man's feat: "straight prying" and otherwise restoring about two miles of rail fences. This was a muscle-straining, spine-wrenching job that even the huskiest of farm hands dreaded. But at nineteen Will Bryan was indeed a strong young man with steadfast convictions. As a fence restorer he was following the history of his now semi-invalid father; with his own sweat and brawn he was seeking to restore utility, order, and fundamental correctness. From fence repairing Will shifted to the wheat harvest, as a full-time helper of the transient threshing crew. Then he began the ruthlessly hard work of summer plowing the "new ground." He finished the summer with sunburn, hand blisters toughened to calluses, expanding muscles, and an improved understanding of the momentous toil of wresting a livelihood from the grim old mother, earth.

He returned to Jacksonville and his third college year in a mood to accept what Julian Sturtevant called the hard, eternal verities. Apparently he had given up his earlier and somewhat diffident willingness to ponder the philosophical discussions at Cousin Hiram's "parlor forums." He avoided what he now described as sophomoric agnosticism. Will Bryan was no longer a sophomore; he was a believing upperclassman. He believed in the omnipotence of God, the integrity of hard work, the implicit rightness of agriculture. He did not believe that the child was father to the man, but rather that God was father of the man.

Will also found the time right to take heed of women— one, in particular. She was Mamie (Mary Elizabeth) Baird, only child of John and Lovina Baird, proprietors of the general store at Perryville, in backwoodsy Pike County, Illinois. Mamie Baird was a healthy, observant, strong-willed, markedly feminine eighteen-year-old. She was well formed and generally attractive, though not conventionally pretty. There was no doubt that she was intelligent and enterprising. She had helped her father keep store and her usually ailing mother keep house.

Following one class-leading year at the Monticello Female Seminary at Godfrew, Illinois, Mamie had now come to Jacksonville to complete the remaining two years of "finishing" at the Presbyterian Female Academy, where she again began to prove herself a class leader.

The academy environment was restrictive; Principal Erastus Bullard claimed that he regarded all his students as daughters and trusted them accordingly—practically not at all. He did not permit dating. One evening a month the academy held open house. It was then or never for the young men of Illinois College.

At Mamie Baird's first experience of the open house, she was introduced to a group of Illinois College students. Bryan recalled that he stood staring speechlessly at her. Mamie's impression of Bryan is best told by herself:

> I saw him first in the parlor of the young ladies' school which I attended in Jacksonville. He entered the room with several other students, was taller than the rest, and attracted my attention at once. His face was pale and thin; a pair of keen, dark eyes looked out from beneath heavy brows; his nose was prominent—too large to look well, I thought; a broad, thin-lipped mouth and a square chin completed the contour of his face.

> He was neat though not fastidious in dress, and stood firmly and with dignity. I noted particularly his hair and his smile—the former black in color, fine in quality, and parted distressingly straight; the latter expansive and expressive . . .

The courtship of Mamie Baird and Will Bryan began right away. A big elm tree grew on the corner boundary between Dr. Hiram Jones' yardway and the abbreviated campus of the female seminary. Through the tree branches, at least after the leaves had fallen, Will could reputedly look out from his own upstairs bedroom and see the discreetly shaded windows of the second-story dormitory room occupied by Miss Mary Elizabeth Baird. In due course Will and Mamie exchanged messages by hanging signs or symbols in their windows. The time-faded back files of the *Jacksonville Female Academy Register* say:

> One tradition is especially dear to the . . . girls who now occupy the old Academy as a dormitory. Near its southern wing grows a large, wide-branching old elm. The story goes that "Billy" who lived with a relative on the opposite corner, did much of his courting from a branch which grew conveniently near to "Mamie's" window. In memory of this the girls have named the tree "Elizabeth," for . . . Mary Elizabeth Baird, who duly completed the Academy's course in 1881. She also stood first in her class. . . .

Mary Baird had set her cap for William Jennings Bryan.

As an upperclassman Will Bryan was doing a great deal besides courting Mamie Baird and no other. In fraternity meetings he began to lead improvised floor discussions. His interests continued to center on the principal political issues of the time: the hardships of farmers, tariff legislation, the gold standard versus bimetallism, the rights and wrongs of pensions for veterans, and others.

During his senior year, the young believer from Salem moved determinedly to attain the presidency of his literary fraternity, generally recognized as the most prestigious political post in the college. As chaplain for the society, Bryan had performed well. As critic he had aroused criticism. Early in his junior year he had been appointed sergeant-at-arms, and here his qualifications were beyond dispute; he was peacefully inclined, yet big and sturdy enough to heave out any troublemaker.

By no subtle means did he maneuver his way toward the presidency. The precedence here was to win the vice-presidency during the junior year; that attained, election as president for the senior year was substantially *de facto*.

Bryan won the vice-presidency, receiving nineteen of the thirty-three votes.

As faculty adviser, Professor George R. Poague noted that Vice President Bryan did not succeed in quelling dissension any more than he had as critic. "It was possible," Poague recalled, "that the executive incapacity which is said to have characterized his services as Secretary of State was already manifest."

But whatever his way or direction, even on the undersize campus of a very small college, Will Bryan was no trail-following politician. He was impressively a believer and a converter. He was also an indisputable son of dispute. He remained a poor young man who championed the poor in the company of other poor young men who almost ritualistically championed the rich. He chose to be a dissenting idealist among conforming pragmatists. He was a bafflingly tolerant prude, a fundamentalist who would revere all creeds and deplore only the lack of a religion, and a poet only by means of the spoken word.

He continued to break through fences, now ideological ones, even the best-built and strongest, and in due time, to pick his way home again, having made exploratory sallies into engaging landscapes he did not know well but liked nevertheless. Intermittently moving forward, backward, or sideways, Bryan was getting ahead in his own strange way.

4. The Seeker

Whatever else it was or sought to be, Illinois College was a workshop, and Will Bryan was one of its busier students. Its average workday was twelve hours. Classes were held from 8:00 A.M. to 4:30 P.M.; studying was done at home or in the dormitory room. Monday evenings were for fraternity meetings that usually lasted at least two hours. Wednesday and Sunday evenings were for compulsory worship services. Saturday mornings were for special courses and makeup work, Saturday afternoons for elocution practice and study. It was a concession to permit Bryan to work Saturday afternoons at Hofra's Hat Store; he needed the earnings.

To this already obese schedule Bryan added two additional activities: athletics, for the glory of the school, or so he hoped; and oratory, for the glory of William Jennings Bryan. Oratory and debating, as noted, were part of the tradition and bill of fare. Early in 1880 the administration cautiously admitted two sports, baseball and track, on an experimental basis. Bryan went out for both.

At Whipple's his one notable contribution to the exercise team had been jumping backward. In this rather bizarre pursuit he had no competitors, but in college track he tried out for the broad jump and sprinting, where there were competitors. The former sometimes took him as far as third place, but in sprinting he failed to score.

The Salem youth's drive for a place on the baseball team was partly successful; he made it, but only on an off-and-on basis. But it was that kind of team. The Illinois Defenders lacked uniforms, playing field, and an experienced manager. Bryan tried out with a dogged lack of success as pitcher, then as catcher; then he shifted to the outfield. His fielding and batting remained deplorable, but his energy and team spirit were almost compensatory.

By contrast, the Bryan efforts at oratory showed promise and won followers. When the Sigma Phi annual open house was held on March 5, 1880, Bryan delivered his oration, "Master Motives." *The Journal,* leading newspaper of Jacksonville, recorded in its College Notes that the speech was the "crowning exercise of the evening." Early in May, Will entered and won a junior class contest. This triumph was of special importance—the winner of the "Junior Oratorical" would represent the college at the much-heralded interstate oratorical contest at Galesburg the following autumn.

Because of the rigidity of the female academy rules and the frustrating alertness of its principal, the Baird-Bryan courtship progressed mostly by letter. Mamie was conspicuously the better writer:

> . . . All the old concepts, of how [what] men are, the distrust, the bitterness is gone and their place is more than filled with pleasant thoughts of you. . . .

Principal Bullard had firmly restricted the once-a-month open houses to "group callers." When Miss M. Baird requested permission to call on Dr. Hiram Jones (for medical reasons, naturally), the answer was "No." Right after that and somewhat mysteriously, Miss Baird received an invitation to pay an evening house call on Mrs. Mary Tanner, wife of the math professor and the then acting president of Illinois College. Principal Bullard granted permission. When the young lady was ushered into the sedate parlor of the college president's home, there waited a neatly combed and lately scrubbed Will Bryan. The invitations began to recur weekly. Bryan called it the luck of the Irish. More realistically, Mamie attributed it to the feminine compassion of Mrs. Tanner.

Early in May the Irish luck took a turn for the worse. Silas Bryan came to Jacksonville for one of his medical confrontations with Cousin Hiram Jones. As usual, Silas complained of dizziness, headache, and "dyspepsia." Dr. Jones asked his guest to stay over a couple of days and rest. That evening, after a brief visit with Will, Silas strolled into the kitchen for a visit with Cousin Mattie. When he reached for a chair, he fell to the floor. The doctor's wife hurried to him, then called for her husband. Cousin Hiram found his patient dead. The diagnosis was death from apoplexy.

With his usual competence, Dr. Jones summoned the undertaker and sent word to the widow. That done, he took his young and deeply shaken second cousin to the depot and set out by train for the hundred-mile rail journey to Salem to comfort and aid the widow and the four younger Bryans. Will recalled that for many hours he could think of absolutely nothing to say. The first overwhelming grief of his life canopied him with silence.

Back in college, he set about drowning his grief in his work, and Mamie Baird was eager to comfort him. A discreet exchange of messages produced another meeting in the Tanner parlor. Word of this finally percolated through to Principal Bullard, who awakened to the fact that his grant of special privilege had been abused, that other, older female conspirators were also involved, and that behind-the-back giggling was going on. Rumor had it that Miss Baird, wearing a heavy veil, had gone so far as to join her suitor for a ride in a rented livery stable rig!

At the dormitory stairs Bullard waited with verdict ready-made. Miss Baird had willfully violated academy regulations. The fact that she was leader of her class in grades only made the offense the more deplorable. Miss Baird had the choice of accepting her punishment or facing expulsion.

Mamie declined to reveal the name of her suitor. But Principal Bullard already knew. He had unraveled the outrageous duplicity. He would be in touch with the tree-climbing Lothario and the conspirator-in-the-parlor hoax. Miss Baird would be punished by being sent home for the remainder of the term. If properly repentant, she *might* be readmitted for the following fall term.

By devices best known to herself, Mamie managed to have a note delivered quickly.

> Am going on the seven o'clock train, but it would not be safe for you to go down, would it?

Principal Bullard also found time to write a sir-you-cur letter to the culprit. Early the next morning he escorted his erring pupil to the depot, bought her a ticket to Perryville, and saw her properly seated in the coach. As the train pulled out, Mamie suffered in painful anxiety. Where was her Will? Why hadn't he appeared? At that very moment the answer was emerging from the baggage car. Will came out of hiding, took the seat next to Mamie's, and insisted on riding with her to Perryville to ask her parents' consent for their immediate marriage. Mamie insisted that he leave the train at Giggsville, the next stop, and return to morning classes. She would handle her parents.

Bryan obeyed, but wrote a flowery letter of apology to Mamie's father. John Baird replied graciously, suggesting that "a mistake had been made" and granting that Will Bryan was "not a fast young man." Some might have regarded the latter as the understatement of the century; Principal Erastus Bullard apparently regarded it as insidiously untruthful.

Will pondered his moves with evident caution. His most forthright way would be to finish college, take over the homestead, marry Mamie, and settle down to serious farming; he liked farming, particularly livestock raising. If he were going to take over the farm, there was no time like the present. His mother needed his help. His two younger brothers were still not big nor strong enough to replace him. Will had long been convinced that the best farming is accomplished by an entire family working together on their own land. But Mamie Baird did not wish to be a farmer's wife, and that was that.

Even so, the big young man with big problems went home for the summer and began the round of much-needed farm work. This was the last of his college vacations; 1880 was also a national election year. The beginning of summer saw the takeoff of thousands of political campaigns, including the presidential. The customary swell of talk about the national conventions was rising. The Democratic Convention was being held in distant Cincinnati, and Will Bryan could find no way of getting there. But he could dream about it, and he did.

When his mother repeated her wish that he take whatever way he deemed best for his own interests, the senior male member of the family decided to compromise—he would try his hand at mixing farm work with local politics. In Salem Village was the newly reawakened Marion County Democratic Club, which Silas Bryan had helped found. With no clear idea of what a county political club is expected to do, Will was not exactly delighted when he found himself given the task of collecting contributions, largely in dimes and quarters. However, grown more handsome as well as more confident, he began to prove that he could persuade and at least mildly amuse the contributors.

As it usually does, news of this devotion got around. Early in July a notable caller appeared in the Bryan yardway. He was their congressman, William Springer, a longtime friend of the family, who had for a time read law in Silas Bryan's Salem office. Incumbent Springer revered the widow Bryan, but he revered nothing more movingly than his own determination to win again. He advertised himself as the Wheel Horse of the People, and had already stiff-armed his way to a place on the mighty Ways and Means Committee. This was all the more reason why he was in no mood to take re-election for granted.

Congressman Springer made a forthright overture for Will Bryan's services as a junior campaign assistant. He liked the youngster and perhaps recognized his potential crowd appeal. But Springer's proposition was cautious; the Bryan boy could keep on with his farm work, but would be permitted from time to time to go along with the congressman's campaign squad as a bush beater. He would receive free meals and lodging and a chance to try spellbinding a rural group here and there as opportunity permitted. It would be good, reasonable basic training.

Will accepted eagerly. His first speaking assignment turned out to be what had been advertised as a farmers' picnic some miles west of Salem. Dressed in his Sunday best, he arrived on foot. The picnic had not materialized. Four people were present: two rival speakers, the owner of the grove, and an obnoxious-looking figure who had come with the intention of setting up a pitch game. Without introduction, Bryan stepped forward and began his speech. To his surprise and quite possibly its own, the tiny recalcitrant audience listened. Sam Kagy, who was there to speak in behalf of his father's candidacy for the state legislature, recorded that the young Bryan made a pleasant appearance and "bonged out every word clear as a bell."

When word got back to the candidate, Bill Springer urged his unsalaried helper to take over as principal speaker at the county Democrats' rally scheduled for a Saturday night at the Salem courthouse. Bryan knew of that event; he had helped plan it, but the congressman's recommendation opened the way for him as principal speaker.

Will was evidently pleased. He wrote Mamie to ask if she would read and criticize his efforts at speech writing. Her reply was warmly affirmative; in a letter dated July 21, she said that she "enjoyed reading the orations of eloquent men. I wonder," she added, just possibly with tongue in cheek, "if students will be studying the orations of Bryan as they do those of Cicero's at the present time. . . ."

Conceivably Will was thinking of that. So was P. W. Kendricks, a Salem resident also helping Congressman Springer, who recorded the Salem spellbinding for the newspaper in nearby Jacksonville.

The county seat shindig drew farm people from various parts of the county. The speaker's platform was raised at the head of the courthouse steps, where Bryan had often sat watching the proceedings of his father's court. By sundown the fore lawn was well filled with patient loungers. By seven or thereabouts, the crescent of folding chairs the Democratic Club had arranged for distinguished guests (who included Bryan's mother, his ailing brother Russell, his strengthening brother Charlie, and his two younger sisters) was filled to or beyond capacity.

There was spirit abounding. The rally opened with a torchlight procession, headed by a marching or trudging throng of Democrats who carried flaming torches and wore blacksmith smocks to protect themselves from falling sparks and cinders. Following on foot were what Kendricks listed only as "the local fraternal orders," probably Woodmen of the World, and Grangers, or National Farmers'

Grange. Will was already a Granger. He joined the Woodmen the following summer. But on this special Saturday
night he was not beneath a flaring, cinder-dripping pine
torch. He was perspiring (the chronic condition seemed to
grow worse as he grew older) and sitting with his family,
feeling quite ill. His urge was to lie down.

Kendricks estimated the crowd as more than three times
the resident population of Salem. One gathers, in any case,
that the majority of the audience was farm people, that
along with the voting males were their families, including
farm wives and daughters in gingham and sunbonnets; and
sons, hired hands, and other men in loose-fitting overalls
and high-crowned, low-priced straw hats. Following the
invocation Will Bryan was "on." Observer Kendricks noted
that his voice carried well and evidenced a peculiar "undertone of music." The oration continued for at least an hour,
and the crowd listened.

Although the entire text was not quoted it seems safe
to guess that Congressman Springer came out no worse for
the treatment and that Wall Street and the hard core of
people-cheating Republicans got what was coming to them.
But we do know that the address began with, "If ye have
tears prepare to shed them now," and closed with "Give
me liberty or give me death!" We also know that a cogent
appraisal was made by Mariah, who had coached and
endured those first recitations by the speaker, across a
tabletop. She pointed out that there were several good
places where her son might have stopped a lot sooner than
he did.

In the final two weeks of campaigning, Will spent several
days at bush beating in the company of the campaigning
congressman. When voting day came both Salem and Marion County went Republican, although Bill Springer was
re-elected. Bryan returned to Jacksonville in a determined
state of mind. He was going to lead his class, to proceed
from Illinois College to law school. His choice was the
Union College of Law at Chicago, a poor man's school

that one of his lawyer uncles, Charles Jennings, had attended and strongly recommended. For the time being at least, Will was resigned to staying poor. In view of his mother's financial situation, he quietly abandoned his pleasant daydream of a year of "finishing" at Oxford or Cambridge. He again took on the Saturday afternoon job at the hat store in Jacksonville and accepted Cousin Hiram's generous hospitality.

In what may have been an additional effort at conformity, Will made a first bold try at growing a beard. More than half of the student body at Illinois College were wearing beards; all the rest of the senior class were at least mustached. The first Bryan beard turned out to be rather remarkable—at least in color. The curly stubble was a pale, fawnlike brown, by inexplicable contrast with the wearer's coal-black hair. After more weeks of growth, the beard assumed a cast that Mamie described as buffalo brown. The senior student resumed shaving.

He also resumed intensive study. In order to take first place in political science he was obliged to score a perfect grade. He made it.

Fraternity politics took a surprising turn for the worse. Bryan, vice president of Sigma Phi, served as acting president for the first five meetings. He stood for routine election as president. Since the founding of the fraternity, every duly elected vice president had been confirmed as president in his senior year. Vice President Bryan lost the election by two votes. It was a two-fisted, hard-jolting defeat.

But there was no time for moping. The interstate oratorical contest at Galesburg was scheduled for the first week in November. As winner of the Junior Class contest, Bryan saw a gleaming opportunity to win what no other Illinois College representative had ever won before—first prize in the "Intercollegiate." He began to memorize and polish a series of three orations: "True Oratory," *"Ducamus non Sequarmar,"* and *"Ad Perpetuum."* Late at night he lay in bed whispering the eloquent texts. Early each morning he held solitary rehearsals in the open. Rumors spread that his locale for practice was an open wood adjoining the state insane asylum. To win the big meet at Galesburg meant a first prize of one hundred dollars and enduring fame; second place would deal fifty dollars and lesser fame. William Jennings Bryan aimed for the first prize.

The Galesburg Oratorical Meet assembled with entries from nine midwestern colleges. The judges and auditorium were ready and waiting. So was a photographer. Separately and in a stiffly posed group, the contestants stood for their pictures. Eight of the contestants were young men. Three of them wore full beards, four were mustached; only Bryan, far and away the most handsome, was clean-shaven. In posing for the group picture he stood rigidly, his right hand hidden in the front folds of a tight-fitting Prince Albert, or "consort" style, morning coat. All the other male contestants were similarly garbed. One gathers that the suits were rented, probably by the host college. None fitted particularly well. The ninth contestant, who remained seated in the picture, was a determined-looking and wide-eyed young woman. Jane Addams, representing Rockford College for Women, appeared somewhat less frozen than her companions, but her expression suggested the unseen but painful presence of photographers' braces.

Four, including the woman who would become known as Jane Addams of Hull House, failed to survive the preliminary trials. The five finalists included Bryan of Illinois College. For the "grand trial" he saw fit to shift to an oration he had composed himself: "Justice." The finals filled an entire day, with each contestant allotted one hour.

Unquestionably the Galesburg *Plain Dealer* sensed the importance of the event, and assigned a gifted and thoughtful reporter to cover it. The latter dwelled lucidly on the intrinsic importance of oratory in college curricula, pointing out that a third of the U.S. public still could not read and were therefore particularly dependent on the "living and expressive personality." The cogent reporter appraised the offering of William Jennings Bryan as the best of the lot:

> There was something magnetic in the way in which W. J. Bryan of Illinois College stalked out to deliver "Justice." His full voice, his clear articulation, good and not affected modulation, his natural style of gesturing and delivery made him a favorite with the audience. His style was matter of fact. Though an occasional hyperbole stole in, his figures were good. While at times declamatory, on the whole he delivered his oration finely. . . .

But Bryan of Illinois College did not win first place; he barely made second place and its consolation prize of fifty dollars. He presently learned that two of the judges had rated him first, but the third judge had placed him fifth and last.

Bryan's initial reaction was heartbreak. After all, he wasn't just another contestant. He was a man with a very special destiny, which included being engaged. Still, there were real consolations with the award. There would be other contests, and the fifty dollars prize money was the most he had ever earned or owned. He put aside most of the winnings to buy a ring for one Mary Elizabeth Baird.

Here, of course, the decision was bilateral; yet there were impediments. Though quartered within view of each other, the young couple, by decree of Erastus Bullard, were still reduced to keeping in touch wholly by correspondence across the one hundred yards. They made plans for Bryan to spend the oncoming Thanksgiving holidays at Mamie's home; there Will would formally ask John Baird for his daughter's hand in marriage. When the permission was granted, as Mamie was certain it would be, they could reach a verdict on the engagement ring. This was the proper procedure. At about this time Mamie wrote to him reflectively:

> . . . Being a girl has a few advantages after all. When you ask J.B. [John Baird] and if he fails to arrange matters satisfactorily there is a party concerned who can and will manage *him*. . . .

Will and Mamie traveled together by train to Perryville. Bryan knew that his prospective father-in-law was an able Bible student, and had readied what he regarded as a suitable quotation from the part of the Bible he knew best. Nervously and with unusual stammering, the young suitor began: "I have been reading *Proverbs* a good bit lately and find that Solomon says, 'Whoso findeth a wife findeth a good thing and obtaineth favour of the Lord.'"

John Baird listened solemnly. "Yes, I believe Solomon did say that. But St. Paul suggested that while he that marrieth doeth well, he that marrieth not doeth better."

Momentarily Will was quelled. Then with a flash of inspiration he countered, "Solomon would be the best authority on the point because St. Paul never married, whereas Solomon had a number of wives."

The parrying seems to have ended. John Baird gave his consent. The Thanksgiving festivities proceeded. The engaged couple then returned to school, each with a class to lead.

As his year of graduation (1881) began, Will was doubly determined to win the valedictory and in all ways to stand independently. He would take no more money from his mother. He succeeded in adding five hours weekly, at ten cents per hour, to his work stint at Hofra's. When the spring serenading season began in late April, he kept selling hats. He explained that he didn't really mean to be a killjoy, he simply couldn't sing; besides, he needed the money. When Mamie suggested that they could get

married right after graduation and "keep separate accounts," Will firmly declined. He wrote sagaciously that
no woman could love a man "if she performed her domestic
duties and also paid for her own support. . . ."

With deeply feminine concern, Mamie wrote of her wish
to make a favorable impression on Will's mother. Mariah
Bryan and her other children would be down for graduation.

> . . . I tell you, if I stood in her shoes I would just
> hate the girl who dared fall in love with my prize
> —the "staff of my declining years." I won't blame
> her if she tries to make us quarrel and separate. . . .

Will was not worried on that score. He seemed to sense
—correctly—that of all the strong-willed women in his life,
his mother was the most generous.

The final college year hurried along, and the sturdy
young believer from Salem Village continued to lead his
class. Apparently without exception, the teachers liked him.
The reaction of students was mixed; but the senior class
prophet was disposed to prophesy, "1900 sees Bryan in
the White House."

Then graduation came. Illinois College issued another
batch of diplomas, seven in the "arts," four in the
"sciences." The oratory of William Jennings Bryan received a double billing. His graduation oration was entitled "Character." His valedictory was a warm and emotional farewell to his alma mater. Both orations were
cluttered with redundancies and hyperbole. Nevertheless,
each carried a recognizable ring of sincerity and an exceptional, somewhat muted compassion. They were documents of youth and age-old belief, and again a strange
poetry of the spoken word.

5. The Lawyer

By his twentieth birthday Will Bryan had thoughtfully announced his decision, abetted by Mamie Baird's, to be a lawyer. As a wife and sister of lawyers, Mariah Bryan openly doubted that her first and, as she believed, her most gifted son, would find complete fulfillment in the profession. She continued to believe that his first talent was for "believing," and that whatever other profession he might choose, his destiny was that of preaching. Mariah was aware that effective ministry can be fitted in with other professions or trades; Will's father had earned respect and proved great usefulness as a preaching judge and lawyer and a believing, sermon-prone legislator. Her own father had left a revered name as a church-leading farmer.

No less understandably, Silas Bryan's widow was grateful for her son's determination to put himself through law school. As financial matters stood, she had little to offer him except her prayers, good wishes, and moral encouragement. Silas Bryan had left a very modest estate—one mortgage of about sixty-five hunded dollars was still outstanding, and, as the local saying went, the true value of farm lands and buildings depended on the owner's immediate condition of spirits. Silas had also left with his executor, his brother John, his conviction that a widow is ethically bound to share her late husband's liabilities as well as his assets—in keeping with the "for better or worse" clause, which is of the decisive rootage of what the late Judge Bryan had termed the civil marriage contract.

Furthermore, and in ample company, Silas Bryan had died not only "land poor," but poor-land poor. Certainly his estate at best was only skimpily adequate for the minimal needs of the younger children, of whom Russell and Charles were still listed as "frail." Although well aware of this, the widow also remembered vividly that her late husband had directed that his eldest son should be "helped along" through a reputable law school; in the last letter he wrote he had expressed deep gratitude for the offer of his admired friend, Lyman Trumbull, to assist in "steering" Will to and through the Union College of Law at Chicago.

"Union Law" would one day be absorbed by Northwestern University Law School, but at the time it was the oldest law college in Illinois and one of the more highly respected in the Midwest. Union was also a "work and learn" school; each student was encouraged, indeed expected, to work twenty hours or more weekly in an accredited law office in Chicago or its immediate area, thereby earning a "subsistence honorarium" averaging somewhere near five dollars per week.

Regardless of the fact that Judge Trumbull still maintained his own law office and "participated" in others (he had accepted a post as special lecturer at the newer University of Chicago Law School), his youngest son, Henry, was enrolling at Union. "Young Harry," who was close to Will's age, had made a rather stormy beginning in higher education; he had been expelled from Yale for drinking and related transgressions. He would be striving to "begin anew" at home. (One gathers that the reference here was to gentlemanly study, not boozing.) Will Bryan could surely be helpful to Henry Trumbull, the prematurely dark sheep in an illustrious lineage, which, even if not as the driven snow, had remained at least on the whitish side.

Following graduation from Illinois College, Bryan worked on the farm until the final week in August, then traveled to Perryville for a three-day visit with Mamie Baird. Having returned to Salem to say good-bye to his family and attend an improvised reunion of kin, he joined two of his boyhood friends on a frugal day-coach ride to Chicago. Don Kagy, the son of another local lawyer, planned to follow in his father's footsteps; Gran Huett was Chicago-bound to study medicine. Kagy, who had a flair for metaphor, later described the train coach as a baking oven on wheels and mentioned the train meals, which consisted of penny candy bars, as being symbolic of what the young men would face in Chicago, the Big Sister of the West. They reached the city on the sweltering night of August 31, 1881, and took refuge in a Y.M.C.A. "shelter," a polite term for flophouse, while searching for more permanent quarters.

From the moment of his arrival, Bryan disliked Chicago; this was the beginning of a long career of detesting big cities. In the beginning 1880s Chicago offered a great deal to detest. By then it had slightly more than half a million people—some five hundred times as many as Salem, Illinois. Salem was as rural as a homemade hoe handle; Chicago, to Bryan's eyes, was a monstrous thing of almost terrifying urbanity. Within a few hours he found a source of outrage. The city was at once witheringly poor and ridiculously rich. Salem was a county seat village of poor people accustomed to accepting "reasonable" poverty as a way of life. In Chicago, virulent contrast was the order of the day and night. Plutocrats' mansions backed into beggars' rows. The newcomer found the appalling contrast antisocial and distinctly ungodly.

Back in Salem Village the cattle and hogs roamed in comparative tranquillity and with a marked degree of liberty. In Chicago the cattle and hogs bellowed, grunted, and stank in huge, imprisoning enclosures called stockyards. In all, Salem had about one mile of sidewalks, for the most part built of wood. Chicago, so the give-away folders proclaimed, had eighty-three miles of sidewalks, including at least eleven miles made of the newfangled artificial rock called cement. As yet Salem had no pavements. Chicago was boasting two hundred miles of paved streets, including what were listed as "improved avenues." As Will saw them, they could stand further improvement. During his first day he crossed several streets ankle-deep in horse manure and other excrement. He watched ragged children playing, or rather chasing, in and through the street filth. Unpainted lean-tos and oversize shacks called tenements seemed to rise like evil mushrooms. Ragged beggars peered out from the alleys; stumbling drunkards flocked the sidewalks; prostitutes spat and catcalled from doors or windows.

When the young travelers parted, Bryan searched for the Trumbull home. After squandering several nickels on erroneous trolley car rides, he found his way to suburban Grand View. However grand the view what impressed him most was Lyman Trumbull, white-haired, kindly featured, proudly erect, yet blessed with a strange, warm humility. The gentleman judge had others to counsel besides young would-be lawyers. He was helping to organize public demonstrations, including street parades, in behalf of such radical causes as the limitation of working hours for children, state control of railroad freight rates and passenger fares, the enactment of federal pure food and drug laws, and the creation of labor unions. (In the Chicago of September 1881, a shaky embryo amalgamation of railroad workers' unions was attempting to set up a strike for a basic trainman wage of twenty cents an hour.)

The newcomer was deeply interested. Within a few hours

his repugnance for the big town found a counterbalance in his virtual adoration of Lyman Trumbull. Although Judge Trumbull was not in a position to invite his young caller to live in his home, he gave Bryan a standing invitation to spend Sunday afternoons as a house guest. He had also arranged for the son of his old friend from Salem to report for work as student helper in the downtown offices of Davidson and Gray, a law firm with which Judge Trumbull had lately been associated. He also introduced Will to his problem son Henry, whom the new arriver also liked.

In searching for a room to live in, Will strayed far from the prominent landmark of the law school—the then new Moody and Sankey Tabernacle. He bypassed the many inexpensive rooming houses in that area and prowled on and on, with shoulder valise weighing more and more heavily, until he arrived in the neighborhood of Hyde Park, then the far South Side. There, in a tenement within smelling distance of stockyards, he rented a hall bedroom for one dollar a week. The dissolute-looking rooming house was filled principally with other new arrivals, immigrants who were slaughterhouse workers.

The dismal little room was connected to the law school by a reasonable trolley car ride, but most of the time Bryan chose to walk. This was one of the surer means of saving money. His years at Jacksonville had been etched in frugality; from its beginnings his law school interval was one of heavy, grueling poverty. He not only tolerated it, he deliberately tied himself to the city's most extensive stronghold of poverty.

Here all his earlier experiences with penny-pinching seemed compounded by immediacy. At twenty-one he was on his own in a hard, strange land. He seemed aware that throughout most of his earlier life he had been diligent most of the time, but in the main steered or pushed or helped along by those more perceptive and determined.

Now, for the first time in his experience, he was on his own.

Almost instantly food became his primary want. Food was cheap, but Will was a heavy eater. Simple arithmetic directed him to keep his food budget below fifty cents a day. A first policy was to pay no more than a dime for breakfast. Many eating places in Chicago were serving one egg, toast and coffee for a dime, but the lean youngster from downstate required more satisfying bulk. After shopping around, he located an establishment that dispensed three large sweet rolls for ten cents, as against the usual nickel apiece. What followed was unquestionably a comfort to the Bryan hunger pains, but it could have contributed to the beginnings of his diabetes.

Dime lunches were readily attainable and perhaps less damaging than the three-sweet-roll breakfasts. Bryan looked to the pushcart peddlers who offered such bargains as nickel sandwiches, two-cent half cantaloupes, and the ten-cent wonders including gastronomic heroics like thick onion rolls stuffed with sliced cheese, corned beef, or boiled ham. For supper, he could squander up to twenty-five cents.

There were complications and moments of strain. Will recalled a grim Sunday when he found himself obliged to treat three fellow students to lunch. With a quick hitch at his distressingly thin wallet, the victim led the way to a bargain food counter. There he pondered the available "specials," among them immense servings of apple dumplings for ten cents. He invested in four of those and delivered them to his clamoring guests. When all the bowls were empty there were, as he had feared, mumblings about dessert. After a painstaking view of the dessert counter, Bryan returned to the table with four portions of apple pie. By then the tab had grown to the serious dimension of sixty cents, but at least nobody complained about being hungry. "I figured that two servings of apples would fill us up, and I would save a little on the meal," their host explained.

Down on La Salle Street, the Union College of Law was

demonstrating comparable frugality. In its twenty-seventh year, the school occupied approximately three-fourths of a drab four-story office building. The ground floor was crammed with small shops and commercial offices. On the second floor were the lecture hall and study hall, with a side tier of conference rooms. The third floor was given over to a library and adjoining reading rooms, the top floor to the convocation or "club hall" and a skimpily furnished student lounge. The faculty consisted of three regulars and an aged and sad-featured former court clerk, T. A. Connelly, who was registrar, monitor, and director of student employment. The senior faculty member, John Cassius Maroney, occupied a figurative settee as professor of jurisprudence, dean, and acting president.

Classroom hours were from eight to ten in the morning and, excepting Saturdays, four to six in the afternoon. The remaining weekday hours were for "earning stints." The loud, odorous, and growing city served as campus.

For the 1881 opening a total of eighty-seven students, including two young women, reported. As was his custom, the sad-featured Mr. Connelly called the roll alphabetically, without differentiating between first- and second-year status, then assigned study hall—two-man benches with flat-topped desks—to the enrollees. Since there were no A's, Bryan's name was the first listed; with orderly matter-of-factness the monitor assigned him to the first desk. When the chairman came to the T's, all the benches had at least one occupant.

"Talbot, Adolphus!"

Bryan became aware that a blocky young man was slipping into the seat beside him. He smiled and Adolphus Talbot smiled back. "Liking Bryan came easy," "Dolph" recalled.

Later that morning the neophytes reported to their respective places of work. Will was generally pleased with his clerking job, menial as it was. "Clerking" included sweeping, dusting, furniture polishing, tidying the library, emptying waste baskets, filling inkwells, and other janitorial chores, but there were also more professional endeavors, such as copying briefs. The beginner soon became exposed to the recent invention called the typewriter, and formed an immediate, lifelong dislike for it. To the end of his days he remained a pen-and-ink man, his handwriting and propensity for splashing ink tending to grow worse and worse.

Will was not really pleased with Union College. He did not like the grading system, with its three attainable marks of "passed," "failed," or "incomplete." The young man from Salem failed no courses and left none incomplete, but he felt that in such entries as jurisprudence and constitutional law, in which he excelled, he deserved more than a hastily scrawled "pass." Even more disappointing was the complete lack of a campus life. Union Law had only one student organization, a misnamed literary society that held occasional evening meetings. But these were largely confined to impromptu discussions of the toils and problems of studying law, or to "addresses" by visiting lawyers or politicians. After listening to several of those, Bryan moved to organize a debating team. The meeting voted no. When young Henry Trumbull headed a drive to elect Bryan to the newly invented post of Society Orator, the honoree responded with his rendition of "Eternal Vigilance Is the Price of Safety." But the membership reacted coolly.

Bryan's efforts to bestir classroom debates also failed to fire interest. In time, and it would seem with real disappointment, he became resigned to the fact that most of his fellow students were primarily interested in passing the state bar examination. The majority was several years older than Will, and most were local residents who saw law practice as more inviting than clerking in a haberdashery or driving a delivery wagon. Dolph Talbot recalled that a substantial number of the enrollees relaxed by group invasions of *biergartens,* burlesque shows, or the even naughtier diversions called Tableaux, or Living Statues, in which shapely young women, largely unimpeded by clothing, displayed themselves in groups *"for the sake of art."*

Bryan took no part in these or similar entertainments, but he made no display of sanctimony. He simply lacked the appetite, time, and money for such diversions; he spent most evenings in his dingy little room, alone with his law texts and the drifting stench of the nearby stockyards.

But the solitude was not absolute. Gradually Bryan won friends. On a day when the handsome youngest Trumbull came to school drunk, the acting president suspended him for a week and placed him in Bryan's personal custody for the ensuing month. There appears to be no record of the precise aftermath, except that the two remained good friends.

Through the lean, grim months Bryan apparently subsisted almost wholly on his earnings as a law office flunky. He continued writing regularly to his mother and to his beloved Mamie, who continued to report progress in cooking and baking and attending to cows, even while helping her father keep the store and her mother enjoy delicate health. During his first year of law school Bryan mentioned only one extravagance, the purchase of a slightly used notary seal. Early the following year, by virtue of a footnote on the precinct ballot, the shaggy and lean student was elected a notary public. This, as demonstrated by a document dispatched to his sweetheart, found a use for his seal:

I, W. J. Bryan, a Notary Public in and for the County of Cook, State of Ill., do hereby certify that I this day appeared before myself and being duly sworn, deposed and said I loved and do love Mamie E. Baird, better than I do any one else in the world, and further that I always will love her, will be good to her, and contribute as largely as possible to her happiness and usefulness.

In testimony whereof I witness my hand and notorial seal

s/s W. J. Bryan
Notary Public

As a mere pass-or-flunk school, Union Law permitted each graduating class to elect its own valedictorian; this was the only elective office available to the student body. Bryan made a try for it. His efforts revealed what he found to be the rather disillusioning truth that even though most politicians are lawyers, most lawyers are not politicians. "By definition politics is, or should be, Godly work," the eager and somewhat seedy young man from Salem insisted. "Politics is the duty of God's children."

The explanation did not exactly strike fire. Bryan also noted that in the main his fellow law students were not deeply interested in any of the social problems that crowded about them. They tended to see poverty and wretchedness as the fault of individuals rather than of government, a point of view Bryan would not accept. Many of the students looked on constitutions as mélanges of verbiage that aspiring lawyers were obliged to study; not, as Bryan saw them, as the Magna Carta incarnate. They tended to speak and feel more seriously about legal rights than legal obligations, and much more of privilege than moral mandates. Bryan did not comprehend this, either.

Such breaches of viewpoint conspicuously widened upon the election of the class valedictorian. Bryan had been nominated with recommendations of the faculty, but when the votes were counted, he lost the election by a single vote. He demanded a recount, but again the effort was in vain.

As he entered the final stretch of Law School, Will Bryan became even more solitary and his financial situation ever shakier. There is reason to suspect that he often went hungry; at best his bargain-counter fare was far less than sufficient. His clothing supply dwindled to a shabby serge suit for winter wear and a creaseless alpaca for summer. At one period the former hat store salesman didn't even own a hat. He gave up wearing starched collars and cuffs and shifted to common blue or gray workshirts without benefit of ties. His neglect of haircuts became chronic, and his lengthening black hair seemed to be in ceaseless revolt against comb or brush.

His distinctly perfunctory letters of the period (almost exclusively to his sweetheart or his mother), suggest that Bryan was spending more than a little of his time arguing with himself about whether or not he really wished to be a lawyer. Apparently his negative debate tactics were gradually leading to an affirmative decision. He *would* be a lawyer. He would not rule out his prospects as a politician, preacher, orator, author, lecturer, farmer, or any combination thereof. He would go to Congress. He would be a Christian statesman. He would labor to better the lot of the common people. But first, so help him God, he would be a lawyer.

Henry Trumbull, newly changed to perhaps the most scholarly member of his class, announced that he would be going west to start his law practice. He was resolved to break away from his father's orbit of eminence and strike out for the fabulous wilds of New Mexico Territory. Dolph Talbot was disposed to choose the already booming Great Plains country, preferably Nebraska. (This "westward-hoing" was a trend of the times in law as well as in most other professions.) Though Bryan did not confide his choice of a site for practice, he pointed out quite knowledgeably that the Illinois Constitution (of 1871), which his father had helped draft and which the students had been virtually required to memorize, had strongly influenced constitutions subsequently adopted by several newer states, including Nebraska and Kansas, which suggested that these places might be of interest to him.

Shortly before his twenty-second birthday, Bryan managed to squeeze together enough money for a bargain day-coach journey to the booming border town that had recently been renamed Kansas City. Like Chicago, the place was too big and loud for his liking. He came back visibly disappointed, and confided to his seatmate that he just couldn't seem to get his feet on the ground in Kansas City.

Union Law's second-year class, meanwhile, was driving hard to prepare for the state bar examination; passing this was a prerequisite for formal graduation. Bryan had barely settled to the final marathon of study when he received sad news from home. His next younger brother, Russell, the more sickly one, had taken a turn for the worse. Early in the year, which was Russell's seventeenth, the frailest of the Bryan boys had been accepted by Whipple's Academy for admission the following fall. He had never before been well enough to leave home, but it was hoped that his tuberculosis had been arrested. Then, late in March, Russell suffered what may have been appendicitis and did not survive the seizure. His was the fifth death in the immediate family of Silas and Mariah Bryan. Mute with grief, Will again journeyed to Salem to attend a funeral.

Back in Chicago, he once more submerged himself in work. Late in May he and his classmates took the Illinois State Bar examination. His rank was fourth; Henry Trumbull's was highest; Dolph Talbot was second. Their tenure in law school ended as matter-of-factly as it had begun. Marshall Ewell, newly promoted to the chairmanship of the school, had taken time to jot down his professional estimate of the strengths and weaknesses of each of the graduates. He appraised Bryan as one with proven ability in "basic" jurisprudence, English-Roman common law, and American constitutional law, but recommended that he strive to develop himself as a jury lawyer.

Following the modest graduation exercises, Bryan and his friend Henry were honored by a small "lawyers' dinner" at the Trumbull home. In an exceptionally long letter to his mother, Bryan dwelled on his belief that his association with Lyman Trumbull had been the most valuable gain from his long—at least it had seemed long—grind of law school. He was especially impressed by the Trumbull devotion to social justice, which the great man called "the peoples' law." He pointed out that "Sir Lyman's" lifelong belief was that the brotherhood of man and the equality of privileges should be attainable both legally and politically; also that the uncontrolled amassing of wealth diminishes the freedom of the individual and destroys the integrity of private property. Will Bryan reverently agreed.

He also agreed that such socially just but as yet unattained legislation as the graduated income tax and the protection of the public good by means of effective antitrust laws was indispensable. In all, young Will Bryan saw aging Lyman Trumbull as a particularly able embodiment of the Christian statesman at work. He was more than a poor law student's hero; Trumbull was a Messiah for justice as the word of life, God's word.

Will insisted that God's word was not being spoken by enough Chicagoans. Even so, he could not and did not brand it a godless city. At least its church life was almost frenziedly active.

Despite or because of his poverty and loneliness, Bryan had made a diligent practice of dividing his church attendance among various and contrasting denominations. During his nineteen months of law school he had sampled further the fare of the Greek Orthodox, Catholic, Moravian, Jewish, and at least a dozen other congregations. He was welcomed alike at synagogues and Y.M.C.A. club rooms, at "conscience wakes of Quakers," and in at least one instance at Mormon services in a private home. How deeply or how regularly he "felt God's presence" (to quote his own words) is somewhat conjectural, although he wrote his mother that he regarded the shopping around among different denominations an enlightening adventure.

But he intimated that he came out less than satisfied with the total "spiritual harvest." All too few Chicagoans appeared to be "true and deep believers." He expressed some degree of gratitude for being within what he could term communication distance of sizable even if not great numbers of fundamental believers.

Will Bryan continued to associate the survival of his own fundamental faith with specific places or environments. This credo appears to have been a principal force in drawing him back to his homeland, if not to the perennially open-range village of Salem, then to Jacksonville, which at least for the time was Mamie Baird's first choice of a place in which to begin their married life.

Subsequent correspondence confirms that Will confided the foregoing to his seatmate and particularly good friend Dolph Talbot, who was already Nebraska-bound as a junior attorney, or "resident legal retainer, junior grade," to use the more formal designation, for the thriving Southern Pacific Railway. When his friend insisted that fundamental faith in an omnipotent God was not really a regional attribute but could obtain in Nebraska as well as in Illinois, Bryan solemnly repeated that he had made up his mind to go back to what he knew for sure was God's country. For that most important privilege he would not hesitate to make financial sacrifices; he was entirely willing to take his own chances on building a law practice in Jacksonville. Even if his earnings should be no more than five hundred a year, all he really required was enough to marry Mamie and support her and their family, even if only very modestly. Dolph Talbot's argument that Jacksonville was no doubt already saturated with lawyers, whereas the New West needed lawyers to grow up with it, went unheard.

By then Will's and Mamie's matrimonial plans were set. Throughout his hard stay in Chicago she had continued to favor him with love letters of warming sincerity. She sprinkled her letters with such reassuring intelligence as the news that she had proved herself a passable cook, that she had mastered the knack of milking a frequently unwilling cow without getting either the milk pail or herself kicked over the shed, that she was helping her father keep store, and was in various and sundry ways preparing to be Mrs. William Jennings Bryan.

He repeated his willingness to have Mamie continue to "help out" her father, who was surely if gradually losing his eyesight, and her mother, who was a far advanced hypochondriac—the local term was "spleeny"—after Mamie became his wife. Bryan did not expect his fiancée to abandon her parents. But when Mamie wrote of her father's willingness to provide a dwelling suitable for two families—wherever the newlyweds directed they wished to live—and to help at least temporarily with paying their bills, Bryan continued to answer emphatically that he would support his own family, and as soon as he was able, pay for their own home.

Having stated his intentions, Will made ready to leave Chicago the day his stint at law school was ended. Breaking camp was the epitome of simplicity. He had more than enough room in his one valise for what remained of his wardrobe; the rest of his burden was law books. Mamie had urged that he bring home the books; she had a "girlish curiosity" to see them.

Following a brief visit to the Baird home, Bryan put in the ensuing June working on his mother's farm. When the farm was at least partially in shape, he accepted wages of forty dollars as a loan. He spent twelve dollars for a suit, ten dollars for a contribution to the local Presbyterian Church, and the rest for setting up his law practice in Jacksonville.

Once more he found himself a welcome guest in the home of Hiram Jones, M.A. and M.D. Cousin Hiram seemed as unchanged as his big white house and his unquenchable ramblings into philosophy. He was happy to learn of his favorite second cousin's decision to hang out his shingle locally. He expressed perceptive regret that 1883 was an off-year politically; for the time Jacksonville had only one controversial issue—municipal referendum to decide whether or not milk cows would be confined to quarters or continue to stroll at large. Correctly Will predicted that the outcome of the voting would be decided by two counts—the tally of local citizens who owned cows and those who did not. Cow owners were more numerous than nonowners, and their interests prevailed.

Bryan thus proved his first premise of American politics: Voters are inherently partisan. Political views are colored by personal desires. A winning political issue is one that accommodates more personal or private advantages than it frustrates.

He was also to learn that, in general, Jacksonville favored cows more than it did young lawyers. After making the rounds of law firms, then numbering sixteen, he discovered that none required a junior partner. The leading firm of Brown, Kirby & Russell, which had spoken the most emphatic "No," did admit that it might find a place for a compatible bill collector. It had an unused revolving chair and a scarred but still usable rolltop desk for which there was unoccupied space in the waiting room. The firm would be willing to permit a personable young man with a new and unblurred law license to occupy the desk and make himself useful as a collector of unpaid debts. Both the law firm and the town had plenty of them. While trying his hand as a collector, Bryan would be permitted to drum up an occasional law case independently, in no instance at the expense or embarrassment of Brown, Kirby & Russell. Affably, Will accepted, and announced that he would open his "practice" on July 4, so that the entire nation could help celebrate the historic occasion.

It was the tired old story of a young lawyer striving to get his best foot on the bottom rung. Throughout the first sultry week no client appeared.

On July 13, a customer came in—John Sheehan, whom

Bryan had met and befriended while Sheehan was Cousin Hiram's hired man. Recently transformed into one of the town's more active liquor merchants and saloonkeepers, John was being bothered by too many customers too much disposed to writing IOU's for their libations. He required some capable collecting.

"I don't approve of drinking liquor," the new lawyer answered. "But I believe that people should pay for what they drink." And so the law practice of a man destined to be the most renowned of the prohibitionists began with a liquor account. John Sheehan propositioned that if Bryan could collect an especially noxious arrears of $2.60 he would follow with all the rest of his collection business and, as opportunity allowed, some nondrinking clients.

Instead of calling in person, Bryan wrote the delinquent a courteous letter. The debtor called and handed over the $2.60. The novice lawyer placed the money in a separate envelope, thus making certain that he could settle in full with the creditor without delay. Some twenty-five years later the practice of holding client's funds separate and apart from any other monies was formally included in the code of ethical practices of the American Bar Association. Envelope in hand, the ethical collector walked to the door of Sheehan's saloon and, without entering, handed the proprietor the sum in hand less fifty-two cents, the standard 20 percent fee for collecting.

The new lawyer was off on six months of paltry collecting chores. During the first month, his gross earnings were $2.53. At year's end, his total earnings had reached sixty-seven dollars. From that he began repaying the loan from his mother.

But matrimony with the prearranged condition that he would earn five hundred dollars a year still seemed remote. From the sylvan spaces of Perryville, Mamie continued to send messages of love and encouragement. Her father had already set about selling his store, his home, and other real estate holdings in preparation for inevitable retirement because of blindness. The groom-to-be answered:

> . . . I am practicing on "and with all my worldly goods I thee endow" so as to make it duly impressive. If you dare laugh when I say that, I won't kiss you when he tells me to salute my bride. . . .

Mamie wrote of such important subjects as how a husband and wife may best spend leisure time together. She also had a variety of cogent reflections:

> . . . I hold the theory that if a wife does not show interest in her husband's work and does not go with him when he asks her, the time may come when he will cease to ask her. . . .

Among liquor man Sheehan's several debtors was a tippling but well-intentioned livery stable proprietor who vowed he would pay what he owed if his debtors would only pay him. On that basis, Bryan began collecting unpaid livery stable bills for the settlement of liquor bills. He succeeded; the purveyor of rented horses and buggies was able to settle his saloon debts, pay Bryan's commissions, and still have money in his pocket.

This dual achievement led to a next case. One morning the livery stable proprietor found himself missing a horse. Believing the animal had been stolen, he offered a twenty-five-dollar reward for its return. A policeman, meanwhile, had found the horse only a few blocks from the stable, returned it, and demanded the reward. The stableman contended that this did not come within the "spirit" of the reward offer. Bryan counseled his client to pay the reward and sue for a refund. After careful search he found a city ordinance that made unlawful a reward to a policeman for work done in the line of duty. He pleaded the ordinance and won the suit on grounds of "constitutional responsibility." The somewhat Pyrrhic victory won a cordial following among the local livery stable set, offset by a marked coolness on the part of the police force. In any case, Bryan felt he was defending the underdog and preventing the wrong.

After ten months of little other than bill collecting, Ed McDonald, Sr., an old-time court lawyer, astonished Bryan by inviting him to assist the defense in an assault case. After the noon recess, Bryan made his first address before a real jury. With bubbling enthusiasm, he wrote Mamie of the adventure:

> . . . I was complimented by the judge and several attorneys. The *Courier* said, "W. J. Bryan was highly complimented on Monday for his success in his first speech before a circuit court jury!"
>
> I think Mr. McDonald was real kind to keep me in this way. . . . I am to help him in the case of Russell who cut his wife's throat. . . . Will tell you of my practice, do you want me to? . . .

As he began to emerge as a defender in jury cases, Bryan reverted to his tactics as a negative debater, projecting the prosecutor as the affirmative. His bearing and voice were gentle and, as some said, almost womanlike. But he was holding the courtroom's attention, and his efforts appeared to help in lessening the prevailing cruelly severe sentences.

During his first year in Jacksonville, the new lawyer resumed his career as a joiner by seeking membership in the Knights of Pythias. Promptly, he began campaigning for election as president or grand chancellor of the local lodge; more surprisingly, he won the election.

Other endeavors confirmed the adage that the road back is hard. But Bryan's mood was one of compliance. The following spring, when the county bar association set about organizing a lawyers' and courthouse workers' baseball club, two adversities appeared almost instantly. One was the team's unfortunate nickname, "the Court House Black-legs"; the other was the eager appearance of William Bryan as a candidate for any available position on the team. The inept college player was now playing disas-trously. When the lawyers lost the season's opener to a local lumber workers' club, the newspaper suggested that Bryan had contributed more than his share to the score of 13 to 1, strongly intimating that the lawyers' third base-man, who openly admitted that he could not sing, dance, drink, or shoot straight, had demonstrated that he couldn't play baseball, either. The *Courier* was at least impressed by the fact that Bryan tried; he shone most vividly while chasing fly balls with shirttails flying in the wind.

But the bill-collecting lawyer was faring somewhat better in his work. John Sheehan, the neighborly saloonkeeper, brought him his first substantial client, the source of a two-hundred-dollar fee. Bryan was delighted, the more so be-cause that represented income to marry on. By the end of his second summer the slender but sturdy young lawyer was reaching his quota of five hundred dollars a year. Dur-ing August the Bairds of Perryville announced October 1 as their daughter's wedding day. It was less than breath-taking news. The couple's engagement had been recorded in the college newspaper, *The Rambler,* almost four years before; the groom ordered a wedding ring with the inscrip-tion: *Won 1880—One 1884.*

The wedding was held in the Perryville Federated Church; kin and in-laws of the groom alone reportedly numbered close to seventy. The less-numerous Baird fam-ily and friends packed the remainder of the church, with onlookers overflowing into a nearby oak grove. Charles, the groom's fifteen-year-old brother, served as best man, and with rather surprising presence of mind handed over the wedding ring when asked. Aboard the train to St. Louis, where the newlyweds intended to spend a weekend honey-moon at Planter's Hotel, Mamie was embarrassed when her new brother-in-law, apparently in a seizure of adolescent nervousness, admitted to a prying fellow passenger that theirs was a wedding trip; the bride was deeply mortified by the ensuing stares and sniggers.

After Charlie left the train at the Salem depot, the honeymoon seems to have progressed most successfully. Mr. and Mrs. William Jennings Bryan returned to Jacksonville agreed that never before had any bride and groom been so happy as they. The honeymoon was to continue for a long time; as Bryan estimated, about forty years. John Baird had already purchased a presentable, modest cottage on College Hill in Jacksonville for the use of the newlyweds, though in due time the Bairds would arrive as permanent guests. The young bride and groom moved into the old place and set about making it young again. They lived there alone for the first three months.

Will returned to his rolltop desk and his sidewalk law practice. For the time at least he seemed to move in a blissfully happy dream. He smiled even more than usual, and according to his youngest sister Mary Elizabeth, he looked as if he were hearing the voices of ten million angels.

Despite this, or possibly because of it, the groom began finding himself with an increasing number of clients. His earnings steadily grew until by the year's end he had recorded a gross income of about seven hundred dollars, somewhere near the prevailing wage of an Illinois College professor.

Bryan was happy as an earning lawyer, and even happier as a husband. But fellow lawyers and others were noting that most of the Bryan clients were from the wrong side of the tracks. Instead of pursuing the well-off or socially elite, the smiling neophyte seemed to attract and welcome the riffraff. Careful readers of the newspaper could note that the William Jennings Bryans, personable as they were, simply were not swarming with the Jacksonville social bees.

Both continued to dress very modestly; Will usually looked like a backwoods farmer come to town for a brief turn of shopping. This fact appeared to add to his rural following. At home, Bryan donned overalls and worked like an energetic hired man, building a fence, clearing and spading a garden, planting a row of apple trees, and building a hen pen and chicken house that he eagerly stocked with white Wyandottes.

It was his Sunday behavior that evoked the most audible comment from his fellow townsmen. He and his bride attended the Cumberland Presbyterian Church. Rather frequently, Bryan appeared as a guest speaker or guest Sunday school teacher in other churches, and for good measure, he took over leadership of the Bible study group of the local Y.M.C.A. Nobody doubted his competence as a Bible scholar; there was general agreement that in particular areas of Biblical literature, such as the Book of Proverbs and the Psalms, he could quite probably hold his own with, or better than, any preacher in town.

On that point all was well, but in local church circles the Y.M.C.A. membership was far from being acceptable. Furthermore, by local estimates, Bryan's church-hopping, now more elegantly known as "interdenominationalism," was hardly discreet procedure; the prescribed course of the leading citizens of Jacksonville, Illinois, was "one wife, one church." At least, if one might occasionally stray afield and mix with Methodists or Adventists, or even Catholics, one oughtn't be so vulgarly obvious about it, or behave like a church-prone tramp.

In his church associations Will Bryan was for most of his life a baffling man. In his politics, Bryan's behavior was comparably odd. First and most impractically, he persisted in being a Democrat—in this resolute stronghold of Republicans. An upcoming and poor young lawyer, had he the brains God gives to baby field mice, would naturally have become a Republican.

There were other conspicuous paradoxes. Bryan was a teetotaler who steered clear of saloons. Yet, as mentioned, liquor dealer John Sheehan was his best client. Further, Bryan did not, as was then usual, keep away from Negroes. Again and again he was seen roaming and conversing in "Niggertown." That, quite aside from being avoidable, was extremely inept social behavior in Jacksonville, Illinois, in the 1880s.

His persistent habit of rubbing elbows with sidewalk riff-raff was still another cause for comment. It was getting so this rather tall man with the contrasting black hair and brown beard could be seen practically any day surrounded or tagged after by loafers. W. J. Bryan was getting to be a local landmark. The wagonyard crowd not only knew but obviously cherished him.

Ed McDonald, a man in the early months of a lifelong friendship with Bryan, was deeply concerned. He granted that there are times when a man who aspires to political office elbows with the country clodhoppers and town riff-raff. But deliberate or otherwise, Bryan's slumming was getting chronic. He was not overly concerned with dignity or distance. Take, for example, a Saturday afternoon, when a wheel bounced off a farm wagon right in the middle of Main Street. Who was there, big as life, strong as a mule and twice as muddy, lifting and propping the axle, then using a borrowed crowbar to try to force the wheel back in place? None but William Jennings Bryan.

Early in May 1885, Jacksonville suffered an embarrassing mishap relating to enforcement of law and order. On a dark night, Tiny Childress, the assistant police chief, shot and killed a local Negro named Thomas Bell. Reportedly, Ole Tom had been burglarizing a food store. But the principal was dead before he could be interrogated.

Bryan seemed deeply concerned. Ed McDonald, Jr., temporarily serving as attorney for the council, centered his concern on how to get the victim buried. The town had no funds for such purposes; none of the white preachers wanted any part of it; the only Negro preacher was seriously ill.

William Jennings Bryan "received" the body, paid for the funeral, and preached the service. And his bride was expecting their first child, a daughter who was born the day after their first wedding anniversary. Yet there was Bryan paying out $48.50, still the best part of a month's earnings, for the burial of a superannuated second-class citizen who probably hadn't earned $48.50 in ten years, and certainly hadn't a dime to his name.

Attorney McDonald attended the funeral in line of official duty. The service was oddly eloquent. Instead of merely reading over the remains, Bryan stood in the pulpit of the shabby little church and preached an entire sermon. He spoke of the peace of heaven and God's decree that his children are, indeed, their brothers' keepers. Then the young man who at times babbled about being a Christian statesman swung into a text that was not as Ed McDonald expected it to be (from Proverbs), but from the Revelation of St. John the Divine. McDonald was not too well acquainted with that Scripture; he had always looked on it as rather far afield from preaching texts, more prophetic than Christian, more godly than Christly. Yet as Will began to speak, the verses seemed to glow with life: the clear and crystal river of the water of life that proceeded out of the throne of God; the tree of life that bore twelve manner of fruit and leaves for the healing of the nations of men.

As a truthful man, Ed did not hesitate to affirm that he had never heard a better sermon. Bryan's words came forth with a strange and ringing poetry. Nevertheless, when the service was ended, the younger McDonald saw his duty and did it. He asked, in a nice way, if Bryan realized what he was doing to himself and to his future. Bryan answered that he waited God's ever particular instructions.

How does one go about counseling such a man? Ed

McDonald, Jr. honestly didn't know. But two things he did know, or believed he knew, for sure. The first was that in Jacksonville, Illinois, William Jennings Bryan was getting nowhere. He still appeared to see it in the misty haze of a college student's daydream. The second thing was that the big, likable oddball whose words poured out like music was beginning to find or otherwise acquire a particular resource for which young counselor McDonald could think of no better word than "character." Yet somehow that character just didn't belong in Jacksonville, Illinois.

To McDonald the situation seemed the more serious because Will Bryan was on the verge of becoming a father. Early the following month, November, Mamie bore him a first daughter, an extremely thin baby whom the delighted young parents named Ruth—her people would be their people, her God their God. And the child was healthy; the father was burbling that lean babies are the best kind.

6. Lincoln, Nebraska

For purposes of permanent establishment, Horace Greeley, popularizer of "Go west, young man!," went west almost exactly three hundred miles from his birthplace, Amherst, New Hampshire, by way of East Poultney, Vermont, to New York City. William Jennings Bryan's formative westward journey was from Jacksonville, Illinois, to Lincoln, Nebraska, approximately the same distance. It began on June 30, 1887, and involved no outlay of Bryan's own funds. The primary mission was to look at a plot of land in lower Iowa that his father-in-law owned and wished to sell. His related mission was to visit his law school friend, Adolphus Talbot. Talbot was settled in Lincoln as a resident attorney, more precisely a retained lawyer for the then largest western railroad.

With his customary frugality, Bryan learned that by deft routing and by buying a round-trip ticket from Jacksonville to Mason City, Iowa, he could make a stopover at Lincoln without a cent of extra expense. Accordingly, on July 1, the traveler found himself greeted by his blocky and balding former seatmate. Dolph picked up his friend's "V-bag," which Bryan confessed to having closed by pressing on the contents with his large right foot, and began leading the way across an outrageous clutter of seep holes, open ditches, pavement excavations, and partly blocked sidewalks. The new capital of the new state was undergoing an orgy of civic improvements, but Will was even more impressed by the young feeling of the town. At twenty-seven, Bryan was ten years older than Lincoln itself.

Dolph led on to the Burr Block, 12th and G Streets, where he had optioned a three-room office suite on the third floor of the Wilson Building. Here was room enough for a law partnership with living facilities for one of the partners, provided he wasn't too choosy about those facilities. When Talbot renewed his invitation to join him as law partner, Bryan impulsively accepted. "Talbot & Bryan" would be the name of the new firm, and Bryan promised that he would close shop in Jacksonville and return to Lincoln no later that the coming October 1. He repeated that he would come poor; the most he could hope to raise as a beginner's grubstake would be three hundred dollars.

Dolph, as usual, was understanding. For the beginning Bryan could make the waiting room of the prospective office his living quarters. There was already running water on tap, and Dolph had recently bought a used sofa that expanded into a reasonably good bed. He was also bargaining for another good-as-new rolltop desk. Bryan was obliged to board a late morning train to Mason City, but he vowed he would be back the following October to settle into the partnership. He had bridges to burn, but he had quite a pocketful of fire matches.

Dolph Talbot recalled that by 1882, or perhaps earlier, Bryan the Democrat had remarked that the rapid settlement of this New West would certainly change the political balance of the entire nation. Young Republican Talbot had agreed; he had a liking for statistics, a bent his partner never shared. By 1887, Dolph Talbot could point out that according to the U.S. census, the population of Nebraska had grown from 112,993 in 1870 to 452,402 in 1880, a decade's increase of about 267 percent. He expected, and quite correctly, that the 1890 census of the new state would be well over the million mark (it turned out to be 1,058,910). Adjacent states were growing in a comparable way. But Talbot was confident that new Nebraska was destined to remain Republican country, even as Will Bryan was bent on remaining a Democrat.

Although William Jennings Bryan was known to rely heavily on his feelings, his move west was a well-pondered decision. The first bold step called for parting with his homeland and for parting, at least temporarily, with his family life. His wife had their infant daughter to care for and, no less demandingly, her parents. Practically speaking, John Baird was now blind, and his wife Lovina was a resigned invalid. Mamie could not pack up and leave at a moment's notice.

Bryan went west alone; it was the eve of his third wedding anniversary. Early on the morning of October 1, 1887, Dolph Talbot again awaited his arrival at the grimly ugly railway station. Once more the partners-to-be picked their way along, amid the outrageous clutter of street-paving-in-progress that made downtown Lincoln look like a battlefield. Once more Bryan found himself liking the town, finding it exciting and reassuringly young, even younger than the strayed plow horse that, in a most fraternal manner, accompanied the two young men to the doorway of the Wilson Building on the Burr Block.

Early the following week Bryan easily passed the Nebraska State Bar examination and again received a license to practice law. Meanwhile, he had set out to learn all he could about the rather astonishing new capital. It was his first direct acquaintance with a body politic in the making.

Capital living was distinctly country style. Most families in the town kept their own horses and milk cows, and the state capital, which by then included the even newer state university, was generously dotted with haystacks, manure piles, unsightly small barns, sheds and pigpens. Plumbing was the out-of-door kind. Water was taken entirely from private wells and cisterns. Pending a public waterworks, the town council was "authorizing" rock-lined cisterns or "water catches" under principal street corners to facilitate firefighting.

But there had been progress nevertheless. Four years before Bryan's arrival, the newly founded Lincoln Gas Light Company had contracted with the town council to install and tend a first line of gas street lights and, as the contract stipulated, to "light and keep said lamps burning from early dusk until twelve o'clock midnight during the dark of the moon, and when it shall be too dark to pass along the streets with safety by reason of cloudiness. . . ."

The newest lawyer in town also noted other enlightening civic developments. The council had regulated the use of bicycles ("velocipedes") on the sidewalks by requiring riders to carry a bell in the daytime and a lantern at night. No less salubrious was the new ordinance that forbade riding or driving horses faster than six miles an hour, on penalty of a maximum fine of twenty dollars for each violation. However, for the benefit of the local sporting bloods, one street had been set aside for "fast horsing" and William Jennings Bryan was soon to prove himself one of the better horsemen of the area.

The town council had already splurged on one of the new telephones for the special use of the volunteer fire department and had instructed the police department to do its telephoning only when the set was not being used by the fire department. In addition, a municipal dump had been established, plus a manhole drainage program. Already, schoolchildren were receiving free vaccination for smallpox, one of the first such provisions anywhere in the nation. Also, the town had completed an isolated refuge for the treatment of contagious diseases, and a first public "lying-in" hospital.

Bryan was deeply impressed by these civic strides. He also formed a special attachment to another facility, a public library. Lincoln's enlightened pioneer mayor, William Hardy, who considered a public library as a primary municipal need, was shortly to become Bryan's first political hero in this New West. His stand for a public library was a typical exhibition of Hardy forthrightness. Lincoln already had a church-sponsored library, and shortly before Bryan arrived, the mayor had proposed that the town take over support of the library and make it a creditable public facility. The council seesawed and evaded. When the mayor persisted, two councilmen submitted that book reading was a frivolous and arbitrary diversion that no town government was obligated to encourage. When the council again voted him down on grounds of lack of revenue, Mayor Hardy said, "If and as necessary we will do away with the street lights and put that money for the library. Anybody can carry a lantern as a substitute for street lights, but there's no substitute for good books." Thus began Lincoln's first public library.

Shortly before Bryan's arrival Mayor Hardy had caused the new capital to take a brave, precedent-breaking fling at labor legislation. The street railroad company, operating horse-drawn cars, was compelling its employees to work sixteen to nineteen hours a day. The mayor investigated, and bluntly advised the street railroad company to mend its ways or hand back its franchise. Not long afterward Lincoln set another historic precedent by establishing eight-hour workdays for all municipal employees and for concessionaires or contractors performing work for the town.

Greatly impressed by his ensuing close look at labor protection "with teeth," Bryan studied other significant controversies with interest. One of these was the Bill Hardy move to persuade the town to give building sites to three denominational colleges, including one projected by the customarily scorned Seventh-day Adventists. "Any sincerely kept college," Presbyterian Bryan (temporarily attending the local Methodist Church) noted in one of his first letters to a local newspaper, "is . . . a meritorious and noble enterprise."

During the year of his arrival Lincoln had acquired its initial Board of Trade, eventually to emerge as the Chamber of Commerce. As a beginning project the board had set up a "freight bureau" and employed a veteran railroad freight solicitor to manage it. The objective was to reduce the discriminatory rates the new capital was suffering; prevailing freight rates were as much as four times higher west of the Mississippi than east.

Bryan promptly resumed his vehement stand against railroads. This position was hazardous. It was common knowledge that most of Nebraska's major politicians as well as substantial numbers of minor office-holders were on railroad payrolls. Bryan regarded such fundamental discrimination as unjust, and, he did not hestitate to add, ungodly. As the local saying went, this was pretty loud chirping from a snowbird who might not last through his first Nebraska winter.

Certainly the bird had not yet proved himself a financial eagle. His gross earnings from three months of law practice in Lincoln, practically all from bill collecting, amounted to $82.50. Young Mr. Bryan was still sleeping on an expandable sofa in the waiting room of his partner's law office, and by his own admission, he was indulging in lunches at the desk, lunches consisting of a nickel box of ginger snaps and a penny apple. Otherwise, he was subsisting on the produce of discounted meal tickets dispensed by O'Dell's Restaurant down the street.

In the course of his first address delivered to the assembled Board of Trade, the newcomer asserted that he had given painstaking and expert study to the entire issue of abusive rail freight rates. He had found that in the Lincoln area the railroads were taking about two-thirds of what the farmer got for his corn when he sold it in Chicago.

Lawyer Bryan could regard this only as the outrageous aftermath of a public-hurting conspiracy of vested interests.

The speaker did not approve the Board's dickering for a local branch of the Beat 'Em All Barb Wire Company (this name is actual), of Cedar Rapids, Iowa. His disapproval took the form of discreet quotation from the local sidewalk commentators, who were pointing out that barbed wire was already cutting the living guts out of the American Great Plains. Bryan stated that as a much-interested onlooker and as a horselover, he regarded barbed wire as inhumane. As an erstwhile dirt farmer he favored the use of rail or board fences and felt that most barbed wire enclosures were really unnecessary.

The young man with strong opinions listened alertly to store-counter discussions, and gave opinions with generosity and vigor.

One of the many vehement interests related to water supply. Bryan confided his resolve to become a Lincoln homeowner, a seemingly bizarre ambition for a bill collector with a meal budget held to fifty-two cents a day. But with the wonderful practicality of the apparently impractical person, Bryan cited water, second only to spiritual faith, as the first requirement for successful home building.

At the time the new Nebraska capital was better supplied with faith than drinking water. Five years earlier the town council had voted a ten-thousand-dollar bond issue for digging a public well sixty feet deep and five feet in diameter. The venture, though temporarily successful, could not long keep pace with multiplying needs. As the Lincoln *Call* had noted, the strain on well rope and muscle grease arising out of drawing water from sixty feet down had been known to lead normally abstemious citizens to quench their thirst from bunged barrels or brown bottles. Three years prior to Bryan's coming, the council effected another bond issue of ninety thousand dollars to establish a "decent" waterworks, to cover deepening the public well, installing a power pump, and raising an elevated tank (pressure standpipe) some seventy-five feet above ground level. As a hoped-for remedy, the council contracted with a well-digging firm to deepen the water source. The contract read, "to extend a hole in the bottom of the old well."

Unfortunately, the new water turned out to be salty and contaminated the central water supply. Frenziedly, the council continued digging additional wells. When Bryan arrived Lincoln's water system stemmed from eighty wells, of which twenty-seven were known to produce salt water.

"There's nothing more inspiring," Dolph Talbot grimaced, "than going home hot, tired, and dusty, turning the faucet knob, and having yourself a nice warm drink of salt water."

The other more demanding liquid problem was no less self-perpetuating and of no less compelling interest to the newly arrived lawyer. Lincoln, Nebraska, had been born a "liquor town"; by 1885, it had eighty-five saloons or other drinking places. The dry forces, headed by the multiplying Protestant churches, had succeeded in needling through an ordinance requiring all saloons to close no later than 10 P.M. But there was no prescribed method for checking barroom timepieces, which somehow kept running more and more slowly. The council responded by ordering local police to check and as necessary regulate saloon clocks during each business day.

Under duress the council also enacted an ordinance prohibiting the use of blinds, screens, awnings, or any other devices for obstructing the ready view of saloon or barroom interiors. The strategy here, of course, was to permit the passing public to see who was tippling or being led astray. Bryan regarded this as unfair; he doubted that the resulting Peeping Tomism was constitutional. In early Nebraska argot, it was being pointed out that the eccentric young lawyer's views on liquor appeared to be as mixed up as a mad dog's guts.

For all that, Will Bryan continued to view the toils and quandaries of municipal government sympathetically. He had readily established himself as a personable curbside counselor. In lobbies, offices, stores, wagonyards, and livery stables, at the post office, on the courthouse steps, and at the railroad depots, he talked with fellow townsmen, wagon-loading shoppers, visiting farmers, miscellaneous transients, and college students. He was further improving his conversational talents. And he had by now developed a distinctive stance that was in itself expressive. His slate-gray eyes peered intently, appreciatively, and in most instances downward into the eyes of all he addressed. His big hands gripped other hands with warm firmness.

Mr. Bryan still looked more like an energetic young farmer newly arrived in town than a lawyer in the process of setting up a practice. His brown beard, even when moderately well trimmed, helped establish that appearance. So did his shoes. High-button shoes were invading the realms of spike-toed saddle boots and clomping plowman's shoes. Bryan compromised by wearing necessarily large walking shoes, black, square-toed, and theoretically laced to the ankle, though he demonstrated an aversion to lacing his shoes.

Townsmen were adopting full-length box-shouldered overcoats. Bryan was not an overcoat man; he didn't have one with him during his first three months in Lincoln, and more often than not he wore a lightweight alpaca suit instead of the orthodox dark woolen one. Country style, and regardless of season, he spent much of his time in shirt sleeves. As he freely admitted, he was the perspiring kind.

He was also the striding kind. He walked with the long, swinging gait of a plowman intent on turning that second acre before sundown. He often whistled while walking, but he rarely sang; he was still unable to carry a tune. Nor could he carry what the more fastidious termed a neat collar front. Even when he submitted to stiffly flanged starched collars, his short, heavily muscled neck tended to squash them askew. His black string tie was forever slipping out of bow and dangling like an untethered shoelace. Nobody could take the country out of this winsome young man. Apparently nobody seriously wished to, least of all Bryan himself.

Yet as a townsman *pro tempore* his intense interest in the new capital was at least in some part reciprocated. As more and more Lincolnians, from garbage men to the mayor and beyond, came to be pleasurably acquainted with Bryan, some felt inclined to listen to what he had to say. Many of the Bryan positions were hard to comprehend. He continued to insist, for example, that the liquor issue was one to be met and decided on a basis of "inward scruples and good conscience," and not by formal legislation at any level. He stated this view as if wholly unaware that such a stance would inevitably be regarded as fence straddling, at the time lethal to anyone with political aspirations. In this, a vehemently opinionated community where the drys were fanatically dry and the wets were splashingly wet, there was no station for in-betweens. But Bryan was distinctly choosing the role of an in-between. He said and demonstrated that he was a teetotaler, yet he was seen in saloons and otherwise in company with drinkers.

As anyone could see or hear, Lincoln, Nebraska, had plenty of politics and plenty of openings therein. Bryan appeared to be bypassing all the openings. But why did he not just lace up his shoes and step ahead? Why, too, could young Mr. Bryan not take a good go-ahead stand regarding church membership? Lincoln was then a town proliferating in Protestantism; five new churches were being built. Bryan watched the progress of each as if primed to try out for the post of Sunday school superintendent. He made a near-fetish of befriending every preacher in town, including the newest arrivals. But instead of tying in exclusively with one or the other of the available Presbyterian churches, again Bryan was playing the field.

His first church appearance was as a guest "lecturer" in the pulpit of the new Methodist Church. Within a few days of his arrival, Bryan joined the recently founded Y.M.C.A. and volunteered his services as "active helper." But again, as in Jacksonville, the "better" church people of Lincoln were not disposed to accept the "Y" as a front-door caller, and they could not approve of a Presbyterian openly hobnobbing with Adventists, Mormons, and those invading Catholics!

None too discreetly, either, this Bryan, whom many called O'Brien, was also spending much time around such Josh-and-Rube facilities as the public wagonyard, which would naturally take business away from the commercial livery stables, and a public or farmers' market that, of course, would rob the proper merchants of trade. Not that there was necessarily anything wrong with farmers; the real point was that when a young man comes to town to get ahead, he benefits by coming to town all the way.

It wasn't that Bryan was taking unpolitic stands on all prevailing issues. Now and then he appeared to go far out of his way to support a "responsible" cause. For example, he strongly advocated the building up of the annual Lincoln Fair as a statewide drawing card. This showed commendable civic spirit. Ultimately, it involved a lot of hard work.

First, the already acquired fairgrounds had to be properly cleared, fenced, and lighted. Newcomer that he was, Bryan was among the volunteer workers who joined without hope of pay in scything weeds and grass, cleaning the streets, setting up barrels full of drinking water (salt-free) with racks of tin cups on top, on all principal street corners. That, admittedly, was a good show. It would have been better had Bryan not spent practically all his time at the fair in the company of farmers.

Impecunious as it was, the ledgers of Bryan's beginning

law practice might as well have been written on the wall. His first client in Lincoln had been a fellow migrant from Illinois who had heard Bryan speak back home. Another was a grocer whom the lawyer had met at the Methodist Church. The grocer had bills for collecting, and Bryan chose to write letters to the debtors instead of hounding them in person. He was interested in learning how effective such efforts really were. One morning when the grocer strode into his office, Bryan inquired if there were any results from his letter to the delinquent customer. There were. Sighing loudly, the grocer removed his hat to show an egg-size swelling on the side of his head. "Seems my customer read *your* letter, thought that *I* wrote it, came after me, and hit me on the head with a brick."

But Bryan continued writing letters. From a local source, which might well have been Lincoln's Democratic newspaper, *The Call,* he obtained the names and addresses of other Democratic papers throughout the state, along with those of their editors and publishers and the names of the leading Democrats in other Nebraska counties. One after another, he began favoring them with polite paragraphs of introduction.

It is doubtful that this effort was worth the postage except to indicate the expedience of abandoning one's membership, or allegiance to, the Democratic Party. At the time a Nebraska Democrat was almost synonymous with an election loser. "Nebraska Democracy," to use a somewhat scrambled phrase, was a house divided against itself. The less destitute and less numerous faction was called the Packing House Democrats. They had headquarters at Omaha and tended to conform to the whimsical rules of the national party. The dissenting and less cohesive faction, scattered widely throughout the state, was called the Slaughter House Democrats. Included among them was a high percentage of incorrigible individualists and veteran opponents of any political party yet formed.

The Nebraska newspapers were preponderantly Republican; most of the Democratic papers were country weeklies in central or western Nebraska. Bryan continued writing letters to practically all of them and supplementing this with letters to local or county Democratic bosses and functionaries of various state or county Democratic committees.

Presumably the uninvited correspondent began each letter by describing himself as a new Nebraska Democrat who hoped to see the party get ahead. On that basis he was asking the expert opinions of important and respected party members regarding the most imporant issues for the upcoming elections. As Bryan pointed out in a letter published in *The Call,* the consensus was that the tariff or "free trade" issue would be foremost in the 1888 elections. Significantly, the diligent young letter-writer subscribed to and began reading the *Congressional Record.*

Dolph Talbot's letters show that his junior partner continued to demonstrate a great zest for life in Lincoln, Nebraska. Talbot recorded that Bryan was an early riser, one who met the dawn by rolling out of his makeshift bed in the waiting room and washing or at least splashing himself in the combination lavatory and sink that, along with the commode, was shrouded by improvised curtains.

Then, having slipped into a white shirt and his light suit, Bryan would comb his hair, don his black string tie, lace his shoes the first fraction of the way, and stride downstairs and out into the waking town to O'Dell's Restaurant three blocks down the street. The full breakfast, i.e., twenty-five cents regular or twenty-two and one-half cents by meal tickets, included an overture of hot coffee plus the customer's choice of "candy-dipped" doughnuts or a stack of the house's specialty, buttermilk hotcakes or "flannels." Next came the main course choice of a breakfast steak, or thick bacon and eggs, or red-eyed country cured ham splashed over with the "natural" ham gravy. The special sourdough biscuits, propped open with butter or homemade fruit jelly, came without extra charge, along with as many additional cups of coffee as one could accommodate.

Such a deluge of morning calories could sustain one through a long and diligent day of plowing, cattle roping, well digging, or practically any other form of labor. Although he was known as one of the heartiest eaters in town, the broader issue was not how much lawyer Bryan ate. Rather it was how O'Dell's, or any other local restaurant, could manage to serve up so momentous a feast for a maximum of twenty-five cents. Farm prices continued to sink. This was not because of any lack of consumers. For the time, the Great Plains population was increasing at the rate of about 5 percent a year, and Nebraska's even more rapidly. In the main, and in defiance of fatigue, loneliness, drought, floods, blizzards, grasshoppers, chinchbugs, and the demons of Wall Sreet, American farmers were growing more and better food than they had ever grown before. U.S. tilled acreage had approximately doubled during the twenty-two years following the close of the Civil War. Demand for foods was increasing as larger towns changed to cities and home workshops changed to factories.

U.S. farming was gaining a new measure of productivity with the momentous improvement of crop-growing implements and machines. A generation earlier, the machine age had begun to invade agriculture. Though all were still powered by horses, one after another, the moldboard turning plow, the gang or grouped plow, the disc harrow, the multiple plow cultivator, the cog-driven grain and grass mower, and the mechanical cereal harvester, moved over the greening earth, pushing back earlier fences and frontiers, and cramming to overflowing a new generation of oversized barns, bins, and elevators. During Bryan's boyhood, "making" an acre of wheat had required about sixty man-hours of labor. Here in flowering Nebraska, less than two decades later, the labor requirement was no more than ten hours.

Yet, despite all those epochal advances, farm prices and profits continued to slip backward. The agricultural population, still some 60 percent of the U.S. public, kept growing poorer and poorer. Back in 1870 to 1874, when Willy Bryan was first putting in serious work on his father's estate near Salem, the average market prices of the three greatest farm crops of the United States had been: wheat, $1.06 a bushel; corn, 43.1 cents a bushel; cotton, 15.1 cents a pound. But now in the late 1880s, wheat prices averaged only 74.8 cents a bushel; corn prices, with their influence on beef and pork prices, dipped to an impoverishing low of 35.9 cents a bushel; while cotton limped along at around 8 cents a pound.

The purse-thinning story persisted as additional hundreds of millions of acres of tillable, or supposedly tillable lands yielded to the plow. In the United States farm lands remained the No. 1 bargain. Never before in history had so much tenable farm land been offered to a restive public. For good measure or bad, a billion acres of public domain still awaited the homesteaders. So crop prices kept on plummeting. The farm price index base—100 as of 1860—had already melted away from 132 in 1865 to about 49 in 1887–88.

The New West had special cause for anguish. Its industries, apart from mining, were still trivial. Its resources in circulating currency were among the lowest the nation had ever known. The nation at large had about three times as many people in 1887 as it had in 1860, the year of Bryan's birth. But the total currency in circulation was barely half what it had been twenty-seven years before, and in money terms the New West was the poorest of the poor. In community after community Great Plains farmers were keeping warm in the winter by burning corn in their chunk stoves.

Who was to blame for this pauperizing of American agriculture? Throughout the nation farmers were asking this of their elected officials. In the main they were not being answered, and with particular grimness the Great Plains farmers were demanding answers and seeking ways out. Bryan was intensely aware of this. Farmers were still the American majority, but both the major political parties were evading that majority.

Bryan felt certain that beyond the spirited confines of Lincoln, Nebraska, a new political creation was emerging. This party could assume a shape that would presently take over the New West. It would have to be bold enough to tax the rich and defend the poor, to damn the rascality of Wall Street, to admit the constitutional rights of initiative and referendum, to tame the ruthless and ravaging railroads, and in all ways find and justify life as the party of everyday people. The seed was planted. The roots were reaching thirstily into newly turned soil.

There was need for a prophet. Bryan, somewhere along the line, resolved to be that prophet. Even more boldly he proposed to try his own hands at remolding his own party, the Democratic, to fit needs that were of God's will.

7. The Uncommon Commoner

Toward mid-December 1887, Bryan took leave from pioneering his second law practice to spend the holidays with his family in Jacksonville and his kin in Salem. By then he was reflecting the ways and "feel" of the New West in contrast to those of his homeland, which he now spoke of as the Old West.

Even the first blurry glimpses from the train windows reminded him that his homeland seemed to have shrunk most peculiarly. What he remembered from childhood as the greening hills of home were not really hills but merely rises or knolls. By Nebraska measures the grain fields of lower Illinois seemed hardly more than garden size. The brooks that had once seemed so engagingly deep now appeared to be mere "runs."

A stop at Salem showed the same old village, which had grown old in little-changing tininess. The human census seemed frozen at about one thousand; the roving animal population appeared to be gaining. At the depot he met his Uncle Russell, who was still tending the railroad stockyard, dealing in live hogs and cattle. He inquired how soon Will intended to come home and settle himself to useful work, such as raising livestock.

His mother, who seemed to be little changed, asked if Will felt the same "trust and faith" that he had earlier known. His answer was a cheerful affirmative; a change of address had not changed his total belief in a total and unchanging God.

He could not overlook the immediate mortal changes. His youngest sister, Mary Elizabeth, whom he recalled as a diminutive crawler who had traversed the kitchen floor leaving trails of wetness, had changed into a very attractive young lady.

He was no less amazed by the metamorphosis of his younger brother, who remained his very special admirer. Nearing twenty, Charlie was a gangling, nervous six-footer who struggled with an engulfing shyness. Despite his undependable health, which in turn had frustrated his successive attempts to attend Illinois College and the Union College of Law, Charles Weyland Bryan seemed wistfully determined to study law and follow his elder brother in the West.

Will welcomed his resolve. He sympathized with the fact that Charlie was another facile young man who was finding himself stranded in old country and eager, as he explained, to touch hands with tomorrow in new country. With his recurring nervous smile, Charlie pointed out that even if he also migrated to Nebraska, there would still be plenty of Bryans in and around Marion County, Illinois.

Will could not debate that observation. He was meeting kin whom he could barely remember. At the Jacksonville home, where his own daughter had passed her second birthday, Little Ruthy was learning to pray: "God bless mommy and daddy, and grandmommy and granddaddy, and Grandma Bryan and all her folks, and Uncle Russell and all his folks, and Uncle John—" and so on until she collapsed into sleep.

Undeniably, God had provided Illinois an enduring abundance of Bryans. But God had not decreed that all be confined there. Will reflected on that truth while viewing his most exceptional daughter. "She is a very precocious child," the young father repeated with sparkling originality. Ruthy could already walk, trot, and skip. She could talk proficiently and almost continuously. She was slender and active. "Babies are best off slender," Bryan continued to observe; with his next, who turned out to be as round as a butterball, he would presently affirm, "Babies are better off fat."

Bryan had other causes to regard himself as a winner. His wife was functioning admirably as a homemaker and as nurse and companion to her dependent parents. For good measure Mamie was getting along with the neighbors, a feat not too easily accomplished in a college town. And she was intensely loyal to her husband, whom she saw if not literally as a prophet then certainly as a man with a special destiny as a defender of his faith, an admirably fundamental faith.

Although he had resigned himself to total blindness, and although his late-autumn endeavor to mow the lawn had left telltale lapses that showed that practically speaking he was already blind, John Baird also saw his son-in-law as a noteworthy crusader. He was humbly determined to add strength to Will's armor of righteousness.

John and his ailing wife Lovina agreed to move to Lincoln, Nebraska, in company with Will and Mamie and their baby. He made plans for financing the building of a commodious home in Lincoln, big enough for both families, including future Bryans, and deputized his son-in-law to purchase a suitable lot. "Whatever suits you and Mamie is right for Lovina and me," he insisted. Mr. Baird would sell the house in Jacksonville and advance whatever additional funds were needed for building a new house for the merged families; it turned out to be a fourteen-room house at the formidable cost of $3290. By Christmas Eve the plans were final; Jacksonville's loss would be the gain of Lincoln.

During the course of his holiday visit Bryan made half-hearted and unsuccessful efforts to solicit law practice for the new firm of Talbot & Bryan, along with diligent and generally successful efforts to advance his own political future. One after another he approached local dignitaries who had politician friends in Nebraska. His most valid find was when Congressman William Springer, who was home for the holidays, affably provided his former protégé with a letter of introduction to a certain J. Sterling Morton of Nebraska City. The founder of Arbor Day, Morton was destined to become better known as Grover Cleveland's second Secretary of Agriculture. But for the time he was less widely known, his reputation that of the bellwether or lead goat for Nebraska Democrats on their way to recurring Election Day slaughter. Congressman Springer was customarily generous with advice. "Keep ever in mind," he said, "that a political party is like a set of plant roots. It has to grow. When and if it stops growing, it has to die."

Mid-January of 1888, the upcoming national election year, found Bryan dutifully returned to his new hometown. To say that he himself was unchanged is a safe premise. But he didn't look the same. His full brown beard had abruptly vanished, never to return. In its stead there re-emerged the well-molded and strongly determined jaw, the broad chin and the unencumbered and easily smiling lips of a strong man coming into prime. The dark gray eyes handsomely large and the high, unwrinkled forehead told of strength and devout determination.

The Bryan gregariousness was showing rapid expansion, too. With the help of his law partner, Will set about organizing what he termed an easy-open discussion club. He named it the Monday Evening Club and inveigled Dolph into serving as its first president. Among the charter members was the slender and rather fiery young bookkeeper for Buckstaff & Company, Wholesale Harness Dealers; his name, Charles G. Dawes, in time to be noted as one of the more vehement Vice Presidents of the United States. Another was an erect, laconic young Army officer newly returned from the Apache Indian Campaign in Arizona and more recently detached on leave to the University of Nebraska as professor of military science and tactics. John Joseph Pershing, West Pointer and Army politician extraordinary, was far more approachable than he would be thirty years later as Commander in Chief of the American Expeditionary Forces in France. It was during his stay at Lincoln that Captain Pershing, formerly of the Tenth Cavalry, received the nickname of "Blackjack"—from the tough, wiry scrub oak which provided very effective switches. William Johnson, whom history would remember as Pussyfoot Johnson, the gentle-voiced proselytizer for national prohibition, was another and perhaps more influential charter member of the Monday Evening Club.

Meanwhile, Bryan's office journal or memorandum book began showing significant changes in content. The customarily dismal listing of many collections attempted and few accomplished was being interspersed with jottings of lines of intended oratory and brief references to interesting law cases then in preparation. One of these dealt with the constitutionality of bounties paid by counties and other component bodies politic to private industries as inducements for locating factories or other works within their boundaries. The Bryan tenet was clearly a direct lift of his father's. The railroads, of course, had been growing fat and mighty from the collection of such "inducements," including the vast land grants the federal government continued to hand out from the public domain, proceeding downward to cash bounties taken from the most impoverished country crossroads. In many instances railroads had gotten by with the shakedown of public monies on grounds of providing "valid public improvements."

Although he was admittedly aching to attack what he

sometimes termed "the arrogant Goliaths on rails," Bryan chose to begin with a more readily accessible defense of taxpayers who were protesting the county court's rather arbitrary appropriation of public money for subsidizing the building of a sugar-beet refinery. As attorney for a citizens' committee, Bryan produced a carefully worded court brief holding that the proposed plant could not be truthfully described as a work of internal improvement since it was a component of a profit-seeking establishment and, therefore, according to the constitution of Nebraska, not entitled to receive public money.

The local circuit court ruled with the plaintiff. With that victory under his belt, Bryan readied himself for a more audacious tilt—with a major railroad. The Burlington Line was seeking to move the established county seat of Greeley County, Nebraska, to a community along its already built trackage. Again using his negative debating tactics and his sound knowledge of the state constitution, Bryan won another, far better publicized victory. Politically it was also audacious bear-baiting. The Burlington was a formidable force in Nebraska politics; it had substantially influenced the vote in the northern half of the state, while the "Pacific System" strongly influenced the south. Every time anyone succeeded in hitting either railroad in a vulnerable spot, one or more Republican office holders cried out in pain.

Bryan next moved adroitly from law to politics, specifically to analyzing the perennial feudings between the two principal factions of the party, the Packing Housers and the prairie-roaming Slaughter Housers.

Discreetly and lucidly, Dolph Talbot pointed out that a divided political party, like a divided house, cannot stand against itself and that the best way for a perceptive young man to get ahead with the Democrats in Nebraska was to join the Republicans, as Dolph himself had done. Pleasantly, Bryan disagreed. He was resolved to remain a Democrat. He was quite certain that party unity could be attained in Nebraska by bringing together the dissenting factors in the fraternity, so to speak, of a common and righteous cause.

Relying in some part on intuition, the young and incorrigible Democrat said that a solid agreement regarding the tariff issue was surely the best handle for grasping Democratic solidarity in Nebraska, when it was achieved. He admitted that at this point he knew little about either the political or economic backgrounds of existing tariff legislation. But he was resolved to learn more and to marshal support in the course of learning. He chose impromptu discussions as his medium of learning, and in the advancement and nurture of discussions he came up with several graphic metaphors. One was that the Republican-originated tariff legislation (he did not dwell on the fact that a Democratic administration was perpetuating the tariff) was functioning like a giant cow that the agricultural West was feeding and the industrialized East was milking.

From the Book of Proverbs he recalled pithy exhortations for the practice of moderation and of impartial social justice and supplemented them with pithy adages of his own origination or selection. One, scrawled in his daybook or work journal, noted that "The great masses of our people are interested, not in getting their hands in other people's pockets, but in keeping the hands of other people out of *their* pockets . . ."

In an effort to better comprehend the effects of the tariff on the violently backsliding fortunes of western agriculture, Bryan continued to read the *Congressional Record* as well as increasing numbers of magazine articles that sought to interpret the enormously complex subject. From *The Forum* he gained what seems to have been his first acquaintance with the then widely heeded and hard-working sociologist, Washington Gladden.

Gladden's views were deep black; he pointed out that the American farmer was surely losing ground not only in the West but nationally and internationally as well.

Could rural America ever succeed in forcing either of the major parties to serve it competently? Washington Gladden said no. He glumly insisted that the more intelligent and capable American farmer was already devoid of any confidence in his own economic solvency.

Another popular economist, C. Wood Davis, who had taught at Yale, insisted that the "barn door prices" of the prevailing farm crops, such as oats, 9 to 12 cents a bushel; corn, 7 to 10 cents; wheat, 40 to 50 cents, etc., removed any real assurance that American farms could ever pay off their indebtedness. Davis contended that the prevailing interest rates on farm mortgages, whether 8 or 9 percent yearly as common in the East, or 12 to 14 percent as prevalent in the West, were beyond the farm lands' capacity to repay.

Davis and Gladden were being joined by many other respected economists in their belief that abroad, mostly in Europe, were at least potential markets for great quantities of harvests from American farms. But they tended to agree that prices paid by European buyers could never be on a par with the past levels of U.S. farm prices because of the need to compete with lower-priced European labor and tariffs.

Accordingly, Bryan deduced that quickly and sharply reducing all tariffs, and in the case of farm crops completely removing them, would inevitably better foreign sales and improve crop prices. This, of course, was wishful thinking, but it was not entirely irrational. Consider wheat, for example: for seven successive years, U.S. wheat crops had been very large. From a seller's standpoint, American wheat was disgustingly plentiful. Even so, during 1887–88, about 37 percent of the entire harvest had found markets abroad, whereas only 3.7 of the corn crop had been so marketed. Bad as they were, wheat prices at barnside in Nebraska were four times better than those of corn.

There was common agreement that circulating currency was also a crucial factor in the farmer's perennial depression. The more exclamatory insisters here were the burgeoning associations of farmers, including the rapidly expanding National Farmers' Alliance.

The Alliance was clamoring for what it termed cheaper money, specifically enactments by the U. S. Congress of legislation to increase the quantities of currency in circulation, particularly of silver coins. The latter, of course, had intrinsic or metallic value that, as the saying went, could stand up and walk away on its own strength.

Whether used for making money, or spoons, or filling teeth or wrapping fractured bones, silver has true and implicit value. The same, admittedly and to a degree, holds for gold, granting that the latter goes better in jewelry than in spoons and serves better on the outside of watches than for broken bones. The real and lamentable point as the Alliancers saw it was that Congress had made principal metal coinage a restrictive package deal. By prevailing federal statutes the dollar-value ratio was sixteen to one, i.e., silver to gold. The restrictive feature was that gold supply was substantially limited, both in terms of mining and of world prices of the bar metal.

By contrast, the silver supply was highly expansible. Silver, in fact, was the veritable touchstone of the crucially important western mining industry. An increase in silver coinage was not only attainable but was one of the most convenient and economically feasible means for increasing the currency supply—and would encourage mining. The statutory perpetuation of a fixed relation of per-ounce value of the two principal monetary metals, so the Alliance contended, could only shackle and impede the progress of silver mining and hand over unfair advantages to the producers of and speculators in gold.

Without dipping too profoundly or cerebrally into the complexities of monetary science, the spokesmen for the Farmers' Alliance kept stressing the point that the total supplies of valid monies then in circulation were grossly inadequate for meeting the life-or-death needs of a rapidly expanding agriculture and a very rapidly growing New West. They submitted that the monetary policy of the U. S. Government remained cruelly and hurtfully orientated to the advantage of the East and the detriment of the West.

In a like mood and with a predisposition to broad and carefree assumption of appearances as absolutes, the Alliancers were urging the abolition of all national banks, the outright federal ownership of railroads, the reinstatement of graduated income taxes by both federal and state governments, and the statutory limitation of land ownership by nonresidents.

Bryan was impressed by the boldness and depth of the Alliance credos; he felt certain that they were adding new dimensions and new impact to what Alliancers were terming "the crusade for the common man." In letters and journal notes that would soon reappear as speeches, the ambitious young man on the third floor of the Wilson Building was gaining awareness that Nebraska, in considerable part pioneered by veterans or dropouts from the Colorado and other gold rushes, was a particularly good place to learn about the chronic inadequacy of the American gold supply and the benefits attainable from the use of much greater quantities of silver. Bryan was quickly convinced that silver mining had become a key industry of the New West; Nebraska and her growing neighbors were in desperate need of more fluent credit and a far larger supply of touchable money. Silver, he agreed, would best meet these live-or-die needs.

"That's as plain as the nose on one's face, which in my case is saying a great deal," he would shortly be telling his sunburned rural audiences, while pausing to exchange smiles. Bryan would add, factually, that he spoke and would ever speak as a farmer at heart. For even in late winter he was watching with yearning interest the beginnings of brave young leaves, the first awakening of the waiting prairies. More and more impressively, Bryan's letters and spoken words proved his awareness of the ever-engaging partnership of earth, air, rain, and sun. As he jotted in his journal and later asked in successive speeches, "Can the rosebud blooming in beauty despise the roots through which it draws its life's blood from the soil?"

But for the time the young man was obliged to heed his commitments to effect the building of a town house for his own family and the Bairds. In February 1888, he arranged the purchase of a building lot out on D Street and let the contract for building and completion by the following June 1 for what was duly specified as a "permanent dwelling with due appurtenances and likewise a backyard barn." That done, he returned with vigor to what had to be construed as political fence building. He put to use the letters of introduction he had acquired during his holidays back in Illinois. He used one letter to make the acquaintance of a Jefferson Broady of Omaha, who confessed to being Nebraska's leading Democratic lawyer. Broady was not responsive, but the "organization leader" of the administration or Packing House Democrats, James E. Boyd, a member of the Democratic National Committee, responded amiably, sizing up Bryan as "a likable young hayseed."

Meanwhile, Will held onto his most impressive letter of introduction—from Congressman Bill Springer, of the Ways and Means Committee, to J. Sterling Morton, who was being described as the laziest newspaper publisher, the most proficient railroad lobbyist, and the most unsuccessful office seeker in Nebraska. Whatever his designation, Morton could not be listed as a political bargain package. His association with the National Democratic Party by way of the Packing House group caused him to be detested by the more liberal and rural Slaughter Housers. He was necessarily prorailroad, since he was still drawing pay from a railroad lobby in Washington, D.C. Morton knew or cared little about farming as such, though he had made a hobby of what he called roadside and yardway forestry. He published a kind of weekly newspaper called the *Arbor*

Journal. He dressed handsomely, carried a swagger stick, and wore spats—all of which provided a less than politic reminder that he was a one-time New Yorker, a fact of life that his advocacy of such agrarian measures as growing seed potatoes at home and planting trees where trees never grew before could not effectively camouflage.

Even so, and for reasons he never clearly revealed, Bryan chose to join J. Sterling Morton; he mailed him his letter of introduction from Congressman Springer and offered his unsolicited support. That done, and with comparable inconsistency, the unusual young man of unusual political strategies began selecting a prospective farm home even while his already committed town house was materializing. About three miles southwest of Lincoln he located a "rise" of land that showed a crescent of tall trees. Through this grove, rainfall permitting, flowed a brook called Antelope Creek. Beyond the corn field that lined the brook's course stood a shabby 1½-story farmhouse, and Bryan, at first sight, was convinced that this was the kind of place he would most like to live in.

He estimated the distance as right for a brisk horseback ride to and from his office. In a discourse at the Monday Evening Club he stated his absolute conviction that farm living is the "ever fundamental American way of life." In this revelation he apparently overlooked the fact that, even in and around Lincoln, industries were rapidly gaining on farming as new factories and shops were causing more and more farmers to move to town, and steadily crowding out the countryside mills, smithies, stores, and other farmside trades.

Appropriately and traditionally, while he stated his affection and esteem for country living and country people, Bryan continued to build relationships in town. He resumed his binge of joining town clubs. Already a past chancellor of the Knights of Pythias, an Oddfellow, Mason, and Modern Woodman, he almost simultaneously joined the Moose, Elks, and Royal Highlanders, then took over as president of the newly formed Lincoln Democratic Club—thereby counterbalancing his law partner's presidency of the Lincoln Republican Club.

He was finding little free time for his law practice, although he found time to make frequent speeches to local clubs, including the newest one, the Rotary, which he would presently join. Late in April he made his first open-air or bandstand oration to a gathering in Seward, Nebraska; his subject was "Less Tariff and More Farm Prosperity." He was generously applauded. On April 30 the Lancaster County Democratic Convention assembled at the Cornhuskers Hotel in Lincoln and, one gathers, within easy reach of the taproom. Bryan was on hand, vocal but not drinking. The primary objective of the meeting was to elect delegates to the state Democratic Convention and to endorse a representative-at-large to the national convention. The choice for state delegate was between the incumbent, James E. Boyd, and the perennial loser, J. Sterling Morton.

To the astonishment of practically everyone present, Bryan took the floor to support Morton. His move may have given the win to Morton; in any case, it was reciprocated by Bryan's last-minute election as delegate-at-large to the state convention and, in due course, to the national convention. When the state convention opened on May 3, the promising youngster from Lincoln gained the floor and spoke on "Lower Tariff and Higher Prosperity for the West."

His text and reasoning were wobbly, but his oratory was impressive. The central committee responded with an invitation for Bryan to try his talents with a speaking tour of the state "in support of the purposes and principles of the Democratic Party" both state and national. There would be no pay other than for barest expenses. But there would be "exposure" that Bryan eagerly welcomed. And as an initial dividend, there would be the chance to officially attend the Democratic national convention shortly to be held in St. Louis.

While these bright mirages gained substance, so did the new town house on D Street. It was taking form as a three-story, fourteen-room wooden mausoleum with a rash of baroque ornamentation. The first and second floors bellied with oversize front porches, and the steep roof was topped with a slightly mosquelike observation tower. Architecturally the one creditable attainment was the barn.

By late May, Mamie and her parents were ready for the big move. Bryan, in turn, was ready to receive them and to set forth for the national convention, which would convene on June 5. The moving was successful. But the convention turned out to be absolute frustration for the Nebraska and all other western delegations. The "eastern wing," under the aggressive leadership of the incumbent President, Grover Cleveland, had the entire function tightly in hand.

Although it was conceivably an omen of oncoming eminence, Bryan's gleaning of public attention was related only indirectly to the convention. On the first morning, when the Nebraska delegates strolled out of Planter's Hotel, the youngest member noted a curbside mishap that the sidewalk crowds at large apparently overlooked.

A legless cripple, who had been hand-pushing his four-wheeled box-cart across the street, had met with near disaster. The wheels of his cart began to fall apart on the rough cobblestones. Bryan went to his assistance, and lifted up the crippled man, who tearfully pointed out that unless his cart could be repaired he was stranded.

Bryan made a hurried inquiry about a repair shop, and after being directed to a bicycle shop, he carried the legless cripple and his cart to it. The shop mechanic managed to rebuild the cart, and Bryan paid the bill. A roving newspaper reporter picked up and wrote the story, briefly mentioning the charitable passer-by as "W. J. Bryan, a youthful convention member from Nebraska."

For his first hour or so in the convention, the delegate looked on in wonderment, like a child at a big and loud circus. But his wonderment changed to disappointment when the platform came up for approval. The first-timer from Nebraska observed that all the "planks" were obnoxiously vague. One advocated the "betterment of employment and labor wages" without even suggesting how this could be accomplished. The desperately serious farm depression was conveniently bypassed. The platform contained no clear statement of the party's stand on tariffs other than a recommendation of "moderation." Under the circumstances, this was almost meaningless verbiage. The platform spoke of "ample currency" without specifying a gold-to-silver ratio. Otherwise, the platform gurgled along for some forty thousand suave and almost meaningless words. Bryan was painfully reminded of the repressive power of platform drafters; he was determined that next time he would try his own big hands as a platform writer.

Bryan was happy to arrive home again. After a prayerful housewarming, he reported in person for an interview by the state central committee at Omaha. He listened in affable silence while Acting Chairman Prescott Smith listed him as an "entertainment attraction" and directed that he tour the thirty-four counties that were known to have Democrats in residence. Already the Republicans were airing their own special orator, John Thurston, who was billed as the "New Demosthenes of the West." The New Demosthenes now had a competitor.

Tom Calfer, an irrepressible Democrat who happened to be heading the fledgling McCook County Fair, took the cue by delivering an open invitation:

> . . . Can you come and meet the Enemy for us? The Republicans will have Thurston if he can be gotten—if not, the next best. You are our choice— *Bryan, the Invincible.* . . .

Bryan accepted, and in the course of the halcyon, green summer he made eighty-three other appearances before audiences, for the most part rural. Where practicable the "entertainment attraction" traveled by train, but to more remote engagements he rode by livery stable rig or rented or borrowed saddle horse, or sometimes by farm wagon. His own continuing preference was for horseback travel.

On several of his early sallies, immediately following the convention, Bryan found himself overtaking weather-delayed Easter parties. These rather incongruously delayed events were usually held at churches and included the inevitable egg hunts. At the prairie village of Ewarts he recalled having ridden away with all his pockets stuffed with dyed eggs. He missed the once-a-day train and reached home the following night after three consecutive meals of hard-boiled eggs.

But that was the untoward exception. Most of the time the effervescent young entertainer ate well and formed a cherished image of the Nebraska farm kitchen as the provident throne room of the Great Plains domicile. He fondly remembered the unpainted walls kept bright with long strings of red peppers, and the great bunches of drying seed corn and garlands made with dried husks of popcorn with the tiny ears peeping downward.

The food was in the pattern of an American epic. Venison was still plentiful, but to the delight of William Jennings Bryan, so were catfish, wild turkey, duck, and quail. Upon occasion there was buffalo meat, juicy and lusty red. The perennial staples included dried or "jerky" beef, salt pork, potatoes, hominy, sourdough biscuits, wheat breads, cornbread, johnnycake, flapjacks, and buckwheat cakes, all in prodigious abundance.

Sweet sorghum gravy was made by "browning" flour and lard together, adding water and "sweetening." Barley coffee, ground of crisply roasted barley grain, was standard fare in the sod hut homes and in many others. Wild honey, home-boiled sorghum molasses, and wild fruits such as chokecherries, plums, wild grapes, and mulberries were among the lighter standbys. By any standards the home cooking was magnificent, and Bryan enjoyed it to the last bite. Photographs indicate that during the summer of 1888 he began gaining weight.

Grease lamps with cotton flannel wicks still lighted many of the prairie homes. Dried gourd dippers filled with dry corn or meal, beans or peas, and a score of other commodities, adorned back walls. Giant outside kettles, high windmills, lye barrels for use in making hominy and soap, all were among the standby accouterments of backyards, as were the hollowed log watering troughs, and the split-log wash racks. To Bryan, all were heroic facilities.

There were lusty country weddings and birthday surprise parties, such as the one at Red Cloud, where the new preacher, having been showered and fêted, was heaved bodily into the cattle-watering trough. There were shivarees —the merry hazing of country brides and grooms—and no traveler could avoid the "nationality parties," where the man was expected to pin a dollar bill on his dancing partner's gown. One gathers that the nickel-counting Bryan was thankful he was not a dancing man.

Much more to his liking were the church "sociables." These included pound parties for the benefit of the preacher, and meat hunts for the same cause; also custard treats, strawberry festivals, mixed suppers, and box suppers. Girls and their beaux drove from house to house soliciting knickknacks and fancy work for church benefit auctions and contributions of the ingredients for church suppers.

There were also taffy pulls and watermelon "feeds." Bryan fell for both of these, and the same held for the rural and village "speakin' societies." According to the Fall City *Broadaxe,* he once joined in an impromptu debate, "Resolved that men and women should be equal before the law in respect to legal rights and liabilities." For a change, Bryan took the affirmative. He won the judges' decision, but the crowd's reaction seems to have been that women were best off in a subordinate role.

This free-for-all debate at Fall City may have been the engaging young visitor's first public defense of female suffrage. His subsequent stump appearance at Grand Island was certainly his first lengthy public address in behalf of tariff reform and, even if vaguely suggested, his first presentation of the merits of reciprocal trade agreements between nations. For the time this "tariff talk" was also his best-reported public address. A correspondent for the pro-Democrat Omaha *Herald* recorded the thesis respectfully:

> W. J. Bryan spoke for two hours in a clear and forcible way, dispensing with the usual stump oratory but illustrating his address with apt stories and bright quotations.

At Weeping Water, Bryan took over as "follow-up man" for J. Sterling Morton. The Arbor Day promoter spoke for an hour and a half, then yielded to his shirt-sleeved protégé, who "would speak but a few words." The neophyte spoke for ten minutes; then, in response to insistent applause, he continued for another hour, and presently another, as the sweating audience applauded and shouted for more.

By August 10, Morton was inviting his voluntary henchman to represent him directly. He was sent first to the mass meeting and flagpole raising at Verdas in Richardson County. Following a rousing success there, the young exhorter rode on alone to Barada, Palmyra, David City, and elsewhere in the short-grass prairie. Again and again he held and won the crowds. More and more invitations started to pour in. Back at Lincoln for a two-day breather at the state Democratic convention, Bryan heard his name placed in nomination for lieutenant governor, then for attorney general. With benevolent stubbornness he declined. Two deductions were easy: Bryan did not believe the Democrats could prevail in Nebraska in 1888, and he had

already decided to seek at the subsequent election the one
public office he most wanted. He would admit later:

> Certainly from the time I was fifteen years old I
> had but one ambition in life, and that was to come
> to Congress. I studied for it. I worked for it. And
> everything I did had that object in view.

For the time, however, he could afford to wait; or as
he stated it in his preferred semantics of the negative, he
could not afford not to wait. Meanwhile, as a transient
Democrat evangelist he was winning friends, influencing
voters, and establishing an exceptional image of unselfish
devotion to the party of his choice.

Happily, at Chadron, the new county seat of outlying
Davis County, Bryan had met the sheriff and thereby won
his most durable and effective political champion for the
oncoming twenty years. An indigenous man of politics who
had spent his youth as an open-range cowboy, James C.
Dahlman was rail thin, leather brown, bow-legged, and
had the general appearance of a spur-jangling, pistol-toting
leprechaun. As a frontier rancher, village mayor, and surviving sheriff, Jim Dahlman advocated helping people, not
shooting them, and on this basis he confessed to being a
steer-wrestling Democrat. He also confessed that he had
taken a special shine to hard-muscled, garrulous Will
Bryan.

Dahlman revealed that a big rally—at least the Democrats hoped it would be big—had been arranged for
Gordon Village in nearby Sheridan County following the
Chadron appearance. There would be need for a good
"tall talker," at Gordon, too, and the sheriff proposed that
Bryan take the assignment. Since there was no time to
waste, the two set out on horseback and rode across prairies
to the two-street village, where they found a crowd of
several hundred citizens already assembled and milling

about. Sheriff Dahlman led his perspiring guest to the perspiring chairman.

"Young man, can you make a speech?" the latter inquired.

"I'll try," Bryan answered.

He tried. His announced text was lower tariff, but his evident cause was people, the poor people of Nebraska. His voice rang clear, without distinguishable bass or tenor, but with a bell-like lilt. Each word, clearly enunciated, seemed to stand momentarily alone, then join in a rhythmic, almost lyrical, current of words. His big hands moved in spontaneous, sweeping gestures, left to right, right to left. Sweat poured from his forehead and his cheeks, and even from the sides and tip of his large nose. His shirt, originally white, clung to his powerful chest and arms. He looked directly at his audience, pausing frequently to accentuate with silence. This Bryan was showing himself to be a dramatist and at times a poet, who sang of greening earth and love and hope and the invincible dreams of the common man. Between skillful pauses his words poured forth like the clear waters of the nearby Mobrara River.

For more than two hours Bryan held his audience of tanned farmers in fading work shirts and hard-used overalls, and farm wives in faded calicos, ginghams, and homemade sunbonnets. None took his leave. Again and again Bryan sought to conclude his speech. Again and again those efforts were frustrated by tumultuous applause.

"They would of listened all night," Sheriff Dahlman summarized. But they couldn't. Bryan was pulled away in time to board the eastbound train. Early next morning he picked his way to his bedroom and wakened his wife. "I have had a strange experience. Last night I found I had power over the audience. I could move them as I chose. I have more than usual power as a speaker. I know it." He bowed his head in prayer. "God grant I may use it wisely."

The prayer befitted the developing William Jennings Bryan as a political evangelist. While proselytizing for a party, he was preaching a fundamentalist's devotion to what he deemed the vitally related causes of frail people and an almighty God. From the usually fragmentary accounts published in weekly newspapers one gains the sustained impression that Bryan's speeches were primarily sermons—tending not always consistently to interpret political issues according to the inferred light of an Old Testament God of might and wrath and benevolence.

In great part he was preaching what his rural listeners wished to hear. Even if he wasn't winning votes, he was winning audiences.

He was a fundamental believer, and other fundamental believers were starting to show that they were willing to applaud and to elevate him into public notice.

8. The Loser as Winner

The national campaign of 1888 was a notable chronicle of losing winners and winning losers. The year's premier political contest would be consummated by an unprecedented and outrageously undemocratic paradox. Presidential nominee and incumbent Grover Cleveland would win the popular vote by 5,544,337 to 5,440,050 for his Republican opponent, Benjamin Harrison. Yet the electoral college vote would go 233 for Harrison and 168 for the Democrat Cleveland, and so frustrate the people's will—as sustained by the counts of bona fide ballots.

Behind this dispiriting paradox, which Bryan deplored as a most regrettable blot on the escutcheon of democracy, were a number of grass-roots developments that the evangelist and agrarian entertainer of Lincoln, Nebraska, was assiduously heeding. The two principal parties were confronting formidable forces of dissatisfaction. Each was being diverted by increasingly vehement conflict between the articulate haves and the less articulate but increasingly protesting have-nots.

Four years earlier as Democratic nominee for the twenty-second Presidency of the United States, Stephen Grover Cleveland, a New Jersey-born son of a Presbyterian minister, and a lucidly compromising New York State politician, had triumphed as an eastern Democart who professed willingness to compromise with western Democrats. Cleveland had won his first try for the Presidency by utilizing what he called the solid core of an enduring party augmented by extensive recruitment of the distressed agrarian vote, which was widely available in the South, Border South, Midwest, and substantial areas of the Great Plains, or New West.

Meanwhile, if, as many believed, Cleveland did not understand the New West, those who were beginning to follow the movements of Bryan surmised that he did not comprehend the "Old East," that he was less than adequately aware of the urban shifts and early-stage industrialization then incubating in his native Midwest. Clearly, too, he did not comprehend the merits and faults of Cleveland's somewhat stoic philosophy of federal government and his Administration's occasionally erratic practice of *laissez faire* by the federal government. To a fundamentalist such as Bryan, God was neither a practitioner nor an advocate of hands-off policies. In his eagerness to evangelize and convert the politically neglected, chronically poor farmers of Nebraska to what he regarded as Democratic beatitudes, Bryan devoted himself with customary vigor. On that basis, whatever the total vote count, he could not, certainly he did not, see himself as a loser.

By his own acceptance he was an audience politician. His technique of conversion was to simultaneously entertain and nurture a common, at least a potential, listener's faith in God and hence in mankind at large. As his speeches followed, and as the rural or small-town audiences responded more and more warmly, Bryan continued to reduce his wobbly discourses on national political issues as such and to concentrate unashamedly on entertainment and sermon-style exhortation. The crowds desired entertainment and recognized that insofar as the engaging young man with the unusually beautiful voice was willing and eager to fulfill that desire, they would permit him the affable vagaries commonly allowed any working evangelist. Accordingly, with his distinctive talents for easy transition, Bryan moved through such entertaining topics as female suffrage, the particular merits of hogs as a farm crop, the superiority of woven-wire fences over barbed wire, the roles and responsibilities of country schools and churches, the "fundamental goals" of living, and the merits of a self-cultivated faith.

At a county fair at Crete, Bryan opened his advertised address on "The Tariff Issue" with a "listen, friends" discourse on education:

> The value of an education, both to one's self and the world, depends very deeply on the purpose behind it. The buzzard and bee serve to illustrate. The buzzard soars high, but it is never so high that it is not looking for something to eat, and when it dies it leaves nothing to perpetuate its memory. The bee lives on the best that there is while it lives and leaves a legacy of honey when it dies. Some imitate the buzzard— some the bee. . . . Man is free to choose—will you pattern after the buzzard or the bee?

Then, with untiring zest for the engaging *non sequitur,* he swung into a free-wheeling discussion of what many now decry as the school dropout:

> The boy who drops out of school under the delusion that the money he can earn will be worth more to him than an education makes a fatal mistake. As the wood chopper can afford to stop chopping long enough to keep his ax sharp, so the student can af-

ford to postpone money earning long enough to complete his education. . . .

And long before the two-hour address was over, the prose poet was eloquently blasting the evils of plutocracy, which to Bryan then meant the grabbing and holding of unearned wealth:

> This plutocracy is already sapping the strength of the nation, vulgarizing our social life and making mockery of our morals. . . .

Neither the speaker nor the majority of his listeners was grievously threatened by any of the maladies of excessive riches; but Bryan knew well that the theme of great wealth and extreme poverty is a taproot of American interest and moral evaluation, and he was never disposed to overlook the Ciceronian principle that "the orator who would arouse others must himself be aroused." Thus, as the long, hot days of volunteer speaking followed, he went on arousing others with words that visibly aroused him. As the rural audiences grew, so did the skill of the strong young man with the waving mane of black hair. By varying procedures slightly he continued to learn that an assembled crowd is an emotional phenomenon markedly different from an individual or a small group.

Visiting newspaper reporters and local correspondents began to note that Bryan was a self-powered crusader who repeatedly caused crowds to "blaze," even "explode with enthusiasm," but not destructively and only rarely acrimoniously. Bryan was determinedly improving his public speaking techniques. He was learning to sound syllables precisely and to enunciate with determined clarity. He was overcoming his earlier and erratic traces of stammering and lisping. Fully aware that his speaking voice was not and could not be made "deep" (as later recordings proved, the Bryan voice was almost completely lacking in bass), he resigned himself to what elocutionists called "natural intonation," and an impressive contrast of volume, from melodic murmurs to trumpeting shouts.

He was learning, as well, to look continuously at his audience ("their heads should move as the speaker's eyes move"), and was beginning to develop the use of the pause into a fine art. ("Pauses give your listeners time to catch up—to absorb what you've been saying and to think for themselves, in case they wish to.") For good measure, he was making more effective use of his broad and quickly produced smile. "People say," he confided, "that when I smile my mouth spreads out far enough for me to whisper in my own ears. I think that's possibly an exaggeration. In any case, I've learned that when there's nothing better to do, and there rarely ever is, it's good to smile at your audience."

In the course of his zigzaggings across Nebraska he dispensed with all attempts at satire and substituted the slow-smile routine and jokes that were usually directed at himself. These included exaggerations of his own stride or stance and confiding in the crowd his late father's suggestion that if his son only had four more pounds of brains Will would be his father's size. One can sense in the early Bryan at least a potential talent for emerging as a humorist; but one also finds himself wondering whether Bryan was leading his crowds, or the crowds were leading Bryan.

In any case, with the passing of the summer the laughter diminished. Rains came and the harvests were plentiful, but crop prices dwindled ruinously while the burdens of debt grew and foreclosures multiplied.

There were other prophets of agrarian disaster, but for the time the mobile William Jennings Bryan was proving himself the most attractive—at least in Nebraska. By October he had energetically stumped twenty-four counties, including eleven in the First Congressional District, which he was already viewing with an especially personal interest.

Then with a quickly gained second wind he "worked" nine more counties during the final month of the campaign. He was being deluged with invitations for additional appearances; again and again he expanded speaking appointments from one a day to two, or three, or four. His energy was all but colossal.

At his final public appearance at the Crete fair, Bryan found relief from his chronic perspiration problem. After a warm month of Indian summer, autumn frost was browning the great prairie. The sky was ribbon blue, the air was crisp with materializing autumn. Even the flooding sunlight and the short-grass prairies, brave green as they still were, could not hold back the onrush of winter or another Republican victory. The would-be prophet of democracy for Nebraska sensed this; with a gentle frankness he assured the Crete crowd that there would be other elections, and the cause of "Nebraska democracy" was invincible because it was the people's cause.

In a mood of beaming, and to certain other Democrats baffling, satisfaction, he returned to Lincoln and the third-floor office in the Wilson Building. He assured his law partner that his side had won a considerable victory even though it would lose the election. At his new home on D Street the returned crusader made a similar revelation to his pretty young wife. Mamie, too, may have been a shade baffled when her glowing husband revealed his absolute certainty that the congressional nomination for 1890 waited within his easy reach. Sure, the independent vote would certainly continue to grow, and by latching onto just a fair number of the wavering Republican votes, her Will would be as good as in Congress—on voting Tuesday, 1890. But Mamie recalled that the Republican plurality in the First District was still heavy; also that a campaign for a place in Congress was said by experts such as Will Springer to cost at least three thousand dollars. Where would the money be coming from? "God will provide," said William Jennings Bryan.

Election Tuesday confirmed the Bryans' observations. J. Sterling Morton lost by thirty-four hundred votes. Republicans easily carried the governorship of Nebraska and all other principal offices, excepting only one of the congressional seats, which had been won by a most independent western Democrat. As already noted, the national Democratic ticket also lost—in a painful and unprecedented manner.

Cleveland had lost his lucid and diligent try for re-election primarily because he failed to carry his adopted state; New York had gone Republican by a small edge, barely thirteen thousand votes of the 1.7 million counted. Certainly a shift of as few as thirty-five thousand votes could have returned Grover Cleveland to the White House, Electoral College or no. With freely splashing ink, the youngster who was certain he had won even though his party lost wrote his standard-bearer, "Why not come to Omaha or Lincoln [to live]? As a western man with friends you have in the East we can elect you . . ."

The hero worship was not as bubbly as it sounded. The potential strength of the New West could not be denied, but as far as the Democrats were concerned, it had not yet been won.

In his personal life Bryan was wading a stream of happiness. Back in Lincoln he was again earning a livelihood and making friends. He was gaining recognition as a man of politics. He had even attained a measure of newspaper support, which he cherished. Congratulatory letters came in from many parts of Nebraska and a dozen other states.

More surprising was Sterling Morton's move to have Bryan chosen as secretary of the Nebraska State Railway Commission. Understandably there were interested onlookers who regarded this as the incongruity of the year, but in any case the Morton move was unsuccessful.

But William Jennings Bryan had a great deal for which he could be and was thankful. Dolph Talbot joined him in reorganizing the Monday Evening Club into the some-

what better integrated Round Table Club. The expanded
membership included such notables as Dr. J. H. Canfield,
chancellor of the University of Nebraska, and Charles H.
Gere, editor of the *Nebraska State Journal*. The club admitted wives, and male members took turns at preparing
and reading papers—literary, philosophical, or religious;
not surprisingly, Bryan's discussions were usually centered
on religious subjects. By contrast to the discussion group
sponsored by his eminent cousin, Dr. Hiram Jones, the
Bryan-propelled Round Table Club accentuated the intake
of calories. Each meeting began with a hearty Nebraska-
style "supper"; the Round Table feasted first and philoso-
phized afterward.

With typical generosity John Baird had provided his
daughter and son-in-law with a small two-seater surrey and
a capable little Morgan horse that Bryan named Silas and
subcaptioned the Bryan weight controller; the utmost capacity of the undersize horse and rig was two comparatively slender couples.

Helpful reserve forces were in the offing. Stealthily, like
a prairie dawn, Brother Charlie arrived to take a place
in events. The younger Bryan boy was in the throes of
becoming a Lincolnian. Although still gawky and shy, and
possessed of a sometimes startling talent for showing up
unexpectedly, like a confused comic who emerges on the
wrong cue or in the wrong theater, Brother Charlie showed
up as announced. He fitted easily and usefully into the
extra chair in his brother's law office and into a spare room
of the big, new, ugly house at 1425 D Street. In the little
horse barn in the back lot he had quartered his one luxury
possession, a well-behaved mule named Sam. Charlie
Bryan was fond of mules; as a free, grown man he proposed to be a mule-raising Nebraska lawyer.

The younger Bryan's one nagging worry was his dread
of baldness. It was a rational concern; even in his beginning twenties Charlie was already practically bald. While
complaining that the glare of his balding head was begin-

1. The birthplace, built in 1852, of William Jennings Bryan.

2. Schoolmaster Silas L. and his wife Mariah E. Bryan, Willie's parents.

3. Willie at ten.

4. William Jennings Bryan's wife-to-be, Mary Elizabeth Baird, as she appeared when he fell in love with her as a student.

5. Bryan in top hat, the badge of the junior class at Illinois College at that time.

6. Bryan at the age of twenty-three; his experiment with a beard was short-lived.

7. A. R. Talbot, of the Bar Association of Lincoln, Nebraska. He was Bryan's first law partner and encouraged him in his early political career.

8. Bryan's close crony, James C. Dahlman—also a strong influence.

9. The first family portrait: Mr. and Mrs. William Jennings Bryan, their daughter Ruth, and their son William, Jr.

10. Mr. and Mrs. Bryan at home in the library of their D Street house.

ning to adversely affect his eyesight, Charlie could nevertheless see what was going on. For one thing, he could see that if Brother Will intended to stay with the law, he required a lawyer; Charlie proposed to be that "working lawyer." He could also see that Mamie Bryan was "something very special." Through the now more than four years of her marriage Mamie had been keeping the home, caring for her baby, her parents, and her distinctly messy, cluttering, and frequently absent husband with remarkable devotion. And somehow, on the side, Mamie had been studying law.

It followed that on November 29, 1888, Mary Elizabeth Baird Bryan, twenty-seven and again with child, appeared for the "open court" bar examination at Lincoln, as the only female "candidate." She passed the examination with an honors score, taking third place among the seventeen participants. She told the Omaha *World-Herald* correspondent that she had no serious intention of practicing law; she had qualified as a lawyer "in order to better understand my husband and help him with his work." As Brother Charlie saw it, she was already accomplishing the latter, but understanding Will Bryan would be the neatest trick of anybody's lifetime.

When the Round Table Club got around to honoring Mamie's emergence as a lawyer, Brother Charlie was seen taking his mule for a moonlight stroll. On cross-examination he explained that he found the mule more thoughtful and much less noisy than the Club.

With Charlie as his law assistant, Will again settled himself to political preparations. For this he chose as principal reading matter the Atlanta *Constitution*, which he regarded as speaking for the South, the magazine *Public Opinion*, and, as before, the *Congressional Record*. His intensive study of tariff legislation presently resulted in his first book-length manuscript, entitled "Tariff Essays."

He sent the script to Walter Page, then an associate editor of the New York *Post*, who passed it along to

G. P. Putnam's Sons. When the vehemently Republican publisher rejected the script, Bryan responded that he could love practically anything, even, God forbid, Republican publishers.

That charitable viewpoint underwent another test at the ensuing St. Patrick's Day program in Lincoln. Nebraska's glum Republican governor, John M. Thayer, presided, and in due time announced, "The next number will be by W. J. Bryan." Bryan stepped forward with extended hand. When the governor clutched his hand, Bryan interpreted it as a gesture of forgiveness for the many whacks he had handed Thayer in the course of his orating tour of the previous summer and early fall. He was almost withered when the governor pulled him close and whispered wetly into his ear, "Do you *speak* or *sing?*" Without answering, Bryan began his speech.

On concluding, he heard himself being designated as "O'Brien." "My name is Bryan, sir," Bryan explained. " 'Tis all the same," the affable dunderhead answered. "It's of being Irish, it is. . . . When the great Bryan Borow got to be King of Ireland, his descendants put on the 'O,' leavin' the Bryans as just the common, ordinary, shanty Irish. . . ."

As the year 1889 hurried along, Bryan continued to feel doubly blessed. Intuition or, more probably, wishful thinking reassured him that his next offspring would be a son. By way of further blessings he was earning a tolerable living, which, with Mamie's frugal management, permitted the saving of a few dollars for the next year's campaign. He was greatly enjoying his church work, and he was receiving invitations to speak, in most instances to rural audiences. Charlie urged him to keep with sermons on fundamentals. "Tell 'em what you believe and they'll believe what you tell 'em," he exhorted.

Will accommodated with vigor. But he was more and more cognizant of the hard-crowding political issues: the multiplying antagonisms between capital and labor; the

Republican resumption of high tariffs; the appalling Republican favoritism toward insurance companies, packing houses, power companies, and, of course, the railroads.

Bryan also resumed his open-forum letter writing, peppering Democrats throughout the state for their opinions on issues and their suggestions for feasible candidates. One gathers that he was not heartbroken to note at least occasional mentions of his own name as a possibility for the next Democratic congressman.

June turned out to be a most wondrous month, a golden-green June with Nebraska prairies shining in the sun like ten billion emeralds. Then on June 24, there was born to the Bryans a son, William Jennings Bryan, Jr. He was a big, fat baby; the enraptured father confided that fat babies, as practically everybody agrees, are the best kind. He also confessed that this newborn was the spitting image of his father. "Fiddlesticks," said Uncle Charlie.

But here at least was the first of another generation of Bryan males. William Jennings Bryan, Sr., admitted that when he heard the first cry of his first (and only) son, he truly heard the jubilation song of a host of angels.

On the more literal side, Bryan also heard what his brother pointed out as especially memorable political news. In South Dakota, directly to the north, a voter group that had chosen the name Populists was already taking form. Its rootbeds were primarily of revolt, a Westerners' revolt of distressed farmers and unemployed or direly underpaid laborers. Across country, in St. Louis, the still rapidly growing organization rising out of the merger of the Agricultural Wheel Union and the Farmers' Union was holding its first convention and finding resurrection as the Farmers' and Laborers' Union of America—ready groomed for a lively plunge into state and interstate politics.

The Farmers' Alliance, meanwhile, continued to multiply as the most vocal protest group in Nebraska. Its Chicago headquarters publication, *The National Econo-*

mist, was claiming a total membership, including northern and southern "divisions," of three million. Conceivably that number, if it held together, could decide the next national election, and almost certainly the oncoming Nebraska elections.

Other ruralists' associations were blooming out like wild flowers on a rain-blessed Nebraska prairie. Perhaps the most significant of these was the Colored Farmers' National Alliance and Cooperative Union, which was standing up to the fact that Negroes in general were being robbed of or tricked out of their voting rights; CFNA&CU, with a claimed membership nearing the million mark, proposed to do something about it. Bryan granted openly that Negroes do, indeed, have the constitutional and moral right of franchise, adding that he was game to say so from any platform he mounted.

During 1888 the Union Labor Party had also come on the interstate scene. Founded in Cincinnati on Washington's birthday of the previous year, the "Unioners" had already made entries on state tickets in Kansas, Missouri, Arkansas, Iowa, Wisconsin, Illinois, and Texas. In all seven of these states they had demonstrated ability to attract protest votes. With somewhat baffling reasoning or lack of reasoning, Bryan chose to frown on the incubating labor party as being "special favors seekers," but he could not and did not overlook the concurring throngs of emerging protest groups of farmers.

One of these was North Dakota's new Independent Party, comprised largely of frustrated prohibitionists and protesting farmers. Fusions of farm and labor groups were emerging in Colorado and Michigan. But Bryan was much more impressed by the "one-man Democratic revolt" that was flourishing in Nebraska. Its decisive "one man" was the state's only non-Republican congressman-elect. He was the former homesteader, dirt farmer, and Indian counselor, Omar Kem, of Broken Bow, who had stood against the

Republican tide of 1888 to take over Nebraska's Third Congressional District. In keeping with his vehement motto, "Fair Deals for Farmer," Congressman-elect Kem made no pretense of being a my-party-right-or-wrong Democrat.

While granting that independent parties were unquestionably in the western air and drinking water, Bryan was determined to remain a Democrat. But he was resolved to proceed as what he termed a revivalist Democrat. Later, in his *Memoirs,* he reflected that just as association with fellow worshipers is implicit in joining a church, so is group action in building a political party. For quite inevitably a valid political party is a congregation. It must share a faith; it must recruit or convert in order to survive, and it must sustain group activity.

He was already convinced, too, that political parties, like churches, cannot long endure without participation by women. Having spent his life among, or never far from strong-willed females, he had never doubted the power of a woman. By now he was appreciatively aware of the already evident place of strong-willed women in the dramatically changing political scene of the New West. As yet women could not actually vote, but they could and were organizing and otherwise influencing voters.

An outstanding instance was Ireland-born Mary Ellen Lease. During 1889, "Battling Mary" had taken over as "lecturer at large" for the Farmers' Alliance. As an Alliance voice Mary was proclaiming, "What you farmers need to do is to raise less corn and more hell."

Other feminine voices were also preaching the inevitables of political change. Elizabeth Barr, one of Kansas' more capable historians, points out:

> Women with skins tanned to parchment by the hot winds, with bony hands of toil, and clad in faded calico, could talk in meeting, and could talk right to the point.

One of these, Annie L. Diggs, was taking over as a widely heeded crusader. Twelve years earlier, this birdlike ninety-pounder had led the march against saloons in her hometown of Lawrence, Kansas, where, so she proclaimed, the college boys were being "ruint" by liquor. Annie was still very much in public view both as an apostle of church reform and as an Alliance speaker, or, as some saw it, "agitator."

Large, plump Sarah Emery, also of Kansas, and strong-willed and attractive Billy Gay of Texas, were among the female spellbinders no upcoming male orator could afford to overlook. The same held for the prettiest of the lot— Eva Valesh of Minnesota. Eva "worked" the street corners, social clubs, farmers' markets, wagonyards—wherever she could find the makings of an audience for a well-presented fighting talk on a fairer deal "for us working men *and women.*"

Protest was in the air, and American women were beginning to dip effectively into the politics of protest. Throughout the New West, particularly in Kansas, Nebraska, and the Dakotas, farm wives and daughters were learning how to make banners, invent and letter mottos, provision countryside rallies, march in processions, and, alas, sing in chorus such typical gems as:

> We voted with our party no matter where it went,
> We voted with our party till we haven't got a
> cent. . . .

Faithful husband that he was (he had already made an absolute rule of never being alone in a closed room with any woman except his wife), Bryan was distinctly aware that whoever succeeded in getting along with the determined independent voters would necessarily have to get along with their determined women.

Another October found the pleasantly ambitious young

Democrat accepting another obligation of practical politics—rubbing elbows with the "state organization." The Nebraska "total Democratic committee" assembled at Bohanan's Hall in Lincoln on 10th and N Streets, only three blocks from Bryan's office. The hopeful tenor of the meeting was that despite all their fighting and feuding, Nebraska Democrats were on the up and up—much more so than those snide, snickersneeing Republicans realized.

A particularly revealing example was the G.O.P. First District congressman, Bill Connell of Omaha, who openly boasted that his next re-election was in the bag; that the big towns, Omaha and Lincoln, were so solidly for him that he wouldn't bother to canvass the rural counties. Bryan had heard all this before, and every repetition made him feel better. But as a mere delegate, he carefully avoided airing his aspiration for taking on and over in Bill Connell's district. Instead, with the help of Sterling Morton, he maneuvered to win places for himself on both the credentials and resolutions committees. This was to become a standard opening play for William Jennings Bryan.

He also moved adroitly to make friends with some of the less approachable committeemen such as George (Square Boots) Hastings of Crete and "them smart Martins"—Euclid of Omaha and Frank from the prairies of Richardson County. With their counsel, Bryan joined in drafting a tentative state platform that opposed high tariffs, special interests legislation, and the use of public monies for subsidizing profit-seeking private business. As a document the recommended platform turned out to be rather weak soda pop, but as Square Boots Hastings noted, it could be livened up with some harder stuff, as required.

In private, Bryan was totally convinced that (a) the crying inadequacy of American government could be remedied only at federal levels, and (b) William Jennings Bryan could help memorably as a congressman. But first he had to get to Congress. To attain that he had somehow to melt away the competition. As 1889 drew to a close, there were only two visible rivals for the Democratic nomination from the First District—Sterling Morton, and Charles W. Brown of Omaha, a loyal worker for the Packing House or administration Democrats. In his correspondence Bryan opened by giving out the word that he would not try to lift the nomination from either of the senior contenders. Rather, he would urge all to consider the good of the party and the "cause of the people." "If we ever desert the cause of the people we have nowhere to go except the grave," young Will Bryan of Lincoln solemnly advised old Charlie Brown of Omaha.

9. God and the Tariff

The long, hard winter of 1889 had barely given way to the first spring thaws when Nebraska began awakening to an unprecedented outbreak of political rallies, conclaves, parades, and brief but vehement encampments. A "wake-up rally" at Hastings was typical. The village elders had anticipated a crowd of between one thousand and fifteen hundred. When the "big speakin'" began, more than sixteen hundred visiting farm wagons were on hand, and the waiting crowd totaled at least twelve thousand.

It was the largest crowd that the political hopeful, Will Bryan, had yet addressed. "I offer myself as a Democrat," he began, "as a believer in God and the party that is best qualified to serve the people of Nebraska. . . ."

He pointed out that the people of Nebraska were arrived at a Rubicon from which they could not retreat and that the invincible, eternal, Almighty God would never retreat. In due course, and by way of anticlimax, to which he was prone, Bryan pointed out that as a child of God he had no intention of retreating. He could have added, but did not, that he had recently been imparting that message to several political leaders.

Back in his law office, Bryan again settled at his rolltop desk, which was bulging and cluttered with longhand correspondence. Here he noted that in a mood of exceptional caution the Democratic state central committee had chosen to defer all Democratic conventions, including those of the five congressional districts, until both the Republicans and the Independents had held theirs. Since the brand-new Peoples Independent Party had booked its first state convention at Omaha for July 28, the Democrats had named 2 P.M., July 30 at Lincoln as the convention time and place for the First Congressional District nomination. It was a long wait, and seekers for the congressional nomination were left to scramble for themselves.

Bryan had accepted the decision calmly. He sought no support from industrial or other vested interests; he would stand or fall independently, and he would write his own platform. It was a bold move; if the convention should not accept his platform, the candidate would almost certainly be barred from nomination. Out of deference for what the Peoples Independent convention might devise as a statewide platform, Bryan decided to postpone his first venture in platform drafting until the Independents had compiled and published theirs.

On the sultry morning of July 30, Dolph Talbot walked into his office to find his junior partner engrossed with pen and paper.

"Hello, Will. What are you doing?"

"I am writing the platform for my race for Congress."

As Talbot knew, the Independents' platform had been released late the previous day. His partner's longhand, ink-splashed draft was taking form, and in it was the gist and spirit of a long and historic parade of Bryan-written platforms.

We, the Democrats of the First Congressional District in convention assembled, reaffirm our faith in Democratic principles and invite to our standard all who believe in free citizens, just laws, and economical government.

We arraign the Republican Party for its failure to fulfill its pledge solemnly made to the people, its reckless extravagance for the past two years, its tyrannical rules, and its unblushing efforts to reclaim supremacy by fraud and force.

Believing that the object of government is to protect man in the enjoyment of life, liberty and pursuit of happiness, unaided by public contributions and unburdened by oppressive exactions, we denounce the tariff policy of the Republican Party as contrary to the spirit of our Constitution, inimical to the best interests of our country, and especially unjust and unfair to the people of the Great Plains. . . .

We demand that wool, coal, lumber, sugar, salt, and iron ore be placed on the free lists; that the tariff on articles of necessary use be greatly reduced, and that articles of luxury be subjected to the heaviest duties. . . .

We favor an amendment to the federal Constitution which will take the election of the United States Senators from the state legislatures and place it in the hands of the people, where it belongs.

We favor the Australian or some similar system of balloting which will assure to every citizen the right to cast his vote according to his own judgment, free from corruption or intimidation.

We are opposed to the "trust" in all its forms, and favor vigorous measures for its prevention and suppression.

We demand the coinage of silver on equal terms with gold, and denounce the efforts of the Republican

Party to serve the interests of Wall Street as against
the rights of the people. . . .

We believe in the right of local self-government—
home rule—and we believe the so-called federal election bill an encroachment upon the rights of the citizens, an attempt to perpetuate the Republican Party
in power by overruling the election laws of the state,
and we denounce the congressman who misrepresents
the district for his support of that measure.

The public domain should be preserved for the
actual settler and we demand the enactment of a law
by Congress prohibiting the acquiring or holding of
lands by non-resident aliens. . . .

Discreetly, Bryan left part of the final page blank to
accommodate possible last-minute additions. But the body
of his thesis bore the William Jennings Bryan hallmark; it
was engendered not only by his years in Illinois College
and Whipple's Academy, but by his boyhood improvisions
for the mock senate in the vacant store across from Jackie
Chance's and later in the big parlor of his father's "mansion."

Bryan was wearing a dark alpaca suit, which was much
too hot for comfort; certainly the jacket appeared to cling
to his big chest. He wore his customary white shirt, wing
collar, and black string tie. His blunt-toed black shoes
showed additional half soles, apparently attached while the
shoes were still new. Shortly before two o'clock, with his
manuscript bulging his right-hand pocket, he walked alone
to the entrance of Bohanan's Hall, where the 159 accredited delegates would shortly be arriving, mostly on the
noon train, which as a rule was late.

The candidate quickly sighted the three men he most
wanted to see: his younger brother, whom he was beginning to regard as a very special luck piece; Sterling Morton,
who could still command at least a few Packing House

votes; and Will Cundiff, an elderly local rancher and henchman of former sheriff Jimmy Dahlman, then headquartered at Omaha.

The newspaper pictures made that day and published
on the following showed the boy daydreamer who would
not grow up and the fundamental believer who would never
change. But the pictures showed, too, the exceptional
young man who would be prophet-defender of his people.

At about two-fifteen the candidate strolled into the stifling hot meeting hall and seated himself in a back-row
folding chair. He shucked his jacket, resolved to make his
speech in shirt-sleeves.

John Owen, a local storekeeper, went to the platform
to make way for the chairman. The floor manager began
exhorting the delegates to move closer. For the moment
a quorum was not countable, but a distant puffing and
bell-clanging told of the belated arrival of the noon train.
Moments later a heavy tramping of feet announced the
arrival of the rest of the delegates. Bryan recognized with
visible discomfort the appearance of several railroad lob-
byists and henchmen of the sugar-beet companies that he
had earlier frustrated.

Brother Charlie and Will Cundiff took chairs on either
side of the obviously disturbed candidate. Both seemed to
be performing a feat in thought transference. Rancher
Cundiff, sensing a conspiracy of opposition, whispered to
Bryan to move for a recess for the examination of credentials. The motion carried routinely; the ensuing wait helped
break the timing of the opposition maneuvers while permitting Bryan to memorize his newly written platform text.
When the recess was finished, Bryan gained the floor and
recited the document with great conviction. Hastily Cundiff
moved to accept the platform. There was a spat of argument between the "sugar men" and the Omaha administration Democrats, but the platform was adopted. Now
that the convention had accepted Bryan's platform, re-
jecting its author would not be easy.

Bryan retreated outside quickly while Chairman Paddock called for the nominations. Sphinxlike W. R. Vaughan of Omaha moved to nominate his fellow townsman and ward heeler, M. V. Gannon.

"Who's he?" Charlie Bryan called out in his innocent but carrying tenor.

Obviously angered, Vaughan turned abruptly from extolling the merits of his nominee to an attack on Bryan. He shouted that the big-headed boy from Lincoln was an elocutionist, not a statesman. His platform reeked of wild and untried notions. E. F. Moriarity, who kept a saloon on Omaha's ever-moist Harney Street, seconded Gannon's nomination and continued the lambasting of Bryan. Then Cundiff and Brother Charlie beamed as they watched the sugar men challenge the Omaha "machine men" by placing two of their own members in nomination.

When the opposing forces had fought themselves to a virtual standstill, Will Cundiff "placed in nomination the name of William Jennings Bryan." He recalled the young man's valiant "crusade" of the previous campaign year and closed with the reminder that Bryan was part and parcel of the platform already adopted. Sterling Morton seconded the nomination. For the first time there was hard-slapping applause and the stamping of feet.

A first ballot showed eighty-six for Bryan, thirty-three for Gannon, and only five for both the sugar candidates. Cundiff moved for a written ballot of all delegates actually present. This time the secretary's count showed 137 for Bryan, twenty-one for Gannon, and one for Bebb, a sugar lobbyist. Again there was vigorous applause, followed by a motion to make the nomination unanimous.

Chairman Paddock appointed a committee to escort the nominee into the hall. It wasn't hard to do. Bryan, drenched with sweat, waited at the open side door. Jacket in hand, confident, he came swinging toward the platform; his forehead gleamed, and as the newspaper cameras presently revealed, his flanged collar was completely wilted, and his black tie dangled hopelessly. But his acceptance speech showed evidence of painstaking rehearsal. "The standards of democracy" would never through any act of his be "found trailing in the dust." He vowed that, win or lose, he would personally visit the everyday citizens throughout the district.

> . . . I will visit you in your homes. I will call upon you on your farms and help make hay while the sun shines, and I shall expect you to help me make votes all the time. It is no small task to shake hands with seventy thousand voters and remember the names and ages of twice that number of children. . . .

"Kiss all the babies!" a rustic voice boomed. "You've got mouth enough for it!"

With a broad smile in confirmation, Bryan finished his speech:

> If you will work as hard as I, your congressman elected from this district will bear the name which thirty years ago last March my parents gave to me. . . .

Measured in newspaper space, Bryan's campaign was off to a bad start. Measured by weather, the farming season was even more distressingly begun. A wheat harvest seriously damaged by drought was being followed by a corn crop already twisting and graying for want of rain. Brooks, ponds, and rivers were failing; livestock were starving on ruined pastures. Country churches were supplementing prayers for rain with prayers for better markets.

Bryan could and did sympathize. But his hoped-for crop of votes was also drying up because of financial drought.

With his brother Charlie as his unpaid but devoted assistant, he began drawing up further and extremely frugal campaign plans. His campaign "chest" held only seven hundred dollars that he, with much help from his money-competent wife, had managed to save. Nobody could doubt that this was their own money, but insofar as it was less than one-fourth of the minimum outlay for even a modest drive for Congress, the lack of funds involved peril, the greater because of a veteran and highly combative opponent.

Congressman William J. Connell, who had held public offices longer than Bryan had lived, abandoned his loose boasts about dispensing with an active campaign. Bryan had anticipated this, but he recognized that he would be obliged to win several thousand independent votes in order to defeat Republican Connell.

To that end he moved resolutely to open his campaign in the rural districts, where he already sensed his surest support. For his opener he chose Gretna, a village where he had met with gracious acceptance two summers before. He rode out on horseback, arriving during a still and stifling noon to find the rally in full swing. From a bandstand he faced his first voter audience in his first open quest for office. Beyond the listeners and the drought-seared green, he noted a newly raised flagpole. Below the Stars and Stripes a banner lolled in the slow, hot breeze. Crudely lettered on the banner was "W. J. Bryan, M.C."

Bryan was deeply touched; as he put it, "inspired to speak my heart out." The next day and the next he rode on, speaking to all who would listen. Many listened, for many remembered his appearances of two summers ago, and in the sultry loneliness they came to be entertained. They were not disappointed, for once more he was crusading in behalf of "poor folks and everyday people."

On returning to Lincoln he was astonished by the accumulation of cards and letters from ardent, and in the main, volunteer followers. Omaha's eminent Bible scholar,

Eli H. David, for example, whom Bryan had never met, revealed that:

Among the sturdy bullrushes of Democratic faith a Moses has been discovered to lead the chosen people out of their bondage to trusts, tariffs, and irrational taxation. . . .

Others were beginning to see Will Bryan as he saw himself.

At the state Democratic convention, which opened in Omaha on August 14, Bryan avoided the fumings and fighting of the wets and drys and hastily returned to campaigning. For the next sally he took the horse and surrey, and while Charlie drove, Will practiced his exceptional talents for almost instantly going to sleep in any imaginable position, and for waking on a moment's notice, refreshed and ready to make another speech.

Wherever he found people, in fields, in shops, or at the roadside, he addressed them. Without invitation he spoke in creameries, grain elevators, and sugar-beet plants, to the crews of sawmills, stockyards, and grain threshing rigs. He spoke from courthouse steps and store porches, wagon beds and the front porches of residences. From time to time he addressed lodge meetings and professional clubs, but his first goal was that of meeting and mixing with farmers.

Arriving without plans, he would stride forth, shake all hands within reach, then step to the nearest elevated location, which quite frequently turned out to be nothing more than an empty or partly filled wagon bed. One blistering noonday at Crete, he searched in vain for an empty wagon to serve as a platform. All he could find was a lone, rusty, manure spreader. He climbed aboard and smiled triumphantly at a gathering of onlookers: "Friends, this is the first time I ever spoke from a Republican platform. . . ."

As opportunity allowed, he wrote ahead to postmasters, country newspaper editors, and storekeepers to announce his arrival and to invite the attendance of those who had first helped with the "arrangements." The crowds became larger, and Bryan began making an average of three speeches every day. The Omaha *Bee-News* observed somewhat obliquely that the young spellbinder from Lincoln was not obliged to talk down to the prairie farmers because he was one of them. That, of course, was a figurative statement, but the report that he was fresh out of money was quite literal. Despite his thriftiness, Bryan had exhausted his law-practice savings in the first six weeks. By August he was borrowing from both his partner and the German National Bank, and before the campaign was ended his campaign debts totaled almost three thousand dollars.

As he shaped plans for town invasions, the country evangelist hardened his phrasing, lambasting more aggressively the Republican "merchants of patronage" and "swiggers from the pots of privilege," and defending his own position:

> They call that man a statesman whose ear is attuned to the slightest pulsation of the pocketbook, and they describe as a demagogue anyone who dares listen to the heartbeat of humanity.

Whatever he was being called, Bryan's crossroads oratory was establishing him as a symbol, as a prose poet singing in the sun, a mystic who seemed to listen to the hosts of jubilation, and as a special prophet of and for what would now be termed the underdeveloped American. In farm homes, whether sod huts, log cabins, or ranch houses, he was the family's friend, the giver of sympathy, counsel, and prophecy. He joined in rejoicing for rain and good harvests, in lamenting outrageous and undue losses.

When a child died, Bryan was the one to comfort and weep. When a child, or a lamb, or a calf, or a colt was born strong and well, he was the one to beam and congratulate.

However, as the cruel drought lingered and the campaign waxed hotter and rougher, the press responses grew more negative. Edward Rosewater, editor-owner of the Omaha *Bee-News,* declaimed that the young spellbinder from Lincoln was as effervescent as a bottle of soda pop. "Two-faced, too," stormed editor Gere of the Lincoln *State Journal,* a recently alienated member of the Bryan-founded Round Table Club. "Mr. Bryan went to church leaving his mouth in the backyard practicing a new tariff speech," Gere announced, then suggested that Bryan equip himself with a newly invented automatic regulator for windmills.

But not even the gruffest Republican papers denied that Bryan was winning votes, and, from all appearances, the most concentrated rural following in the entire state. Even the Independents agreed. With acumen that was growing chronic, Charlie pointed out that all Brother Will required for sustenance was three square meals and one fresh shirt a day and some kind of solid object to lie down on at night. On this basis he could win town votes at perhaps a tenth of the cost of winning country votes. Will did not entirely agree. Gilbert Hitchcock, the editor of Nebraska's largest Democratic newspaper, the Omaha *World-Herald,* pointed out that Bryan was repeatedly drawing crowds of three thousand people in hamlets or crossroads with censuses of no more than thirty. He wondered what would happen when Bryan saw fit to invade Omaha.

Unquestionably Bryan was wondering the same thing. During September he authorized his younger brother to arrange for appearances before several luncheon clubs and fraternal orders. Congressman Connell proclaimed his eagerness to take on the wonder boy from Lincoln in open debate, adding that as one of the more respected Republican voices in the House of Representatives, he certainly had nothing to lose by an open confrontation with his oddball opponent. He proposed to meet Bryan first in Republican Lincoln, then in his own hometown, Omaha. As his brother's emissary, Charlie Bryan gawped his agreement. It was sure mighty neighborly of the Great Statesman and could his brother Will, please, debate the negative side of that tariff is-sue?

On the sultry evening of Monday, October 12, the first Connell-Bryan debate took place in Bohanan's Hall in Lincoln. Bryan took his place on the platform, sweating mightily, and conspicuously pale. He had confided in his brother that he was suffering a "touch of dyspepsia." Charlie diagnosed it as stage fright and self-curable. Despite the withering heat, the lodge was jampacked, with the audience spilling out onto the sidewalk, even into the street. As senior candidate, Congressman Connell spoke first. He opened with a carefully prepared brief of the prevailing platform of the national Republican Party, including the gold standard and "moderate" tariff for the protection of American business in general and "new" business in particular. He confessed with considerable eloquence his many attainments in the Congress, and reminded all present of the dangerous folly of massaging the vanity of a novice spellbinder and reciter from the *Book of Proverbs* and/or the *Prairie Farmers' Almanac.*

The crowd was respectfully attentive, though less than enthusiastic. Bryan remained pale, and stumbled on his way to the lectern. He opened shakily with an abstract appeal for justice for the common man of Nebraska and the New West; "our brothers whose welfare is our first obligation before God, mankind, and Nebraska." His voice began to gain steadiness.

When the crowd applauded, Bryan's nervousness began to abate. With slashing gestures he began tearing into his opponent's somewhat pompous defense of "moderate" tariff. What moderate tariff? In terms of the living needs of impoverished Americans and the children of God they must sustain, who dared call any wealth-benefiting tariff "moderate"? "Consider the most humble of household necessities, the knives, forks, and spoons with which we eat our food; the bread knife, the meat-cutting knife; yes, dear friends, even the baby's spoon! . . ."

The trap was beautifully baited. With the deft assistance of his brother, Bryan had compiled and memorized the prevailing tariff rates on all manner of tablewares. "And my esteemed opponent would not challenge—" It was like spearing fish in a rain barrel. Quite emphatically Connell challenged.

Innocently, Bryan called for Jim Staples to step forward and settle the argument. Staples, who kept a local hardware and household furnishings store, had shown him that in many cases the tariff payments represented half or more of the retail prices. By a remarkable happenchance, Mr. Staples was seated directly below the platform with an attractive showcase of cutlery in his lap. He handed it to Bryan, then hurried across to his store and returned bearing a tasteful exhibit of an imported Cheltenham carving set—bearing import ladings neatly attached. Staples exhibited all the wares and read off the import tolls. The crowd applauded lustily as the congressman made a red-faced retreat to his chair.

Storekeeper Staples confirmed all Bryan had said about tariffs from the standpoint of a "practical merchant" who was obliged to penalize the blushing bride, the frail grandmother, and the harassed breadwinner with the tolls of conspiring tariff grabbers.

The crowd continued to applaud as Bryan resumed his speaking. He did not mention the Democratic presidential candidate nor the antics of eastern Democrats. Instead, he intermixed the cause of hard-used Nebraskans, children of frustration and political betrayal, earners being cheated of their earnings, with an eloquent verbal massacre of the Republican platform, which Bryan appeared to have memorized. Discreetly, he did not compare it with the national

Democratic platform, since the two were appallingly similar.

As he spoke on in his strange, unrhymed poetry, with what the anti-Bryan *State Journal* described as a "quality of strong and beautiful music," the crowd continued to cheer and stamped and cheered again. "Please save part of your applause for my most eminent opponent. He needs it and I need to talk to you—"

Two nights later, when the adversaries met again, this time in the Paxton Hotel "Hall" in Omaha, Connell's headquarters had arranged for the crowd to be seeded with hand-picked Republicans. But this turned out to be utter futility. Again the hall was hot and jammed to capacity and overflowing onto nearby sidewalks, as well as into the hotel bar. But this time Bryan was not afflicted with nervousness, pallor, or nausea. As first speaker, he took his position with pride and assurance. His voice rang out bell-like, and again his words poured out in torrents. The audience began to sway, to applaud, at first during pauses, then continuously.

Once more Bryan asked that the crowd hold its applause. The best efforts of Connell were self-destructive.

Late October brought continuing drought, dust blows, and the intensified uproar of campaigning. Unhappy Republicans and determined liquor men joined forces to meat-ax Bryan. But he simply would not be cut. The meetings of Connell and Bryan dwindled into mere open platform appearances, with Bryan the invariable winner in terms of crowd appeal. As an indication of how far the young contender was straying from "straight party lines," the black-haired youngster began reciting Gray's "Elegy Written in a Country Churchyard," and followed with a poignant monologue about the poem's tribute to the "mute Miltons," the unsung and noble yeomen who were the deceased counterparts of the noble hosts of poor people the Republican party had betrayed. At the conclusion of each performance Bryan solemnly and magnanimously presented his opponent with a bound copy of the inescapable poem.

For the final lap of the campaign Bryan again struck out on his own, diligently intermixing town and city appearances. In a last desperate play, Congressman Connell gambled all he had left on support from the "wets," but it wasn't enough. The Nebraska G.O.P. lost on all sides: the governorship, the legislature—which the Independents took over—and the three congressional seats, one to an Independent, one to a fusion Democrat-Independent, and one to Democrat Bryan.

When the dust and fog lifted, the winner of the First Nebraska Congressional District checked and rechecked the vote count: Bryan (Democrat), 32,376; Connell (Republican), 25,663; Root (Independent), 13,066. There were outraged charges of fraud. According to the best-accredited counts, Bryan lost Omaha by 3003 votes, and carried his adopted hometown, Lincoln, by a puny 89, admittedly a near-miracle. More importantly, he had won his first election to public office. Insiders guessed the actual plurality at 3500 to 4000 instead of 6713 as officially reported. But nobody could deny that Bryan had won.

He had won in part by proselytizing for an eastern-based party in graphic terms of prevailing western needs; in greater part by establishing himself as an impoverished champion of the poor and as a fundamental believer among fundamental believers. Otherwise his strategies were of invincible youth, not wholly shorn of mischief, abounding in partisanship and prejudice, yet permeated with poetry and an implicit and even then unusual intensity of faith.

In all his life Bryan had never been nearer to absolute bliss. He had fought a good fight. By his own reckoning he had kept the faith. As a crowd persuader he had proved his ability to lure new followers into his fold. Even in Omaha, the newspapers were terming him the Henry Clay of Nebraska and a new musketeer who had succeeded in holding the Rochelle Infantry at bay.

Bryan preferred to see himself as a "Christian statesman who says what he believes and feels what he says."
He responded with special warmth to an unexpected letter
from the great Henry Watterson of Louisville, who conveyed the compliments of the Democratic National Committee, and from his first advocate, Congressman William
Springer of the Thirteenth Illinois, who now volunteered to
recommend Bryan for membership on the ever-important
Ways and Means Committee.

Otherwise, regarding his future in national government,
the winner recorded only three ready-made decisions: he
would continue to work for the "upraising of agriculture,"
he would give his younger sister Nancy a job as his congressional secretary, and before leaving for Washington he
would try very hard to pay off his campaign debts.

Meanwhile, the youthful congressman-elect was respond-
ing to a growing urge to mold words and phrases that
might better carry beyond home boundaries his feelings
and beliefs regarding what he had begun calling "the new
American revolution." "Nobody's with us except the people." "The rightful purpose of government is *not* to nail its
citizens to a cross of gold." "A dollar approaches honesty
as its purchasing power approaches stability." "The [Re-
publican] party that boasts it struck the shackles from four
million slaves insists on driving its fetters deeper into the
flesh of sixty-five million free men. . . ."

By now, and with finality, the young man whom the
revered St. Louis *Post-Dispatch* labeled an "emerging national symbol" saw and felt himself to be a Westerner.
To Bryan the East still meant New England hillsides
studded with the mansions of plutocratic mill owners,
and sinister henchmen—God forbid!—of New York's befouled Wall Street. But the voice of the West, particularly
of western Democrats, was strong and clear and righteous.

While yielding to his need to earn money, Nebraska's
youngest congressman-elect was determined to nurture his
faith. His first post-election address was made as guest pas-

tor at the local Methodist Church. His thesis was more of
fundamentalism than of politics as such: Insofar as Christ
had died to save all people, not any preferred groups such
as, say, First Methodists, or Second Baptists, or even Cumberland Presbyterians, but all of mankind, sectarian Protestantism was not doing an adequate job of following its
Savior. The time was long overdue for a more literal and
robust living Christ, not for lip service to a peripatetic
pool-hall Jesus; and ever more basically, a more absolute
acceptance of the eternal, all-powerful God. The actual
choice is between fundamental belief and passive atheism.

His speeches for a fee to a convention of retail merchants in St. Louis, and a conclave of real estate brokers in
Denver, were less impressive discourses on the evils of
"high tariff." In Cincinnati, his "fraternal salutation" before a convention of Woodmen of the World resulted in
his being carried bodily back to the platform for a two-
hour encore. In Chicago his appearance before a panel
discussion set up by the Cook County Bar Association may
well have been his most thoughtful and lucid public discourse. There Bryan set forth his conviction that the "era
of the common man" had finally arrived, that the common
American had no choice other than standing against the
conspiracies of greed that could, and, left unchecked,
would destroy him.

There were indications that Bryan was displaying well-
studied improvements in his platform techniques. These included more effective opening sentences and greatly improved summations. But the impressive hallmarks remained
intact: the gushes of eloquent emotionalism and the real if
primitive lyricism. He was becoming the unquenchable
bard of the still daydreaming American West.

Returned to Lincoln, Bryan turned to his brother again.
Charlie would be taking over his law practice, helping look
after the John Bairds and the big white house on D Street,
and completing the purchase of the coveted Bryan farm

site out on Antelope Creek. "I favor building it up as a mule farm," the younger Bryan confided.

Another factor in his stimulation and inspiration was the fortunate birth of the second daughter and third child of the William Jennings Bryans. They named her Grace, and the name, even though it promptly degenerated to Gracie, was well chosen. From the first, the third child and second daughter was the most beautiful member of the family—there were those who vowed the only truly beautiful member. Bryan was seen passing out cigars with hard-to-believe extravagance; as a rule he secreted only a handful in or about his cluttered desk for his own occasional, private enjoyment. He noted that Grace was just petitely plump, and, as anyone knows, that's the best kind of baby to have.

When another autumn came Bryan began shaping plans for the exodus to Washington, D.C. His next younger sister and secretary-to-be had been helping with preparations and with the new baby and the two other children. The young father noted sagely that not everybody's secretary could do double duty as governess and infant nurse. It was agreed that Will's favorite sister would escort the baby on the long trip while Mamie and Will herded the older two and located a place to live in the ever-wondrous capital. As an economy measure the Bryans would dispense with the extravagance of a preliminary hotel stay. It was Bryan's understanding that the capital rooming houses were always eager to take in new congressmen and their families; after all, that was what prestige was made of in the capital.

That point of view was duly shared by James L. Kelley, who was keeping a rooming house on Sixth Street, N.E., within easy walking distance of the Capitol. Kelley had named his hutchlike establishment the Congressional House, but to that time it had never housed a congressman. The nearest facsimile had been the person and family of Joseph E. Abrams, the senior secretary ("administrative assistant" is now more frequently used) to Congressman William Springer of Illinois.

Late in the afternoon of October 11, 1891, Joe Abrams, who vowed that nothing ever really surprised a congressman's secretary, found himself at least slightly surprised when without warning a couple with two young children entered the waiting room of Congressman's Springer's office. The family head carried a V-shaped valise in his left hand and a sleepy thirty-month-old son in the bend of his right arm. Under the circumstances he was unable to remove the broad-brimmed, pale gray, western-style felt hat, which appeared to have been welded onto his exceptionally large head. The new arrival was otherwise rather tightly encased in a black alpaca suit, portions of which suggested that he had lately taken a plunge in the Potomac. His white shirt was sopping wet; his black shoestring tie was dangling abjectly; his creaseless breeches were wrapped vengefully around his large legs.

Having provided chairs for the lady and the little girl, each of whom wore somewhat wrinkled traveling dresses of black silk, Abrams relieved the family man of his valise and lifted down the dozing young son, who promptly awoke and began complaining of heat rash.

"I am Will Bryan of Nebraska," the man explained. "We just now arrived and are on the lookout for a lodging place."

The secretary remembered the vacant new apartment next to his own. (Bryan's youngest sister, Mrs. Mary Elizabeth Allen, recalled that Abrams later confided he was at least a trifle surprised when a congressman-elect with a wife and two young children accompanying arrived from far Nebraska without a hotel reservation.)

Mr. Kelley was mowing the front lawn when he saw Abrams, his star roomer, carrying an overweight valise and followed by a slightly overweight couple with two attractive children, both of whom Bryan was carrying. The rooming house keeper liked the looks of the prospective tenants. When introductions were completed, Mamie explained sadly that Junior seemed always to be dirty. Mr. Kelley observed that such is a generic characteristic of the Irish male. He also had an eye for likely patients for his young brother, a doctor, and it was to their mutual and lasting good fortune that J. Thomas Kelley, M.D., presently became the Bryans' family physician.

More immediately, and at long last, Kelley's Congressional House had a congressman under its roof.

10. "O'Brien" Greets Tammany

The Fifty-second Congress was not officially convened until January 5, 1892. The opening was about as confused as it was late. The freshman member from the First Nebraska District was confused, but he was not late.

Since his arrival in Washington almost three months before, Bryan had busied himself by learning the human and physical geography of the national capital. He began his explorations alone and afoot, a country boy having a first look at a state fair not yet open to the public. First, he made the acquaintance of the already multitudinous parks, monuments, and statues. This "exercise" also helped Bryan work at his worrisome inability to remember names. The newcomer extended his strolls to include the Arlington National Cemetery, which generously accommodated the new congressman's urge to read the inscriptions on headstones.

The story goes that he also rehearsed speeches to the silent, subterranean hosts in Arlington. Certainly in a letter to his brother Charlie he confided that when his own mortal course was run, he hoped to be buried there.

As a hot October led into a wet and somber November, Will and Mamie enjoyed many Washington walks together; both felt that they were renewing their too often interrupted courtship. By late November, when congressmen began flocking back to the capital like migratory birds, the Bryans settled themselves to a more expedient home life. Mamie sought to make more of her time available for helping her husband pick his way around the many pitfalls waiting directly ahead. She decided that the Bryans would move from Kelley's rooming house to Daniel ("Cotton") Bride's more prestigious and convenient Congressional Boarding House. Mr. Bride, who had worked his way up, or, as he said, down, from a White House messenger and assistant secretary to the assassinated President Garfield, was something of a Capitol counselor.

Mamie knew that her Will could use some counseling. As of January 1892, he was merely one of seventy-eight new Democrats and eight new Populists then on the House roster. Nearing thirty-two, he was only the seventh-youngest member, and since his political inclinations appeared to be much closer to those of the Populists than to the going order of Democrats, his immediate future seemed less than secure.

Granted, Will had already shone brightly as an orator, but the Fifty-second Congress was studded with accomplished orators, including the lame duck Ohioan who was chairman of the Ways and Means Committee and the most able spokesman for the Grand Old Party. Bryan and the world at large would shortly be hearing much more of Major William McKinley, Jr. Other gifted speakers at hand included young Henry Cabot Lodge of Boston; Henry Cheatam, the scintillating mulatto from North Carolina; the vehement Populist, "Sockless" Jerry Simpson from Kansas; Tom Watson of Georgia; also the brilliant and winsome "Silver Dick" Bland of Missouri; and of more immediate benefit to Bryan, the cagey and aggressively ambitious William Springer of Illinois.

With discreet insistence, Cotton Bride admonished his new and already favorite boarder to begin by saying little or preferably nothing for public consumption. He had noted that Bryan was a highly vocal advocate of the free or unlimited coinage of silver. That, certainly, would not better his lot with administration Democrats, including Grover Cleveland, who might very well be returned to the Presidency before the year was finished.

Apparently the amiable boardinghouse keeper did not feel qualified to counsel on press relations, but he was somewhat concerned about the forwardness of young Mr. Bryan in exposing himself so openly to the Washington press corps. Already the working press was giving attention to the engaging freshman from Nebraska; Capitol columnist, J. E. Edmonds, for one, noted that Bryan appeared to be "everywhere" in downtown Washington, in hotel lobbies, barber shops, and restaurants frequented by "important people," naturally including the press. The need for caution was accentuated by the fact that in his audacious drive for the chairmanship of the Ways and Means Committee, Congressman Springer of Illinois was already using young Mr. Bryan as a novice missionary.

Instead of driving directly for his goal, Springer made a show of presenting himself as a foremost contender for the post of Speaker of the House, which he knew he could not attain. Even so, the facile Springer had succeeded in making a deal with Congressman Charles Crisp of Georgia for an inside track to the chairmanship of Ways and Means in return for his support of Crisp's bid for the speakership. In repayment for his part in the diffuse maneuver, Bryan would be made one of the new Democratic members of Ways and Means. The campaign worked.

Though exhilarated by his first apparent victory, the

freshman from Nebraska fared badly in terms of drawing his assembly seat (by lots) and his seniority-based assignment to an office. His office looked out on a temporary garbage dump, and his House seat turned out to be in one of the more dismal and cavelike rows to the left rear.

Bryan's initial venture as a speaking congressman was even less salutory. The first session opened with the rereading of a long-bruited carryover or "mop-rag" bill that was an ambiguous ancestor of foreign-aid bills. The Russian Ukraine was in the throes of a virulent famine. The "relief" bill, which, as Springer noted, hadn't a short spit of a passing chance, would appropriate U. S. Treasury money for collecting and transporting unsalable American wheat to the famine-stricken area—on the principle that U.S. farmers would be better off—they could hardly be made worse off—if some of their "stagnant" surpluses were given away.

Bryan gained the floor to oppose. What justice could there be in aiding an alien and distant people when the U.S. government was failing to help its own? Consider Nebraska! Like the magnificent grain bowl in and about it, Nebraska was perishing of willful neglect. The novice next broke continuity and struck out at the "cruelty and corruption" of the Czars and the outrageous folly of trying to benefit "those subjects of the Czar who bear the double burden of want and persecution . . . with the economic life's blood of the American West. . . ."

The foreign aid bill and the Bryan oratory died limply. Obviously, as in the rabbit hunting of his boyhood, the youngster had blasted off at a wavering target without adequate preparation. His next move was to advance a petition to impede the spread of cigarettes, which Bryan sparklingly termed "silly little paper tubes with a little fire at one end and a little fool at the other." This was an oratorical dud. The few who chose to listen were not even entertained.

Subsequent newspaper mentions were hardly less vexing

to an eager newcomer. At the first White House reception for the Congress, gossip columnists noted the "boy M.C." from Nebraska filled a frock coat quite impressively, but his wife wore a high-necked, big-sleeved, black cashmere dress that wasn't even "fashionably cut." However, the more cogent Washington *Post* (of March 20, 1892) observed that Mrs. William Jennings Bryan's "instrument of self-expression" was her husband and that her recognizable revision of his speeches was notably improving both the lucidity and congressional future of Mr. Bryan.

Early in March the controversial subject of tariffs re-emerged. The tariffs-modifying Wilson Bill was again reported out of Ways and Means, where Bryan had had an opportunity to gain conversion to its text. He knew, of course, that the tariff remained the No. 1 party-splitting issue for the Democrats. In the main the agrarian South and the New West were passionately antitariff, many believing that only free trade could aid farming. By contrast, the eastern folds of the Democrats as well as the Republicans were topheavy with manufacturers, industrialists, and banking interests strongly advocating "a firm groundwork of tariffs." Bryan was opposed.

The early afternoon of March 15 found the House of Representatives in committee of the whole. Almost instantly after the call to order, Bryan was on his feet shouting for recognition. As he edged toward the aisle, he noticed that the galleries were still filling; well to the front, he sighted Mamie wearing a high-collared, plain blue gingham dress with gently flapping bag sleeves, and white gloves. (By her own admission she soon clutched her chair arms so tightly that she split one of her gloves.)

Other alert onlookers included H. A. Sommers, editor of the Elizabeth, Kentucky, *News,* who was spending a few days in Washington. The journalist had met Bryan in a downtown barber shop, taken a shine to him, and had therefore decided to report the speech that the young con-

gressman had confided he would be making. His report
turned out to be readable as well as highly laudatory:

> He had hardly been speaking more than two min-
> utes in that wonderfully clear silver voice of his when
> Democratic members from the cloakroom and else-
> where began filing into their seats and in less than five
> minutes . . . there was not a vacant seat hardly,
> either on the Democratic or the Republican side of the
> Chamber. . . . In a few minutes the galleries were
> well filled also.
>
> The young man . . . did not seem to appeal to the
> gallery until his clear notes were heard ringing out—
> and then every correspondent was soon in his place
> to listen to this great orator.

Undeniably, the young orator was playing for keeps.
He had moved into the great aisle and, still spraying a wonderful cadence of words, began striding toward the speaker's desk. The poetic fire of his speech seemed to draw
men on all sides. As if in hypnosis, Democratic members
began rising and trailing after him. Within minutes the
aisle was packed with congressmen who were following or
surrounding the speaker as if to take communion from his
words.

Republican opponents sought to disperse the torrent by
firing questions, for the most part barbed. Readily, volubly, Bryan answered, and with considerable skill at improvisation he kept on with his fusillade against the tariff
and its economy-ruining, people-degrading partisanship.
The clustering standees began to sway a little with the
compelling rhythms of his words. Once more, William Jennings Bryan was the sidewalk prophet, the bard of the
courthouse steps, of the open wagon beds of Springdale,
Springfield, Spring Valley, and Spring Hill, of Bald Knob,
Nellie's Apron, Prairie Grove, Goose Pond, of the American hamlets, villages, and country towns.

In his report to the home folks back in Elizabeth, Kentucky, H. A. Sommers jotted: "No one can time a great speech like Mr. Bryan made on this occasion, but if I was to state the length of time that he spoke I would say that it was about an hour and a half. . . ." (The actual time was three hours and four minutes.) When the speech ended, Bryan of Nebraska was smiling engagingly, almost in the face of the Speaker of the House. There was a moment of silence; then the gathering, including the press section, broke into a tremendous roar of applause that spread all over the floor of the House, where most of the membership was standing, shouting, and in substantial part crowding about the sizable person of William Jennings Bryan. They shook his hand, slapped his broad back, poked and probed, whacked and exclaimed. Bryan found himself being eased into the lobby and toward the bar.

"Have a drink, for God's sake," a New York member rasped.

Bryan smiled. "I don't use liquor, sir. I'll have a glass of buttermilk. . . ."

In its next issue (of March 16), the New York *World* burbled beneath a Washington dateline:

> Today, almost with the effect of an ambuscade, the Democrats uncovered a ten-inch gun, and for . . . hours shelled the surprised enemy so effectively that the protectionist batteries . . . were silenced. . . .
> This speech has been a revolution. . . .

Now that he had scored with a negative onslaught against the tariff, Bryan began maneuvering to strike out similarly at the gold standard and the Wall Street "conspiracy." To this end he sought to resume his often interrupted study of the immensely complex quandaries of U.S. currency—prefabricated defense of a far more liberal coinage of silver.

Bryan also moved to make himself known to new audiences. As a warmup, he addressed and delighted the Young Democratic Club of Philadelphia. Then, well in advance, he accepted an invitation to attend the national convention of the Populists, whose forthcoming platform would include: unlimited coinage of silver, government ownership of railroads, the abolition of national banks, the institution of a graduated income tax, and the election of U.S. senators by popular vote instead of by state legislatures. The young Democrat recognized all these as strength-building proposals that he would not disdain or neglect.

Meanwhile, the mail response to his tariff speech had grown impressively; it included letters from Nebraska and about twenty other states. "I don't rightfully know your age," one communicant declared, "but in case you are old enough to be President of the United States, I sure favor it." Bryan was not, in fact, old enough to be President, but he certainly cherished and favored the "gracious sentiment."

Timing put him in a quandary. Here he was, barely beginning his first congressional term, when another formidable campaign, including a presidential election, was already beginning. Back in Nebraska, the word was that the political corn was already popping. The Populists, known there as the Alliancers, were heatedly at work and unquestionably gaining in forcefulness, while the Democrats were digging in for the fight of their lives. Once more J. Sterling Morton was seeking the Democratic nomination for governor, and, to Bryan's chagrin, had announced himself as a gold standard man.

In Nebraska for the Democratic state convention, Bryan was renominated by acclaim, then mentioned as a possible Democratic candidate for Vice President of the United States. Affably, he bypassed the tall talk. His all-important goal was re-election to the Congress—as a Democrat. Certainly it wouldn't be easy. The Nebraska political horizons were ominously murky, and this would hold so long as

Morton and the Packing House crowd controlled the state organization, or what remained of it. Abruptly, Bryan's congressional district had been revised to leave out Omaha and include five rural counties instead. He welcomed that, but knew no Democrat could hope to win on registered Democratic strength only; to gain re-election he would have to win over both Republican and Independent voters, in all no fewer than eight thousand.

With this clearly in view, Bryan wrote his own platform for his candidacy. Implicitly, it was a bid for Populist support. Again he included a spirited free silver plank, well aware that the Nebraska state convention, obviously controlled by the Grover Cleveland crowd, headed by Morton, had condemned free silver. Bryan could not escape the absolute that as a Democratic candidate he was obliged to pay lip service to his party's presidential candidate, Cleveland; certainly he could not openly support General James Baird Weaver, the Populist candidate, even though his platform was in essence Populist. Yet unless he could dip effectively into the potential Populist vote, he simply could not win re-election.

Furthermore, this time Bryan's Republican opponent would be a truly formidable competitor. Judge Allen W. Field was an experienced political gut fighter. He stuttered badly, was no competition in silver voice and charming oratory, but he had proved his talents for recruiting votes and serving in public office. The judge was a moneyed man; he had the Republican organization behind him and open access to Republican patronage, which dipped all the way down to fourth-class postmasters and federal building janitors.

For the time Bryan was almost completely fundless and without access to patronage. His Washington expenses had far exceeded Mamie's careful budgets; the oncoming campaign would require no less than five thousand dollars. Bryan simply did not have that kind of money. The Washington *Post* reported that Judge J. H. Broady, whom

Bryan had successfully placed in nomination for election to the Nebraska Supreme Court two years before, would serve as the youngster's campaign manager and fund raiser.

Bryan sought to earn money as a lecturer, and in the quest another apparently ripe plum was dropped into his lap. By way of Tammany man Richard Crocker, an astute in-and-out congressman from New York, he eagerly accepted an assignment to serve as special Fourth of July speaker for "Tammany Hall" in New York. The fee was substantial; so was the likelihood of displeasing Grover Cleveland, who detested Tammany, which in turn detested him.

Bryan arrived in New York by train on July 3, and found the metropolis antisocially hot and noisy. Even so, he reported to his assigned room at the Waldorf-Astoria and settled to assembling a speech. Next morning the loner walked out early, viewed a Tammany-sponsored parade on Fifth Avenue, then strolled down to Tammany's own Madison Park, which flamed with festive bunting and pretty girls—wasp-waisted enchantresses who were serving free beer and sausages. Having had a touch of the latter and some amiable conversation, the young man returned to his hotel to polish his speech and to dress for the prolonged appearance. Back in Washington he had splurged on a long-tailed velveteen frock coat. It was obnoxiously moisture-provoking, and even before the committee-in-waiting called, the speaker was pouring out perspiration as well as greetings to the curious press, who pictured him afterward, in words and photographs, as a handsome, if sweat-blotched, figure.

On the platform Bryan was seated beside Tammany's own Honorable Richard (Dandy Dick) Crocker, whom Bryan would inadvertently refer to as Honest Richard Crooker. The two frock-coated guests of honor found themselves outshone by the long tableful of Tammany chieftains (sachems) all but entombed in black coats with high collars of velvet striped with gold, flaming red silk chest badges with the glaring inscription, *Tammany Society of New York,* and tightly fitting black velvet breeches. Their costumes seemed to cause an unquenchable thirst, which was obviously shared by the lowlier Gaelic saints at the less elevated tables.

The working press, meanwhile, particularly reporters and photographers for the *Sun* and the *World,* was having a field day. They noted that when Bryan was introduced, all tables, from the speaker's down through the sublevels of minor importance, broke into almost deafening applause. When Bryan smiled and bowed, a mighty and besotted voice boomed, "Whasha matta wid Wilshon?" The interrogation was echoed and answered in ardent repetition. "Whasha matta? Nuffin's a matta, Wilshon's aw right!" By then, Bryan was aware that he was being mistaken for William L. Wilson, the venerable, tariff-fighting Democratic House member. Loudly and somewhat profanely, Dandy Dick Crocker set about correcting the besotted error. Thereupon at the head table someone whooped, "Hoo-ruhh for O'Brien!" The uproar of welcome began anew, and Bryan swung into his hour-long speech on the Decade of the Common Man. Again and again the audience chorused, "Whatsa matta wid O'Brien? O'Brien's aw right."

11. The "Second Declaration of Independence"

In Omaha, Nebraska, July 4, 1892 was also an exceptionally sultry and a memorably noisy day. But whereas Tammany Hall in New York was merely convivially loud, the Omaha Coliseum was roaring with the nonalcoholic fervor of a second Declaration of Independence and a New Birth of Freedom.

Nearly seven thousand shirt-sleeved men and several hundred women, for the most part sunburned or wind-browned and impecunious of dress, were assembled for the first national convention of the Peoples' Party, more commonly known as the Populists, more derisively known as the Knuckleheads, the Wild Jackasses, or worse.

The report of the platform committee, billed as the Second Declaration of Independence, was forthcoming. All was to be in readiness to accept and publish it on this most appropriate date, the Fourth of July. Leaders were hopeful that before midnight the convention would name its nominees, and with them the next tenant of the White House. Delegates, many accompanied by their families, came at their own expense, naturally, from every state except Delaware. Since most were poor folk, each additional day of convening represented added strain on the prevailingly thin wallets and coin purses.

The mood of the body was enthusiastic, a readiness for historic action. This was loudly evidenced by the fact that the assembled convention had spent practically all morning singing. The slightly melodic uproar was not, in the Tammany manner, fueled from brown bottles or platters or other contrivances of and for parasitic slobs in quest of special privilege. For the most part, and ever so sincerely, the Populists saw themselves as patriots assembled to save the nation from the greedy and otherwise evil forces and interests that would destroy it. For Populism's own Ignatius Donnelly, the head draftsman of the forthcoming platform, had asserted: ". . . I tell you no greater body of men [than this] has ever assembled upon this continent since those men who formulated the immortal Declaration of Independence. . . ."

Having expressed agreement by means of almost deafening applause, the assembled convention had returned to singing. The Populists were already renowned—visiting reporters were using the adjective "notorious"—singers. There were those who questioned that they sang well, but not even the deaf could doubt that they sang loudly. Many were experienced in hymn-shouting revival meetings, and here in the steaming confines of the cow-town coliseum they had not only the communion of ardent spirits but the merging brass of two bands placed on opposite ends of the large, flag-draped platform. Even the immense overhead rafters seemed to quaver from the tumult.

The noise was certainly not without purpose. Practically all the numbers were parodies of well-known songs of the period that the Party planners had painstakingly prepared and distributed; only the wording was changed to protect the purpose. "Good-bye, My Lover, Good-bye," for example, came out:

> I was raised up in the kind of school,
> Good-bye, old party, good-bye,
> That taught how to buy with money rule,
> Good-bye, old party, good-bye,
> And made of me a doggone fool. . . .

"Robin Hood" had been similarly rewritten:

> The robber of old was simple and bold
> And rarely put on any frills,
> But the robber today has a different way,
> And the taxpayers foot up the bills. . . .

By noontime, convention chairman Henry Loucks had taken the platform with dignity despite his missing leg, his weighty crutches, and his almost incredibly robust beard, which reached to his waist. Moments later Ignatius Donnelly, then sixty-six, who was scheduled to read the platform that he had had most to do with drafting, hopped to the platform but gestured to the crowd to keep singing and to its delight began jigging and capering across the big stage in time with the music.

The roar of applause soon shifted to the comely Mary Ellen Lease of "raise less corn and more hell" fame, who called out her deep-voiced conviction, "The people are at bay; let the bloodhounds of money beware!"

The final forensic warning carried more truth than originality. Whether the Republican leadership was or was not composed of the bloodhounds of money, most commentators were convinced that the Populists held in their sunburned hands the outcome of the oncoming national election. It was commonly forecast that the new third party could and almost certainly would carry at least six states, viz., Colorado, Idaho, Kansas, Montana, Nebraska, and Nevada; these thirty-one electoral votes could very well spell the defeat of the Republican presidential incumbent, Benjamin Harrison, who in his dubious 1888 victory had carried all but three of the then crucial "New West" electoral votes.

By three that afternoon the perspiring crowd settled to hear the long-awaited party platform. In an unexplained shift of plans, Tom Crator, a towering Californian, strode forward to begin reading the "second Declaration of Independence":

> . . . Corruption dominates the ballot box, the legislatures, Congress, and touches even the ermine of the bench. . . . The newspapers are largely subsidized or muzzled; business prostrated; our homes covered with mortgages; labor impoverished. The fruits of the toil of millions are being stolen to build up colossal fortunes. . . . A vast conspiracy against mankind has been organized. . . . We believe that the time has come when the railroad corporations will either own our people or the people must own the railroads. . . .

Plank followed plank, with vociferous applause:

> Labor forces represented at the convention will be permanent components of the Peoples' Party. . . .
>
> The Peoples' Party demands free and unlimited coinage of silver and gold at a ratio of 16 to 1 and a minimum currency issue of fifty dollars per capita in actual circulation.

Other "demands" included the graduated income tax; postal savings banks; public ownership of telegraph and telephones; return to the government of all railroad bounty lands and the opening of these to settlement by the people; Australian-style secret ballot; eight-hour work days; laws forbidding use of "Pinkertons" and other mercenaries in quelling labor disputes.

When the reading was finished and the applause somewhat abated, Chairman Loucks put the question. The platform was accepted in toto by an ear-splitting shouting of "ayes." Women threw their hats and parasols into the air. Men showered the rafters with their straw hats and other headgear. "Yankee Doodle," "Dixie," and "Old Hundred" were roared out as interlocking or overlapping numbers by the two bands. "Victory stacking" of hands, effected by clusters of celebrants who ardently joined in multiple hand clasps, occurred throughout the hall. Pretty girls danced solo on the huge stage even while delegates knelt individually to ask God's help in the crucial struggle directly ahead. A farm contingent paraded the master placard: WHAT IS HOME WITHOUT A MORTGAGE?, while a white-bearded patriot skipped along the aisles tweeting "Yankee Doodle" on a fife.

When the nominations opened, the old protester standby, General James B. Weaver of Ohio, came forward from the shadows to accept the party's nomination for the Presidency. The general was a graying, white-bearded warrior in many causes, some few of which he had won. He had been a pioneer champion of Abraham Lincoln; he had served in Congress as a Greenbacker and had been a presidential candidate for the now vanquished Greenback-Labor Party. The incorrigible champion of the underdog and the poor man's cause would fight again and that with a Confederate colleague, General Jim Field, who would stand for the Vice-Presidency.

Bryan, meanwhile, although more than two thousand miles away, was not conspicuous because of his absence. For the most part, even the congressmen who admittedly owed their elections to the emerging Populist or Populist-prone voters of 1890 were not present in person. Among the more prominent absentees was the well-dressed and astute "Sockless" Jerry Simpson, the particularly able Populist House member from Kansas. Tom Watson of Georgia, the poet-congressman, who had definitely won his congressional seat with Farmers' Alliance support, also stayed away even though he was then writing *The Peoples' Party Campaign Book*. Populists-supported U. S. Senator William A. Peffer of Kansas, also House members John Otis and Ben Clover of Kansas; Omar Kem, the almost fabulous "calamity howler" from Broken Bow, Nebraska, and Swedish-born K. Halvorsen of Minnesota were among those who were deliberately elsewhere.

One who is disposed to weigh their motives for being absent is entitled to surmise that all had taken for granted that the noisy conclave at Omaha would be little more than a safety valve for vocal amateurs. It was therefore not a fit place for professional politicians, who must live with the truism that vehemence and voters are not synonymous.

For his own reasons, almost certainly including his intuition, Bryan, even while seeking Populist support, did not and would never envisage the Peoples' Party as a national winner, or even as a durably trustworthy regional winner. He would never explain his reasons, but he would certainly enact them.

On his return to Lincoln, the most renowned citizen of that town found that all was not right. Judge Broady, securely planted as his campaign manager, had already set about obtaining speaking dates in the principal towns of the district, leaving his candidate to again play the rural communities by ear. But Broady pointed out firmly that the campaign could not even be started rolling with less than four thousand dollars, or preferably five thousand dollars. Accordingly, he had "approached" a likely source, former Congressman Charles S. Thompson of Denver, who was serving as attorney for an association of silver mine owners. Thompson had already raised two thousand dollars for Bryan's campaign from his clients and was seeking more. Having collected the first substantial offering and firmly explained that his protégé was fighting for his political life and without adequate financing would almost certainly lose it, Broady determined to extend the reach of the offering plate.

He took the next train for Salt Lake City, where he solicited openly from silver concerns headquartered there. Within a week he was back with a campaign chest totaling well over five thousand dollars. Bryan's reactions were mixed. He could not, as he put it, relish the fruits of mammon. But he was confident that the "silver men" were justified in their efforts to convince the nation, in some part by way of Bryan, that silver money was not only the poor man's boon but that it could be produced dependably and in adequate quantities—something U.S. gold mining, except for the brief intervals of gold rushes, had never actually done in support of the gold standard.

In the course of an early speech at Auburn, Nebraska, the incumbent with problems said, smiling, "I don't know anything about free silver. . . . But the people of Nebraska are for free silver, and I am for free silver. So I will look up the arguments later. . . ." He recognized that this statement was naïve and unbecoming of an economist. But who had ever called Will Bryan an economist?

He was not obliged to "look up" the arguments that the Republicans were far better financed than the Democrats and that his advocacy of Populist tenets, which were popularly favored in his district, particularly by its majority of agrarian voters, would bring forth Populist cries of "copycat."

In response, an obviously childish response, Bryan developed a story about a pious old lady, who, in spite of being a devout and lifelong Baptist, once attended a Methodist camp meeting and promptly began outshouting the loudest of the Methodists. When asked how she, a devoted Baptist, could rise up and go shouting around like a rude, unsophisticated, leather-lunged Methodist, the dear old thing answered, "It's true I was born a Baptist, but I have strong Methodist tendencies."

Bryan smiled. "I was born a Democrat, but I now have strong Alliance [Populist] tendencies."

Bryan's first move to meet his Republican opponent in open debate was instantly regretted. His fluent oratory could only cruelly mock the incurable stammerings of Judge Field. So "the Voice" returned to his old routine of proselytizing for votes. He continued to find the people virtually unchanged and the dogging poverty of the Great Plains farmers unimproved. Yet despite his augmented experience, his expedient and money-coaxing manager, and his confidence that he could serve effectively in Congress to prevent the wrong, Bryan felt that he was losing.

Certain that he was breaking with his party, both statewide and nationally, the tiring young spellbinder began making pilgrimages to seek what he deemed expert counsel. Two weeks before Election Day, Bryan paid a brief visit to a new political friend, Governor John Peter Altgeld, the Prussian-born and courageously progressive governor of Illinois.

In large part Altgeld's stature as a liberal had risen from the tragic aftermath of the Chicago Haymarket Square Riot some six years earlier. On May 3, 1886, Chicago police had clashed with embattled strikers at the McCormick Reaper Works and killed at least four of them. The next day saw the fairly peaceful assembly of a protesting group that supposedly contained a number of members of what was then called "I.A.I.—International Anarchism Incorporated." When police sought to break up this meeting, a bomb was thrown, killing seven policemen and wounding twenty-seven others. Eight alleged Anarchists were arrested and charged with being "accessories to a fatal bombing." Seven were sentenced to death by hanging, the eighth to a long prison term. Of those seven, four were hanged, one committed suicide, and the sentences of two were commuted to life imprisonment.

The state had failed to prove beyond a reasonable doubt that any of the defendants had actually thrown the fatal bomb, and in other respects the trial was unprincipled and deplorable. Altgeld had termed it "massacre by malfeasance," and on that basis made it a prime issue in his successful quest for re-election to the governorship of Illinois. Recently he had boldly pardoned the surviving victims. As a result of his action, any candidate who called openly on the Illinois governor, if only to exchange handshakes and small talk, did so with virtual certainty of being marked a labor sympathizer, therefore a "liberal."

Apparently Bryan's pilgrimage to Springfield was a deliberate, symbolic gesture to tell friends and foes alike that he stood for impartial justice and the degree of courage required to redress a miscarriage of justice, however belatedly.

For better or worse—in terms of the still stumbling campaign—the governor of Illinois publicly predicted victory for the young congressman from Nebraska. Privately he twitted Bryan for bearing an entirely normal desire for conscience balm. The governor could understand why "practical" politics is hard on the "Christian conscience" and hell on a fundamentalist.

Bryan spent his final days of campaigning on the sidewalks and in or around the stores, shops, and wagonyards of his beloved Lincoln. The voting was medium, but the counting was excessively slow. By the night of the day after election, there was reason to believe that Cleveland had won, that the Populists had slipped considerably, and that the eastern Democrats had won decisively in several key states, including New York. But the final national count showed no semblance of a landslide: Cleveland's popular vote was 5,544,415 against Harrison's 5,190,802; by contrast, the electoral vote was 277 for Cleveland and 145 for Harrison. It was common agreement that continuing hard times had severely penalized the Republicans. As usual, there were notable exceptions, and in Nebraska most Democrats fared badly. As Bryan had anticipated, Sterling Morton took still another formidable beating. With the exception of twenty-one counties, ten of them in Bryan's district, the state had gone whole hog, even if less than enthusiastically, Republican.

Bryan's own shaky position was best described by his deeply concerned wife. Mamie had previously agreed to attend a political hen party on the Thursday following the election. She knew that most of the women who would be present were the wives of Republicans, and although the count showed Bryan ahead by a few votes, a rumor was circulating that he would lose to Field. The final returns were not yet in, and Mamie felt too shaken to attend the party. She went anyway, recording the event later with typical forthrightness:

> My pride let me dry my eyes, dress as nicely as I could, and go to congratulate the enemy. I had a little speech ready. The [supposedly] successful candidate's wife was there, surrounded by friends, all happy and smiling. . . . I was called from the room. Word had been telephoned up from headquarters that later returns gave the election to Mr. Bryan by 75 votes. What a load off my heart. I could smile, too. I did not make any speeches of congratulations. . . .

As the late country vote dribbled in, Bryan's small lead climbed to 140 votes and finally to 154, but there it died. He was back in Congress for another two years, but his return was begrudging and there were sound political reasons for predicting that the skimpy winner would not win again.

The imperiled victor retreated to his country home on Antelope Creek for a few weeks of what he called "massaging his soul." For a full month he worked with a seemingly boundless rush of energy, backing this up with a shopping spree that worried Mamie. First he finished purchasing the 120 acres, mortgaging the whole to raise the money to buy the final forty acres at $150 per acre, a then preposterous price. There was instant use for the land. Brother Charlie, as earlier revealed, was raising mules. When Will first arrived at the decrepit farm house he found a trustful young mule dozing at the front steps and another standing complacently on the front porch. When he glanced out of the front room window he saw two more mules peering in at him.

That served as a reminder that the livestock cadre should be completed. Personally Bryan favored cattle, any kind of cattle so long as they were red beef cattle. Mamie favored Jersey milkers. "We reached a compromise and settled on Jerseys," the congressman explained solemnly, failing to add that he had bought only one Jersey. Chickens came next. While in Illinois, Bryan had preferred white Wyandottes, then an upcoming breed. He hadn't changed his mind, and at "Fair View" he built a very special house for the initial colony of eight Wyandotte hens and a rooster. Charlie found the entire procedure baffling. Charlie's brother devised a special slip-out board in back for liberating the birds, although they seemed to have no serious problem breaking out through the front. Next he tried building a new contraption called a trap nest.

Bryan completed only one, but that was plenty. The trap nest was a slightly sophisticated version of the old-fashioned rabbit trap—with a straw-padded nest placed in a box. The hen entered the box from the front. When she got up during or after laying her egg, she supposedly pushed against the parallel bar or stick of a figure-four trigger. This caused the door to drop shut. The attendant in due course—trap nests require attendants in due course —would take off the top, release the hen, after first having noted *which* hen, and recover the egg. It was unpleasant for the hen and not exactly a bed of roses for the attendant, but it showed the owner which hens were actually laying.

Not the Bryan trap nest, however. The whittled wooden triggers didn't function as they were meant to, and neither did the hens. On the very first tryout the falling door had jammed, the laying hen got out, and a curious skunk got in, ate the egg, and took over the nest as a permanent apartment. The builder did not undertake gentle eviction measures; he only pushed over the nest and ran like the wind.

The temporarily impoverished young congressman who would champion all other poor Americans was finding a yeoman's joy in building for himself. For the time, at least, he was not confronting audiences of ragged, sun-beaten, despairing men and women. For the time he was not peering into the sad, pleading eyes of ill-fed, insecure children. He was building a tangible measure of American security, not with beautiful words, but with board, nail, hammer, and tar paper.

At the betowered oversize piano box of a residence on D Street, life went on with assurance. Mamie was in charge once more. The Bairds were doing tolerably well, and the Bryan children were flourishing. Ruthy, aged eight, discarded dolls in favor of serious reading. Junior, beginning his fifth year, was affectionately nicknamed Dirty Boy. In dry weather he moved about the premises like a small, portable dust storm, in wet weather like a combination of mud turtle and flash flood. He scared his frail grandmother half to death by sliding down banisters, and Mamie once found him swinging from the telephone wire thirty feet above the cement drive. But his mother would not be discouraged. "Our Junior is so sweet and clean and well-behaved when he's asleep," she told her husband. Little Gracie, the pretty one, was just beginning to walk; in a few years she would turn abruptly from rag dolls to croquet.

They returned to Washington, and once more Mamie found time to help her husband. Again there were deluges

of mail that Bryan encouraged and sought to attend to with
his own hard-scratching steel pens. Again there were the
seekers of patronage to heed, and again his pallid sister-
secretary was almost never feeling well.

The stream of callers caused Capitol correspondents to
exclaim about Bryan's impressive talent for attracting people, including the exceptional or odd. On that list was an
easy-spoken, handsome young man from Indiana, whom
much of the working press had already branded as a "notorious figure." Although not yet forty, Eugene Victor Debs
of Terre Haute was president of the newly established
American Railway Union and a widely recognized leader
in the labor movement.

Understandably less than *persona grata* with most of the
party-loyal Democratic and Republican congressmen, Gene
Debs was a pre-eminent student of American railroads and
Americans. Forthrightly, he sought and received the support of Congressman Bryan of Nebraska. The warm friendship would endure even as Debs moved on into the jungles
of American prejudices to mark trails for what would be
termed "socialism."

Undeniably, Bryan of Nebraska gained from his quickly
formed friendship with Debs of Indiana. He acquired, for
one thing, a source of responsible information about American railroads and their policies of employment.

Meanwhile, what he was learning about the head of
the national Democratic party was profoundly discourag-
ing. As Bryan appraised them, Grover Cleveland's basic
policies and dislikes had not changed during the latter's
four years of unwanted retirement, nor had they improved
in terms of western needs. Cleveland, as he openly admitted, believed in letting the children settle their own quar-
rels. At the same time, like Mountaineeous Mary Lemen,
Bryan's "whuppin'" teacher, the President was never far
away from his flogging stick. Others, including responsible
historians, would presently contradict this concept of Mr.
Cleveland as a whip-wielding schoolmaster, but as a working politician Bryan continued to see his President as a

breeches-wearing Mary Lemen patrolling grimly within easy reach of a box of switches.

In Bryan's estimate, the President was sustaining a gold standard to implement the interhemispheric greed of the British Empire, yet simultaneously was whacking Her Majesty's Government for its defiance of the Monroe Doctrine by meddling in Venezuelan affairs. Democrat or no, Grover Cleveland was effectively spanking the silver mine interests and the proponents of lowered (or eliminated) tariff barriers. He was slashing away at the legitimate self-realization of western Democrats and standing ready to apply the rod to any disagreeing party member on the all-applicable theory that a loyal Democrat was necessarily a conservative Democrat.

These, to repeat, were Bryan's own estimates, but they were not wholly divorced from fact. The more so now that Cleveland had reached into Nebraska to make J. Sterling Morton his second-term Secretary of Agriculture. Bryan could not see his former sponsor plowing corn, but he correctly assumed that Morton would shortly be under presidential orders to plow under William Jennings Bryan, another reason why the last named was already describing the President as the most completely orthodox Republican ever to occupy the White House.

As anyone could see, Morton's appointment to the Cabinet placed Bryan's future as a Nebraska Democrat in profound jeopardy. The one rational hope for saving his imperiled political hide was that Nebraska's Slaughter House or "Free West" Democrats, more specifically Jimmy Dahlman and company, might come to the maverick's rescue and, as Dahlman put it, "settle the ropes" on Morton's and the administration's Packing Housers. The former cowboy sheriff was headquartered purposefully in Omaha, where he was organizing the "Real Nebraska Democrats."

Bryan resumed his political fundamentalism. Just as he held totally with one God, he resolved to cling totally with one political tenet, which he saw as covering all like a giant revival tent. That, of course, was the limitation, re-

duction, and eventual erasure of tariffs. Though he was
still no profound scholar of tariffs—he had not actually
dug into the enormous complexities of the subject, its many
paradoxes and counterbalances—Bryan was convinced
that he knew enough to justify branding tariffs, per se,
as evil, as Satan's instruments, and to continue to urge their
obliteration as the just and godly thing to do. He would
further supplement his crusade with a correlated crusade
against the "gold standard" and a revived championship of
"free silver."

It followed that when Cleveland called a special session
of Congress for mid-August 1893, Bryan, who had spent
most of the interrupted legislative vacation traveling the
drought-seared, agriculturally distressed West, returned to
Washington loaded for bear, by his own admission. On
the afternoon of August 16 he took the floor to speak
in defense of free silver. Once again he peered up to
crowded galleries and saw his Mamie sitting well to the
front, clasping her chair arms tensely. Once more he spoke
over the heads of the Congress to the world beyond.

The Washington *Post,* which usually controlled its enthusiasm for anti-Administration and most other Democrats, was effusive is praising Bryan's speech. "It raised
the young Nebraskan to international renown. . . ." Bill
Springer of Illinois did not restrain his own superlatives:
"The greatest speech I ever heard in either branch of Congress. . . . It will take rank with the speeches of Clay or
Webster. . . ."

At 1600 Pennsylvania Avenue the response was quite
different. Quaking with fury, the President, so the telling
story went, called in his Secretary of Agriculture and commanded him to kill off "that young upstart from Lincoln,
Nebraska." J. Sterling Morton was still ineffective as a
party disciplinarian, and perhaps did not find joy in meat-
axing an estrayed protégé. In any case, Bryan did not
waste time bleating with alarm. He began paying affable
calls on Democratic senators. He expanded his correspondence to include warming letters to Democratic gov-

ernors and state chairmen, particularly in the South and West. When an association of silver-mine operators asked permission to distribute half a million copies of Bryan's "remarks" on silver, as published in the *Congressional Record,* he happily gave permission.

October 1893 brought the interim convention of the Democratic party of Nebraska. If Bryan ever doubted having been marked for slaughter by his own party, his doubts quickly vanished. Like a kangaroo court victim, he was given no chance to defend himself or his actions. He was an accused party saboteur. Hour after hour the condemnations proceeded. One after another, major and minor henchmen of the Administration Democrats joined in the flaying. When he was finally permitted to speak briefly, Bryan calmly stated that he proposed to go his way alone, doing right as God made him see it, and that without fear or favor.

Early in January, 1893 Bryan had made headlines with a speech that was a renewed defense of the hard-used, much-punished Wilson Tariff Bill:

> The poor man is called a socialist if he believes that the wealth of the rich should be divided among the poor, but the rich man is called a financier if he devises a plan by which the pittance of the poor can be converted to his use. . . .

Once more the voice was speaking to America of her sons and daughters in rags and hunger and despair. Once more Grover Cleveland permitted his displeasure to be known. The President was not mollified by Bryan's subsequent discourse on corporations:

> But, Mr. Chairman, we are not hostile to corporations. We simply believe that this creature of the law, this fictitious person, has no higher or dearer rights

than the person of flesh and blood whom God created
and placed upon His footstool. . . .

The Nebraskan's first plea for a graduated income tax,
which Cleveland had opposed on grounds of constitutionality, won strong following from representatives out of the
hard-battered South and West. Bryan was substantially,
even if intuitively, in step with the changing credos of the
time. The President again plowed cross furrows with his
attempt to offer a "financier's substitute" for the long-delayed but carefully weighed Wilson Bill. Bryan waited to
defend. Bill Springer stood by to assist him in baiting the
eastern Democrats. When the hour neared, the cagey Il-
linoisan moved for unanimous consent that the doors be
thrown open to the public and that all otherwise vacant
seats be made available to the ladies. (Bryan's House seat
was being shared by a young lady, his then nine-year-old
daughter Ruth, who, in time, would also be a member of
Congress.)

Once more the Nebraskan bowed to the Speaker and
gained recognition. Then he moved into the aisle and
opened with an almost thunderous broadside against "pro-
tectionism" by way of a pretended compromise bill, the
Administration's less than particular hoax to use presidential prestige to coddle the industry and finance of the East
at the ruinous expense of the South and West. He began
to shift from regionalism to plead that all Americans claim
and validate their rights as citizens.

Again the membership of the House came spilling into
the aisle to surround Bryan. Again gallery listeners began
cheering like collegians at a football game. In answer to
opposition by Representative Bourke Cochran of New
York, Bryan apparently improvised what was presently to
be the opening of the Cross of Gold speech:

If this were a mere contest in oratory no one would
be presumptuous to dispute the prize with the dis-

tinguished gentleman from New York . . . but clad in the armor of a righteous cause I dare expose myself to the shafts of his genius, believing that pebbles of truth will be more effective than javelins of error even when hurled by the giants of the Philistines. . . .

Bryan emerged further as the knight defender of the American masses, the preponderance of have-nots. The New York *World* called him the orator of the century.

The fight for the Wilson Bill reached its climax on the following Ground Hog Day. With painful deliberation, the clerk began to call the roll. The count was close. For many minutes the "Nos" were well ahead of the "Ayes." The Carolinas, Tennessee, and Virginia made the race neck-and-neck. Then came the remnant of Westerners—Texas, Utah, and Washington. The "Ayes" had it; the "Wilson Tariff Moderation Act" had carried. If Cleveland chose to veto, he would be openly defying the decision of his own party and inviting the subsequent passage of a more emphatic tariff reduction act. Again pandemonium took hold of the House of Representatives. The New York *World* recorded:

It was a scene unparalleled in parliamentary history in America. The Capitol police were powerless and the regular police force of the city had to be sent for. . . . It was the greatest crowd ever assembled in the Capitol. . . .

The New York *Sun* recounted that the air of the House was cluttered not only with uproarious sounds but with high-thrown hats, papers, and, more dangerously, umbrellas and books. Representative Bill Wilson was hoisted bodily into the air; his short, slender body somehow settled on the shoulders of a delirious throng of Populists. They carried him down the aisle, and when they could find no place to set him down, they tossed him into a cluster of fellow celebrants. Discreetly, Bryan retreated to the cloakroom and locked his strong arms about a coat rack.

But in his own distinctive way, Bryan also celebrated. He quietly announced that he would not seek re-election to the House of Representatives; he accepted that so far as the First Nebraska District was concerned, his throat, politically speaking, had been cut from ear to ear. But he would never forsake his party.

Perceptive Bryan-watchers soon noticed that the young congressman from Nebraska was spending more time with his family than before. Intimates noted that in the Bryan living room the congressman was leading family prayers before breakfast each morning and holding household gatherings for Bible reading each evening.

But Bryan did not substantially reduce his work in Congress. When the Cleveland administration devised a plan for large issues of gold bonds which, of course, would commit the government to restrict the coinage of silver, Bryan hounded the move relentlessly, pronouncing clearly that at least in his own mind he identified free silver with free men, and the gold standard with the contrived crucifixion of free men.

As the year and the life of the session grew late, the Cleveland forces again brought up the gold bond bill. Bryan struck. In the early afternoon of December 22, he once more gained the floor, and his voice filled the chamber:

I shall not help crucify mankind upon a cross of gold. I shall not aid the pressing down upon the bloody brow of labor the crown of thorns!

12. The Long Odds

When Will Bryan was eleven and his father was seriously considering making his all-out try for Congress, Lyman Trumbull favored Silas Bryan with a characteristically thoughtful letter. The gist was that an officeholder could not expect to be permanently immunized against political dormancy from time to time. Out of his own experience Trumbull believed that political growth was subject to the natural limitations of other kinds of growth—vegetable, animal, or ecological. The illustrious Chicagoan pointed out that vote crops, like farm crops, must necessarily survive the phenomena of leaf shed and winter waiting and revive or be resurrected with the oncoming season, in an environment of growth.

On his own rather vivid recognition Bryan was finding his career compellingly dormant. At least, that is, in terms of visible progress in his second congressional term. Though he felt deeply, spoke volubly, and continued to gain in the scope of national attention, nevertheless his presence in Congress as the Democratic representative from the First Nebraska District was in the yellowing sere. The congressional exodus of William Jennings Bryan was pre-assured.

During February 1894, Bryan said that he would not seek re-election to the House of Representatives. Stubborn as he was, the eloquent young Nebraskan admitted that the gaining root power of the Nebraska Alliancer-Populists, the firming of the Republican strength, and his continuing bludgeoning by the Cleveland administration and its henchmen in Nebraska combined to obliterate the political future of any Democratic House of Representatives nominee in his district.

He explained in his subsequent announcement in early August that he would nevertheless seek election as United States senator as a restatement of his unfaltering belief in God and country and his confidence that he could help the economically and socially oppressed American majority. The statement carried a ring of sincerity, along with what many saw as a rather appalling lapse of logic. The Bryan chances for being elected U.S. senator by the Republican-dominated Nebraska legislature were frozen at an unrelenting zero.

During 1891, when the 130-member Nebraska legislature made an off-year (temporary) selection of a U.S. senator, Bryan's name, along with fourteen other "off-the-cuff" nominations, had been duly entered. On the ensuing ballots he had received as many as sixteen votes. The forthcoming selection, in 1894, for a full six-year senatorial term promised no substantial change in political status or preferential mood. Legislative head-counters were agreed that however vigorous his campaigning efforts, Bryan could not expect to win more votes than those of twenty legislators, and probably considerably fewer. The Republican-faithful governor, John M. Thurston, however colorless, could and did count on at least a hundred votes. The Populist-Alliance candidate would almost certainly receive more votes than Bryan. These forecasts, as made by the Omaha *Bee-*

News late in 1893, turned out to be substantially correct; to nobody's surprise, Republican Thurston received ninety-seven legislators' votes, Populist-Alliance D. A. Jones, eighteen, and Bryan, seventeen.

This was Bryan's first major and bone-jolting defeat. But the young man was not bitter; his meditative, slate-blue eyes continued to see greener horizons. He remained convinced that he could and in time would help powerfully in reshaping the federal government to fulfill the needs of the American people. He refused, therefore, to accept this interval of dormancy in a lethargic manner. He revealed that he was working harder and praying harder than he had ever worked or prayed before, and his nationwide publicity was unquestionably catapulting. One of the strongest causative factors was the President's lambasting of the volatile young Nebraskan as a party troublemaker, with and without specific mention of the lame duck's name. During his twilight days as a member of Congress, Bryan continued to hammer away at the thesis that Cleveland's prejudicial treatment of silver and his outrageously mis-named "tariff control" could only make the poor poorer and the rich richer.

During April 1894, when the pitiable "army" of jobless men led by Jacob Coxey of Massillon, Ohio, staged its pathetic "invasion" of the capital, and Cleveland disdained as "crack-brained" the Coxey proposal that the federal government refurbish employment by means of public works, principally the building of much-needed roads, Bryan veered from direct participation, explaining that with only a "twilight hour" of his congressional term remaining he was in no position to function effectively as a young David, temporarily lacking a slingshot.

But he continued to proselytize for the cause of the common people, most of all the depression-tormented farmers, the unemployed laborers, the ill-paid teachers and preachers, and the independent shopkeepers. In this pursuit Bryan at least indicated that he had the will, the words, and the audacity to build his own rural road to the White House. When opportunities permitted—and he worked astutely to create the opportunities—Bryan spoke for the record, all kinds of public records, including newspapers, reviews, and house organs or pamphlets that would heed him:

> In the name of those who still believe "all men are created equal"; in the name of those who still believe in equality before the law; in the name of those who still believe the harvester has the same rights as the hat makers, and that the farmer is entitled to the same respect as the factory owner, I protest against the arrogant and impudent assumption that it is the privilege of any particular class to make laws for our people, or that any of our citizens, whatever their residence or whatever their occupation, are excluded from an equal voice in the affairs of government. . . .

The Silver Voice continued to engineer strategic side trips out of Washington. One preliminary harvest was notable during June 1894, at Springfield, Illinois, when the liberal and grandstanding Governor Altgeld, looking ahead to the 1896 presidential campaign, boldly recommended Missouri's old-line Congressman "Silver Dick" Bland of Missouri as the Democratic nominee with Bryan as the vice presidential candidate.

In Bloomington, Illinois, the gentle-voiced, sad-featured Eugene V. Debs, by then winning the big strike against the Great Northern Railroad and planning a much larger "sympathy strike" in support of Pullman employees, was "all for Will Bryan." So, one might gather, was Debs' youthful and dour but quite competent lawyer, Clarence Darrow, who had first met Bryan at the Trumbull home. From Chicago the now feeble Lyman Trumbull continued to encourage his former protégé to accentuate his prevailing devotions: a graduated income tax, state inheritance taxes, direct election of U.S. senators, and female suffrage. Bryan agreed all the way, but steadfastly declined to join the Populists, toward whom the aging Trumbull was veering. "I'm forever a Democrat," he repeated, adding with his slow smile, "even if only a fading Democrat."

The burgeoning "associations" of silver miners were in no mood to contradict. Two other Chicagoans, William Clark and Marcus Daly, both directors of the Associated Silver Miners, Inc., joined in the first distinctly partisan move to further "build up" their silver-voiced orator and champion of silver. They agreed and presently proclaimed that Bryan required a forum. They had learned that Omaha's and Nebraska's largest Democratic newspaper was available for purchase.

That was an understatement. The Omaha *World* had been fumbling and bumbling along at the edge of bankruptcy for more than a decade. The paper could now be bought for twenty thousand dollars; the silver propagandists decided to buy it by proxy, but short of assuming full ownership. Their plan was to make Bryan editor-in-chief, on an admittedly honorary basis, meanwhile retaining most of the regular staff. In that manner, directly after his exit from Congress, Bryan would take over an established platform. He would not be expected to run the paper; he would be privileged to speak through it, and his honorarium would be thirty dollars a week. The fringe benefits would include hotel rooms, rail transportation, and other accommodations then regularly receivable in lieu of cash payments for advertising space. This advertising barter would help the young upcomer keep on the lecture trail. Time would shortly prove that William Jennings Bryan did not excel as a doctor of a sick newspaper. He did perform brilliantly as a temporarily unofficial advocate of social justice and upbuilder of his own already impressive image.

The engaging young Nebraskan with the remarkable

voice that could thunder Jovian wrath or mellow sweetly also excelled as a letter writer. The ever-expanding marathon of Bryan correspondence for 1894 and 1895 shows exchanges with scores of influential Democrats throughout the nation. His correspondence with church leaders was also increasing. And his correspondence, like his versatile speeches, was more than affable gush. In most of his letters he was taking emphatic, even hazardous, positions. His eloquent defenses of the Eugene Debs leadership of the nation's first major railroad strike, his castigation of Cleveland's and federal court's move to break the strikes by claiming the federal government's right to maintain uninterrupted transmission of the mails, and his ringing protest of the subsequent sentencing of Debs and his colleagues to jail terms for contempt of court were among significant examples.

Bryan shuttled adroitly from his editorial office in Omaha, where he rarely spent more than one day a week, to his lectures and back to his developing farmstead just outside Lincoln. There he was no dilettante. On his prairie-edge farm he joined actively in haying, well digging, fence building, and harvesting, and even as a hard-toiling member of the wheat-threshing crew. Stripped to the waist and clad in black-striped breeches and high boots, he swung a pitchfork with authority and lifted towering armloads of cord-bound grain bundles.

The family in the main was thriving. Mamie was again keeping house on D Street and doubling as a farm wife at Fair View. Some said that William Jennings Bryan, Jr., now six, was improving his behavior, and although others vowed it was getting worse, none could deny that he was around, alive, and drawing his ample share of attention. Ruth was proving herself a stellar student; she was leading the fifth grade in a local public school. Little Grace, though only four, had learned to play an impressive game of croquet; she beat her father practically every time the two met in competition. Only one member of the family was waning; Lovina Baird was even more than customarily convinced that she was not long for this earth.

As the months hurried along, Bryan spent more and more time "on circuit" as the quasi-official voice of silver. In great part his itineraries were related to his political aspirations. The emoluments were obviously catch as catch can. Where silver advocates or similar groups had arranged for a hall and audience, Bryan eagerly took his cue and focused on winning friends and potential voters. He spoke and charmed at home gatherings, public lyceums, hotel lobbies, courthouse conclaves, Masonic and other lodge halls. Frequently he lectured at churches, rallies, and county fairs. When an honorarium was available, Bryan usually accepted—even modest ones. When no honoraria were available, he spoke for free. Again and again, he used his newspaper advertising barter to pay for a hotel room and, when possible, his next railroad ticket. Frequently he arranged his own appearances, hired or borrowed the hall, and on repeated occasions, drummed up his own audience.

With passing time and experimentation, Bryan centered more effort on appealing to small-business people as well as farmers and laborers, the better to show his respect for their real importance as voters and citizens. He kept on rebuking the "plutocracy of the gold standard" who would regard only major manufacturers, bankers, or utility magnates as "real businessmen." He continued to speak to and for the occupants of some nine million homes and farms that remained under mortgage and to devise a more inclusive definition of the American businessman.

We say to you that you have made the definition of a businessman too limited in its application. The man who is employed for wages is as much a businessman as the merchant in New York; the farmer who goes forth in the morning and toils all day, who begins in the spring and toils all summer—and who by the application of brain and muscle to the national resources of the country creates wealth, is as much a businessman as the man who goes upon the board of trade and bets upon the price of grain. The miners who go down a thousand feet into the earth, or climb two thousand feet upon the cliff, and bring forth from their hiding places the precious metals to be placed in the channels of trade are as much businessmen as the few financial magnates who, in a back room, own the money of the world. . . .

As the days and nights continued, Bryan shaped and tried out other approaches. He had already polished the "cross of gold and crown of thorns" metaphor. In his *Memoirs* he jotted: "I had used it a few times before . . . recognizing its fitness for the conclusion of a climax and had tucked it away for proper occasions. . . .

Bryan struck aggressively at the man he was virtually certain would be the Republican presidential candidate—Major William McKinley, Jr., governor of Ohio. That determined native of Niles Village had moved into politics early with a commendable background of Union Army combat service, and had won his first political office at twenty-six (prosecuting attorney for Stark County, Ohio) and his first election to Congress at thirty-three. There, in 1890, McKinley had lost while Bryan was winning. Now the fifty-two-year-old Ohioan had staged a forceful comeback. He had strongly organized backers in Ohio politics as well as a personal talent for political pulse feeling and for forwarding his case as an economic rainmaker. In that area McKinley and Bryan were whacking away at the eastern Democrats with a common fervor and apparent effectiveness. The Cleveland administration in general and the Nebraska Packing House Democrats were aware of that, the latter so much so that there was already very real doubt that W. J. Bryan and other "Slaughter Housers" would be permitted to hold their places as official delegates from Nebraska to the Democratic Convention of 1896; certainly they could anticipate vehement challenge by the party regulars.

Even so and without correlating his dispersed energies and diffused strategies, Bryan was looking forward to the oncoming election as an underdog's year of promise. He knew that by the start of 1896, the United States had approximately forty prosilver groups or lobbies, and at least five of these were already contributing to Bryan's buildup. The silver front was by no means his only bright promise. In Nebraska old Jimmy Dahlman, unquestionably the state's dominant politician of the year, was saying openly that he was all for hustling Will Bryan. Dahlman pointed out wryly that the Democrats were obliged to pick a real Democrat for the next round, one who could really get out the country and poor folks' vote. He looked on Will Bryan as such a vote getter. He conceded, too, that a man seeking a toehold in national politics requires homeland support.

Beginning late in 1895 and through the following winter Dahlman had assembled gatherings of what he termed straight-talking Democrats; the largest of these was held at the Paxton Hotel in Omaha. In unvarnished cowboy language he spoke out for Bryan as a potential presidential nominee. His "boy" was now of presidential age, i.e., thirty-five. In the West at least he was already well-known. More important, he had proved himself of championship caliber as a country campaigner, and a majority of U.S. voters still lived in the country.

Bryan next lectured south and east, going into the Carolinas, Georgia, Louisiana, and Mississippi. He also continued to study possible Democratic nominees for the Presidency. One was a young congressman from Missouri, Champ Clark. Bryan found Clark easy to like, but not easy to believe in. He also erased the name of Cleveland's Vice President, Adlai E. Stevenson, from his list, believing

Stevenson's association with Cleveland to be the kiss of
death. Among fellow silverites there were at least two
other possibilities: Senator Stephen M. White of California
and Senator Henry M. Teller of Colorado, a changeover
Republican. But Bryan saw none of these as probables. As
he traveled on, he grew more confident that a man "sell-
able" to the hard-used farmers and laborers would be the
forthcoming Democratic nominee; himself, say.

On a brief return to the towered white house in Lincoln,
Bryan found his mother-in-law seriously ill. After half a
century of believing herself an invalid, Lovina Baird's conviction was borne out. She died quietly in her sleep three
days after Bryan's thirty-sixth birthday. Mamie was grief-
stricken. Bryan tried to comfort her; so did Junior. Putting
his arm about his mother's neck, Junior said, "Mamma,
whenever you are feeling sad, just think of me."

Another month of diligent lecturing and political track-
ing took Bryan to St. Louis, press card in hand, to "report" the Republican convention. He said smilingly that
he was going to add to the confusion. That wasn't easy to
do. From beginning to end, the St. Louis convention was
a cauldron of confusion; even Boss Hanna and his protégé
William McKinley seemed dazed.

Bryan was convinced that Marcus Alonzo Hanna of
Cleveland was the man in charge. It was as obvious as a
country washday that the Republicans were seeking to
build up tariffs as the decisive issue of the campaign and
to bypass as far as possible the silver-gold controversy.
Bryan estimated that the Republican party was about as
near to an open split as the Democrats. Now that the Republicans had both a silver "wing" and a gold one, McKinley
was making noises like a bimetallist; for the silverites
he was prosilver, for the gold faction he was progold,
to those who exclaimed, "But you can't be for both!,"
he was saying, in effect, "You are absolutely right!"

The platform was being drafted by Melville Stone of
the Associated Press because, so the wiseacres reported,

Stone was the only person present who knew how to spell "inviolable." Beneath its froth of purple rhetoric, the Republican platform carried a recognizable pretty-please undertone, inspired, perhaps, by such developments as the recurring pleas of the New York City Police Commissioner to the city's plutocracy to refrain from "social events" that might bestir the despairing riffraff to rise up violently. Whatever else they were, the "Gay Nineties" were not gay. Most Americans were painfully poor. Farming was increasingly pauperized. The "inexhaustible" American frontiers were, in fact, showing signs of outright exhaustion. The country's natural resources were being ravaged by the privileged few, and the first of these resources was people.

"The second American revolution" was being talked about with fervor, and Henry Cabot Lodge, widely noted at the best "intelligence" in the Congress, saw his Republican party rapidly becoming indefensible in its chronic avoidance of the needs of laborers and farmers. Appeasers, including prominent university faculty members as well as politicians, were advocating the establishment of overseas colonies to replace the expiring home frontiers. There was a fervent public interest in Spain's appallingly bad management of affairs in Cuba, her "key" colony in the American Hemisphere. High brass in the U. S. Navy were beginning to seize on overseas conquest as the best attainable means for inviting a buildup of sea power. The mismanaged, badly led, badly paid, ill-equipped, ill-fed, and politically mildewed U. S. Army could see overseas conquest aimed at weak Spain as the one remaining device for returning its twenty-four thousand men to respectability.

Many axes awaited sharpening, Bryan thought, but the Republican platform of 1896 was no grindstone for public well-being. In a fifty-thousand-word outgushing, the text revealed only vague and aged shapes in its planks—"firm" tariff walls, peace by means of withdrawal from international covenants, severely controlled currency supported by a restrictive gold reserve, undefined encouragement of international trade but without reciprocal tariff agreements, confining Indians to assigned reservations as wards of the government, minimized federal taxes, and so on.

Bryan left St. Louis with the conviction that if the Democrats could hang together, they had a chance to win again. He also left with the congealing hope that he might even yet find a way to lead his party to victory. Checking out of his hotel, the self-described reporter met a fellow Democratic eavesdropper. "Bryan, we are going to Chicago to nominate Senator Teller," Senator Towne began. "You had better come and help us."

Bryan smiled broadly. "I can't do it; I am going to be nominated myself."

13. Cross of Gold

At about 9 A.M. on July 13, 1896, Samuel P. Martin, Jr., sixteen, of Poplar Bluff, Missouri, headed for the local railroad station to find out what was new in the world outside. For most residents of Poplar Bluff, that wasn't easy. At the time the town had no daily newspaper; the St. Louis papers, which usually arrived at least a day late, were for a minority of the affluent.

But Sammy Martin had solved his own problem with the recalcitrant communications. On his own initiative the Martin boy, who would grow up to be one of the most revered physicians of southeastern Missouri, had learned Morse code. He could translate by ear all that came over the telegraph wires.

On weekday mornings, as line loads permitted, Western Union carried a brief summation of the principal news of the previous day. This was known as the pony service of the Associated Press; the so-called line slop was dispatched at special rates to the smaller member newspapers.

Already interested in politics (as Dr. Martin he became

a lay politician and convention delegate), Sammy was particularly curious about the Democratic Convention assembled in Chicago. He found the depot waiting room empty; even the dispatcher-telegrapher had stepped away from his desk. But the keyboard was clacking away, and the Martin boy listened. What he heard next made his hair stand practically on end:

YOU SHALL NOT PRESS DOWN UPON THE BROW OF LABOR THE CROWN OF THORNS; YOU SHALL NOT CRUCIFY MANKIND UPON A CROSS OF GOLD.

As Sammy Martin sensed, and as history would confirm, those twenty-four short and well-chosen words, however metaphoric, were destined to catapult a poor and supposedly failing ex-congressman to international fame. For William Jennings Bryan this combination of commonplace words was both the symbol and living proof of his resurrection from political death. This came from what he regarded as God's will and his own diligently developed techniques of crowd persuasion.

The twenty-six days that separated the closing of the Republican convention and the opening overtures of the Democratic convention had been the most emotionally upsetting of Bryan's lifetime. Following his somewhat less than objective reporting of the Republican session in St. Louis, the ousted Congressman had set out to seek the support of key Democratic leaders. To that end he moved aggressively into Atlanta and Louisville to seek support from two supposedly bellwether Democratic newspapers. He returned to Omaha where the *World-Herald* was doing badly, as usual. The man who genuinely liked law practice but couldn't find time for it was becoming less certain that he genuinely liked newspapering, even as an editor-in-chief customarily *in absentia.*

In Lincoln for a "get-reacquainted" visit with his family, Bryan received a telegram advising him of the death in Chicago for his revered friend and hero, Lyman Trum-

11. A lithographed campaign copy of the famous "Cross of Gold" speech.

12. The presentation of the speech: the Chicago Convention.

13. A hometown celebration of the 1896 official nomination—Lincoln, Nebraska, on September 8 of that year.

14. Eastern papers wanted photos of "Bryan the Farmer," so he obligingly posed with his son and a young friend.

15. A literal stump speech in the slash-pine country of the Southeast, 1896.

16. At home on D Street: Ruth on the bike, Grace next to Mrs. Bryan in the chair, Mr. Bryan, and young Willie, Jr.

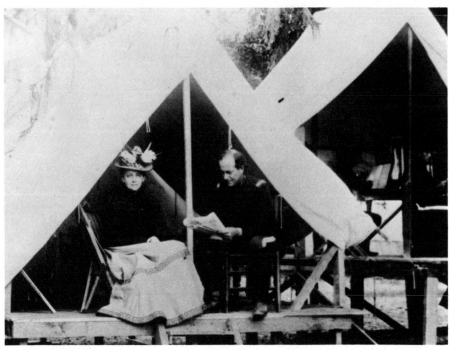

17. Bivouac for Cuba: Colonel Bryan and Mary in Camp Cuba Libre, in north central Florida.

18. Home from the hostilities, Colonel Bryan addresses the Jacksonian Club of Lincoln from the back of his prize horse, Governor.

bull. Shaken, Bryan boarded the next train for Chicago. There young Henry Trumbull awaited his arrival with the request that Bryan speak the eulogy at the graveside.

Profoundly honored, Bryan managed to improvise an eloquent but largely puerile tribute to Sir Lyman and his people-benefiting devotion to social justice and the American legacy of reform. Later he recalled his sincere inability to check his tears while speaking. He also remembered meeting another protégé of Sir Lyman's, the restless, tense, peering young lawyer named Clarence Darrow.

Bryan next answered an urgent request from his friend, Jimmy Dahlman, the hard-riding herder of liberal Democrats in Nebraska, who had important party business to discuss. Dahlman had word that the Easterners, headed by Stephen Grover Cleveland in person, were conspiring to disqualify most of Nebraska's convention delegates on grounds of party disloyalty. Bryan, of course, was the best-known of those imperiled. The Nebraska delegation was his only assured backing for the Democratic nomination. There were many other complications, but Dahlman reiterated that he was wearing his long-roweled spurs and as necessary he would use them on certain onery rumps.

When he was again free, Bryan returned to his big ugly home on D Street in Lincoln to be met with the news of his mother's death back in Salem. Mariah Bryan was sixty-two; presumably she had died of an apoplectic stroke.

At first Bryan seemed unable to accept the report as real. He shut himself in his bedroom for several hours of prayer. When Charlie arrived to help the family make ready for the journey to Salem, he found his brother unable to stand alone, and he almost carried him to the carriage and literally lifted him aboard the train. At the Salem depot Bryan seemed unable to recognize kinspeople and others who waited his arrival. In the homestead his grief gained intensity. To the distress of his three sisters he declined to eat, this for the first time in anyone's recollection. Throughout the funeral service at the local Baptist Church he wept silently. Going into the cemetery, as he followed the glass-topped funeral wagon on foot, he remarked only that he had never seen the grass so green at that time of the year.

Charlie once again took over as his guardian and counselor, reminding him of the need for his proceeding to Chicago where important, probably decisive, preconvention parleys were in progress. Only after being put aboard the Lincoln-bound train did Bryan seem to shed his heavy haze of grief. In his hometown he called at his law office to borrow a hundred dollars from Dolph Talbot; then, with Charlie still at his side, he took the train for Omaha. Jimmy Dahlman had already made arrangements for a Pullman car for the Nebraska delegation, but it would not leave for Chicago until the following Sunday. Bryan left his brother to serve as his proxy in Omaha, boarded the first train for Chicago, and in solitude resumed his speech writing.

He bypassed the de luxe Palmer House, where rooms had been reserved for all the Nebraska delegates, and sought quarters at the small and inexpensive Clifton Hotel, within easy walking distance of the Loop. The only single room available was Number 13. Bryan declined it, and took a double room without a bath. He confided that his wife would shortly be joining him and that, as usual, he was obliged to be economical. In his *Memoirs* he wrote:

> . . . I took $100 with me and after paying the hotel bill for Mrs. Bryan and myself during the convention week I had about $10 left, a sum probably as small as anyone has spent in seeking a Presidential nomination . . .

Many others sought the Democratic nomination. Advance patrols for at least six possible candidates were already in action. At first glance Bryan adjudged that Bland of Missouri and Lucas J. Matthew of Indiana were among those with the most "sentiment" in their favor. Except within himself he found little enthusiasm for Bryan, and with an unusual and temporary flair for understatement, he noted:

> . . . As I looked over the situation I did not think the outlook for my candidacy was promising . . .

At that point, there was no evidence that Bryan was even in contention. The threat of disqualification placed even his favorite-son status in doubt. A first overture to gain support from other delegations was rewarded with kindly words from Joel Watson, the senior member of the two-man delegation from Oklahoma Territory. But even that pennywhistle chance was far from solid. Although the probing hopeful from Nebraska had written at least an initial draft of a convention speech, he could not find an opening as a platform speaker.

Following another day of apparently fruitless solicitations, Bryan switched tactics. He abruptly entrained for Crete, Nebraska, where he had a standing invitation to debate the merits of silver with a widely publicized advocate of the "gold standard," John Irish of Iowa. Presumably Bryan had canceled all other lecture appearances, but had held onto the appointment to debate the garrulous Mr. Irish. Any onlooker at the materializing Democratic convention could be certain that the case of gold versus silver, which was doing most to divide eastern and western Democrats, would be argued on the convention floor. Bryan, it appears, had decided to rehearse before a living audience what he hoped would become a floor debate at the convention.

Following the debate at Crete, where Bryan again used his Cross of Gold line, he hurriedly went to Omaha and boarded the special Pullman coach that would carry the Nebraska delegation to Chicago. Mamie waited at the station to join him. The takeoff was gay, even boisterous. The Cornhuskers were uniformed in broad-brimmed straw hats and red bandanas, and most were wearing blue denim overalls and puffing corncob pipes. Bryan wore his usual clothing without impediment of jacket. He continued to scribble on bits of paper, and to talk with his wife, who sat beside him, and to Charlie, whose head seemed permanently positioned beside his own. Thus togetherness may have been encouraged because of the ten-piece brass band that Jimmy Dahlman had employed for the delegation's entertainment.

Making a second entrance at Chicago, Bryan sought out Josephus Daniels, who headed the North Carolina delegation. Daniels could give no quick commitment. His delegation would vote by the unit rule—all or nothing—and Bryan would not be its first choice. Next he probed the Kansas delegation; it was committed to Bland of Missouri, but might consider Bryan in the event the Bland balloon failed to rise. The Oklahoma and Indian Territory votes were similarly set: Bryan on the second ballot, *maybe*.

Refusing to be discouraged, Bryan next maneuvered audaciously and somewhat bafflingly for the post as permanent chairman of the convention. Success here would have assured his chance to speak and appear openly, but convention chairmen rarely receive nominations. Such weighing of advantages and disadvantages was superfluous; Bryan got nowhere.

Yet the darkest of all the dark horses at hand would not be balked. "I have as good a chance as anyone," Bryan insisted with wonderful naïveté. Considering that the Nebraska delegation was not yet "officially accredited," his position remained that of a maverick. "The exclusion of my delegates was a good illustration of machine politics," he fumed. "The gold and corporation factions had control of the Old National Committee."

During the first morning of the convention, Dahlman called an emergency meeting of the Nebraska delegation, opened the fight before the accreditation committee, and listened approvingly while, again acting prematurely, the delegation voted Bryan its representative on "Resolutions and Platform." Though unaccredited, Bryan headed for the closed-door committee room. He was not challenged, but the platform drafting was practically completed. "Colonel" Charles H. Jones, editor of the St. Louis *Post-Dispatch* and principal writer of the upcoming Democratic platform, was a proponent of the progressive ideas of the party. Jones was also annoyed by the apparent attempt to disqualify the Nebraska liberals. Aware, too, that Bryan had exceptional experience as a platform drafter, the *Post-Dispatch* editor invited him to join in writing a tentative "money plank" favoring bimetallism. That accomplished, Bryan tried his hand at writing a "sympathy plank" directed toward the "oppressed peoples" of Cuba and Venezuela. As a very warm Tuesday ended, the Bryan prose, even if not the Bryan voice, was on its way to being noted. Next morning, after two hours of sweating and waiting outside the Coliseum, the Nebraska delegation tramped to its assigned place—duly, begrudgingly accredited.

Thursday marked the planning of the already scheduled floor debate on the obviously crucial issue of silver or gold coinage. More or less simultaneously, the two Joneses on the Platform (Resolutions) Committee showed their awareness of Bryan's presence. Senator W. C. Jones, the chairman, sent a note by a pageboy to ask if the leader of the Nebraska delegation would care to serve as "arranger" for the upcoming debate. Bryan scrawled his answer: *Yes, gladly.* "Colonel" Charlie Jones of the *Post-Dispatch* moved to expand the invitation by permitting Bryan to participate in the debate. After all, nobody could now reasonably doubt the Nebraskan's devotion to his party, or that Will Bryan was the only gifted speaker who at this point had not been given a chance to address the convention.

Senator Jones explained to Colonel Jones that the available speaking time was already more than taken. Two and a half hours—seventy-five minutes for the gold men and a like time for the silverites—was the absolute maximum. Old-line party dignitaries were clamoring for every minute of it. Two prominent ex-governors, David B. Hill of New York, who had also served briefly in the U. S. Senate, and William E. Russell of Massachusetts, and an irrepressible senator, William F. Vilas of Wisconsin, who had also been Postmaster General in Cleveland's first cabinet, were set to defend the party's gold standard forces. Senator ("Pitchfork Ben") Tillman of South Carolina was demanding at the very least an hour for defending silver on behalf of the party-loyal South. The Pulitzer editor urged Bryan to use his prerogative as "arranger" to supplement Tillman's anticipated storm of would-be persuasion. The young Nebraskan was willing.

Bryan moved deftly to claim a place for himself as "close-out man" for the silverites. "Pitchfork Ben" Tillman repeated with warming vigor that he required at least an hour to close the case for silver and was fully competent to do so. When Hill joined Bryan in pointing out that an hour was much too long for a closing speech, Tillman reluctantly agreed to permit Bryan to close with a brief summation. These and other arguments forced postponement of the big debate until the following day.

Bryan was in luck. He had the entire night to polish his speech—at least as well as he could shape a closing argument without any knowledge of what would go before. He spent most of his grace evening filling in his definition of a "businessman" and polishing his crown of thorns, cross of gold for a conclusion.

The next day was sultry and otherwise oppressive, but at least and at last the convention had an effective drawing card. The grim fortress of the Coliseum, with a rated capacity of fourteen thousand, was jampacked with about twenty thousand, with many more crowding nearby streets, sidewalks, and entranceways. Bryan saw and felt the multitude. It was an inseparable composite in which delegates were but a minor entry. Here in a great, heated blob were the American people. But he was no less distinctly aware that the prevailing mood was more of discontent than of passing curiosity or the quest for entertainment. The people were weary of poverty, with which the issue of silver or gold was symbolically if ambiguously related. As he took his place on the convention floor he was feeling distinctly ill. Later he recalled:

> . . . I felt as I always do just before a speech of unusual importance. I usually have a feeling of weakness at the pit of my stomach. . . . I wanted to lie down. But this being impossible in the convention, I got a sandwich and a cup of coffee and devoted myself to these as I waited for the debate to begin.

He prayed and munched simultaneously. When young Clark Howell, the son of one of the silver leaders, handed him a note scribbled on the back of an envelope, *This is a great opportunity*, Bryan penciled back, *You will not be disappointed.*

But throughout the ensuing two hours Howell and apparently almost all the uncomfortably crowded audience were disappointed. The debate dragged. "Pitchfork Ben" Tillman, after an appallingly bad opening in behalf of free silver, bellowed lengthily and angrily about northern abusers of the South. He damned Wall Street, Grover Cleveland, the "uppity Niggras" who would never learn their places. When the tirade reached its vituperative ending, Chairman Jones took the platform to announce that the "sectional arguments" of Senator Tillman were not approved by the committee and were not recommended to the convention at large.

Hill of New York followed with a hard-rocking attack on what he flayed as irresponsible silver promotion; both his text and vocal fervor suggested that he was directing himself to the disbanded Republican convention in St.

Louis. Hill was short and bald; he had a sharp, pointed nose, a huge, fierce voice, and his gestures pantomimed the swinging of an ax against a hard log.

Bryan watched the audience uneasily. Closest at hand, the Nebraskans—though still wearing their blue denim overalls and red bandanas—were losing their picnic mood. The sergeant-at-arms had directed them to leave their brass band outside. There was to be no exhibition between speeches, and the crowd showed no inclination to applaud.

Bryan had completely destroyed his ham sandwich and slipped his coffee cup beneath his seat. For the moment he seemed lost in thought. Senator Vilas, a ranking protectionist or high tariff advocate, opened verbosely and overran his time allotment. Bryan waited with closed eyes. "I couldn't say for sure," Charlie later noted, "whether Will was praying or squeezing his rabbit's foot." (Earlier that morning a Mississippi delegate had slipped the luck piece into his jacket pocket.)

Bryan was aroused by a whispered controversy. Russell of Massachusetts, third and final speaker for the gold bugs, was complaining that Vilas was ratting into his own time. Bryan slipped quickly across the aisle and stated his willingness to extend Russell's time provided the same period could be added to his own. Not too happily, one gathers, Hill and Russell agreed. As the youngest participant recounted:

> I cannot say that it was entirely unselfish on my side, and I think I would have made the suggestion if the extension of time had fallen to someone else, but it added about ten minutes to my time and I needed it for the speech I was to make. This was another unexpected bit of good fortune. . . .

The former governor of Massachusetts was afflicted, or as some believed, blessed with a soft voice. From the beginning of his speech he was unable to make himself heard throughout the restless and noisy hall. He mumbled along without pause or applause. Bryan listened intently. The frail young man from Massachusetts was advancing no new arguments; Bryan was convinced that what the crowd wanted and needed was a cause for applause and agreement. Preponderantly, the listeners were poor people being sprayed by rich men's platitudes.

At long last Bryan heard the chairman calling his name. He got to his feet with a suffusing certainty that God was surely and ably on his side. The Nebraska delegation was, conspicuously. The rising hero felt strong hands slapping his back and tugging at his rumpled clothing. He did not mind at all. His suit was already wrinkled and his black string tie was customarily out of kilter; even his breeches legs were sodden with sweat. Lawyer-reporter-poet Edgar Lee Masters saw him only as "slim, tall, raven haired, and beaked of nose."

Bryan walked rapidly like a confident prizefighter heading for the fray. His stride was long. At least momentarily his expression was that of one awakening from a dream too beautiful to last. Still smiling, he mounted the platform, turned about to face successively the entire floor of delegates, his arms held forth like a young boy reaching for a large, irresistible slice of watermelon. Then he began speaking. With bassless clarity his words began to carry to and across the great floor of delegates and on the farthest and highest galleries. He gambled all at first on his natural voice, enunciating with care, pausing audibly between syllables at times and pronouncing every word with rhythmic clarity.

As the result of the careful care accorded it, each word seemed to come alive. *"But this is not merely a con-test between persons,"* he confided almost shyly. With gentle insistence he began to emphasize each word: *"The humblest cit-i-zen in all the land . . . when clad in the ar-mor of a right-eous cause . . . is stronger than all the hosts of error."*

As a first rumble of applause materialized, Bryan waited in accommodating silence, aware that for hours his listeners had not been given any real reason for applauding. In this speech there was no occasion for laughter. Even so, the young Nebraskan ventured a brief, appreciative smile, then shifted to a deft evangelism by way of a Bible-based reference—the zeal that had inspired the crusaders to follow Peter the Hermit. Effectively if not subtly, he was using Biblical precedence for establishing the mood of a crusade in behalf of his God and his oppressed people.

He went into shorter sentences, improvising brief and abstract refutations. Then, relying on his sort of strange verbal poetry, he began to identify himself with his audience. His listeners were tending to respond "like a trained choir." Even the sultry shadows seemed to wait on bended knees. His audience, certainly a major part of it, was beginning to stand spontaneously to cheer. Bryan recounted later:

> . . . The audience seemed to rise and sit down as one man. At the close of a sentence it would rise and shout and when I began upon another sentence the room was still as a church. . . .

His sentences seemed to weld together the speaker, the listeners, and underprivileged humanity at large. He began to employ the first-person plural to mark the changeover from the heavy semantics of metallic currencies to the common cause of the poor. *"We do not come as aggressors. . . ."* His cadence of lament changed to one of protest. *"We have pe-titioned and our pe-titions have been scorned. We have en-treated and our en-treaties have been dis-regarded. We have begged and they have mocked us when our hour of ca-lamity came."*

There was no need for spelling out the idea that the "they" were swiggers from the pots of privilege, the Wall Streeters, the imposers of a gold standard that could only make the rich richer and the poor more pathetic. Emphatically, the "we" meant the sons and daughters of unrelenting poverty, incessant toil, sweat, and fading dreams. For a long moment Bryan viewed his audience respectfully, then resumed:

"We beg no longer. We en-treat no more. . . . We petition no more. . . ."

When the shouting and foot-stamping abated, Bryan added firmly, *"We de-fy them!"* With the massive hall aquaver, cheering, Bryan paused again. Then he began striding toward the outer rim of the platform, naming the supporting forces: *". . . The pro-duc-ing masses of the nation; the com-mer-cial in-ter-ests; the la-bor-ing in-ter-ests; and toil-ers eve-ry-where."* Breathing deeply, shortening his pauses, he closed in for the climax, in a strange, diamond-edged finality: *"We shall answer their demands by saying to them,* 'YOU SHALL NOT PRESS DOWN ON THE BROW OF LABOR THE CROWN OF THORNS, YOU SHALL NOT CRU-CI-FY MANKIND ON A CROSS OF GOLD.'"

For many seconds a stunned, hollow silence prevailed. Bryan walked down the platform stairs, and made for the almost empty main aisle. Then he heard a tremendous shout. "The next thing I knew," he recalled, "I was pulled up and bedlam broke loose."

The Nebraska delegation rose as one man and lunged toward him. He became aware of throngs of other delegates crowding into the side isle, of being hoisted to a wavery seat on shoulders and heads. The madly surging processional went on and on. He saw the platform being vacated. Below him and on all sides a new American epoch was splashing and mewling into birth. Again and again the black-maned poet of the spoken word strived to regain his footing, but the maelstrom of enthusiasts would not abate. Inside and outside the auditorium the uproar of voices kept on gaining, old and young, shrill and deep, fanatic shouters, infidels and praisers of God, and despisers of the rich.

Bryan became aware of the "Battle Hymn of the Republic," blared out by the Nebraska brass band, somewhere in the hall. When at last he was lowered to the floor, delegation heads charged forward to pledge their support, and he saw jogglings of improvised placards bearing the messages, *Bryan for the People, No Crown of Thorns, No Cross of Gold.* Arthur Sewall, a national committeeman from Maine, and already being mentioned as the vice presidential nominee, sought the hero's attention. The banker and shipbuilder was weeping openly. "These people certainly do love you," he said. As he wiped away his tears, he explained that if Bryan so desired he would ask the chairman to "recall" the convention so that he, Sewall, could personally place the name of Bryan in nomination.

Bryan asked for a raincheck, switching easily into Aristotelian rhetoric: "If the desire to nominate me will not last until tomorrow, would it last through the campaign?" As soon as he was able he joined his brother and another champion, "Jedge" Thompson of Grand Isle, Nebraska, and they headed back to the hotel.

The next day Bryan chose to stay away from the convention hall. But he sent Mamie to act as his informant. He had slept well and breakfasted on an oversize bowl of milk toast, undismayed by peering passers-by. Then he proceeded to the hotel barber shop. "I wasn't excited, but the barber was; he could hardly hold the razor."

As the day was to prove, the barber's excitement was widely shared. The telegraph wires were melting with news loads. Jimmy Dahlman vowed that in all his born days he had never had such a workout. The red-bandanaed Nebraska delegates, at least the other sixteen of them, were scurrying about serving the convention crowds with newly

stamped Bryan buttons, snatching placards from the sten-
ciling brush before the ink could dry. The Nebraska band
boomed away, especially strong in its "Onward Christian
Soldiers."

Clearly, the rival candidates were in trouble. Despite his
Catholic wife, Bland of Missouri was the next most likely
contender. The first ballot was mere sparring, the second
showed Bryan gaining strongly, the third found Bryan and
Bland neck and neck, with seven delegations holding out.
The fourth saw Bryan well ahead. On the fifth he was
named the convention's unanimous choice. Mamie had
phoned after the fourth ballot to tell Bryan that he was
"as good as in."

During the afternoon a committee arrived to perform
the traditional pageantry of "notifying" the nominee. Bryan
cordially agreed to appear at the convention the following
day. Next he found himself whisked off on a brief and
wildly cheered carriage ride down Michigan Avenue. As
usual, not all onlookers were in the same mood; police
detected three teen-age boys at an open third-story window
hurling eggs at the nominee's carriage. The demonstrating
youths were promptly arrested and hustled to jail. When
word percolated through to him, Bryan refused to press
charges, and as a favor asked that the boys be released immediately. Moments later he was told that the youngsters
had asked to be permitted to make in-person apologies.
While uncounted thousands waited to behold the Cross-of-
Gold candidate, Bryan chatted amiably with three egg-
throwers.

The victorious blur continued. Bryan and Mamie accepted an invitation to spend Sunday as guests of the
Trumbull family. On Monday they rushed off to Salem,
recovered their children, and took them home to Lincoln.

Bryan left Chicago with only one principal regret; the
Democratic convention had largely bypassed the possibilities of fusion with the Populists, who could very well
muster as many as a million votes. This round-number es-

timate was of special consequence. In his habitually rough-and-ready arithmetic, the nominee foresaw the need for winning at least a million "new" Democratic votes; he estimated the "as-is" popular vote ratio as seven million Republican to six million Democratic. The importance of Populist support was evident. And before the month ended Bryan found himself named the Populist candidate for President. He declined to accept the latter nomination "officially," i.e., being formally listed as a Populist. But he welcomed the support.

Having accorded exceptionally thorough coverage to the nomination, the press viewed the nominee with a dizzying range of yeas and nays. Among the first publicity seekers to deliver a smear was Elihu Root, who labeled the Democratic nominee a Populist, anarchist, blasphemer, and an anti-Christ. From Louisville, publisher, editor, and Democratic national committeeman Henry Watterson of the *Courier-Journal,* whose friendship Bryan had sought so diligently, lashed out with inexplicable fury:

. . . Mr. William J. Bryan has come to Kentucky and Kentuckians have his measure. He is a boy orator. He is a dishonest dodger. He is a daring adventurer. He is a political faker. . . . He is not wanted in Kentucky. . . .

(Bryan was to miss carrying Kentucky by fewer than three hundred votes.)

By July 25, the Chicago *Chronicle* was branding the Democrat standard-bearer as a "paid agent and spokesman for the silver combine."

. . . He has not since his retirement from Congress had any visible means of support. The richest men in the world, the proprietors of the Big Bonanzas, hire "orators" like Bryan exactly as other men hire fiddlers and value them as highly. . . .

The New York *World* took exception by noting that the silver lobby was notoriously slow on the pocketbook draw, adding that Bryan, like many millions of fellow Americans, sincerely believed in the issuance of more silver money, and that when accurately appraised he was about as wealthy as a starving red rooster summering on sawdust. Philosopher Tom Johnson, at the time a Democratic national committeeman from Ohio, listed Bryan's nomination as the protest of the American people against monopoly, the first great struggle of the masses of our country against the privileged classes.

Bryan himself, still clad in black alpaca suit, boiled white shirt with low collar, and black string tie, which would be his working uniform for a spirited presidential campaign, revealed some personal thoughts in simple words: "There is nobody on our side but the people. . . . We could win with only the West and South, but we can lose no state south of the Mason-Dixon Line or west of Missouri. . . . Our guidance is optimism based on factors confessedly outside of human control. . . ." To all this his nearly-eleven-year-old daughter, Ruth Baird Bryan, made a prophetic addition: "I don't know about the country, but here on D Street in Lincoln, it looks as if my papa will get quite a few votes."

Mamie made an immediate observation as well. When she and her family returned to 1425 D Street they found their house garnished with flags and bunting and crepe paper. "Interested persons" had taken over with conspicuous energy and without invitation. Intuitively Mamie saw in this the imminent demise of privacy for all the family.

In his adopted town of Canton, Ohio, Major William McKinley, Jr., who had won the Republican nomination on the first, Hanna-engineered ballot, was trying out a front-porch, stay-at-home campaign for the Presidency. Before its formal opening he had announced that he would leave Ohio only to move into the White House. On that basis, between July 1 and November 1, the Republican candidate made about three hundred speeches in his hometown, and it was said that somewhere near a million people listened to the Republican candidate in Canton. There was common agreement that the local hotels had never before been favored with such an effective stimulus to trade.

Bryan's reputed bonanza, meanwhile, was related to the possible drawing in of votes from across party lines. As already noted, without effort or even the expression of willingness on his own part, the Democratic standard-bearer found the Populist nomination thrust upon him. He repeated that while he did not wish to read his name on any ballot as a Populist candidate for the Presidency or anything else, as the Democratic nominee he would, of course, welcome converts from any or all other parties. But he would not plead the case or cause of Populism; he was and he would remain William Jennings Bryan, Democrat. Further, he did not repress his belief that the Populist Party was going nowhere rather rapidly.

Early on Saturday, August 8, Bryan officially opened his presidential campaign. His initial rostrum was the rear car or "platform coach" of the Rock Island day train to Chicago. Several hundred people crowded into the depot to watch the candidate and his wife take off. Mamie wore a plain black suit and a broad-brimmed black felt hat to "harmonize" with her husband's traditional apparel. After they had posed for trainside pictures, Bryan smiled engagingly at the applauding audience and spoke in boyish solemnity:

> All I can promise you is that, whether what I do meets with your approval or not, I shall do my duty as I see it and accept all consequences which may follow. . . .

As became the opening of a poor man's campaign for the poor man's vote, Bryan and his wife had chosen to begin their journey as plain, everyday coach passengers. More luxurious accommodations would be provided at the discretion of the National Committee. Meanwhile, the candidate began making typical entries in his journal:

Lincoln to Chicago over Rock Island railway
555 miles

Chicago to New York over Pennsylvania railway
913 miles

New York to Buffalo over New York Central
440 miles

Buffalo to Erie & return over Lake Shore
and Michigan Southern railways
176 miles

Buffalo to Niagara Falls over electric line
22 miles

Kent to Toledo over Toledo and Ohio Central
72 miles

Short trips in neighborhood of Upper Red Hook, N.Y.
100 miles

Beginning that first morning, and at each train stop, however brief, Bryan hurried to the rear platform and addressed the waiting crowd. He continued speaking until the train was on its way again. He recorded with evident pleasure that as the day progressed the crowds increased in size and the train crew frequently trotted back to join the listeners until it was time to go. At Canton, Ohio, Bryan made a short public appearance in deference to his opponent. After reading from his hard-used Bible the parable of the good neighbor, the couple went on to New York. At Madison Square Garden the "notification" ceremony was large, loud, and without mishap. The desultory New York press coverage reiterated that the candidate's heart was in the country.

This platitude was again confirmed when a group of reporters joined in hiring a surrey and team for escorting the Bryans to Sleepy Hollow and Newburgh for their church services. Came Monday, the candidate and party proceeded to Upper Red Hook, where the Bryans were house guests of Mrs. E. C. Perrine, one of Mamie's former and favorite teachers during her academy years in Jacksonville. Will was particularly delighted by Red Hook, which then included a post office, a hotel, two stores, three churches, and a girding of shaded country roads. It was late summer. Roasting ears were waiting the boiling pots —Bryan's own kind of corn, big, firm, field corn ears, shucked directly from thriving stalks. The happy campaigner jotted:

> . . . When my fondness for green corn became known, the farmers generously supplied our table, and justice compels me to add that the quality was fully equal to the Nebraska article.

The climax was a village rally with Bryan as guest speaker and a red-uniformed hometown band. The concert featured Bryan's favorite number, "El Capitan," by John Philip Sousa.

At Utica, the plaza crowd was so large and widely spread that for the first time Bryan had difficulty in making himself heard. While he was working at it, the hastily built speaker's platform collapsed, spilling the Voice of Silver and some twenty other prominent citizens into the cheering throng. Three similar platform collapses would follow. Perhaps the symbolism was economic; the Democrats were restricted by an almost unbelievably small budget. The total amount for waging the national campaign was less than fifty thousand dollars, and some 40 percent of it would be left unspent. In most instances local committees were responsible for building the outdoor platforms, not a few of which turned out to be perilously flimsy.

Local newspaper reports suggested that the same held for many of the Bryan speeches. Most were winsomely improvised sermons fringed with generally engaging conversational essays. The entertainment value was impressive; so was the grounding of faith in a firm and righteous God. But the political specifics were frequently, almost habitually, as ephemeral as windblown cobwebs.

Not without cause, Bryan continued to see himself as a typical American in communion with the American majority. As a fundamental believer, he felt surely that he was among tens of millions of such believers. And among other virtues, spontaneity redounds from such belief. It followed in the course of a brief station-stop talk in upstate New York that Bryan pinpointed one whom he considered a "typical American citizen." A sturdy farmer hitched his plow team to a fence post nearest the halted train, strolled into the observation car, and without introduction shook Bryan's hand and explained, "I have always been a Republican, but I am for silver. We farmers know what is good for us." With that the typical American made a quick exit and went on with his plowing.

As August ended, Bryan returned home with his wife for a rest preparatory to the Long Trip. There he reviewed approvingly the white satined and gold braided company of the Bryan Home Town Guards. (Brother Charlie had been the moving spirit.) Smiling, Bryan assured the volunteers that what he felt was like the farmer who said of his favorite horse: "If somebody starts the wagon first, he pulls real good."

His subsequent three-speech stand at St. Louis showed the presence of willing pullers. Charles H. Jones of the *Post-Dispatch* served as master of ceremonies. At the opening rally at Concordia Park the Horseshoers Association of America presented the candidate with a silver horseshoe. At Convention Hall Bryan was accorded almost deafening applause. In his final appearance at Sportsman's Park, the makeshift platform collapsed, continuing the tradition, and again "prevented any extensive speech." With his almost unbelievable poise, Bryan extemporized from the wreckage.

Heading east again in the company of the diffident vice-presidential candidate, Arthur Sewall, the standard-bearer began speaking more pointedly. At Morristown, New Jersey, where the railroad station crowd gave an appearance of exceptional affluence, Bryan opened without smiling:

> Ladies and Gentlemen: In a city like this, where there are so many evidences of plenty of money, I do not know whether you understand or feel the need of more money. But I want you to remember that all the wealth of the country is first derived from those who toil, and you cannot destroy the prosperity of those who produce the wealth without undermining the foundation upon which all society rests. . . .

The first team pressed on into New England. On an open square near the Yale campus, Bryan faced a dour audience of factory workers. Before he could begin his speech a group of Yale boys swarmed across the green, cheering for McKinley and booing Bryan. It was the first crowd abuse he had encountered and, without success, Bryan tried to speak against the uproar, slashing away at the "gold crowd." The Yale boys booed all the louder. The episode grew into headline news. Professor Henry P. Wright, acting president of Yale, explained, "Boys will be boys, you know, and it was really nothing more than a boyish outbreak. . . ."

Bryan amiably agreed, but many did not, including the

first citizens of Muskogee, Indian Territory. On September 30, the Associated Press noted:

At a mass meeting of the Cherokees, Creeks, Choctaws, and Seminoles, held here yesterday, the following resolution was unanimously adopted:
"Resolved, that we contemplate with deep regret the recent insulting treatment of William J. Bryan by students of a college in the land of the boasted white man's civilization, and we admonish all Indians who think of sending their sons to Yale that association with such students could but prove hurtful alike to their morals and their progress toward the higher standards of civilization. . . ."

In Boston, Bryan met with one of the most gracious receptions of his entire campaign. The noontime rally at the American House was among the largest and loudest in Boston's history. By seven-thirty Boston Garden was the center for a crowd estimated as one hundred thousand, and, as Bryan observantly suggested, 99,999 derby hats. His evening appearance at the Music Hall was another lusty success. For a brief and quickly forgotten interlude, the Commoner had only the warmest praise for New England.

By October 3 the Democratic Clubs of the United States were in flamboyant convention at St. Louis. There Bryan received a hero's welcome. He developed finger bleeding from the hard-pumping handshakes. He moved into the Great Lakes states (which Bryan called the Northwest). There, in Minneapolis, Duluth, Milwaukee, Detroit, Lansing, and other principal towns, the winsome invader drew record crowds. At Springfield, Illinois, he led a tremendous parade in the company of his friend and counselor, Governor John Peter Altgeld. Among the tens of thousands of onlookers was a slender, fidgety high school student named Vachel Lindsay, who in time would write the greatest of the Bryan adulations in verse. Mamie's appraisal, though offered from the confines of their home, was more querulous. Were those tremendous crowds supporting Bryan or merely in quest of free entertainment?

Following still another uproarious welcome in Chicago, the presidential candidate moved toward home base. His journal logged twenty-eight thousand miles. On November 1, Bryan arrived at his home on D Street tired, hoarse, and permeated with almost masochistic satisfaction of an activist who has survived the feat of driving himself to the utmost limits of endurance. Bryan stated by way of rather complacent summation that he had fought a good fight, kept the faith, and he waited God's decision.

The more level-headed news coverage of the campaign, by contrast to the frequently intemperate partisan editorials, while not overtly confirming the capitulation to Bryan, did not contradict it. Except in the Deep South, American city or larger town newspapers of 1896 were preponderantly Republican-owned and -orientated, at least editorially. For the most part, the urban press was strongly anti-Bryan in editorials. But the news coverage showed impressive improvements. In terms of reporting techniques the oncoming golden era of the city daily was at least foreseeable.

Accordingly, one going through the back files of 1896 newspapers is likely to find himself discovering that the nation's twenty most heeded city dailies tended to agree in several reportorial—not necessarily editorial—details about the unusual and prolonged presidential campaign. These were that the two major nominees had performed competently, at least by the measure of their respective métiers. There was little doubt that Bryan had outplayed McKinley both as a crowd pleaser and as a one-man crusader. Neither of the vice-presidential candidates had proved worth a whoop. Both McKinley and Bryan had played almost exclusively to domestic issues without registering heavy body blows or specifying specific remedies.

The McKinley stay-at-home performances were considerably more repetitious and less adroit than Bryan's road shows, which were far better as entertaining whimsy and in folkish appeal. On-the-scene reporters stressed that McKinley's sometimes suave eloquence was less impressive than his earlier and more mellifluous proselytizing for veteran and business votes.

Some of the more astute papers, particularly the St. Louis *Post-Dispatch* and the New York *World,* winnowed the pertinent truth that both Bryan and McKinley were functioning not so much as compelling leaders as symbols for the two mass echelons of voters. McKinley was receiving and welcoming acceptance as hallmark for the haves and those supporting the establishment as such. Bryan was being hoisted on the shoulders of the have-nots and the protesters or challengers of outrageous forces that would destroy them. "There is no actual leader," the St. Louis *Post-Dispatch* editor wrote gloomily in the issue of September 19. "Rather there are two contrasting and publicly halyarded symbols."

Colonel Jones of the *Post-Dispatch* and editorial writer Abel Gorman of the New York *World* chorused the common contention that neither candidate was leading or being towed by the still somewhat nebulous labor vote, which, as both reflected, was like God in that it surely existed but for the most part was not visible. They did not dispute the common understanding that the G.O.P. candidate was again drawing labor votes via employers who got the word to their hired help to vote Republican or else.

Many reporters and miscellaneous appraisers doubted that Bryan was adequately leading, or if one preferred to say, being held by, the Populists and their Alliance cohorts. During the election of 1892 all these protesters had polled about a million votes for the Populist nominee, "General Jim" Weaver. The Peoples' Party vote for 1896 was being expertly guessed at 1.5 million. But the Populists were still preponderantly harassed farmers; their labor following was not as predictable, and many commentators doubted that it would prove to be consequential.

Not surprisingly, the Chicago papers took the lead in pointing out that the presidential race would be decided, not by New York nor any close-by "beehive of American population," but by the Midwest, particularly Ohio, Indiana, and Illinois. In those states, many villages were growing into comparatively big towns while thousands of small shops were mushrooming into sizable factories with rapidly growing rosters of employees. No doubt a portion of these would vote as their employers or foremen told them, but the industrial labor of the Midwest was not decisively unionized or predisposed toward a "protest" party.

McKinley, perhaps by way of his advisers, in the main better experienced than Bryan's, had recognized this fact, which had much to do with the G.O.P. decision to risk a stay-at-home or front-porch campaign. Bryan, as the minority party candidate from the Great Plains, had recognized that he could not possibly win by staying home or by limiting his principal efforts to the Plains; he knew that he would have to carry all the South and Border South and most of the West, practically all of it beyond the Mississippi.

Bryan kept on speaking for Bryan. Even though he was accompanied by guest speakers, ready to take over when and if the candidate "felt faint," the alternates found out that the nominee was not disposed to yield platforms; also that he was usually about as faint as a young bull.

What the Voice lacked most conspicuously was astute advisers and adequate funds for putting together a coordinated national campaign. Democratic campaign financing was ludicrous; the pecuniary-minded New York *Sun* had suggested that the Democrats were spending substantially less than one cent per hoped-for vote, whereas the Republicans were spending well over a dollar for every hoped-for vote, including those that were virtually assured.

Subsequent reports of the respective national committees supported the *Sun's* estimate.

Neither campaign could be objectively rated as coordinated or well-managed. But reversing the old adage that there is no really bad whiskey, only that some whiskey tastes a shade better than others, it could be and was being argued that while neither campaign was expert, Bryan's was far and away the worse run. Perhaps that was best proved by the fact that the Democratic decision-makers, to use the term somewhat fancifully, were squandering too much of the candidate's time and efforts at the futile invasion of incorrigible Republican strongholds, particularly in New York, the upper Atlantic, and New England, and too little at fighting for the Great Lakes states, the Midwest, the Border South, and California, where Bryan had at least an outside chance.

The feeble but vociferous Democratic press castigated "Republican crookedness," which reportedly included devilish G.O.P. conspiracies to move thousands of stooge voters, principally Negroes or po' white trash, across boundaries into adjoining states where the outcome was nip-and-tuck, and the dastardly stacking of ballot boxes. Or the nefarious device of misadvising the innocent; such, for example, as sending town-comers who inquired, "Whar's the votin' place, neighbor?" to the Yokel Street Saloon or the whorehouse with the player piano.

Many of these made juicy stories, but the rumor crop as a whole would have been more convincing had not the locales of these damnable skullduggeries not been in Missouri, Tennessee, Virginia, Kansas, Texas, or other states that went for Bryan. Certainly there was no sense in describing the election as "clean"; but there was evidence that by the standards of the times the campaign of 1896 was no more than customarily crooked. As usual the dirty doings appeared to have been mostly by way of individual counties or the town or city wards, but to label them as the outrage of one party was not very credible; after all, there were Democratic Tammany and the dubious Democratic mobs of Chicago, Philadelphia, and even, heaven forbid, Providence.

Although the popular vote was somewhat more than usually close, Bryan lost the election. The final count showed him with a popular vote of 6,511,073, more than any Democratic nominee had ever carried before, to McKinley's 7,107,822. The electoral votes would go 271 for McKinley and 176 for Bryan, but the score by states was so narrow that an additional 15,000 votes strategically distributed might have given Bryan the Presidency.

As Bryan had expected and "felt," his surpassing strength was in the West and South. He had carried Alabama, Arkansas, Colorado, Florida, Georgia, Idaho, Kansas, Louisiana, Minnesota, Mississippi, Missouri, Montana, Nebraska, Nevada, North Carolina, South Carolina, South Dakota, Tennessee, Texas, Utah, Virginia, Washington, and Wyoming. He had wrested the entire Populist electoral vote, one from California and another from West Virginia; and his Populist support was apparently of some consequence in the Great Plains and the Rocky Mountain silver states.

He lost grievously in the East. In New York, New Jersey, Delaware, Connecticut, Massachusetts, Rhode Island, and Pennsylvania Bryan fell below the Cleveland tallies of four years before.

But Bryan could look to the future, and he did. He foresaw no shortage of causes, he was convinced that he could and would again gain the nomination of his party, and that he would win on the next try. He was no less certain that he could and would change his nationwide political defeat into his greatest personal victory. William Jennings Bryan would rise again.

14. Remember the Maine!

During an early evening in February 1898, the U.S.S. *Maine,* a light battleship at anchor in Havana Harbor, was blown asunder by unidentified saboteurs. The death list included 260 of the ship's crew. The causes of the tragedy were never surely determined; an official U.S. inquiry blamed "external explosion"; official Spanish inquiry blamed "internal explosion." Neither could deny that the tragedy of the *Maine* was tinder for a war between the buoyantly rising United States and gently rusting Spain.

Bryan's typical American position regarding the multiple tragedy of Cuba could be described as deeply felt and shallowly informed. He recalled from school days the Ostend Manifesto of 1854 in which James Buchanan urged that the United States either buy or seize the Pearl of the Antilles in order to "abolish oppression." The so-called Cespedes-Quesada revolt had begun in 1868 and bled along for ten years. Beginning in that same year the efforts of the Grant administration to buy Cuba like a bunch of bananas and hang it on the lower United States also had failed.

While Bryan was orating through his final year in Congress, the so-called Patriots' Insurrection, led by the Cuban "Generals" Calixto Garcia, Maximo Gomez, and Antonio Macea, flared into lethal reality and was aggressively countered by Spain, which poured a reported 150,000 occupation troops into the beautiful and tragic island. Yet during 1896, while Bryan was evangelizing for the Presidency, the Cubans continued to hold about half of the beleaguered island. Throughout 1897, for Bryan a year of lecture circuits, proselytizing for free silver (both with and without fees), and dabbling occasionally as honorary editor of the silver bloc's bumbling newspaper, the Omaha *World-Herald,* what he termed the "Free Cuba sentiment" was gaining. As usual, the sentiment was genuine in the U. S. West, where the championship of "freedom" seemed to grow out of the struggle to stand against domestic forces of economic enslavement, or, as some vowed, from the air and drinking water of the plains.

For the most part Bryan's occasional references to Cuba's hurt and distress had been garbed in convenient vagueness. As noted, even before receiving the nomination Bryan had joined in the belated write-in of a "Free Cuba plank" for the Democratic platform. There is no reason to believe, however, that he had studied the Cuban tragedy, either before or after his ringing campaign.

Ironically, an understanding was not easy to acquire from American sources. The U.S. press was simply not reporting the story comprehensively. By contrast, the newspapers and news services of London, Paris, Berlin, and other European centers were appraising the island's tragedy competently and, in substantial part, at first hand. Among the youngest and most facile of the British correspondents briefly in Cuba was a cub named Winston Churchill. He saw the Cuban tragedy as "mass crucifixion," stupidly accelerated poverty, and rampant, people-ruining

diseases—interrelated evils, and both substantially avoidable. Winston Churchill, possibly helped by more experienced reporters for the Reuters News Agency, estimated
that by 1897 Cuba had lost at least a half-million citizens,
at that time about a fourth of its total census, to mal-
nutrition or starvation and diseases including epidemic
yellow fever, virulent dysenteries, and long-endemic ma-
larias. Many Cuban towns stank with the unburied dead.
The island's economy seemed almost irreparably upset.
Civil strife was deepening. Cubans were fighting Spaniards
and vice versa, but, more ruinously, Cubans were fighting
Cubans.

Without weighting his readers or listeners with too many
detailed suggestions for remedies, Bryan continued to plead
for a "free Cuba." His general statements were plagued
with contradictions. As a fundamentalist he was opposed
to war. As a perennial champion of the oppressed poor
he advocated "saving" Cuba, preferably by means short
of war, otherwise as a last resort by "military might." He
evaded the facts that at the time the United States had no
military might and no remotely convincing plan for "saving" or even helping Cuba by peaceful measures.

While pondering what Bryan might have done had he
won the Presidency, any contemporary was entitled to wonder what William McKinley was going to do as the newly
installed President. Like Bryan, McKinley was not one to
advocate war against Spain or any other country; as a
one-time battleline soldier he detested war and had repeatedly indicated as much even as a vote-seeking cooer
and at times crower for the Grand Army of the Republic,
as well as the Grand Old Party. Also, like Bryan and
most other Americans, the new President seemed to hold
with the engaging but airy credo that freedom is a condition
that any nation can acquire, somewhat like an alert, long-
armed boarder stabbing a piece of fried chicken.

Certainly no clairvoyance was required to perceive that
a free Cuba would inevitably need such facilities as mer-

chant shipping, roads and railroads, the revival and improvement of its long obsolescent sugar industry, and even more immediately, facilities such as hospitals, clinics, waterworks, sanitation, and epidemic controls. But in view of the prevailing condition of the beautiful island, clairvoyance was indispensable to visualize ways and means for the United States to deliver these facilities without first seizing Cuba.

The new President continued to advocate assistance to Cuba by means short of war. As a first move—one may gather with heed of the more cogent Republicans, including Henry Cabot Lodge, who insisted that permitting the "flaying" of Cuba to continue could cause the party to lose the next election—McKinley turned to what he wishfully termed "diplomatic persuasion." On that basis he had demanded that Spain grant "autonomy" to its long-suffering Caribbean colony. Madrid responded with a cautious expression of willingness to grant "liberation of status" that apparently meant changing the Spanish occupation force to what was discreetly designated as a garrison police force. This gave promise of at least cooling the prevailing civil warfare between the so-called pro-Spain and anti-Spain factors.

Late in 1897, for reasons that were not lucidly explained, Fitzhugh Lee, a field-grade Army officer who was U.S. consul general to Spain, recommended a show of American strength at Havana. In keeping with the chronic sea power shortage, McKinley responded by ordering only the U.S.S. *Maine* to appear at Havana for a "friendly visit" early in January 1898. The death-dealing and mystifying sabotage of the *Maine* was the tragic aftermath.

Developments in March added to the brew. On March 9 Congress voted fifty million dollars for "defense" but barred the disbursement of monies until the nation was officially at war. Eighteen days later, after "inquiries" regarding the *Maine*'s fate were bogged in a deep fog of contradictions, McKinley demanded that Spain grant an armistice to accommodate negotiations with her Caribbean colony by way of the United States. As the month ended, the imperial Spanish government offered to accept "neutral arbitration" regarding the *Maine* and to refrain from what it termed "reconcentration" of Spanish occupation forces on the island.

On April 9 Spain also granted armistice to the so-called Cuban revolutionaries. At that point there was a glimmer of hope for avoiding war. Then, like a tipsy fat man losing his equilibrium on the bar stool, the diplomacy toppled. On April 11 the President asked Congress for authority to "intervene directly" in Cuba. For more than a week Congress mewled and muttered. On April 16, ex-Congressman Bryan in a lecture at Des Moines stated flatly that war with Spain, however deplorable, was virtually inevitable. On April 20 both houses of Congress opened debate on a joint resolution recognizing the independence of Cuba, demanding that Spain withdraw all military forces from the island, and empowering the President to enforce the terms of the resolution and demand. On April 25 the resolution, which by then included the statement that war existed between the United States and Spain (beginning as of April 21), was adopted. Spain, meanwhile (on April 24), had officially declared war against the United States.

During one of the most legislatively muddled weeks in American history, Bryan continued to, as he put it, "think aloud." Again, his "thought" was that as a fundamental believer the war seemed to him unconscionable but perhaps somewhat less than ungodly. He added that while war is an *ipso facto* violation of God's commandment, "Thou shalt not kill," a holy war, faithfully directed to the attainment of a just, God-fearing peace, could at least contain the overt violation of the Commandments to one instance rather than two, three, four, or more. He further indicated that, even though he was a fundamentalist, he would be personally willing to participate in the war effort.

As a measure of the illimitable cranial blackout then prevalent in Washington, the foregoing could qualify as logic. The word in the capital rumor mill was that the first step of the United States would be to put a naval blockade around Cuba, then let the U. S. Navy blast the daylights out of the Spanish fleet in the Caribbean and/ or wherever else it was hiding so that the invincible U.S. bluejackets, Marines, and Army could sweep over the island and give the little brown bastards a real American-size dose of Freedom. Bryan's failure to voice a challenge or strong audible disagreement may have been related to the above "logic" or to the fact that as a congressman he had shown no convincing interest in the armed services. He had accepted as routine the diminishing public interest in the U. S. Army, which by 1898 survived as an encampment force of barely twenty-six thousand enlisted men and officers (Spain's combat troops in Cuba still numbered at least twenty-eight thousand). As of April 1898, the Army's equipment was markedly below the appallingly low standard of Civil War times, certainly of the latter 1850s. Cavalry units were declining to muster for parade because too many horses were unable to walk safely, and time-honored artillery units were vowing that they had not received a bag of fresh powder in ten years or longer.

The U. S. Navy was less pitiably run down, but the rating media, including Jane's *Fighting Ships,* appraised the Spanish Navy as definitely superior to that of the United States. Among those who were most aware of this was a shrill-voiced, volatile young man, Theodore Roosevelt, Assistant Secretary of the Navy. Directly after the mysterious destruction of the *Maine,* the Secretary, John D. Long, took leave of his Washington desk to "shape procedures," whatever that meant. As Acting Secretary, Theodore Roosevelt dispatched orders to the Asiatic Squadron to mobilize its forces at Hong Kong. The squadron commander, George Dewey, from nonmaritime Montpelier, Vermont, reported back that the Asiatic Squadron suffered from one slight deficiency: It hadn't any ammunition. If war came, his force had only a few Navy Colt pistols plus bare fists to fight with. With a Spanish Philippines Squadron breathing down his neck, the Vermont seaman pleaded softly for ammunition.

Late in February the U.S. cruiser *Baltimore* set out to supply the missing ingredient, but she did not arrive at Hong Kong until April 22, when war was already breaking. On the Sunday before "War Monday" (April 25), Dewey, aboard his flagship *Olympia,* led out his squadron, and on official orders of the Acting Secretary of the Navy, headed for undisclosed points within Spain's Philippines colony. Five days later the U.S.S. *Baltimore, Boston,* and *Concord* nosed into Subic Bay, followed in line by the *Olympia, Raleigh, Petrel,* and *McCulloch,* to "probe" for the enemy's fleet. Finding no warcraft, the striking force returned by moonlight to Manila Bay, thirty miles southeastward, passing Spanish artillery placements on Corregidor without challenge. Shortly after the dawn of May Day, the eight-inch rifle on the *Olympia*'s starboard turret roared out an opening challenge to the defending Spanish squadron. Throughout the ensuing three-hour battle, the American force seemed to escape return fire as if by magic. Spain's flagship *Christina* was first to burn, then the *Duero,* then the *Ulloa.* Dewey interrupted briefly to direct with cool Vermont geniality, "Withdraw from action. Let the people go to breakfast."

After the morning meal the Asiatic Squadron steamed in for the knockout. The *Baltimore* led the way, opening a gun duel that silenced the recalcitrant shore batteries. Spain's splendid *Ulloa,* by then without a functioning gun, lowered her flag and let her crew abandon ship to swim for shore. Only the little U.S.S. *Petrel* had a shallow enough draft to steam in upon the shore arsenal, but she was sufficient for the task. Dewey directed the *Petrel* to accept the surrender, then ordered that concerts be given aboard all ships carrying bands. It was a good New England village-style finish to what many regard as the most telling naval victory in American history. The U.S. public rejoiced mightily, and quite erroneously, taking for granted that the Philippines were won.

Back in Washington, meanwhile, the President had issued a call for 125,000 army volunteers. Even though the Klondike Gold Rush was calling and the prospect of wearing a shabby blue uniform and subsisting on Army beans, slime, and gravy and $8.16 a month was less than wholly enticing, volunteers were coming forth.

On the day following the war resolution by Congress, and five days before the beginning of the Battle of Manila Bay, William Jennings Bryan dispatched a telegram from the law office of Talbot & Bryan to the President of the United States, offering his services to his country—"in any capacity desired." The telegram was never answered.

After waiting four days, Bryan announced by way of the Omaha newspaper, which he was in the process of giving back to practically any taker, that he would volunteer as a private soldier. He said that he was neither warrior nor pacifist, and that he had never urged the United States to declare war on Spain or any other nation. Somewhat theoretically, he added that even as men make wars, so do wars make men. Bryan did not point out that while more than a few political figures were accepting upper-grade commissions, no other, so far as he knew, was clamoring to volunteer as a buck private.

The first response was the offer of a colonelcy by another state. Governor Lon V. Stephens of Missouri offered Bryan the field-grade commission in and on behalf of the Missouri Militia or National Guard. Aware of Bryan's love of horses, the Missouri governor sweetened his offer by dispatching express prepaid a handsome black saddle mount that Bryan happily accepted and named "Governor." But he did not accept the commission. He explained that he had no military experience and was not qualified to command a regiment or any other body of troops.

Silas Holcomb, whom Bryan had helped win the Nebraska governorship two years before, was astutely aware of the publicity value of having the past Democratic presidential nominee as an officer in the Nebraska National Guard. Holcomb was seconded by his exceptionally competent military aide, Victor Vifquain, at the time Nebraska's only holder of the Congressional Medal of Honor. The former brevet general was setting out to recruit a test or pilot company of volunteers. Vifquain began his recruiting outside the armory of the capital. The first volunteer in the waiting line was William Jennings Bryan.

The signing up began on May 19. Within three days the roster of the try-out company had 156 names, or company strength. The adjutant directed his volunteers to elect their own officers. Bryan was instantly nominated as captain (company commander) and elected by acclaim. He amazed his fellow enlistees by declining to accept; his explanation: "I am simply not qualified."

When the assembled company sufficiently recovered from its astonishment, it elected the oldest member present as captain, and Bryan was summoned by Governor Holcomb. There Adjutant Vifquain waited to do some volunteering on his own. The sixty-eight-year-old graduate of the National Military Academy of Belgium eventually gave his report of what ensued:

> I told him [Bryan] that a man in his position could not very well afford to become a private and gave him reason therefor. He told me, "But I know nothing about military matters . . ." I then told him that I would help him; that if he who had received 6,500,-000 votes for Commander-in-Chief of the Army and Navy could afford to become a colonel, I could af-

ford to come down a peg or two and become a lieutenant colonel. . . .

The Nebraska governor promptly commissioned the volunteer private a colonel of volunteers of the oncoming
Third Nebraska Regiment, soon to be known as the Silver
Regiment, and assigned Vifquain as his executive officer
with the grade of lieutenant colonel.

The governor expressed the hope that Colonel Bryan
might somehow be able to open the lagging supply lines.
For the time it was a vain hope. Most of the personnel
of the regular Army still awaited issue of suitable uniforms
and carbines; the militia volunteers were left waiting any
kind of uniforms or usable firearms.

The month of May was what Correspondent Richard
Harding Davis termed the rocking chair period; but there
were no rocking chairs for lowly volunteers. And there
was no follow-up of victorious news. The "understanding
from Washington" was that as soon as the U. S. North
Atlantic Squadron could do away with the Spanish Caribbean fleet commanded by Admiral Pascual Cervera y
Topete, U.S. land forces would move into Cuba; the un-
answered questions included, What forces? and How would
they move? At that juncture Caribbean shipping lanes remained unprotected; Spain's Caribbean squadron, if it so
wished, could attack eastern and southern U.S. seaports
more or less at will.

Rear Admiral William T. Sampson, commanding the
North Atlantic Squadron of the U. S. Navy, sought to
quell the alarm by leading a blockade force to the area
of Havana. But there was no duplication of Dewey's victory
in Manila Bay. When the U.S.S. *New York* bombarded
the earthworks at Matanza, Spanish troops returned the
fire with their carbines. Although Lieutenant A. S. Rowan,
then of U. S. Army Intelligence, had carried his message
to Garcia, the ensuing attempt to establish rendezvous with

other Cuban insurgent forces near Cedro Alto in Oriente had failed. So did a first landing attempt by Captain J. H. Dorst and 120 First Infantry regulars. The eventual success of Company E in landing supplies at Puerto Banes suggested to many dejected volunteers that the one dependable way to receive essential supplies was to qualify as a Cuban rebel.

At what was being called Fort Omaha, Colonel Bryan had reason to agree. He had taken up residence in an unfloored tent. Several thousand volunteers were spilling over the surrounding pasture lands; though "regimental strength" was limited to two thousand, more than five thousand were seeking to join "Bryan's Silver Third." The recruiting month was more than half gone, and still the eleven hundred recruits already inducted in the Third Nebraska Volunteer Regiment had no mess halls, barracks, or latrines, and except for fourteen badly worn tents, no shelter. The fact that no uniform issues were available—most of the volunteers continued to wear their farming dungarees or cowboy togs—was softened by the knowledge that their commanding officer had not yet acquired a uniform either.

Early in June, Bryan donned the first military uniform he had ever worn. It was the regulation "woolly blues," with wide white stripes on the seams of the breeches, a tight-fitting jacket, and an almost metal-hard can collar sided with the silver initials, U.S.V. (Only the regulars could wear the initials U.S.A.) Camera testimony indicates that Bryan had not been able to purchase the regulation broad-brimmed campaign hat in the correct 7¾ size. The hat was set rakishly to one side, with his mane of black hair protruding conspicuously; his jacket buttons also appeared to be under strain.

Bryan applied his experience as a Y.M.C.A. worker to the problems of helping "his boys" find themselves and feel more at home. He would "father" them while Vifquain "soldiered" them. Accordingly, Colonel Bryan set up evening song assemblies—with group prayer included. The commander, who frequently admitted that he "couldn't carry a tune in a washtub" (the receptacle changed from time to time), chose the "Battle Hymn of the Republic" as the regimental marching song. His selection of a regimental hymn required greater caution, since the membership of the Third Volunteers included Catholics, Jews, Seventh-day Adventists, Quakers, and Shakers, as well as routine Protestants. After much study Bryan chose "Rock of Ages." From that point on the choice of miscellaneous songs remained a delicate matter. In his now widely scattered possessions Bryan located a compilation entitled, *Favorite Soldier Songs for the Grand Army of the Republic National Encampment, 1883.* His personal selection was "Marching Through Georgia," but out of consideration for the southern sympathizers present he chose instead the moaning old-timer, "The Army Bean," as the regimental song. A more depressing choice is not easy to imagine:

> There is a spot that the soldiers all love,
> The mess tent's the place that we mean,
> And the dish that we like to see there
> Is the old-fashioned white army bean. . . .

As he began learning the timeless ways of soldiers, the novice soldiers began to learn the ways of a most exceptional colonel. "The old man isn't as soft-headed as he looks," Sergeant F. C. Scarborough wrote home. "Yesterday he saw our topkick slap a recruit. The sergeant will be chopping thornbush and tending privies the rest of the month. . . . But I sure wish those birds of civilian Bryan worshippers would stop cluttering us up. . . ." The hometown Lincoln *Evening News* jibed, caustically:

> Military life is having an excellent effect on Mr. Bryan. . . . He made an address to his troops the other evening, and not a word did he say about the

output of silver or the relation of coinage to prosperity.

The *News* could have added that Bryan was not saying a word, either, about the fact that his regiment, with muster books finally closed at 1997 men, was being cited as a model attainment in recruiting.

By July 13, the date of the first regimental parade, barely a third of the volunteers had received uniforms and fewer than half had rifles. In a "direct critique," Colonel Bryan addressed a regimental assembly:

> . . . We are all serving our country as volunteers. I am proud of my regiment of sturdy, healthy fellows. We are all on call for combat assignment. We will hope for this, but we will do our best whatever comes. . . .

As he had hoped, Bryan saw his own family waiting in the reviewing line. Mamie was putting on weight, and her hair was showing streaks of gray. Ruth was wearing her first velvet dress. Junior, nine, was solemn, wide-eyed, and, as his father said, lean enough to slip through a soda straw. Gracie had brought along her croquet set in case her father had time for a quick game.

The reviewing officers were the overweight Major General Fitzhugh Lee, reinstated as a corps commander, and his fiercely bearded aide. Lieutenant Colonel Vifquain sent word that the regiment was ready to march, and God pity whoever got in its way. Bryan had changed to his new and better-fitting dress uniform. Nimbly he climbed into the saddle and rode forward to "sashay" his regiment. He was a handsome figure, and he rode well. Then, rising in his stirrups, he delivered what may have been the shortest public address of his life: "Pass in review!"

Try as they did, the Third's parade turned out to be a

drillmaster's nightmare. Files wavered like prairie grass in a strong wind.

At the conclusion of the parade General Lee congratulated Colonel Bryan, and the colonel in response shook hands with the general, the general's aide, and his own executive officer. That done, Bryan kissed his wife and each of his children. On coming unfrozen, General Lee advised the regimental commander that his belated supplies were en route, and that due to pressure of responsibility the corps commander would forego the pleasure of taking mess with the regiment and push on to his hotel in Omaha.

Later that day a line of Army mule wagons rolled in, bearing the remainder of the uniforms and rifles, along with various other long-delayed issues. An official telegram also came, advising that the Third Regiment would shortly be ordered to an embarcation training area for overseas duty. One routine preliminary would be "culling out" the physically unfit.

Following his customary Army workday of about eighteen hours, Bryan returned to his tent to find travel orders directing the Third Volunteers to Jacksonville, Florida, for final combat training. Next morning five physicans arrived to administer the physicals. Sixteen of the volunteers had already been discharged for health reasons, and the medical examiners disqualified 699 of the remaining 1981. Clearly the "sturdy, healthy fellows" were neither as healthy nor as sturdy as their colonel had assumed. Bryan began the heart-breaking chore of bidding farewell to the disqualified. He was aware that young dreams of glory were being shattered. When the discharged burst into tears, as many did, they took whatever comfort could be derived from the evidence that their commanding officer was weeping also.

On July 19 the remaining Third Volunteers entrained for Jacksonville aboard a string of eighteen day coaches plus a Pullman observation car for the colonel-who-would-be-President and his staff. The regiment soon recognized

that it was riding a campaign train; at almost every stop
a crowd waited to cheer the Nebraska heroes, and Bryan
most of all. Again and again he addressed them, offering
praise of his men, hopes for an early victory with a peace
of freedom for Cuba and an escape from the Poisoning Tentacles of Imperialism, more commonly known as Expansionism. Again the train crew joined in the listening crowds,
finding each address different from the one before. As the
troop and campaign train moved into Illinois, the crowds
grew larger. Town bands blared patriotic marches and at
night the depots were being used as focal points for torchlight parades. Bryan's "responses" soon included strong
exhortations against the putting of a godly cause to ungodly
uses.

On July 21 the on-the-train reporter for the Lincoln
News-Call reported:

> The Third Regiment is having a very hard time of
> it running the doughnuts and cake and ice cream
> gauntlet that the people of the South seem to have
> thrown across its march to Jacksonville. . . .

At Nashville the edible contributions included 1342 pies
and three hundred quarts of coffee. The citizens of Jacksonville greeted the arriving regiment with eighteen hundred
packed box lunches—a full one and part of another for
each soldier. As an added bonus the Nashville *World-
Herald* of July 25 noted glowingly that William Jennings
Bryan made a spendid-looking soldier—"handsome as
Apollo himself." Then came the hot, grim awakening.

About four miles out of "Jax" and seven miles inland
from the coast waited the wasteland that some sardonic
bureaucrat had labeled Camp Cuba Libre. Local maps
still listed it as Rattlesnake Flats, and there were many of
same in residence. There were also sand fleas, chiggers,
stinging ants, and marsh rats; but above all, and on every

side, there were mosquitoes of every known species plus many visiting insect kin, all drooling for a taste of incoming Nebraska Volunteers.

Other, less visible foes developed. The unanticipated train feasting, together with the muddy and foul-tasting drinking water, contributed to an outbreak of diarrhea. There were no Army doctors at hand, which may have been just as well, and the leaky tents required much mending and tarring before the ailing could be sheltered from what seemed twice-a-day downpours.

The diarrhea was alleviated by an epidemic of measles. Before this partially subdued, and before July ended, typhoid struck. Bryan was up to his abundant eyebrows in trouble. There were no hospital facilities nearer than Jacksonville and no enlisted medical personnel. Having already learned that a regimental commander must, above all else, be the acting father of a grotesquely oversize family of volatile human males, Bryan was now compelled to act as lay physician, male nurse, chaplain, and counselor to four hundred sick young men and to double that number who expected to be stricken at any moment.

Once more the Commoner plunged into action with a vigor rivaled only by versatility. As a first quick step he headed a fund-raising endeavor for the purchase of a large tent. While this was being raised and staked he improvised a Y.M.C.A.-style center to fit inside it. The accouterments included books, magazines, games and puzzles, and, of course, Bibles.

With fatherly directness Colonel Bryan lectured his officers and noncommissioned officers on the widening scope of their responsibilities and the need for showing greater compassion for their men. He complemented the effort by employing at his own expense a retired physician to give lectures and demonstrations on sanitation and practical nursing. He presented Bibles to his entire officer personnel and to all those reporting for sick call. Byan instituted twice-a-day visits to all sick men and rented a horse-drawn ambulance for emergency use. His next move was to contribute the money for building a shack to serve as an officers' mess. That accomplished, he personally employed a competent cook and drew up a list of menus for what he, as a food lover, considered "decent meals." After that he determined to make each evening meal an "inspiration hour." Undeniably, the Third Nebraska Volunteers needed inspiration. By his labors and devotion, whatever else he was, had been, or would be, William Jennings Bryan was proving himself a damned good soldier.

In that he had noteworthy company. While the Nebraska Third squirmed and floundered in Florida mud flats, the fighting front had continued to fluctuate in the anguished island to the south. The Cuban invasion was a rapid sequence of ups and downs. Even while Richard Harding Davis continued to popularize the cynical adage "God takes care of drunken men, sailors, and the United States," U.S. forces were at grips with a new warfare. It already included the largest expeditionary force yet to embark from homeland shores. Late in May the then ranking U. S. Army Commander, General William R. Shafter, noted earlier as an Indian fighter, arrived at the badly equipped port of Tampa to direct an expedition to invade Cuba. Although he had most of the available regular Army at his call, the general's struggles against malfunction were even more epic than Bryan's. Practically all the needed materiel was outrageously late in arriving; not even the indispensable Army mules appeared on time. Railroad facilities bogged down, troop units arrived without uniforms, rifles, ammunition, or the luxury of a single day of range practice. Teddy Roosevelt's Rough Riders arrived garbed only in brown cavalry fatigue dress.

The combined forces included the elite all-black Ninth Infantry, and a total of 819 officers, 15,050 enlisted men, 2295 horses and mules, 114 six-mule Army wagons, and, appallingly, only seven ambulances. The artillery, though the best and most of what the Army then had to offer, was suicidally inadequate. It totaled sixty field pieces, four howitzers, a "pneumatic dynamite gun" that never worked, four Gatling guns, and a Hotchkiss revolving cannon that rarely fired. When finally loaded out, the convoy required nearly six days to reach its landing site, Daiquiri Beach near Santiago de Cuba. A pregnant porpoise could have made the sea trip in no more than half that time.

The first land battle of consequence had developed on June 24, when Major General Joseph Wheeler, a former Confederate troop leader, moved a skirmish force to meet and dislodge the Spanish defenders. The Wood-Roosevelt Rough Riders followed in Wheeler's wake for a grim baptism by fire. Their commander, Colonel Leonard Wood, was among the first to be wounded (an insolent Spanish bullet spattered into his wrist, severing one of his cherished gold cufflinks). Lieutenant Colonel T. Roosevelt was obliged to pause momentarily to pick palm splinters from his own head.

A week later, when the twin battles of El Caney and San Juan Hill occurred, the Spanish defenders of Santiago again fought surprisingly well. So did the Rough Riders and the far less publicized black infantry, particularly the Ninth. One of Bryan's favorite restaurant-counter companions of earlier years, Captain John Joseph Pershing, Tenth Cavalry, was most favorably impressed by the gallantry and courage of the black troops and the Spaniards who faced them. As Pershing had predicted, this was no tinfoil war. By July 3, about nine thousand U.S. troops had suffered casualties of 142 killed and 1010 severely wounded. On that day Lieutenant Colonel Theodore Roosevelt managed to cable his Boston friend Senator Henry Cabot Lodge:

> . . . We have won so far at a heavy cost but the Spaniards fight very hard and charging these intrenchments against their murderous rifle fire is terrible . . .

On the same summer Sunday the most historic of Caribbean naval battles was in preparation almost within rifle range of the hard-pressed American holders of San Juan Hill. Spain's Admiral Cervera seized on the carefree force dispersion of the U. S. Navy's Rear Admiral Sampson to make the fight of Cervera's life. Though he had only four battle craft in combat order, the Spaniard charged gallantly into Sampson's guard force, which included the battleships *Oregon, Iowa, Indiana,* and *Texas.* All the U.S. battleships except the *Texas* had cut off engines, presumably to save fuel, and all had raised battle hatches to give relief to the heat-suffering crews below.

In armada fashion the buglers aboard the Spanish flagship *Maria Teresa* sounded "Open fire." The *Teresa* all but leaped into the fray, her sister ships following with blazing guns. The penalty was inevitable. All four of the Spanish warships were set afire by sniper-style American fire, and for Spain's New World sea power it was ultimate disaster. The admiral and about eighteen hundred of his men were captured, for the most part rescued, from waters near their ruined ships; they had another 323 killed and 151 wounded. U.S. casualties totaled one killed and one seriously wounded.

Rear Admiral Sampson's marksmanship in public relations was even more effective than his turret rifles. He reported succinctly:

> The fleet under my command offers the nation as a Fourth of July present the whole of Cervera's fleet.

The rear Admiral could have added that "the nation" was even then offering the world a preliminary view of the emergence of a first-rank power.

Bryan could have no part in the publicity salvos. His daily work record noted only that he spent the historic Fourth leading a church service for his troops and supervising the purchase of potatoes, cabbage, and locally slaughtered beef for his meagerly supplied regimental messes. As he followed the fighting war by newspaper account, the young colonel was particularly disturbed by the July 12 report of a first outbreak of yellow fever among U.S. forces in the Siboney area. Many viewed the insidious killer as a direct result of the formidable stenches of rotted mules and unburied corpses. Bryan admitted to his mess table companion that the outbreak could have been divine punishment by plague.

On July 17 Spain's commandant in Cuba, Captain General Blanco, agreed to make formal surrender of all Spanish forces remaining on the island, in all about twenty-six thousand men, half again as many as the U.S. invasion force then numbered. Blanco explained that Empire law did not permit any military force to surrender so long as it had food and ammunition, but now he could surrender quite legally. The U. S. Secretary of War, Russel A. Alger, announced that the United States would provide return passage to their homeland for Spanish military personnel desiring it.

As he had anticipated, Bryan heard renewed laments that the war was running out before his Nebraskans could get into the fighting. He could and did point out that Cuba was not the entire war. Puerto Rico was next on the invasion list and after that the Philippines. But even as the Nebraska volunteers tramped down the guinea grass on the Florida rattlesnake flats, U.S. forces were being welcomed in Puerto Rico, which waited happily to join the United States.

The Philippines were something else again. As July began their principal native leader and self-declared liberator, General Emilio Aguinaldo, and his diffuse followers were already holding as prisoner some three thousand Spanish occupation troops and were proclaiming themselves masters of the island, with Aguinaldo claiming to be "President of the Revolutionary Philippine Republic." Meanwhile, small U. S. Army expeditions were setting out

from San Francisco for the six-week sea journey to Manila.
The first of these, twenty-four hundred troops commanded
by Brigadier General Thomas M. Anderson, had been
greeted in Honolulu, where they learned that the island
kingdom of Hawaii was also eager to join the United
States. At Guam the Spanish port commander of Port Luis
apologized for not having returned what he construed as
the Americans' salute. (At the time there was no functioning gun on the Spanish-held island.) General Anderson
accepted still another volunteer member of the new American Empire.

Arriving at Manila, and to the obvious annoyance of the
insurgents, Anderson led his force to Cavite. Other American combat groups were following—General Francis
Greene and his command of about three thousand, and
Brigadier General Arthur MacArthur (father of Douglas)
with a force of about five thousand. As June ended, Major
General Wesley Merritt and his staff set out to take command of the Philippine "occupation."

At Camp Cuba Libre, Bryan suffered double anxiety.
The ill health of his regiment was not improving, and
around the globe the onset of aggressive American imperialism was progressing mightily. What was he to do? As
a patriot he could not abandon his men; as a soldier he
could not crusade openly against the imperialistic leadership of his own Army. Yet as a party standard-bearer he
could not wait meekly and indefinitely while all he had
said against imperialism was being willfully violated.

Meanwhile he continued to scrawl hasty journal entries:

> Got up at five, visited the hospital an hour, went
> to breakfast, went to Jacksonville and made inquiry
> about another man, cut a lifeline for the beach, sent
> a telegram, got six men to arrange cots for sixteen
> patients coming in, secured an order for three ambu-
> lances, hurried to the ferry to meet the patients, paid

$4 for a horse and buggy to haul them, then attended
a number of minor details, but this will show what
I did. . . .

Dr. Nicholas Senn, Chief Surgeon for U. S. Volunteers,
called at Camp Cuba Libre and promptly classified the
Nebraska Third as being 65 percent incapacitated; Dr.
Senn recommended that eighty-one more of the worst-off
men be discharged immediately. That left approximately
one hundred stowed in available hospital space, principally
in Jacksonville, and about four hundred more "confined to
quarters," with most of the remainder of the personnel
serving as nurses and medical orderlies.

In more and more ways Bryan was proving his own
dimension of greatness. He boldly cut red tape and relied
on money he continued to borrow to pay for medicines,
physicians' services, and dozens of other needs of his men
that could not be procured from the quartermaster or the
commissary. He signed an endless series of personal notes
on two of the more trustful banks back in Lincoln, along
with several IOU's that his devoted law partner painstakingly destroyed.

As one more device for keeping up lagging morale,
Bryan directed the shaping of a nearby swimming pool
and beach. With his odd, motherly intuition, and again
at his own expense, he remembered to buy a rescue rope.
Almost immediately a young volunteer who could not swim
well was seen drowning. Bryan hurried to the rescue with
the help of two strong swimmers and succeeded in saving
the youngster's life.

He did not succeed in thwarting the onslaught of typhoid fever. By August 8 the newly promoted Brigadier
General, Theodore Roosevelt, and his Rough Riders,
were sailing happily out of Santiago Bay bound for routine yellow fever quarantine (fortunately unnecessary),
and subsequent "mustering out" at Montauk Point, Long

Island. Bryan was arduously fighting malaria as well as the typhoid contagion. The malaria strain was especially virulent. At "surgeon's call" sick soldiers crawled out of their tents and, on trying to stand, quite literally fell on their faces. Bryan was regularly among those who helped them rise. A visiting reporter, J. R. Johnson, confided by way of the Associated Press:

> Colonel Bryan displays little aptitude for formal military duties. . . . [He is], nevertheless, highly popular with his regiment as well as other units, and deservedly so. . . .

At Camp Cuba Libre, as at all other military establishments, August 12 was a memorable day. At about 4:30 P.M. Eastern Time the fighting war ceased. U. S. Secretary of State William R. Day and French Ambassador Jules Chambron, on behalf of Spain, signed a "peace protocol" or armistice, as an overture to a formal peace treaty. At that time, of course, no one could know that the Philippines would remain war torn for at least three more years.

Still concerned about the ominous evidence of imperialism, particularly in the Philippines, Bryan made a series of decisions. He would keep his command at least until his "boys" were able to shift for themselves and until a formal peace treaty was negotiated. The latter attained, the colonel of volunteers could legally resign his commission.

As August ended, Camp Cuba Libre was still a pesthole, and for the first time, Bryan found his regiment difficult to control. Now that the fighting had ended, the boys wanted to go home. So did their colonel, but the motivations were not precisely the same. Even from his interrupted glimpsing of newspapers, Bryan deduced, and vigorously predicted, that the remorseless tentacles of Wall Street would surely be reaching out for Cuba, the Philippines, Hawaii, Puerto Rico, and other terrestrial acquisitions and their exploitable resources. In Bryan's readily congealed belief, another poor man's war was yielding rich man's grab.

The Third Volunteers sweated out the rest of September at Camp Cuba Libre. The sick roster slowly diminished; even so, as the month ended, only about half of the remaining force qualified for what was metaphorically termed "active duty." Toward the end of September Bryan took his first leave. He headed directly for Washington to seek the transfer of his regiment to a more endurable campsite. He called on Acting Secretary of War Meiklejohn, the Army Chief of Staff, and somewhat secretively on the President. There was no change of orders. By coincidence or otherwise, the petitioning colonel became ill. Apparently he had malaria. Mamie hurried to Washington to be his nurse. The couple retreated to Culpeper, Virginia, to spend a few days with some distantly related Virginia Bryans, then went on to Hot Springs, Virginia, where Bryan hoped to "convalesce." It was a vain hope. He received orders from the adjutant general to rejoin his regiment and make ready to "abandon post" on October 5.

The subsequent move was to Fairfield, Florida, no great improvement over Camp Cuba Libre. Word came that the First Nebraska Volunteers would be ordered to the Philippines, but the Silver Third was temporarily stranded on the inglorious mosquito flats. Bryan saw that despite his eagerness to return to fence building for the Presidency and for thwarting imperialism, he could be held gagged in uniform almost indefinitely. Peace negotiations in Paris were progressing slowly.

So was Bryan's malaria. A rough and rowdy Army tent camp was no place for a woman, but Mamie stayed with her husband. On October 23 the Nebraska Third, its number reduced to barely eight hundred, was removed to Savannah. Malaria persisted. Although painfully ill, Bryan spent two weeks "reorganizing" his regiment while insisting that Mamie go back to the family at Lincoln. Returned to his status of Army widower, Bryan became very sick. His temperature flared. For many days he left his milk and soup untouched; his weight dropped from about 195 pounds to barely 150. On October 29 he wrote one of his most thoughtful and self-analytical letters, to his wife:

> I have consecrated whatever I may have to the service of my fellow men. To aid in making the government better and existence more tolerable to the producers of wealth is my ambition. . . .

He wrote to Dolph Talbot of his prayers of repentance. He required God's forgiveness for having participated in the war; his grounds for forgiveness were that he had not directly killed; he had labored, rather, to save the lives of "his boys."

When a long-delayed sick leave arrived and Mamie again joined him, the "silver colonel's" decision to quit the Army began changing from rumor to front-page headlines. Following his leave Bryan returned to Savannah and to his regiment, which by then was under orders to proceed to Cuba at a still unnamed date. Bryan began transferring his work to the able if aging hands of his lieutenant colonel who took over command of the regiment in December.

The official signing of the peace treaty took place on December 12. Two days later Bryan telegraphed his resignation to the War Department. For a change, they acted promptly to accept.

While heading for Washington, the tired former colonel noted forthrightly:

> My reason for leaving the army was that the sentiment in favor of imperialism was widespread and that many Democrats had been led to join in the cry for "expansion" as it was then termed. I believed im-

perialism to be dangerous to the country and so believing I resigned my position in the army to oppose
it.

It required more courage to resign than it did to
enlist for I knew the unfriendly papers would criticize me for leaving the army just as they had criticized
me for entering it. They stated that, having no military experience, I was not fit to take charge of a regiment and that it was unfair to the soldiers of my
regiment to be under my command. When I resigned
they stated that I had deserted my soldiers and that
it was unfair for me to leave my soldiers while they
were still in service.

Bryan was well aware that barely one year remained
for a new try at the Presidency. He was confident that he
could win what brother Charlie called the "big biscuit"
if he could keep himself continuously before the American
people and add suitably to his following among the national committeemen and state chairmen of his party. He
was certain that the key plank in his platform would be a
negation of the American lust for an empire beyond national boundaries.

Bryan doubted that his crowd appeal had waned. He
would not be surprised as of the following May when his
regiment, returning from Cuban occupation duty, greeted
him like an oversize and extremely affectionate family,
the volunteers virtually tumbling over each other to shake
his hand. Nor was he surprised when Colonel Vifquain presently saluted him as his "all-time favorite commanding
officer." When he left Washington to spend Christmas with
his family, he was not surprised to find that the Nebraskans had readied a "Welcome Home, W.J.B." gathering
at the Oliver Theatre in Omaha. Though the rally took
place on the night before Christmas Eve, the house was
jammed beyond standing room to sidewalk overflow.

Bryan, changed back to his all-season, all-purpose alpaca suit, white shirt, underprivileged black tie, and extrasole shoes, had reassumed his image. His hair was still jet black and shiny. His smile was still broad, but his girth had shrunk and the seven Army months had left other marks. Anyone could see that Bryan had aged perceptibly. His hairline was receding; his wide, high forehead was wrinkled; some of his photogenic youthfulness had faded. Army service had not shortened his long, country-style stride nor diminished the firmness of his huge handshake. But it could be noted that the Boy Orator was no longer a boy.

15. Hurrah for Tomorrow

Even before the returns of the 1896 campaign were tabu-
lated, commentators were predicting that the two major
parties would repeat their nominations in 1900. By December 1898, when the Treaty of Paris marked the formal
ending of the Spanish-American War, the acceptance that
Bryan would again oppose McKinley was virtually a consensus.

An editorial writer for the New York *World* yielded to
a brief spasm of cultural French to point out that such a
race was already a *fête champêtre* and quickly explained
that the classic phrase meant an entertainment in the open
air. Senator Marcus Hanna, McKinley's much mentioned
handler and slogan maker, loudly agreed, adding that
"the full dinner pail" assured his man a second term.

Bryan, for his part, even during the most dour inadvert-
encies of his brief military service, had never really ceased
campaigning. His optimistic forecast took for granted that
the Democratic party could and would attract votes from
various dissident groups. These might include substantial

numbers of liberal Republicans, who were already making
their presence known in such outlying areas as Wisconsin.
The Prohibitionists were solemnly moving toward party organization, and there were audible rumors that Bryan's
longtime friend, Eugene V. Debs, might be emerging in
1900 as the first Socialist candidate for the Presidency. But
the more tangible third-party front was still the Populists.
The Peoples' Party was known to be seriously divided, but
valiant and astute James B. Weaver, former Union Army
general and one-time presidential nominee for the Greenbackers and later (in 1892) for the then incubating Populists, was already striving to pull together a pro-Bryan
fusion of the chronically divided Peoples' Party. Bryan
held firmly that he did not seek and would not officially accept the Populist nomination as such, but he respected the
ability of "General Jim" to channel dissident votes to or
toward a liberal Democrat, such as you know who.

Yet without denying Democratic possibilities, any reasonably objective onlooker could see that the McKinley
prospects were strong and, indeed, gaining. The patronage
strength of the incumbent was, of course, formidable, and
as Charlie Jones of the St. Louis *Post-Dispatch* said editorially, the beginning of the Spanish-American War had
found McKinley being damned with faint praise, but the
war's ending found him being praised with only faint
damns.

The *Post-Dispatch* also mused that although McKinley
had yet to prove himself a great President, practically
any American of voting age could remember at least one
worse President. Pulitzer's two papers, the more successful one in St. Louis and the more flamboyant one in New
York (the *World*), continued to appraise the political
scenery with candor and abruptly shifting metaphors. The
Democratic *Post-Dispatch* was admitting, at times begrudgingly, that even while shipping a lot of water, misaligning
the ballast, and feeding altogether too many freeloading

seagulls, the S.S. *G.O.P.* was showing undeniable improvements in seaworthiness.

The *World* veered more to the language of sailing ships to speak of the verbal gusts and intervening stagnant calms of the Democrats and the freshening trade winds for the Republican sails.

Granting that McKinley frequently had little or nothing to say, a winner of wars is not obliged to talk up a storm. And the reminder here, of course, was that in 1896 he had come out second-best in the talking and first in the balloting. Bryan's spine-tingling elocution was of course remembered, but its translation into votes was less impressive.

As 1899 began, Bryan's public statements were negative. He did not see any convincing progress in the total American economy. He did not believe that agriculture, the nation's first vocation, was showing even minimal improvement. He regarded the Republican boast of industrial gains as largely illusionary and falsely magnified by partisan tariff laws. He was most disturbed by the continuing emergence of an ominous and, indeed, ungodly epoch of imperialism. He denied and deplored that in joining the aggressive grab for an overseas empire the United States was merely accepting inevitable status as a world power.

His careful reading of the *Congressional Record* motivated his latent talent for parody. In discussions at home or on the sidewalks he noted that what many congressmen were saying in effect was approximately this:

So we're starting an overseas empire. That's a lot like stealing hogs. But now that we've already stolen some (erstwhile colonies of Spain), why shouldn't we get some enjoyment out of the meat? Surely nobody would argue that we're supposed to give back this pig litter to Spain. She, too, stole the pigs some while ago. Now that we've got our hands on the little hogs, we might as well pass the best cuts to those with the longest and strongest reach.

On lecture platforms Bryan ridiculed the warmonger's

concept that war was inevitable. To a degree McKinley concurred, and he was appalled at the difficulties implicit in trying to deal with Spain's very special problem children, Cuba and the Philippines. Although he described himself as a believer in what was conveniently termed "free enterprise," McKinley viewed with anguish the unrelenting needs of what he referred to as the "empire business." The President admitted his shortage of competent advisers; and while he granted that the desirable course was to bed down with the territorial acquisitions and raise the resulting brood as real, red-blooded Americans, McKinley acknowledged trouble in family planning.

Bryan reiterated that the materializing orgy of American imperialism was unequivocally wrong. As a Christian statesman who was gaining ever-wider recognition he was resolved to make the smiting down of "expansionism" a primary plank in his oncoming political platform. For say what the opposition would, he, William Jennings Bryan, was for all practical purposes the Democratic party, and he would keep on wearing the armor of the righteous. So accoutered, he would seek the support of "the Godly believers, the church people, the good people." He would keep on standing for and marshaling this potentially decisive group. He would supplement with two intertwined majorities, the still hard-pressed farmers and the virtually omnipresent poor people.

Using mass persuasion and his own concept of Christian statesmanship as paired torches, and with God leading him and the common people pushing him or, preferably, bearing him aloft, this time William Jennings Bryan would win the Presidency.

Those who might view the foregoing as oversimplification will recognize that simplification was the Bryan strategy and touchstone. Was this the intelligent course? Bryan regarded it as such. Was he as yet a man of intellect? Bryan preferred not to detail an answer beyond his stock reply that a believing man cannot be a stupid man. He accepted that he had critics who looked on him as a stupid man. One of the more persuasive of these was a politically inclined and somewhat precocious teacher at Harvard. Ellery Sedgwick would emerge as editor-publisher of the *Atlantic Monthly*. As an upcoming oracle of the self-confessed "intellectuals," Sedgwick one day wrote:

> Mr. Bryan is an interesting man with an uninteresting mind. He has none of those powers of generalization which lead to the larger reaches of thought; nor has he that mental flexibility which enables a man to understand a position alien to his own. His ideas are cement hardening to stone before they can take rightful shape. To genius the great gift is given of seeing problems in their simple forms . . . but, like many uneducated men, Mr. Bryan thinks a problem simple because he sees not its complexities. . . .

As a man with good hearing Bryan was aware, too, that others persisted in labeling him a demagogue—bent on exploiting social discontent. But the No. 1 Democrat knew that many onlookers measured fundamental believing as more consequential than "smartness." Included among them was the youthful editor-publisher of the nearby Emporia, Kansas, *Gazette*. William Allen White, as the literate world would presently learn, was already emerging as an exceptionally able appraiser of political leaders. Bill White noted, in due course:

> Now the truth of the matter is that Mr. Bryan is *not* a demagogue. He is absolutely honest, which a demagogue is not. He is absolutely brave, which a demagogue is not. He is passionately sincere, which a demagogue is not. When Bryan came to Nebraska a dozen years ago, his town, his Congressional Dis-

trict and his state were overwhelmingly Republican.
A demagogue would have joined the majority party.
Bryan took up the cause for tariff reform and fought
a losing fight. When he became convinced that free
silver was right, he preached it in his Congressional
District with his party organization and the odds of
battle against him. . . .

As he continued to plan his part in the leadership of the
next convention (this one would be held in Kansas City),
Bryan's basic pillar was unshaken. Whatever else tran-
spired, he would build his case on the championship of
the "common American"—definable in the continuing conflict between the God-made man and the man-made dollar,
and the legally contrived corporation. Lucidly, stubbornly,
devoutly, he had kept with that stand and perspective. Beginning with his homecoming speech at Lincoln on the
evening of December 23, 1898, and throughout the ensuing year, he hammered away at this theme.

The man-made dollar was a problem, though. His
crowd-drawing lectures were steadily taking over as his
principal bread-and-butter enterprise. Inevitably he needed
money. He had resigned from the Army with substantial
debts; including the optioned land plots on or near Antelope Creek he had met 1899 owing at least nine thousand
dollars, by his own estimate a formidable amount. He
could not and did not stay oblivious to the fact that his
children were growing up and beginning to require all
manner of tangibles. Even Grace, the "baby," was no
longer content with her battered croquet set and old rag
doll.

Accordingly, Bryan had turned to lecturing for the dual
purpose of earning money and trying out his political
tenets on live audiences. He was in demand, the more so
because the American renaissance of oratory was selling
like cut-rate pain-killers. He discovered that without de-

pendence on the blow-hot, blow-cold silver propagandists he was able to arrange lecture dates quite effectively. During the February preceding his fortieth birthday he had successfully booked eleven "appearances," for which the responsibly promised fees would total at least two thousand dollars.

But money was by no means the total incentive; Bryan was particularly eager to sustain contact with rural and small-town America. There was a comparatively new and steadily growing facility for attaining this most desirable access; it was called Chautauqua.

Bryan had warmed to the special charms and advantages of this distinctively American and generically church-related phenomenon. Back in 1874 while Will was gaining liberation from Mary Lemen the whuppin' schoolteacher, and establishing entry in Whipple's Academy, a new kind of school was being incubated on the shores of Lake Chautauqua in upstate New York. Its founders were Lewis Miller, an extremely versatile Ohio manufacturer who had produced almost everything from buggy whips to cider presses, and Methodist Bishop Otis Vincent, who confessed to having raised almost everything from unholy hell to Greater New York Methodism.

Miller's avocation was organizing and teaching interdenominational Sunday school classes and objectively deploring the inadequacies of most Sunday school teachers, including himself. The Chautauqua "Assembly" was already a revered site for summertime revivals and Bible-study seminars. With the help and encouragement of Bishop Vincent, Lewis Miller succeeded in establishing there a special summer school and Bible "training" center for organizers, teachers, and superintendents of Sunday schools.

By discreet stages the curriculum was expanded to include church musicology, history, philosophy, and other social sciences. After four successive and fairly successful summers of trials and error-reduction, layman Miller became convinced, in his own words, that the product was good enough to ship out. He therefore provided the funds, with Bishop Vincent providing counsel and contacts, for organizing and providing the expenses of small itinerant teams of working pastors, evangelists, experienced Sunday school organizers, and music directors or encouragers. The invitations were mostly from small-town or village churches or country churches or meetinghouses that had no professional pastors. That, of course, was what layman Miller had anticipated and wished for; his working motto was "Religious-Democratic Faith in the Popularization of Knowledge."

In keeping with that tag line the Miller-Vincent team began to augment their "summertime traveling aides" with voluntary lecturers from colleges or seminaries, or even legislators and volunteer musicians, including instrumentalists, quartets and gospel singers. When the demands began to overwhelm the supplies and melt away the Miller donations, the two founders agreed to offer franchises to commercial booking concerns who would agree to sustain the high intentions of Chautauqua and keep the admission charges nominal, no more than twenty-five cents per adult and in no instance more than one dollar for an entire family, with church workers, teachers, and other public servants to be admitted gratis.

Several Chautauqua "agencies" resulted; four gained substantial size, and one, the Redpath Agency, headquartered in Chicago, presently gained special eminence in the field. The Redpath Agency, by way of its gifted young manager and reorganizer, Charles Horner, came directly to Bryan with a fervent invitation to join the good work—for fees averaging about one half the gates, meaning at least a thousand dollars per ten engagements week. The actively advertised early evening shows were usually supplemented by afternoon or matinee performances. Although the medium was definitely tethered to smaller towns, villages, and country crossroads, its ability to draw capacity crowds at minimal admissions was well proved.

Although Redpath's Charlie Horner enjoyed his unofficial title as the grand master of country booking agents, he convinced Bryan that he would not be averse to making bookings in auditoriums or larger town halls, but that small-audience Chautauqua was the better footing and had come to stay for many years.

When Bryan agreed to book some trial runs during the remaining interval prior to the 1900 campaigns, Horner correctly assured him that he would never regret his decision and might very well meet himself coming back season after season. (The concentration of Chautauqua circuits was in the late spring and summer months. "Like the great Julius Caesar did," he told Bryan, "we campaign only in the most suitable weather, carrying our own accouterments.")

From his very first trouping, in June 1899, Bryan liked Chautauqua, including its green-golden sheen of grass-grown town lots and open countryside pastures and its rarely failing aura of blue-jeans-and-calico neighborliness. By then the distinctive entertainment medium had gained acceptance in at least twenty states and was showing particularly strong gains in the Midwest, the Great Lakes states, the nearer Great Plains, and the Border South. Its "talent menus," as noted by young Mr. Horner, included famous orators (naturally none was as famous as William Jennings Bryan), gifted preachers, and evangelists; public officials, including judges and governors, and intermixings of humorists, singing troupes, and concert musicians, and, occasionally, magicians, jugglers, or other "exotics."

The intermixings were important because the Chautauqua circuits exploited versatility but ultimately won by real and legitimate box-office drawing power, such as William Jennings Bryan's. But it was no soft sop. The trouping was rigorous. Where possible, this included the bookings in public or school auditoriums and opera-less opera houses of the towns, the talent traveled by train, principally at night and, as a rule, necessarily by day coach. But fulfilling the majority country stands required supplementary travel by resort surrey, farm wagon, horseback, or, failing these, afoot.

The talent took meals where and when they found them, frequently in private homes, including farm kitchens, or village lunch stands, or crossroad taverns, or, as a last bet, beside the kerosene heater regularly carried by the transient tent or "striking" crew.

Like the ubiquitous circus, the American Chautauqua was primarily a tenting institution, and most of the "stands" were one-day-and-nighters. The advance crew was directed by an almost fiendishly versatile foreman who was "helped out" by a crew of three or four roustabouts or local laborers. His ever formidable task was to keep ahead of the talent, to pitch the tent and place the seating facilities and speaker's platform or "rostrum," also the ticket stand (the foreman usually sold and collected the tickets), and, when circumstances required, the two portable, canvas-covered outhouses.

The severe living economics consisted of two "drawing houses" per day, with a next-day "repeat," preferably but not always attainably within a distance of no more than twenty miles, preferably less. The prime hazards were rain- or windstorms, serious muscle strains or bruises suffered by the pitching crew, railroad mishaps, and indigestion or lagging enthusiasm on the part of the talent.

But by sustaining averages the hazards were held to minimum. The good people of rural and small-town America attended, shelled out their dimes and quarters, and found entertainment, inspiration, good company, and surcease from loneliness. The Chautauqua was America of its times, which endured until around 1915. It was rugged and repetitive, but in its distinctive American ways it was also good, even beautiful.

From first to last Bryan found it so. He attained and found pleasure in the continuing exposure to agrarian

America which had done much to build up the nation and William Jennings Bryan.

And he did not overlook the accompanying publicity by way of placards, local newspapers, and special announcements to church and school audiences. The financial considerations also invited heed. A mass fill-in of Chautauqua appearances proved more profitable than an occasional and personally arranged lecture date in a major town or city. No less advantageously, his venture into Chautauqua justified another pecuniary decision which actually he had already made. This was to completely sever his front-room association with the still wobbly and money-losing Democratic newspaper in Omaha. The honorarium of thirty dollars a week was less than a fourth of a single minimum-rate Chautauqua fee. Furthermore, the ready established Chautauqua circuit crisscrossed at least a dozen states which the forthcoming President of the United States would have to carry.

One could note, too, that Bryan was taking other gains from his return to platform trouping. He was effectively developing his powers as a public persuader and strengthening his talents as a crowd evangelist. Also, while speaking most directly to the little everyday people he was managing to develop, effectively and discreetly, various distinguishable hallmarks of the rising middle class. Photographs made in 1899 and 1900 show that instead of the wrinkled alpaca suit and the broad-brimmed sombrero that appeared to have been sat on violently only a few minutes before, Bryan had begun to wear a black tailcoat, creased breeches, a black slouch hat of recognizable shape, and a white shirt fastened with studs. He kept his laydown collar and string tie, but his shoes were no longer double-soled, he had a fashionable low-cut vest with an imposing gold watchchain, and a heavy cane of polished black wood. This last was explained by his daughter Grace as a device for self-protection in event of a holdup or assault. (By the time he was forty, Bryan had acquired a distinct dread of holdup men.) His elder daughter Ruth noted that her father's somewhat abrupt upgrading of his apparel may have been a more or less deliberate effort to appeal to middle-class voters. But his offhand and off-platform bearing had not changed. As an easy-to-know sidewalk companion, he retained the amiability of a wholesale shoe salesman.

Even so, the Bryan home began to assume a more impressive measure of distinction. The big downstairs living room was converted into a combination library and office-at-home. He festooned the walls with oversize black-and-white reproductions of Washington, Jefferson, Jackson, and Lincoln, with steel engravings of Webster, Calhoun, and Benton tucked away in odd corners. He acquired a large, flat-topped desk and kept it cluttered.

Directly in front of his high-backed leather chair was a brass eagle poised for flight. On the wall behind the desk an immense steel engraving, about ten by ten feet, showed Henry Clay addressing the United States Senate. Clay's figure loomed the entire height of the picture. The members of the Senate, by contrast, were all dwarfs. But all, like Clay, were wrapped in tight black stockings, tailcoats, and deep thought.

Bryan was beginning to build up a home library. One shelf held the revered Caxton edition of *Standard and Classic Novelists*. Another held the Caxton collection of *Standard Histories of the World*. Nearby was Lord's *Beacon Lights of History and Lives of Statesmen, Old and New*. Flanking them were a set of Beaver's *Great Orations*, and two volumes entitled *Poetic Gems*. Those were the "standards." Most of the other books or brochures looked as if they had been bought from door-to-door salesmen or given by novice authors and do-gooders. George du Maurier's *Trilby* was the only noticeable work of fiction.

At home Bryan remained informal. Regardless of season or weather, he almost never wore a jacket or coat indoors and, as a rule, received all callers in his shirt-sleeves. By

then the Bryans had a full-time maid, but so far as callers
or neighbors could discern, this placid domestic spent most
of her time in rocking chairs embroidering or knitting,
while the master or mistress answered the doors and attended to the chores. Repeatedly Bryan was seen carrying
in coal and kindling for the fireplaces, looking after the
horses in the backyard barn, or mowing the lawn. His
prodigious energy seemed to increase with each passing
month and, except for Sunday, which he called "our Sabbath," the homeowner at 1425 D Street forever seemed the
busiest man in town. On the Sabbath he was deeply involved in church work.

Whatever the day, Bryan continued making a determined
effort to avoid the grandiose trend that President William
McKinley, Jr., said was the American rendezvous with
prosperity. Also, the No. 1 Democrat showed no interest
in the spluttering overtures of the Automobile Age. He
remained an advocate of the horse. He expressed regret
that his son did not have to do the "stimulative" chores of
his own boyhood—such wholesome duties as feeding pigs
and calves, chopping fireplace wood, and building morning
fires. He conceded that the times were changing but they
were changing much more rapidly than William Jennings
Bryan.

Although he did not see a great deal of them, Bryan
was distinctly interested in his children and spoke frequently of what he called their "phases." Ruth was definitely the scholar of the family, and seemed more like her
mother than her father. Junior was a pleasant youngster,
still mildly mischievous at times, soft-spoken, somewhat
lethargic, and deeply interested in church and Sunday
school. He showed no particular interest in oratory or politics. Grace, the youngest, all but worshiped her father and
remained the devoted companion of her blind grandfather.

On the eve of the new century, Bryan invited approximately a hundred neighbors and townsmen for an evening
of prayer and thanksgiving. As he stated reverently, his

cup ranneth over. God had blessed him with a loving wife and engaging offspring, a talent for earning worldly goods, a love of his fellow men, and, as he freely admitted, the preassured Democratic nomination for the Presidency of the United States.

Shortly after New Year's Bryan began compiling the working draft of his upcoming Democratic platform. He renewed his exhortation for a more extensive silver coinage. He determined to stand for lower tariffs for the particular benefit of farmers. He would strike still harder for a graduated federal income tax, the election of U.S. senators by direct vote, stern anti-usury laws, and establishment of a Federal Corporation Commission to help guard against abuses of the rights and privileges of corporations.

He probed for a more effective language for use in evangelizing to protect the individual from the corporation. Confident that the brief rainbow of war-raised prosperity was fading, and that mass unemployment would shadow the approaching months of campaigning, he sought to define more graphically what he looked on as the No. 1 enemy of the individual. Instead of "corporation" he set about choosing a more sinister word, more strongly suggestive of stratagem and evil. His choice was the commonplace noun, "trust." As any dictionary affirms, it is a baffling and more than ambivalent word, with a dizzying variety of meanings and connotations. Then as now, the best-known was reliance on the integrity of another. In the living language, the five-letter noun also means confident hope, person or grounds for reliance, responsible charge or custody, or credit duly given; also that which is committed to one. In its legal sense, "trust" is an equitable right or interest in a given property other than the legal ownership thereof, or a property interest held by one person for the benefit of another. Unquestionably, Bryan was acquainted with the legal definition, and the related meaning of a combination of firms or corporations formed to lawfully establish a management facility operated by trustees. However, he went to one of the least-known and usually the very last of the accredited dictionary definitions: *A permanent organization controlling the commercial policy of a number of establishments operated separately, especially when such an organization is strong enough to control prices by suppressing or disregarding competition.* Bafflingly, he chose the least-known definition of what would be his most-used word in his promising quest of the Presidency.

The five-day convention at Kansas City began and ended as a Bryan phenomenon. The platform, from first to last, was Bryan-written. It was a distinctly oratorical defense and gospel of the poor American majority. Its most conspicuous weakness as a party platform was its repeated overlaps and near duplication of the first platform of the National Socialist Party (with Eugene V. Debs as standard-bearer), which had emerged almost simultaneously.

The Bryan platform did not steal the Socialist thunder verbatim. Rather it indicated approval in principle of many of the Debs-Socialist open assertions and commitments. Included here were such outright recommendations and specific commitments as total government ownership of railroads, telephone, telegraph, and other communications; also the graduated income tax, minimum wage, restriction of child labor, and protection of consumers by means of duly empowered federal commissions. While refraining from duplicating the language of the Socialist platform, Bryan had nevertheless indicated his approval of or marked affability toward most of its more noteworthy tenets.

But he had not written absolutes. And he had not tried diligently to mend the undiminished rift between eastern and western Democrats. However, he had reiterated publicly that in order to win the election he and his party would be obliged to carry all the New West (Great Plains), the South, the Border South, and at least divide the Midwest.

Having so stated, Bryan and his platform substantially ignored the East and the eastern Democrats, who had anticipated the bypassing and in conspicuous part had responded in kind. One after another the more dependable leaders of those commonly designated as the Wall Street Democrats had evaded the "Bryan Democrats." The New York Reids and Whitneys, the banking Morgans, even foxy Andrew Carnegie simply failed to put in an appearance at Kansas City. Several Tammany sachems drolly told the reporters they had come for the Kansas City steaks, and the Chicago and Philadelphia delegations were described as being almost as animated as a morgue at three in the morning.

The newspaper coverage showed comparable vitality. The fact was, of course, that the proceedings were disillusioningly predictable. After five uniquely newsless days, completely lacking in Cross-of-Gold magic or any faintly comparable mass ignition, the convention did precisely what the previous standard-bearer and virtually all others expected it to do; it nominated Bryan on the first ballot.

The campaign take-off was another masterpiece of lackluster. A prime reason was that both majority party platforms were peculiarly lacking in exploitable controversy. The Republicans once more sought to checkmate Bryan's "God-made man versus the man-made corporation ("trust") routine with an intensified revival of the "full dinner pail for everybody" tag line.

Earlier in the season various commentators had predicted that the particular significance of the first twentieth-century national election would be the emergence and testing of a third party. This surmise was predicated primarily on the chance that the Populists might be able to close ranks at least sufficiently to better their score of 1892, when General Weaver actually received about 1.5 million votes as the Peoples' Party nominee.

Bryan had held with his belief that the Populists had long since figuratively burned out their fuses, that the would-be third party had by then lost all of its fire and most of its blood. He had discouraged the Weaver group from again trying to take him as its we-too nominee. Earlier in 1900 Bryan had hoped that he would not again be so embarrassed. Several successful exploiters of Populist followings, in particular Congressmen Jerry Simpson and Ignatius Donnelly, had loudly castigated Bryan as the insidious contaminator and destroyer of their party.

Their reasoning was less than convincing. Nobody could deny that back in 1892, when his re-election to Congress was at stake, Bryan had talked quite a lot like a Populist— at least temporarily. But he had never joined the party or sought to dissipate the reach or thrust of its vote.

As the big campaign took shape, Bryan looked on somewhat apprehensively while the veteran and astute Populist brains, General Weaver and Senators William Allen and Ben Butler, teamed up to shape a Populist fusion in support of the Democratic nominee. This move was temporarily diverted when the declamatory group herded by the Simpson-Donnelly forces set about mustering a "middle-of-the-road" Populist bloc that broke away to nominate its own presidential candidate, a little-known Pennsylvanian, Wharton Barker.

Mr. Barker got nowhere at all. The Populist fusion again tossed its unwanted nomination to the recalcitrant Bryan, who again refused to accept it formally. While again emphasizing that he was a Democrat and only that, the forty-year-old man whom some were now designating as the Peerless Leader, kept a sharp and expectant weather eye for the emergence of another third party that could contribute dependably to his own vote or at the very least melt away some of the all too consequential McKinley strength. The most hopeful prospect was a bubbly protest group in what Bryan saw as fountainhead Republican country. In Wisconsin a second generation of frontiersmen was beginning to take heed of a Republican liberal named Robert M. ("Fightin' Bob") LaFollette. Bryan sensed the incubation of an effective revolt against Republicanism. He felt that LaFollette was a kindred spirit, but he guessed correctly that Fightin' Bob was not yet ready to come forth from the big woods as a trust-walloping independent.

In logistics and over-all planning, Bryan's second try for what his brother Charlie called the "big biscuit" was much better planned than his first. His concentration of effort was much more astute; he was centering the vote quest in regions that he had carried before, particularly the Border South, the Deep South, the Great Plains, the intermountain West, and in the Midwest, where he had fumbled most damagingly in his first try. He made minimal, pleasant, but in the main futile invasions of New England, New York, and the Middle Atlantic. He anticipated that McKinley would offer a repeat performance of his front-porch campaigning of 1896.

By his own choice, Bryan moved boldly into a fabulous circuit of speaking engagements and, in due course, joyously extended his first commitment for four hundred speeches to seven hundred and heard clamorings for more.

As before, Democratic financing was deplorable. By August the Republican National Committee had acknowledged contributions of almost 2.5 million dollars. The best that Millard Fillmore Dunlap, Bryan's campaign manager, could report was a twenty-three-thousand-dollar holdover of 1896 campaign funds and a fifty-thousand-dollar gift from Senator Clark, a Montana mining millionaire, and a few lesser offerings from passing the hat. Once again Bryan and his counselors failed to appreciate the compoundable value of rank-and-file financial participation, the fact that dimes and quarters contributed by the perennial majority of poor voters serve to build up vote totals even more than to reduce party deficits.

But the prime ingredient, William Jennings Bryan, was audible, visible, and at least in handshakes, touchable. The Bryan crowd appeal was gaining—even more so when the entertaining candidate shifted to "concentrated messages." His Chicago speech was a stirring appeal for union labor support; his Detroit "Address to the Ladies" was an outright preachment in behalf of female suffrage; his address in Denver was a two-hour glorification of the merits of silver; his San Francisco stand was a particularly winsome plea for the avoidance of imperialism. But in a broader sense, the talks were not winsome enough. The crowds and the working press continued to show far more interest in Bryan than in his platform.

Bryan struck hard with what he regarded as his two strongest magnets for winning votes, the defense of the majority poor from the greed and contrivances of the minority and soulless "trusts," and against the deep, morally rooted evils of imperialism. But try as he did, the Commoner could not make his vanguard issues strike fire. He drew crowds and he entertained them. But he lacked a Cross of Gold speech with which to ignite them.

Before the fiercely hot summer ended, Bryan began encountering what he found to be the most obnoxious bane that had ever dogged him. Its name was Theodore Roosevelt.

There were rumors and stories galore about how this shrill-voiced young aristocrat from Oyster Bay, Long Island, had succeeded in getting himself abducted into nomination as McKinley's running mate. Bryan was not interested in rumors. Like practically everyone else, he had heard a good deal about "T.R.," whose genius for self-publicizing rivaled Bryan's and at times actually exceeded it.

As the Commoner anticipated, Theodore Roosevelt's assignment as the Republican vice presidential candidate was to badger, wear down, and otherwise worry Bryan. Young (he was only two years older than Bryan), pugnaciously argumentative, and with a flair for rabble-rousing and evangelical preaching, T.R. filled assignments with vigor and audacity.

Bryan was aware that the most famous of the Rough Riders possessed even more impressive talents as a derring-do politician than as volunteer cavalryman. His competence would not be frustrated by his shrill voice, his

19. 1900: A particularly intricate Bryan photo.

20. Bryan and niece pose in front of Fairview in a turn-of-the-century "gas buggy."

21. Back from his post-election world tour, Bryan tells the press how it was.

22. Bryan stands proud in front of *The Commoner* office, 1908.

23. The classic Bryan rhetorical pose of the 1900s.

24. Bryan reads his acceptance of the 1908 nomination in Lincoln; resignation seems to replace some of the earlier enthusiasm.

25. Woodrow Wilson visits Bryan in Nebraska, October 1912; between them stands Ruth's son.

26. The architectural peculiarities of Fairview, the Bryan estate, stand out in this view from the oat field.

homely features, his rampant fidgeting, or his somewhat ghastly display of teeth. Roosevelt had already demonstrated breathtaking versatility in accomplishments. He had won election to the New York State Assembly at twenty-three, followed that with six years on the Federal Civil Service Commission, two years as president of the New York Police Board, and from there he had stepped nimbly into McKinley's "kitchen Cabinet" as Assistant Secretary of the Navy. Most of the nation and much of the world knew of his exploits as a civilian cavalry officer, but few were in a position to appreciate his bold brilliance as a naval administrator. Later in 1898 T.R. had lunged to election as governor of New York. The toothy young firebrand was functioning most effectively to extinguish William Jennings Bryan.

As Roosevelt trailed and leaped ahead of Bryan and otherwise harried and bedeviled him, particularly in the decisive mid-Atlantic and Midwest states, the Democratic standard-bearer grew ever more aware that T.R. was stealing his campaign ammunition, such as it was, with appalling effectiveness. Try as he did, Bryan failed repeatedly to generate the feeling of immediacy and dramatic force by his lambasting of the "trusts." In the matter of direct and authentic acquaintance with the foibles and evils of the wealthy, young Mr. Roosevelt was clearly the better qualified of the two. And he, too, loved people, preaching, and reforming.

Back in Omaha, Jimmy Dahlman, who stood with Bryan as he stood with breakfast beefsteaks, had a masterful summation to offer. It was that that whippersnapper Teddy Roosevelt damn sure was helping the Republican ticket and damn sure wasn't helping Bryan.

By October, and without benefit or encumbrance of polls, a great many observers agreed that Bryan was losing the campaign. Some said that he was losing because he had not come up with a compelling basis for winning. Others insisted that unlike the calendar, he had not been able to catch up with the new century. Charlie Jones of the St. Louis *Post-Dispatch* contended that his candidate and friend had been shoved by an unkind fate into socio-economic quicksand. Rural America was ever so rapidly changing to industrial America, and poor folks were pipe-dreaming about the promise of prosperity. Many Americans still favored saving seed potatoes at home, and most still believed in God. But the appetite for reform recipes was not keeping pace with the appetite for the existing pie, and more and more voters were learning that crumb-snatching from a well-to-do's table beats going hungry.

Bryan closed his most energetic campaign with a valiant train platform onslaught in the Far West, then continued fighting until Election Day eve. Once more he lost to William McKinley; the popular vote was 6,358,071 for Bryan to 7,219,530 for the incumbent. Bryan had lost lop-sidedly in the East. But more tellingly, he had stumbled badly in the Midwest, the Pacific Coast, even in principal areas of the Great Plains and Border South. This time he had failed to carry Missouri, Kansas, and, alas, Nebraska.

Once more the uncommon Commoner accepted defeat with humility, and once more he set about winning from losing.

16. Fair View

The family head at 1425 D Street, Lincoln, Nebraska, was an exceptional American; one entry of confirmation was that in his fortieth year he could look back on two tries for the Presidency of the United States. That, of course, was common knowledge. Exceptional, too, was his casually stated admission that he had never tasted or experienced the aftermath of alcohol and that he had never willfully used profanity. During December 1900, William Jennings Bryan was in the throes of abandoning another avoidable indulgence—cigar smoking.

His eleven-year-old son and namesake was responsible for this belated item of self-improvement. During the early autumn heat of that year's campaign, a Philippine admirer of Bryan and foe of expansionism had sent his hero a wooden drum or "keg humidor" of Philippine cigars. From time to time, Bryan had been enjoying the donation, as his admiring young son had noted. One day when his mother and sisters were not too close at hand, Junior snitched a cigar, and with two visiting playmates as audience he gave a demonstration of the manly enjoyment of smoking.

Moments later one of his callers knocked frantically at the back door and reported to Mamie that her son was dying back of the barn. Mamie located her prostrate offspring, the telltale stogie not far from his side. With her usual competence she carried the limp and slightly greening person of William Jennings Bryan, Jr., to his bed. That evening her husband arrived home and hurried to the bedside. By then Junior was beginning to discover that he was still alive, though he rather regretted it. The father delivered a sympathetic but emphatic lecture on the wrongfulness of self-indulgence. "I don't really mind your taking one of my cigars," he pointed out, "though next time I know you will ask permission. But the important thing is that cigar smoking is bad for you."

Junior writhed, then recovered enough strength to ask, "But if cigar smoking is so bad for me, isn't it bad for you, too?"

William Jennings Bryan, Jr., told the writer that if he lived to be a hundred he would never forget his father's "look of acceptance."

"You are absolutely right. I shouldn't be smoking cigars. Beginning as of now I am *not* smoking cigars," he said.

"My father kept his word," Junior added. "I am absolutely certain he never touched another cigar. That was my one and only contribution to his moral improvement—if you care to call it that."

After quitting cigars, Bryan went back to one of his more conspicuous failings, the planning and building of ugly dwellings. His newest was his long-dreamed-of home in the country. By then, with the astute help of his brother, Bryan had managed to extend his holdings of nearby prairie land, including the first chosen plot on Antelope Creek, to 301 acres. Mamie was concerned that he had signed up to pay the appalling sum of fifteen thousand dollars for the final 110 acres.

There was no serious argument when the head of the household chose "Fair View" as the name of the new estate, but there were extensive though futile feminine exclamations when he revealed his other plans for their new home. They had anticipated the inclusion of a tower, for they knew from earlier experience that a protruding "roof platform" or some other unreasonable facsimile of a tower was par for the course, but Mamie and Ruth, Ruth in particular, were shaken by the planning of *four* towers on the same three-story structure. All were to be midget facsimiles of church spires; none was taller than twelve feet nor more than eight feet in diameter. And, as Ruth pointed out, the ultimate architectural nightmare began with two oversize bay windows on the ground floor. By gradual stages Bryan compromised the original drawings to accommodate what he envisaged as a Nebraska adaptation of Jefferson's Monticello. This designation was less than literal!

While the first drawings moldered in his rolltop desk, Bryan set forth on what would be, at least for the time, his most profitable lecture tour. When May arrived, he came home for a six-week interval of farm development. The itinerant squire of Fair View looked convincing in his tight-fitting overalls, carrying the farm tools that he used with skill and power. The rural neighbors were favorably impressed, too, by Bryan's appropriation of land for corn and wheat, and his bold move to adopt a new, lush-growing clover called alfalfa. They approved of his reliance on horses, including his personal saddle horse, Governor, and his generous sponsorship of his brother's increasing congregation of mules. They found Mr. Bryan extremely friendly, however busy, and quite willing to share sociable moments with local nobodies as well as obviously important visitors. Similarly his visits to town, usually on horseback, showed him to be on good terms with the wagonyard set and the sidewalk loafers as well as prominent citizens, most of whom liked Bryan even while voting against him.

As 1900 neared its end, word got around that Mr. Bryan

was starting still another unusual project. He announced that early the following year he would establish in Lincoln a weekly magazine. It would be called *The Commoner;* Bryan himself would be the editor-publisher. Actually, from the first issue on, Brother Charlie was the publisher, managing editor, and general manager. Will leased a downtown shop and office building for housing the printing plant and the advertising, editorial, and circulation offices. The subscription price was one dollar a year, and many were wondering where the rest of the money was coming from—the total cost of the installation was being guessed at no less than forty thousand dollars.

By January 23, 1901, when No. 1, Vol. 1 went to press, more than seventeen thousand advance subscriptions had been received. Forthrightly, the founder explained, in his own type:

> Intending to devote my life to the study and discussion of public questions, I have chosen this method because it will best accommodate the purpose which I have in view. Through such a paper I shall be able to keep in touch with social, economic and political problems. The paper will at the same time, if successful, provide an income sufficient for my pecuniary needs, and this kind of work will allow me more time with my family than I have been able to enjoy for several years past.

The first issue stated its goal: "Aid to common people in the protection of their rights, the advancement of their interests and the realizations of their aspirations." The publisher defined the term "common people" to include "the rich man who has honestly acquired his wealth, and is not afraid to entrust it to the care of laws made by his fellows." It excluded the poor man "if he fawns before a plutocrat and has no higher ambition than to be a courtier or a sycophant. . . ." Brother Charlie was overheard suggesting that *The Commoner* grant suitable prizes to all or any subscribers who knew what "sycophant" meant.

The appearance of *The Commoner* produced rumors that Will Bryan had finally acquired an angel who was willing to grant his protégé almost unlimited credit. The rumors gained substance when the moneybags personally visited the Bryans. He turned out to be Philo Sherman Bennett, an elderly wholesale grocer in, of all places, New Haven, Connecticut.

Bennett could hardly be branded a "plutocrat"; his fortune was presently probated at slightly more than a quarter-million dollars, but he was probably one of the more wealthy of the ardent Bryan followers. The acquaintance began by an exchange of letters, grew following their firsthand meeting at Hartford during the 1896 campaign, and flowered in 1900 when Bennett began referring to Bryan as the New American Joshua. He shortly set up a list of William Jennings Bryan gifts. One of these was a grant of ten thousand dollars, the interest from which would comprise an annual award to the author of the best student essay on "free government." Another ten thousand dollars would be used to advance the education of poor boys recommended by Bryan; a like amount would be used for the education of poor girls as recommended by Mrs. Bryan; and fifty thousand dollars would be placed in trust for the New American Joshua to distribute or use as he saw fit. Actually, none of the bonanzas was to materialize. Before the monies were granted, the grocer died. His will was vigorously challenged by his widow and kin back in New Haven, and after prolonged court maneuverings and despite Bryan's best efforts as a civil lawyer, the will was eventually nullified by Connecticut court order. Even so, *The Commoner* continued publication and proved itself self-supporting; within four years its paid circulation was above the one hundred thousand mark, and the full-time staff, including printers and press and advertising workers, numbered fourteen.

Meanwhile, eventful weeks and months were hurrying along. On September 6, 1901, McKinley was shot; eight days later he died, and Theodore Roosevelt took the oath as President. Bryan foresaw that Theodore Roosevelt would prove out as an exceptionally progressive President. *The Commoner* viewed this as commendable because of the dangerously conservative trends that were beginning to show in both Republican and Democratic headquarters. As the editor-in-chief of *The Commoner*, Bryan identified many shapes that he could only deplore. He was appalled, for example, by the emergence of U. S. Steel as a "trust" with the fantastic capitalization of 1.4 billion dollars. He was unhappily concerned about the developing giantism of United Fruit in the Caribbean. As a student of constitutions and a crusading foe of imperialism, he was deeply upset by the scintillating decision of the U. S. Supreme Court that the Philippines and Puerto Rico, "while not a part of the United States," were not "foreign countries," either. He mused aloud that once more the U. S. Constitution had followed the flag and the Supreme Court the election returns.

As *The Commoner* began to take root, Bryan deemed the time right to return more effectively to the far more lucrative field of Chautauqua trouping. He found it grueling work, with bookings often totaling as many as a dozen two-hour lectures in a single week, and with at least as many more guest appearances at public lunches, breakfasts, church or school gatherings.

Inevitably he caught side glances and heard offhand testimonials that were indicative not only of a conservative upswing but of ominous power shifts within his own party. Particularly in New York, Chicago, and Philadelphia, the gaining city organizations showed indications of uniting to bring the northern and eastern Democratic wings together and, for practical and policy purposes, to drop the Westerners and Southerners. Rising party bosses including Jim Duffey, who claimed "control" of Pennsylvania Democrats, and the Sullivan-Murphy combine of New York were already grooming for nomination in 1904 the extremely conservative Alton B. Parker, a party cog whose economic principles made those of the late William McKinley seem practically revolutionary.

While the two-time Democratic standard-bearer went about his tangent-ridden business, the so-called Wall Street Democrats gave quiet indications of an intercity conspiracy to scuttle Bryan or at very least to subdue him. But the victim was not cowed. Early in 1902 he stated both in his then-weekly magazine and in his lectures his resolve to fight for the salvation of his party. He was still a free-silver, low-tariff, anti-imperialism man, and the defender of the misused, everyday, poor Americans. For these the No. 1 Democrat would stand or fall; and if he fell, he would go down fighting.

In a hastily written editorial (on May 13, 1904), Bryan noted that his forty months with *The Commoner* seemed like barely forty days. In any case, another national election was coming up.

He arrived early at the St. Louis convention, a full week in advance of opening date, but not early enough to frustrate the presumptuous takeover by the city bosses. Though only a contriving, municipal-level politician (originally from Ohio), Alton Parker, for all practical purposes, was as good as nominated. This deplorable situation was not changed when Parker informed the convention that he was a gold standard man and clearly implied that all western Democrats, including Mr. Bryan, could go and jump into any shaft of any silver mine they might choose.

Bryan made his customary beeline for the committees on credentials and resolutions. After three eighteen-to-twenty-hour stints in angry, smoky committee rooms, he was taken severely ill. When he staggered back to Planter's Hotel, Charlie brought in the hotel physician, who confirmed that

Bryan was a very sick man, apparently flirting with a serious heart attack. After at least two days of bed rest, he should return by Pullman to his home and spend no less than a month in bed. Clearly, Thomas Williamson, M.D., was not joking, but just as clearly he was wasting his professional breath.

Next day the mood of the convention was ugly. Senator Ollie James of Kentucky, as in-and-out chairman of the Democratic National Committee, maneuvered to toss out "this so-called Judge Parker" and renominate "Old Man Bryan." The angry responses demonstrated that those who favored Bryan were for him intensely, while the rest, a majority, were vehemently against the two-time loser. On the second day, Charlie all but dragged his sick brother from the convention hall and tilted his chair against the hotel room door. "There's no point to killing yourself," the taller and balder Bryan repeated. "All that's happening is that William Randolph Hearst is smashing out what's left of his brain, trying to nab the nomination, and he hasn't the chance of a waterlogged ghost."

"I'm the man they're gunning for," Will insisted.

During the evening session and without warning, Bryan suddenly appeared in the convention hall. Sweating and staggering and ominously pale, he groped his way to the platform. Pushing past rude men who would restrain him, he began to explain haltingly that he did not seek the nomination, but he would not see his beloved party sold to the God of Gold. He reminded his hearers that even while losing he had twice won more votes than any other Democrat had won. The unscrupulous Wall Streeters were leading his party to ruin. The sick and displaced standard-bearer was obviously improvising what may well have been the most convincing argument of his career. Gradually the great voice began to gain its cadence.

Some would say that Bryan had run his race. Some would deny that he had fought a good fight, but none could charge that he had not been a faithful Democrat. Even

Pennsylvania's tough old Jim Duffey was seen to shed a tear. Well aware that he held the votes to nominate his man Parker, David B. Hill, who headed the New York delegation, listened with reverence. Sick as he was and admitting that his political career was finished, this mad, wonderful Nebraskan was giving a show so magnificent that no boss chose or dared to interrupt it.

Alton B. Parker won the nomination and lost the campaign ignominiously, with a popular vote of barely five million. Once more Bryan remained loyal to his ruinously beaten party. Once more he had kept what he termed the sacred grain of faith.

Back on the lecture platforms Bryan recovered his health, and, as many believed, his youth. His words appeared to gain an even greater fervor of evangelism and, not wholly by contrast, a renewed poetry, that of a sensitive, life-loving, daydreaming adolescent. Certainly at forty-five Bryan seemed younger than he had at forty.

Shortly before his forty-fifth birthday the most famous resident of Lincoln, Nebraska, who was becoming increasingly curious about the world beyond national boundaries, found a contributing sponsor in the officious, in-and-out Democrat, William Randolph Hearst. Hearst retained a degree of sympathy for Bryan as a fellow editor and a victim of the Democratic convention massacre of 1904. Hearst vividly recalled that directly before bosses Jim Duffey and Dave Hill had joined in cutting Bryan's political throat at the regrettable 1904 regatta of bloody slaughter, Chicago bosses John Hopkins and Roger Sullivan had combined forces to hack to smithereens young Mr. Hearst's bold dreams of moving into the White House.

Trying to explain editorial motives is a notoriously unsafe pastime, but one can at least guess that as a deft merchant of the printed word Hearst saw merit in inviting Bryan to try his hand at preparing a series of newspaper articles about Cuba and the "seething Caribbean." There could have been other motivations, including the tweaking of the sensitivities of President Roosevelt, whom Hearst saw as stealing Bryan's thunder wholesale. Whatever his motives, the newspaper publisher wrote to inquire if Bryan would be interested in taking a brief fling at reporting the goings-on in Cuba and, if that panned out, extending the reporto-rial tour to Europe. Hearst suggested that Bryan would be welcome to republish his "material" in *The Commoner.* Bryan's answer was an eager "Yes."

Journalistically, his Cuban junket began badly. His open-ing tour of Santiago de Cuba ("besmirched with odorous rum mills") and the battle site of San Juan Hill ("not actu-ally a hill, only a rather poor cow pasture") marked the beginning of six exceptionally blotchy reportorial efforts. Bryan did not understand Cuba's complex and subtle merg-ing of past, present, and future. His appraisal of the "everyday Cuban" was virtually identical with his compre-hension of the neglected poor of Nebraska, Kentucky, or the Dakotas. The unique socio-economy of a caste-afflicted island remained beyond the Bryan ken. His reportorial in-adequacy was not helped by the Bryan prose style, that of a hastily written letter to a fellow Moose or Elk.

Even so, a reader could see intervals of competence. Bryan provided a deeply felt essay about the "soul-saving devotions" of an English-speaking Chilean priest who had established and continued a manacca-thatched mission near Havana. In this vignette, and in another dealing with an orphan's school at Puerto Banes, the novice correspondent demonstrated warm comprehension of religious zeal and elemental charity.

From Cuba Bryan returned briefly to Lincoln, presuma-bly for some conferences with creditors, then set forth for a nine-week report on Europe. For those who could afford it the American era of the Grand Tour was in ascendancy; with a Hearst assignment including a generous expense ac-count, Bryan could afford it. Even so, his European dis-patches began and ended as a confused hybrid, an inade-quate Baedeker guide and a flatulent parody of *Innocents Abroad.*

Beginning at Rome, Bryan gained audience with Pope St. Pius X, whom he revealed only as a "gentle old man"! From Geneva the tourist became engrossed in a miniature brass head of Theodore Roosevelt made for use as a nutcracker. In Germany his interest gravitated toward the fairly successful government ownership of railroads and utilities. Here, in fact, may have arisen his forthcoming advocacy of government ownership of railroads in the United States.

But his most ambitious reportorial efforts flowered in Russia, where he could not repress his amazement that, at least in some respects, that far-flung nation seemed almost civilized. At Kiev he saw a flourishing city agleam with electric lights. Next he observed handsome diesel-powered motor ships plying the Volga, and at Baku he caught his first glimpse of a "magnificent petroleum field." At the historic capital he found the Czar Nikolai Alexandrovich (Nicholas II) exceptionally gracious and "surprisingly well informed on international matters." After the traveler had complimented the Emperor of All the Russias on his part in establishing the International Court of Arbitration at The Hague, he was unable to resist getting in a word for the virtues of "free speech." The smiling Czar assured him through an interpreter that even a simple Russian could love peace, adding that speech was probably as free in Russia as in America.

When Bryan was escorted on a brief tour of the Imperial Art Galleries, he confided that Russian art admirably avoided "the nude and the lewd" and excelled in "purity, being largely devoted to home scenes and historic events." In the meeting with the great Tolstoy, one gathers that the enthusiasm was largely unilateral. Bryan jotted rapturously:

> My object in visiting [Tolstoy] was to see the man and ascertain if I could from personal contact the secret of the tremendous influence he exerted on the

thought of the world. I am satisfied that notwithstanding his great intellect, his colossal strength lies in the heart more than the head. . . ."

Though the "Christian aristocrat" of Yasnaya Polyana was hospitable, one gathers he was less than enraptured by the roaming Commoner from Nebraska. "That Bryan certainly does talk a lot," Tolstoy recorded, noting that he had been obliged to present his visitor with a Russian yearbook to serve as a tourniquet for his seemingly endless flow of questions.

En route home Bryan made a personal call on the President of the United States, where once more he was graciously received. Back at Fair View, which was nearing its startling completion, he settled to finishing his travel articles, stringing them together into a book, *Under Many Flags,* and shaping some mellow excerpts for *The Commoner,* which brother Charlie was running efficiently even though he insisted on using folding chairs in lieu of cabinet files.

As Fair View became ready for occupancy, Bryan was astonished to note that his children were rapidly ceasing to be children. Ruth, for example, had entered the University of Nebraska at thirteen; at sixteen she was seriously contemplating marriage. Junior was to be sent away to Culver Military Academy. Gracie was in the throes of acquiring her first party dress. Meanwhile, as a noble venture in the new internationalism, the Bryans were acquiring, short of formal adoption, another son. He was Yamashita, a Japanese farm boy from the village of Kagoshima, who had walked to Tokyo and there stowed aboard a freighter bound for San Francisco; he was in quest of an American education. The young man had heard of the great American Commoner and set forth to find him.

One evening Yamashita showed up at the Bryan door and explained his mission, in halting English. The Bryans opened their home to the youth and helped him gain admission to the local university. Neighbors and townsmen were duly impressed, though not all favorably, by the Bryans latching onto a "yellow boy." Yamashita would stay for five years, complete his schooling, and return to his native village as a school principal.

Bryan's attention was caught by another possibility for interracial relations. At the time, two nearby territories, the Indian and the Oklahoman, were striving to gain statehood. The Indian Territory, with the "Five Civilized Tribes" and some 350,000 other residents, was petitioning for admission to the Union as the "Indian's state" of Sequoyah, while the Oklahoma Territory, with a still unofficial census of about six hundred thousand, was clamoring even more emphatically for statehood.

For personal as well as patriotic and political reasons, Bryan was very sympathetic. Three years earlier he had traveled both territories as a much-applauded lecturer. Much earlier he had begun to correlate the political progress of the territories, or lack of it, with his own.

The great gunshot opening of the "Unassigned Lands" had taken place in April 1889, while Bryan was plowing into Nebraska politics. While he was winning his initial congressional campaign, the Organic Act of 1890 marked the emergence of Oklahoma Territory. Five years later, as a propagandist for free silver, Bryan had gained a close and fond look at the Indian lands; he recalled warmly the welcoming band concert, barbecue, and fireworks display that had been staged in his honor at Smith's Grove, now part of Oklahoma City. He particularly remembered the barbecue: the brick-size chunks of roasted beef and buffalo steaks passed around with thick bread-and-butter sandwiches. There was a background of fireworks, and the event had merged into an afternoon and evening that Bryan would never forget. Nor would he ever forget that when he stepped to the bandstand to make his speech he shortly learned that an imaginative celebrator had set a blacksmith's anvil with the borehole tamped with gunpowder not far away. The resulting explosion almost blew down the bandstand. The structure was still quivering when a local matriarch screamed, "Eee-ek, save my baby!" Her baby turned out to be a veteran countryside cattleman who stood about six feet three in his moccasins. Bryan had tenderly preserved the issue of the Guthrie *Leader* that recorded this folk drama.

Successive administrations, including Cleveland's, had deferred the issues of statehood, in some part because the more desirable territorial offices provided patronage and, in the case of McKinley, the admission of two additional Democratic states was not good Republicanism. Theodore Roosevelt, by contrast, favored admission of the territories as a single state and had set himself to coaxing an act through Congress. The move was regrettably stalled, however, and Indian leaders, including an able Cherokee attorney, Joseph M. LaHay, continued to work on a constitution for the proposed Indian state.

Bryan repeated that he was eager and willing to help with drafting the constitution, but he was quite confident that the Congress would not get around to the enabling act sooner than late 1906. Meanwhile, he was yielding to other enticing daydreams. First among these was a sumptuous reporting tour of the world. Charlie Bryan gently suggested that the first half of the trip be devoted to learning what stray fragments his brother did not already know about the present world and the last half to drafting an appropriate Bryan platform for the next world.

Will did not regard that as particularly funny; there were times when his younger brother's whimsies chafed him, and this apparently was such a time. However, he answered by publishing an editorial on the inalterable loyalty of his brother and the indispensability of Charlie's helping hands. He pointed out that God's Bible comprised a Bryan platform for the world to come.

The planning of the grand tour was expedited by two

contrasting developments. Bryan's income was catapulting; during the first half of 1905 his lecture fees, including those from the Chautauqua circuit, had totaled about forty thousand dollars, and his hastily written, hastily published travel book, *Under Many Flags,* was selling like hotcakes. He would, of course, expect to write and publish another book about his forthcoming global tour, as well as other articles. No less importantly, he would be giving study to Christian statesmanship and developing another "line of thought" too important to be mentioned prematurely at that time.

The other impelling development was the quiet passing, on June 11, 1905, of Mamie's father, who by then had lived for nineteen years in total blindness. Mamie had refrained from long absences from home primarily because of his handicap. Now that John Baird had passed on to his reward, she was more than willing to join her husband in the great adventure he had proposed.

On September 27, Mr. and Mrs. William Jennings Bryan, their son, William, Jr., sixteen, and their daughter Grace, fourteen (Ruth had her own very special reasons for staying at home), paused in San Francisco to have their group picture taken prior to embarking for Japan by way of Hawaii. Readers of *The Commoner* would shortly be favored with specific and enlightening recountings.

Once more the Bryan dispatches from abroad began badly. The warmup story from Honolulu conveyed the impression that the editor was preoccupied with gorging on the quaint native food and indulging in gentle expository burps amid a haze of pious sentiments. His first published letter from Japan carried a strong tinge of heartburn; it dwelt at length on the gourmet merits of giant white radishes (up to thirty inches long) fried in butter, and closed with the somewhat baffling assertion that the Japanese people in general are "Frenchmen done in bronze."

Next was a display of tourist humor *à la* Bryan. In Tokyo he attended a reception-dinner honoring Admiral

Togo, hero of Port Arthur and the newly won Russo-Japanese War. The admiral was being toasted with saki, of course, but Bryan persisted in drinking water. When the American ambassador discreetly suggested that his Nebraskan guest at least taste the rice wine, Bryan answered that Togo had won his decisive sea battle on water; if and when he won one on wine the Commoner would toast him appropriately.

At Waseda University he at least partially redeemed himself with a brief sketch which, for a change, showed more painstaking preparation; its punch line was, "Steam has narrowed the Pacific and made us neighbors. Let justice make us friends."

In a private audience at the Palace of Kyoto he found the Mikado to be a "gracious, bearded gentleman, 53 years old, and standing 5 feet 6." Protocol prevented Bryan's asking direct questions, and the American visitor found that "obnoxious."

If travel is the touchstone of culture, Bryan was finding himself on a stone mountain. At least temporarily, however, neither his Friend Joe prose style nor his capacity for cultural absorption were sufficient to meet the challenge. While building mountains of verbiage from molehills of frequently unchecked information, he continued to play skiphop with nations and cultures. He did not like what he saw of China; Confucianism troubled him deeply. In Korea he found little to recommend except a Protestant mission school. Having made a fifty-dollar contribution, he encouraged his wife to purchase a pair of "symbolic" bronze lions. They had the latter shipped home. Brother Charlie, who was doubling as caretaker of Fair View while running *The Commoner* and pondering Nebraska politics at a local grassroots level, dutifully received what he called the "bronzers," set them up at the front doorway at the country place, grumbling darkly that they would scare the living daylights out of his mules.

Via the Trans-Siberian Railway and an impressive connecting line, the Bryans visited the Russian capital, then St. Petersburg, where they visited the Duma, the skillfully managed agricultural banks, and the still chaste Imperial Art Galleries. Early riser that he was, Bryan called at the U.S. legation at 9 A.M., expressed chagrin at finding the doorways still locked, and later listened dubiously to the sickly explanation that in Russian officialdom nothing ever really happens until 11 A.M.

In Egypt, Bryan found the Sphinx disappointingly small. On the shores of the Aegean he gathered pebbles to remind himself of Demosthenes and to "signalize" the lisp he himself had largely overcome. In Jerusalem he and Mamie strolled reverently. The family traveled to Norway to attend the coronation of King Haakon VII. From Scandinavia they proceeded to London, where the U.S. ambassador, Whitelaw Reid, received them graciously, and at an embassy dinner introduced Bryan as a "typical American whose whole life has been lived in the sunlight."

Only after their arrival in London did Bryan reveal what he later noted as his primary objective of the great journey. That was to develop what would be known as The Bryan Plan for Goodwill and Peace among All Nations. When the Inter-Parliamentary Peace Conference convened in London, the affable provincial from Nebraska was invited to present what was revised by title to The Bryan Scheme for Establishing a Permanent Tribunal of Neutral Powers for the Advancement of World Peace. The gist of the plan was to submit disputes among nations to a tribunal made up of representatives of neutral powers who would serve quasi-officially as arbiters. The tribunal would submit a final judgment or deposition on the issues in challenge. Disputants would be honor bound to refrain from taking warlike action until the dispute was duly "cleared," thereby avoiding the "humiliating impediments of compulsion." Principal London newspapers published the text of Bryan's exposition, and the Conference voted unanimously to incorporate the recommended peace-keeping procedures into a resolution for presentation to the Conference at The Hague.

The following week the Commoner was presented in private audience to His Britannic Majesty Edward VII. From that moment on he was virtually deluged with invitations from important and unimportant followers of the Court of St. James's and his exploits were widely noted, not only by the London press but by correspondents for American newspapers and the news services as well.

When Bryan's former campaign manager, Millard Fillmore Dunlap, arrived for a series of consultations, the conjecture that the Commoner would again be a candidate for the Presidency gained immediate and widespread circulation. Dunlap joined the Bryans for the remainder of the tour through Holland, up the Rhine, and to Italy and Spain. After a brief stay at the Washington Irving Hotel in Granada, where the family occupied the Imperial Suite and Mamie caught up with the family washing, the party moved on to Gibraltar to board the *Princess Irene,* which was sailing for New York.

By then they had been away almost eleven months. In a beaming mood, Bryan devoted a day and evening to charming fellow passengers, then settled to five days of seclusion in his stateroom. There Mamie joined him in the final drafting and rehearsing of a speech that Dunlap and other party factotums had arranged for him to give at Madison Square Garden shortly after arriving in New York.

Once more Bryan appeared to be confronting political resurrection. The western Democrats were buzzing strongly. In Omaha and elsewhere in Nebraska, Jim Dahlman, by now the cowboy mayor of Omaha, had recruited the Bryan Welcoming Committee of One Hundred. It arrived en masse in New York by special train before the *Princess Irene's* arrival. By no coincidence, eighteen Democratic governors and fifteen U.S. senators (none Republicans, of course) were also newly arrived in New York. The Dahlman "Cow Hands" hired a tug on which to intercept the

Irene at quarantine, and on hearing the tremendous uproar of steam sirens Bryan hurried to the port side just in time to feel good old Jim's well-thrown lasso settling about his shoulders.

At Madison Square Garden the homecomer spoke in favor of government ownership of U.S. railroads (federal ownership of interstate lines and state ownership of local lines). Some Republicans, sensing that the talkative traveler had laid down the tinder for cooking his own goose, were pleased. Others, apparently including the President of the United States, were not at all happy about it.

Bryan himself was among the happy ones. Almost as soon as he arrived home in Lincoln he left again for Oklahoma Territory, where the campaigning for delegate posts to the approaching constitutional convention had grown almost as hot as the early September weather. In a matter of days the *Daily Oklahoman* would be announcing that "Bill Bryan, the next President of the United States," would shortly be touring all of Oklahoma on behalf of "Democracy," i.e., the Democratic party.

After delivering at Little Rock what sounded a great deal like a major campaign speech, Bryan on September 26 proceeded to Wilbarton in the Indian Territory. The territorial Democratic chairman had a special train waiting. At Enid and Oklahoma City the self-propelled champion of statehood addressed almost unbelievably large crowds and found the responses little short of riotous. The sun-blistered little three-coach train moved on into Indian country where the chiefs of the Five Civilized Tribes waited to greet Bryan and introduce him to their "nations." His subsequent greetings by Kiowas, Cherokees, and Chickasaws were most enthusiastic; the Osages and Choctaws were at least affable.

At dusk the following day, when the puffing camelback locomotive reached McAllister with whistle cord taut, a mile-long parade had already formed. In a matter of seconds Bryan was settled in an open buckboard before a deafening brass band and followed by about six hundred coal miners dressed in working blues, with their caps fronted by blazing carbon-arc lights. Behind them marched a quarter-mile file of torchlight bearers. An extremely good time was had by all.

At Vinita the next day, the Welcome Bryan Parade was headed by Major J. B. Turner's Horsemen, an unofficial frontier constabulary noted for high spirits, galloping horses, and a playful habit of emptying six-shooters into the vibrant Oklahoma air. Schools were dismissed and shops were closed as the entire population waited to greet its visiting hero. Chairman Bill Dunn felt it necessary to telegraph the remaining local chairmen:

> There will be no more hand shaking. . . . On account of the many meetings Mr. Bryan is holding his hands and arms are now so swollen it is impossible for him to shake hands.

But Bryan shook more hands. After delivering six hour-long speeches in a day, he was again addressing a nearly tumultuous crowd at Clinton by seven o'clock the following morning. The Vinita *Leader* spoke with its customary conviction:

> Bryan is older than he was and looks it, and his voice is hardly as strong as it was in 1896. But Bryan has lost none of his magnetism and his directness.

The marathon of crowd persuasion paid off. Bryan had privately hoped for a Democratic majority of thirty for the constitutional convention; ninety-nine were voted in, along with twelve Republicans and one Independent. Early in November, after his return to an expansive Chautauqua schedule, he provided a thirty-page letter in longhand that unquestionably influenced the text of the forthcoming constitution. Specific Bryan "inserts" included the authorization of a corporation commission empowered to prohibit interlocking directorates, provisions for initiative and referendum, authorization of municipal ownership of public utilities, a state board of arbitration for labor disputes, and legislative authority to fix wages and hours of work.

The completed constitution was popularly adopted by a citizen vote of 180,333 to 73,659. When statehood was finally attained, the first legislature, overwhelmingly Democratic, opened its work by passing a resolution to invite William Jennings Bryan to appear in person to receive thanks for his services on behalf of Oklahoma statehood, and to pledge the support of Oklahoma Democrats in nominating him as the next Democratic candidate for the Presidency.

There was still no capitol, but on December 21, 1907, Bryan stood before the joint session assembled in the Brooks Theatre at Guthrie. The chaplain of the Oklahoma House of Representatives stepped forward to open the session with a prayer:

"Lord, if it be according to Thy will, let Bryan be the next President of the United States."

17. The Challenger and the Challenged

In the last issue of 1907, P. Y. Brinton, the editor-publisher of *The Weekly Chief* of Hobart, far west in the brand new state of Oklahoma, recounted:

> Bryan has come and gone. He will go down in history as one of the truly great, whether he is chosen President of the United States or not, without a blemish or stain upon his character, leaving as a legacy new and advanced ideas and theories of government.

Throughout the birth year of Oklahoma statehood, the deluge of Bryan correspondence had reiterated his desire to keep the national Democratic party for and of the everyday people and free of the selfish chicaneries of city bosses. The fiasco of the 1904 campaign had shown the vote-repelling Alton Parker as a forewarning of the possible extinction of "the new western democracy."

On February 16, 1908, when Theodore Roosevelt first announced that he had decided he would not seek another Republican nomination to the Presidency, Bryan's willingness to go again for the Democratic nomination revived. Bryan took a dim view of the man whom T.R. was grooming as his successor. Bryan could see William Howard Taft as little more than a fat faker. Bryan had not been favorably impressed by Taft's performance, either as governor general of the Philippines or as Secretary of War. He particularly deplored the former as ugly imperialism. Furthermore, Bryan regarded Taft both as politically vulnerable and as a natural-born party splitter.

The Bryan belief that he could serve to reunite the Democratic party may have been personalized romanticism. But his awareness of the reawakening of western Democrats was fairly objective. The same held for the encouraging deductions of Jim Dahlman and Brother Charlie, who were unshakably confident that 1908 was the year for Will to try again.

On the personal side, Bryan's assets were rather markedly restored. He was no longer a poor man harassed by debts. By March 19, 1908, his forty-eighth birthday, the Commoner could look back on his most bounteous year. His gross earnings from lecturing and writing had been about one hundred thousand dollars. Thanks to Charlie, *The Commoner* was better than breaking even. Despite his growing list of donations to church schools and orphanages (including Catholic and Jewish as well as Protestant) in seven countries, and despite the cost of sending his son to Culver Military Academy and his younger daughter to the Sweet Briar Academy in Arlington, Virginia, Bryan now had money to spare. He was in the process of giving his home on D Street in Lincoln to the local Methodists as a church work center even while making real estate investments in Los Angeles, California.

But he had not impaired his image as a plain-living country man. As he grew wealthier he tended to dress more plainly. He still rode horseback to and from town. On a pleasant April day when a party of reporters descended on Fair View for some new views of Bryan the forthright farmer, they were doubly reassured when their overalled host loaded them into the surrey, personally hitched up John and Silas, the "buggy team," and drove them into Lincoln, where he did the family shopping for the coming week. He let the press take turns at holding the horses.

Whatever he said or did not say, by April it was common knowledge that he was again in the running for the Presidency. His campaign motto was LET THE PEOPLE RULE. During May, Bryan revealed somewhat tantalizingly that he would not attend the Democratic convention in Denver, but would await its deliberations at his home. Neighbors soon noted that Squire Bryan was doing some exceptionally pragmatic waiting. Important-looking strangers poured in. Early in June a handsome new tent, almost circus-size, was raised in the Bryan front yard. "My procedure, if you care to call it that, will be one of prayerful waiting," Bryan repeated to the local newspapers, which noted that his brother was moving around like a shot cat, all the way from New York to Denver.

The national press, meanwhile, observed a tendency on the part of the Democratic National Committee to recall with pride the notable vote-drawing records of the Bryan campaigns of 1896 and 1900 without dwelling excessively on the previous Cleveland or the subsequent Parker tallies. Josephus Daniels, the most gifted writer on the committee, pointed out that the party particularly needed a devout leader with readily accredited public appeal and an appreciation of the nation's new and expanding role as a world power; there was need for a man of peace to lead the United States into a renewed Era of Good Feelings.

William Allen White of the Emporia, Kansas, *Gazette,* was reflecting on Bryan's evident desire to rebuild his image as a people's prophet rather than as a real or would-be convention manipulator. Pulitzer's New York *World* reflected editorially that Bryan had nothing to gain by an in-person confrontation with Messrs. Sullivan and Murphy of New York "democracy," or Boss James (Axlehead Jim) Duffey of Pennsylvania. After all, the Nebraskan was getting back in the graces of his National Committee, whereas most of the officious city bosses were doing just the opposite.

Charlie Bryan proved himself an effective proponent of that point of view. With help from Jim Dahlman and Bryan supporters in Philadelphia, Charlie had been bringing together valid proof that several, probably as many as seven, of Boss Duffey's delegates had won their posts by snitching Republican votes. On convening, the Democratic Qualifications Committee, having been acquainted with the evidence, promptly proceeded to disqualify Duffey and his entire Pennsylvania delegation. That was more than a subtle slap at the New York bosses, as well as those from Pennsylvania.

On the second ballot, 888½ of the 994 accredited delegate votes went for Bryan. The unanimously adopted platform meanwhile had been virtually dictated by Bryan via a special telegraph line installed in his front-yard tent.

The 1908 Democratic platform included most of the text of the 1900 platform. As before, it omitted the issue of federal-state ownership of railroads, which again was a foremost plank in the platform of the National Socialist Party, and Debs, its now perennial nominee. But the Bryan platform outdistanced the Socialists' by endorsing Prohibition on a basis of local option and strongly advocating female suffrage, along with the required publicizing of campaign expenses and an emphatic demand for a "just and reasonable" federal income tax.

"It's a good platform," Charlie summarized, "good enough for those pinheaded Republicans to steal again."

Bryan accepted the nomination matter-of-factly, and announced that he would postpone his speech of acceptance and the opening of the campaign until August 24. He would spend the intervening time making "due preparation" at home. Apropos of this he invited his running mate, Senator John Kern, of New Jersey and the entire Democratic National Committee to assemble at Fair View, beginning July 24, for a leisurely planning and discussion session.

As the throng assembled, Bryan astonished at least some of the reporters by giving first emphasis to what he termed campaign honesty. He demanded that no individual campaign contribution in excess of ten thousand dollars be accepted, that all in excess of one hundred dollars be plainly recorded, and that no contribution of more than one hundred dollars be accepted during the final three days of the campaign. The assembled committeemen agreed.

The Democratic and Republican platforms, as Charlie had predicted, were again too much alike for Bryan's comfort; indeed, the scarcity of principal controversial issues was bewailed by both Democratic and Republican newspapers. Even the acridly Republican New York *Herald* admitted that Taft could run on the Bryan platform without discomfort, particularly now that the Ohioan had accepted Roosevelt's "command" to advocate an income tax. The New York *Sun* loudly regretted a "disturbing lack of purposeful partisanship." But this was not literally true. As Bryan made his first sally into the Midwest, the National Association of Manufacturers began flooding the mails with pamphlets exhorting all businessmen, regardless of party, to unite in defeating the irresponsible wild man from Nebraska. From Paris William Randolph Hearst, in an abrupt change of heart, commanded all his newspapers to oppose Bryan vigorously. From Chicago the Hearst-servile and grimly ambitious lawyer, Clarence Darrow, turned venomously against the man whom Hearst had turned against. There were reports of industrial employers notifying their hirelings that any one of them who supported Bryan was inviting discharge. Major railroads offered bar-

gain excursion rates to those who would hear Taft's acceptance speech but not to those who would hear Bryan's.
With customary crusading verve, Bryan swung into
action. When Wall Street Democrats threatened to bolt, he
bade them bolt ahead. He tweaked and quipped at Taft's
weak tea and "reheated" babblings of social reform, affably
overlooking that weak tea could very well be what most
voters wanted. For at least seven years Roosevelt had been
striving for federal reforms, but during the first month of
his campaign Bryan seemed conveniently unaware that the
appetite for reform is satiable.

During September Bryan shifted to his technique of the
eloquent sermon in behalf of righteous causes and deeper
faith. More or less simultaneously he began to concede, at
least by implication, that the righteous cause, however be-
fitting democratic politics, is not inevitably a passport to
victory. With sympathetic concern, Charlie observed that
in the course of his third try for the "big biscuit," his
famous brother was accentuating his role as defender of
the faith rather than a seiner of borderline votes. While
maintaining his public mood of serious fundamentalism,
Bryan surprised those near him with sorties into conspicuous lightheartedness, at times outright prankishness. He
continued to accept literally what Calvin Coolidge would
presently state proverbially—that the American public ex-
pects its President (or presidential aspirant) to be a solemn
sort of jackass; that to the lay onlooker politics must be
presented as a very serious business. But when not actually
on public rostrums Bryan was beginning to yield to a
much-repressed boyish talent for clowning.

For example, late in September the Democratic candidate received word of his election to membership in the
monkeyshining order of the Knights of Ak-Sar-Ben—that
is, Nebraska spelled backward. When he reported for initia-
tion, he heard himself being called on to deliver a campaign speech. As he strode toward the platform, another
knight dressed and made up to look as much like Bryan as

possible, stepped in front of him, lumbered to the platform, and delivered a vociferous imitation of Bryan making a campaign speech. When the applause had abated, the chairman announced solemnly, "We have with us tonight Mr. William Howard Taft, and I now request him to take the platform and reply to Mr. Bryan's remarks." Improvising ably, Bryan waddled to the platform, clasped his hands over his belly, and opened a devastating parody of his opponent. With anxious humility he apologized for leaving out all sensible points; he had not yet been able to gain the approval of Mr. Roosevelt.

Bryan also demonstrated a warming communality with newsmen, including the bevy of a dozen or so regularly assigned to report his campaigning. At Fair View one Monday morning the candidate looked up from his clutter of newly arrived mail and called out to two lounging reporters, Charlie (Charles Willis) Thompson of the New York *World* and "Fat Jack" ("Major" J. J.) Dickinson of the New York *Herald,* "Here's a Minnesota man who says he is going to present me with a bucking mule! He says it's on its way to me now, by railroad express prepaid, and should be here before the end of the week. Now what am I supposed to do with a bucking mule?"

"Send it to Taft," the *World* man suggested. "If you could ever get that barrel of lard to try riding it, you'd be elected by default."

The *Herald's* correspondent spoke up with customary owl-like solemnity, demonstrating again that although his military title was fictitious, his Kentucky accent and predisposition for clowning were real. "I'll ride yo' mool, Colonel Bryan, suh."

Bryan's eyes lighted. "Do you mean that, 'Major'?"

"Did yo' evah know me to say anything in jest, Colonel Bryan?" Nobody could remember for sure anything the "major" ever had said that wasn't in jest.

The candidate's mouth spread into an oversize smile. He announced happily that immediately following the arrival of the uninvited gift, a special mule-riding fiesta would be held in the alfalfa field next to the big barn, featuring "Major" Dickinson of Lou-a-vul as the mule man.

"Any time you want to back out, just say the word," Bryan advised in a fatherly way. "But if you do, I'll be disappointed in you. Remembah the honah of—Loo-a-vul."

On Thursday the bucking mule arrived along with other gifts that included an Indian arrowhead carved with the Lord's Prayer and a neatly crated apple pie six feet in diameter. Early Friday morning Bryan, beaming with satisfaction, began rounding up visitors, including the aroused press, and announced, "The ceremonies await, gentlemen." The photographers closed in.

Arm in arm, Bryan and Dickinson led the procession to the alfalfa field, where a forlorn and drowsy-looking little mule had already been saddled. "Major" Dickinson approached the dismal creature, spoke softly into each of its excessively large ears, then with considerable caution swung a fat leg across the saddle. Bryan clapped loudly. "You've got him tamed, 'Major.'" Confidently the fat reporter eased into the saddle. What followed seemed like a brief optical illusion. Although the mule did not appear to move, other than to arch its back into a wavery, inverted "V," the "major" began going higher and higher until in slow rotation he began to fall.

He landed head first in fortunately yielding Nebraska mud. Bryan turned abruptly pale, dashed over, and lifted up the prostrate, 280-pound hulk, and with an impressive show of muscle power carried it from the field, across the far-spreading yardways, into the house, and upstairs to bed. By then Dickinson was wide-eyed and apparently as near to consciousness as he ever got. Bryan summoned a doctor, who directed that the victim remain in bed at least two days.

They were hospitable days. The "major" was able to sit up and take nourishment, and throughout his confinement fellow newsmen and brotherly Elks continued to call in an almost unending procession. On the second and final day of bed rest the fallen hero found a huge bouquet of cabbages, squashes, and turnips swinging from the chandelier above his bed. On it was a cardboard with the legend scrawled in a recognizable longhand: *From the Amalgamated Mule Riders of America to Our Hero.*

As the hot, tiring campaign moved along, the Commoner continued to leave the use of special trains and private cars to others. Charlie Thompson of the *World* found himself suffering through an unending succession of stuffy day coaches, searching, frequently in vain, for a seat. On one occasion he glanced back dejectedly and saw Bryan beckoning. "Have a seat!" the candidate said hospitably, wagging a large knee. Passengers gaped as the smallish reporter settled himself on the aisle-blocking knee. When Thompson asked why he had been chosen for the signal honor, Bryan answered solemnly, "You have been a *very* good boy."

At Kansas City, Thompson was obliged to leave the campaigner to return to New York. On noticing the *World* man diligently counting his remaining funds, Bryan laid a twenty-dollar bill in his hand to pay for meals and cigars on the return journey. Then he picked up the smaller man's bag, and with a procession of reporters following, escorted Thompson to his train. Having helped him aboard and seated him rather grandly on the observation platform, Bryan reassembled his party, clapped loudly, and gravely called out, "Speech! Speech! Let the candidate speak!" As a station crowd began to assemble, reporter Thompson, in a shy man's anguish, got to his feet, raised his arms, and to the best of his ability began mimicking a Bryan oration. The subject listened with profound gravity, applauded loudly during the rather frequent pauses, and from time to time cheered lustily. As the train pulled out, the inept impersonator watched Bryan holding the pose of an enthralled listener:

> The last I saw . . . was Bryan waving his big black sombrero at me in a slow rhythmic manner, and the crowd on the platform studying him in a sheeplike effort to divine the meaning of his extraordinary behavior.

In his own inimitable ways Bryan continued to sparkle, but once more the campaign simply would not take fire, even while the Bryan crowds were consistently bigger and more animated than the Taft crowds. Bryan seemed more and more aware that those who came to hear him and be entertained by him would not necessarily vote for him.

Once more the balding, weight-gaining, middle-aged man returned to his home after the final Monday of campaigning. Now that the big tent had been removed, Mamie and Charlie waited beside the telephone and the telegraph ticker. The early returns were more punctual than usual, perhaps in some part because they were so top-heavily for Taft. By 10 P.M., early counts from New York, Ohio, and Pennsylvania were averaging almost 5 to 1 Republican. They also indicated that Bryan had carried his home precinct, but had lost most of the rest of Nebraska.

Next day the three-time loser absorbed without direct comment the news of the most crushing defeat of his career. One after another of the so-called key states had gone Republican: New York, Pennsylvania, Illinois, Indiana, Missouri, and sixteen others. Again only the Deep South had remained solidly Democratic. The popular vote was 6,409,106 for Bryan to 7,679,006 for Taft—about 60,000 fewer than he had received in 1896. The electoral vote was 321 for Taft, 162 for Bryan. For several days Bryan evidenced profound, anguished disappointment and bewilderment at the cause of his defeat. Then, as before, he resolved to carry on, and to keep with political tenets in which he believed, whether local, national, or international.

For the remainder of the year at the outrageously disorderly office of *The Commoner,* where the randomly placed straight chairs remained heaped with loose papers, the interests of the editor-in-chief shifted conspicuously to foreign affairs. He noted with concern the restless European Balkans, particularly the ominous dispute between Austria-Hungary and Serbia. He deplored the Franco-German wrangle over Morocco, and confided the intention to renew his one-man crusade in behalf of voluntary and quasi-official peace treaties predicated on arbitration by neutral powers. After the holidays he indulged himself in a brief tour of South America, concentrating on Peru. Upon his return he began writing amiable pleas for the case and cause of "voluntary and goodwill" peace agreements among nations.

News pictures showed that Bryan was aging. He kept on gaining weight. His jowls were beginning to sag, and the front of his big round head was almost bald. Tufts of light brown hair persisted in growing from his ears. His broad shoulders were beginning to droop.

But his crowd appeal did not diminish. Eager to confirm this, Bryan refurbished his Chautauqua bookings by rejoining Charles F. Horner, who had lately reorganized the venerable Chautauqua Agency at Chicago. Horner's decisive shift was from city or large town auditoriums or "opera houses" to portable tent theaters that were effective for trouping smaller towns and community centers. "Striking the tents" involved more modest box office takes (the tent theaters rarely seated more than thirteen hundred people, and twenty-five cents was the going admission). The advantages included accessibility to audiences not otherwise reachable and far more numerous bookings—up to twelve for a major attraction, and Bryan was indeed a major attraction. Horner provided him with expert tent and maintenance crews and locally recruited "Chautauqua maids" to attend to the wailing babies and present invalids.

With good cause, Horner continued to praise the loyalty and compatibility of his star attraction. Week in and week out, Bryan could be counted on to put on his ever-distinctive show. As necessary, he traveled by farm wagon, buggy, or on horseback as well as by train to meet his engagements. Despite middle age and regardless of the hour, a ten-minute nap usually found him refreshed and audience-ready. His "regular" fee was $250 for a ninety-minute address, but he paid his own expenses and declined to collect when attendance fell below one-half the tent theater's seating capacity. His gratis or benefit appearances for schools, churches, or other worthy causes, repeatedly totaled a third of his entire schedule, and during this period he declined to collect fees for appearances in Nebraska.

It followed that even though his net earnings temporarily waned to an average of about a thousand dollars per week for his twenty-two or twenty-three weeks per year at lecturing, he continued to meet all financial commitments, including his steadily increasing charities, and to put aside money for investments in real estate.

His lectures, meanwhile, grew more markedly evangelistic; "Have you heard Bryan speak?" was revised to "Have you heard Bryan preach?"

In this the Commoner appeared to acquire a still greater measure of fulfillment. He confided to his son that he was living a ministry of glancing through train windows and dreaming up more and better ways and means—not for making gardens or cultivating fields on his own but rather of "tilling the faith."

His relations with Junior tended to demonstrate his gradual and inevitable straying from his family. He saw comparatively little of his son (or daughters). At eighteen Junior left Culver and chose to enter the very young University of Arizona, where he had decided to study law. Shortly before his twentieth birthday Junior married

Helen Berger, a fellow student and a Milwaukee heiress. The preoccupied father telegraphed his congratulations, and a year later repeated the felicitation when informed of the birth of his newest granddaughter, another Mary Bryan. At about that time he made the acquaintance of a college youngster, Jack Hargreaves, who was ardently courting Grace Bryan, a coed at the University of Nebraska. Hargreaves would soon emerge as Bryan's favorite son-in-law—though Bryan's affections were inclusive.

"My family is getting to be the whole God-fearing American public," Bryan assured Dolph Talbot, his erstwhile law partner and unfailing friend. "I do love all my family."

Without detailing specific causes, Bryan also confided to Talbot that 1911 would be his year of "special revelation." A succession of events supported the prediction. After completing his early-summer Chautauqua tour, he returned briefly to Fair View and with his wife set out for the Ecumenical Protestant Conference at Edinburgh. At the opening session the Nebraskan heard himself being introduced as the most renowned American layman and the most effective American defender of the faith. The ego massage was less than adequate. Even while listening to scores of addresses and sermons, some of admirable sincerity, Bryan felt a depression of spirit occasioned by awareness of what he termed a "terrifying" lack of effort to build togetherness in living Christianity sustained by a fundamental belief in an omnipotent God. Sophisticated semantics and the clever gymnastics of sectarianism were simply not a substitute for fundamental faith.

Fall was showing on Nebraska prairies when the couple reoccupied their home. Mamie noted that her Will was yielding to an unprecedented seizure of autumn sadness. His efforts to appraise political developments did not lighten his spirits. In *The Commoner* he noted that the Taft administration was replacing his own motto, "Let the People Rule," with "Let the Money Rule." He added that if the trend were not checked both the Democratic and Republican parties would shortly be replaced by the Combined Plutocratic party.

His immediate hope was shaped by Theodore Roosevelt's unmuffled expression of disappointment in his onetime mantle carrier, William Howard Taft. T.R.'s preliminary maneuvers to win the support of the Wisconsin Progressives were being integrated with what would soon be known as the Bull Moose Revolt. At least three months before the Second February Crisis of the national Republican party, Bryan predicted openly that the Republican party would be split asunder and go down to almost certain defeat. In the same mood of finality, he reiterated that the Democrats could win only with renewed unity. He wrote that he himself would not be a candidate for the Presidency, and for the same good reason—sustaining Democratic unity—he would not even consider a vice-presidential nomination. But as the No. 1 Democrat, he was duty bound to aid in the judicious selection of a suitable candidate.

Already, and perhaps too emphatically, Bryan had made favorable mention of his "old friend and colleague," the Democratic Speaker of the House, Champ Clark of Missouri. Just before leaving for Edinburgh, *The Commoner*'s editor-in-chief wrote:

> I have known Champ Clark eighteen years. Never in all those years have I known him to be on any side of the question which is not the people's side. . . .

Then, quite abruptly, Bryan ceased tossing bouquets at Clark. His motivations were less than crystal clear. Some believed the change-over resulted from adoption of Clark by William Randolph Hearst and his papers, all of which had lambasted Bryan vehemently throughout the 1908 campaign. The thought of Clark as a White House puppet for Hearst seemed too much to bear. Bryan also noted with concern certain indications that Clark was also being "adopted" by the Wall Street crowd and the Murphy-Tammany "conspiracy."

From his customarily cluttered rolltop desk in Lincoln, Bryan also weighed reports that the New York forces were aggressively planning to take over the oncoming convention (at Baltimore), and set up a power drive to nominate Clark. Bryan's counterplay was an interval of thinking aloud about other possible Democratic candidates. This tantalizing vagueness began to diminish late in 1911 when Bryan mentioned Governor Woodrow Wilson of New Jersey as an "interesting possibility." Following publication of an agreeing but unsigned "reader's response" (the prose style somehow reminded one of Brother Charlie's), Bryan yielded to the invitation to tell more of this "Democratic upcomer." He answered somewhat primly that Woodrow Wilson, earlier known as Thomas W. and T. Woodrow Wilson, was a man of exceptional intelligence, scholarship, and dignity; not a seasoned campaigner, but one who had proved his competence at working with "legitimate party organizations"; not a compromiser or "merchant of spoils," but a devoted and progressive educator—in public office as well as "revered centers of learning."

The Bryan revelations regarding "W.W." were notable by their extensive omissions. There was no mention of the fact that the Wilson political philosophy as spelled out in his books was definitely more Hamiltonian than Jeffersonian. Or that, however effective the subject's talents for academic politics—certainly Professor Wilson had successively advanced himself from a rather dismal instructorship at Wesleyan to a professorship and presently the presidency of Princeton—Woodrow Wilson had faded from the latter post under aggressive fire from both his board of trustees and consequential portions of his faculty.

A casual reader might have deduced that Bryan and Wilson were long-time friends. Such was not the case. At most they had been only distant acquaintances; certainly

Wilson had never been a Bryan supporter. In fact, during the Cross of Gold campaign Wilson had described Bryan as an undisciplined and untrustworthy spellbinder and/or rabblerouser. Bryan may or may not have known that directly before his 1908 campaign the same Woodrow Wilson had advised Bryan-prone Democratic National Committeeman Adrian Joline of the Wilson wish that "something at once discreet and effective might be done to knock Bryan once and for all into a cocked hat. . . ."

Estimates, of course, can change, but there was no convincing evidence that Thomas Woodrow Wilson, as of 1911, had changed his estimate of William Jennings Bryan. But there would shortly be evidence that the new governor of New Jersey may have been gaining awareness that Bryan was still a real power in the national Democratic party. Also that from Chautauqua and other platforms, including pulpits, Bryan was holding intact his public following.

To step from the probable to the known: When Bryan accepted an invitation to speak at the Washington, D.C. Jackson Day Dinner in 1912, the long-distant acquaintances met again. When formalities permitted, Bryan left the speaker's table, strolled to the side table at which Wilson was seated, cordially shook his hand, and with Wilson's willing permission, posed for photographers with his strong right arm about Wilson's narrow shoulders. The pictures turned out well; in a subsequent interview published in the Washington *Star,* Governor Wilson paid tribute to "W.J.B., the great friend of Democracy."

The ambivalent chronicle of Wilson against and for Bryan and Bryan for Wilson would shortly be headline news. The Democratic national convention, scheduled to open in the Baltimore Armory on Tuesday, June 25, 1912, was what Charlie Bryan characterized as a real double-ply humdinger. Early on Monday, July 24, Mr. and Mrs. William Jennings Bryan, accompanied by their elder daughter Ruth Bryan Owen, and Charles Weyland Bryan,

climbed into an open Maxwell for the ride from the station
to the Belvedere Hotel. When sidewalk crowds noticed him,
Bryan stood up to smile and wave, and lusty and prolonged
cheers ensued. The people knew Bryan; great numbers of
them were aware that the Commoner had come for the
fight of his life, or as the Baltimore *Sun* explained, to
save the Democratic party as he had shaped and lived it.

The "Easterners" had already arrived in force, including
such famous or notorious figures as August Belmont,
Thomas F. Ryan, the J. Pierpont Morgan crowd, and Tammany boss Charlie Murphy. The Wall Streeters had already
chosen their candidate.

Champ Clark also had strong support from Democratic
congressmen and a diligent political lifetime readying himself for this best-ever chance at the Presidency. Governor
Wilson of New Jersey was still as dark as white horses
can be. The best-known name was still Bryan's. Numerous
uninstructed or undecided delegations divided into two
groups: those who, regardless of what else they might do,
would cast out Bryan, the three-time loser, and those who
would follow him and do as he would have them do.

As an opening move, Bryan made a try for the temporary chairmanship of the convention—a play to test his
personal following among the delegates as a group. He was
not surprised when the Murphy forces hurried to checkmate with Alton B. Parker. Any convention buff would
construe this move as an admission that Parker's chances
for the nomination were negligible.

Bryan regarded his loss to Parker by 578 to 509 as
distinctly favorable. As a deft follow-up, he threw his support—which carried most of his following—to electing as
permanent chairman Senator Ollie James of Kentucky,
whom he knew was "friendly" to his man Wilson, as well
as Clark. As he had done sixteen years earlier, Bryan held
the seventeen votes of the Nebraska delegation of which,
as usual, he was the duly elected chairman. Though not
yet pledged, the Cornhuskers were tentatively agreed on

Clark as their first choice, Wilson as second. However, as head of the Nebraska delegation and its official spokesman, Bryan had readied his own interpretation of a rarely tested procedural rule. By tradition, the leader of a state delegation reports to the convention chairman and clerk the previous or most recent canvass of his group. Was the latter practice mandatory or just traditional? Bryan believed it was only traditional, that as duly elected delegation leader he was entitled to cast or withhold the votes of his delegation. He saw this strategy as his only means for thwarting or even delaying Clark's nomination.

Next Bryan fired his first and only salvo at the powerful New York delegation. He introduced as a resolution a documented charge that three of the more able Wall Streeters, claimant delegates J. Pierpont Morgan, Thomas F. Ryan, and August Belmont, had not qualified as delegates. The resolution carried, 882 to 201. It proved most effective as a face-loser for New York and a face-saver for the veteran from Nebraska. Conspicuously shaken, the Murphy forces sought to remuster with their powerful colleagues from Pennsylvania and Ohio. That maneuver revealed even more clearly that the Clark forces still lacked about fifteen votes to nominate; Bryan held seventeen.

For hours to come Clark's chances wavered in midground; with the Nebraska delegation's vote Clark could win the nomination; without it, he would continue to teeter. The three-time loser held the Bryan-loyal Nebraska delegation as his only sword. At each roll call Bryan continued to shout, "Mr. Chairman, the great state of Nebraska passes!" As the ballotings continued, five, ten, fifteen, twenty, and on and on, Woodrow Wilson emerged as the only other noteworthy alternative. No less conspicuous was the fact that without Bryan the "professor" didn't have the shadow of a chance.

As the roll calls went on, Bryan assured frowning protesters that whereas many other heads of delegations were seeking for themselves, he sought only to save his party.

He was making enemies wholesale. The session grew stormier. On the thirty-third ballot the Missouri delegation returned after a brief recess to parade a large banner on which were printed several of Bryan's earlier recommendations of Clark: "Incorruptible," "Ever on the Side of the People," and so on. But Bryan no longer chose or believed in Clark. Accordingly, in grim silence, the "defender of the faith" kept to his uncomfortable chair. Members of Clark's Missouri delegation began waving their fists and shouting protests. Members of the Texan delegation grew so riotous that convention police moved in to form a protective cordon around the heavy and balding Nebraskan. Delegate Stanchfield of New York managed to gain the floor long enough to denounce Bryan as a selfish, bribe-seeking, office-snitching, favor-trading, publicity-hunting fraud.

Bryan maintained his silence and his hold on the Nebraska vote. The successive ballotings showed ever more convincingly that Clark could not win the nomination without it. At his own convenience, Bryan gained the floor. Tranquilly, he explained.

"The vote of the state of New York in this convention represents the will of one man—Charles F. Murphy of New York, and he represents the influences which dominate this convention. I shall withhold my vote *from* Mr. Clark so long as the New York vote is recorded *for* him. And the position that I take in regard to Mr. Clark I will later take in regard to any other candidate whose name is now or may be before the convention. . . ."

The floor again rumbled with angry protests. Once more Bryan settled to resolute silence. He had struck the telling blow, sacrificed Champ Clark, frustrated Hearst and the mighty New York delegation.

Next day the balloting was resumed. Bryan did not give in. In time his chosen candidate began gaining. On the forty-sixth ballot Woodrow Wilson won the nomination, thanks to and by way of William Jennings Bryan.

18. The Secretary of State

The Washington press corps reported with varying degrees of astonishment the President-elect's choice of William Jennings Bryan as his Secretary of State. Several editorialists were in a mood to label it an unreasonable climax to an exceptionally unreasonable campaign.

That Wilson would appoint Bryan to one of the more prestigious Cabinet posts was in no sense surprising. At least in public print few saw fit to deny that without the tenacious support of the famous Nebraskan, the out-of-the-mold governor of New Jersey would not have got within sniffing distance of the Democratic nomination.

The ensuing campaign, itself a kind of odyssey of improbables, had further solidified the unusual dependence of a comparatively little-known candidate on an exceptionally well-known manipulator. Yet even with Bryan's almost fabulously effective help and, at least for the Democrats, an above-average job of campaign direction, Woodrow Wilson had scored rather poorly as a vote winner. Even with the irreparable cleavage of the Republican opposition,

Wilson's popular vote was only 6,286,214—markedly below Bryan's three-time average. As the Progressive Republican or Bull Moose contender, Theodore Roosevelt had received 4,216,020 votes to 3,483,922 for the Taft "regulars." Many appraisers believed that winning the Presidency with a vote count almost 1.5 million short of a majority was not only much worse than Abraham Lincoln had scored in his first presidential campaign, but proof that Wilson had won despite, not because of Wilson. The fact that the New Jerseyan had won the electoral college vote 435 to 88 for Roosevelt, with only 8 for Taft, had again accentuated the fantastics of the American way of electing Presidents.

The person responsible in large part had to be Bryan. Although controversies, arguments, and differences of opinion lingered, to deny or to doubt that the ever-astonishing Nebraskan had earned his just reward here below was less than cricket—indeed, less than American.

The surmise that Bryan's own first choice of post was that of Secretary of the Treasury had been reported. Persons who knew Bryan exceptionally well were confident that Bryan's own first choice would be Secretary of State. A strong basis for this conviction was of course the Bryan fundamentalistic passion for international amity and his remarkable interest in quasi-official peace agreements; "treaties" was not precisely the correct word. This alone would have caused Bryan to practically leap for the first post in foreign relations. Woodrow Wilson had refrained from detailed comments regarding what he rather hazily termed "Mr. Bryan's nonwar philosophy." But the files of correspondence prove that the President-elect had already rewarded his champion with an esteem that was hardly less than boyish hero worship.

Wilson's frequent letters to Bryan invariably began, "Dear Mr. Bryan," yet the texts were chatty, even chummy, and abounding in such whimsical lapses of literacy as "to Day" for "today," "alright" for "all right," and "ect." for "etc." The prim little letters also foretold notable Wilson vulnerabilities, such as extreme sensitivity to editorial criticism and a hard-to-extinguish flair for making meddlesome suggestions. But what Bryan called the "W.W. notes" were full of appreciation and affection. For example:

23 Febry 1913

My dear Mr. Bryan:

How contemptible the efforts of the papers are, the last few days, to make trouble for us and between us—and how delightful it is—to me, as I hope it is to you—to know, all the while, how perfect an understanding exists between us! It has been to me, since I saw you, a constant source of Strength and Confidence.

I have nothing in particular to write you to Day. I have written these few lines merely from impulse from the heart.

Mrs. Wilson joins me in warmest messages to Mrs. Bryan and yourself.

Your sincere friend

Woodrow Wilson

Hon. Wm. J. Bryan

Mamie Bryan was particularly eager to aid with the cultivation of the germinating friendship between her husband and his President. And with no less determination, the graying and plumpening sweetheart from Pike County, Illinois, was bent on proving herself a pre-eminently effective first lady of the U. S. Department of State.

Such determination took form in a marathon of helpful wifeliness. This became widely noted about two weeks before Inauguration Day, when the Bryans took over a sixth-floor suite in the "New" Willard Hotel overlooking quiet F Street. Somewhat earlier the hotel had let its Presidential Suite to an early Texas oil lobbyist who had subsequently welshed on the lease. The management discreetly invited its most prestigious guests then in residence to move into the elite suite at no extra cost.

Mrs. Bryan accepted. She knew, of course, her husband's preference for plainer accommodations, and she agreed that in due time they would move back into the more modest apartment on the sixth floor. But for the time she would compromise with the demands of a more formal front.

Even while bowing to expedience in this respect, Mamie would not try to change her Will more basically. She liked his ways, even those that less sympathetic outsiders saw as ingrown sloppiness; in so many respects her Will was really nice to have around the house:

> I have been reminded of this when Mr. Bryan approached his desk apparently confused and without system to find a certain letter. His eyes would roam over the different piles. Then suddenly he would dig down and he very seldom failed to bring up the required document. . . .

What if her husband did fill his pockets with wadded telegrams? He never lost any. And what if he did occasionally slip one or the other of his feet into his Gladstone bag to tamp down its excessive contents so that he could squeeze in a few more entries? "He got them all in and was satisfied. . . ."

"I think we are going to have a really 'homey' home in Washington," the Secretary's lady predicted confidently. She had already decided that their painting of Thomas Jefferson would hang in the front room, flanked by her own favorites, "Hollandische Dame" and "Beautiful Beatrice." Somewhere in their second home she would also find places for their bust of Diogenes and their two bronze Korean lions. For several years Charlie had taken a more than casual interest in the Diogenes, confessing that he, C. W. Bryan, Will's ever-loving handyman, was beyond reasonable doubt the one for whom the old brass-headed bastard had been looking for so long. But, as noted, Charlie never thought much of those damned corroding Korean lions that had so grievously bothered his mules.

Mamie, meanwhile, had also scouted her husband's future office suite in the then War-State-Navy Building.

> I inspected the gallery of former Secretaries. The portraits do credit to the office, but the places where they hang do not. It is a dingy room. The ceiling has been patched and not retinted in one place. The backs of the chairs have been marred and some of the upholstery is positively shabby. I do hope this room may be put in order during the present regime. . . .

Much else waited putting in order, but Mamie noticed that her husband had become a trifle more orderly. For example, he had grown to be an exceptionally cautious man. He rarely rode in hacks or taxis. He never carried a valuable watch, wore no jewelry, and meticulously refrained from carrying more than twenty dollars on his person. When walking alone at night he now made a fetish of carrying a heavy cane that he called his walking stick.

Characteristically, Mamie reflected that even though her Will was grateful when someone gave him nice handkerchiefs with embroidered initials, he invariably lost them and was content with substituting a bit of cotton cloth hemmed on a sewing machine. Though he now had his square-toed shoes made to order, he had never changed the style. As his wife explained, "His string tie and turndown collar, his alpaca coat, have become a part of himself. . . ."

Inauguration Day, 1913, abounded with omens. The morning began threateningly, but the clouds lifted and the March sun broke through. Street crowds assembled early and greeted the brief appearances of the outgoing and incoming Presidents with polite but subdued applause. Woodrow Wilson was trailed, academic procession style, by his soon-to-be Cabinet. When the audience recognized Bryan, ineffectively disguised in not especially well-fitting formal attire, which included a top hat that was conspicuously undersize, the applause increased. Bryan smiled broadly as he approached the board platform, and stood respectfully, his wife close at his side, while the President-elect took his oath of office and shifted into a stilted oration:

I summon all honest men, all patriotic, all forward-looking men to my side. God helping me, I will not falter if they but counsel and sustain me.

The exeunt worked out better than the entrance, despite the fact that the incoming Secretary of State continued to receive more applause than the incoming President. As the limousines arrived to shape the procession, the crowd continued to surge around the Bryans. Mamie noted that scores of hands were reaching out for her husband's, patting his shoulders and forearms and back. It was as if he had been inaugurated. When she moved to join other Cabinet wives, Mamie felt her husband strengthening his hold on her arm. "You have helped me win and I want you with me," he insisted.

The entire distance from the Capitol to the White House was crowded with people. When the cheers for the new President subsided, the crowds continued cheering Bryan and moving closer to him. Women were shouting and men were waving their hats in salute. Clearly the initials of "Mr. Democrat" were W.J.B., not W.W. Bryan spoke to his wife huskily, "It's worth sixteen years of hard work to have devotion like this, isn't it?" A reporter noted that the Secretary of State was weeping and unable to wipe away his tears since both his hands were clasped by those of the onlookers.

At the White House buffet that the retiring President had earlier tendered his successor and the latter's guests, alert reporters overheard significant opinions about the newest Secretary of State. For one, Wilson's "special assistant," Colonel Edward M. House, had been watching Bryan shrewdly for several months. House noted later that the Secretary was "pleased as a child with a new toy. . . . He is a really fine man, full of Democratic simplicity, earnest patriotism, and religious fervor." Colonel House, however, seemed disposed to regard Mamie as the outstanding talent of the family.

Another incoming Cabinet member, David F. Houston, Wilson's Secretary of Agriculture, commented that Bryan was a "gentle-natured and unsophisticated fellow—unless playing God or bullying a convention." But Albert S. Burleson, the Postmaster General with a predisposition for censoring mail and coordinating patronage, was less tranquil about the crowd-winner. He was informed that Bryan advocated the Jacksonian spoils system, and he would shortly learn without joy that Bryan's Willard Hotel suite was taking on the appearance of an employment agency, with Mrs. Bryan as directress.

William Gibbs McAdoo, somewhat controversially named by his father-in-law, the President, as Secretary of the Treasury, was not willing to accept the new Secretary of State as a cherished friend and colleague, either. In time he would warm to the Nebraskan, but for the moment McAdoo was inclined toward his father-in-law's earlier disdain of the Commoner. McAdoo had taken leave of the Trenton conference at which Wilson had prevailed upon the Nebraskan to become his Secretary of State, with the impression that Bryan was at least amusing. For example, W.J.B. had innocently asked the President-elect if his (Bryan's) moral objections to serving alcoholic beverages at State Department social functions would be upheld. Solemnly, W.W. had advised the Great Plains bumpkin to "abide by his own discretion."

But this March 4, of course, was Wilson's special day. Following the luncheon the punctual President led his guests to the reviewing stand to "receive" the inaugural parade.

It was a most impressive review of more or less everything graphically American, from Indians in war paint and ceremonial dress to the Corps of Cadets from West Point and Naval Academy midshipmen along with such minor show-off groups as cadets from the Culver Military Academy and the Hiawatha Health Maidens. The lines rolled on, and Bryan stood as if hypnotized. But at last the all-time champion of bowing and hat-waving bowed and waved finish to the festival. The Bryans walked to their hotel arm in arm, still with a sizable crowd following. "It was a matter of great satisfaction to me to see democracy so powerful," Mamie recorded.

Those sentiments may have abated slightly the next day when the Bryan hotel suite began swarming with job seekers. Mamie took over what she called the "branch office" and diligently began writing down the names and self-admitted qualifications of the seemingly limitless legion, a great many of whom introduced themselves as Bryan supporters from the beginning. "I saw the undercurrent but was not always impressed," Mamie noted with a tinge of skepticism. Managing the branch office barely permitted her time to hear her Will formally sworn in as head of the State Department, but she simply could not afford to miss the occasion. "I told Will I had never heard him swear before and was interested to know how he would do it. . . ."

She seemed satisfied with what she learned. The same did not hold for her subsequent adventures as first lady of American diplomacy.

> Official dining is a particularly serious business.
> . . . Procedure is rigidly observed. I understand
> dreadful complications have arisen because Mrs.
> Smith went in to dinner in advance of Mrs. Jones. . . .

Mamie wrote, using official State Department stationery for her scratch paper. She noted that they were dining out practically every night except Sunday, and were up early every morning, since "working people cannot lie in bed." Nor could the Bryans be absent from their regular Wednesday afternoon open house, where several hundred miscellaneous Washingtonians and other guests were accustomed to gather, fraternalize, and freeload.

These afternoons had the advantages of informality. More formal dinners and receptions turned out to be what were known in Nebraska as bean spillers. Mamie soon found herself in the line of fire of the society columnists. Following a Pan American soiree, Mamie attended a reception which, according to her journal, "my absent-minded husband had forgotten to tell me about." Visiting news hens did not forget to tell their readers that the Secretary's lady showed at the reception in a country-style, gray taffeta house dress. "I would like . . . to dress well enough and at the same time help by an example of simplicity the . . . people who are tempted to live beyond their means," Mamie explained with a perceptible air of indignation.

If side-glancing Washingtonians did not get her meaning, friends back in Lincoln, Nebraska, certainly did. Despite rain, hail, and outrageous blizzards, their hometown threw a Bryan birthday party on March 19 that was more than worth the long trip home.

They arrived in Lincoln in the throes of a roaring Great Plains storm that continued for a week. Despite the "truly awful weather," about fourteen hundred friends of Bryan, including five governors, gathered for the dinner, locally known as a gut bust, and on the following day the memberships of the Sorosis and Fortnightly Clubs gave a lulu of a luncheon for Mamie. "I do regret parting from these club friends," Mamie recounted. "A more bright-minded, clear-headed lot of women does not exist. I shall miss them sadly when I return to Washington." She also spoke fondly of the Korean lions "which are going to guard our doorway in Washington as they did in Nebraska."

The return to Washington was marked by two significant developments that the ferret-eyed Capitol reporters failed to observe. Neither could be termed good news. Even while noting that the Bryans had abruptly given up their Presidential Suite at the "New" Willard in favor of a rather stringy and much smaller apartment on the sixth floor, they failed to detect the worsening health of the Bryans who were much in need of a more quiet domicile. Following the rigorous trip to Nebraska, Mamie had begun to suffer from arthritic rheumatism in her hands and arms. Her husband, though he continued to eat heartily, reported intervals of what he described as head buzzes, accompanied by dizziness and the urge to pass urine at very frequent intervals —the latter accompanied by a great thirst (for water, naturally) and a nagging hunger for sweets, such as cobblers and candies.

Mamie's physical problems were being aggravated by various social problems, one related to their local preacher:

> . . . The Minister has been a friend of Mr. Bryan's for many years. What he says is good but he shouts it in a most annoying way. I am trying to get Will to speak to him about it. I cannot understand why his wife does not train him a little. . . .

Indications are that Mamie did not succeed in getting Will to speak to the preacher, nor, much more regrettably, to consult the family physician. Even without an opportunity to examine his friend, J. Thomas Kelley, M.D., strongly suspected that Bryan had acquired diabetes. Certainly Dr. Kelley did not like what he heard of the symptoms. He urged that his distinguished patient begin reducing his intake of sweets, and, for heaven's sake, to come in for a checkup, if not to Dr. Kelley then to any other competent physician. Try as she did, Mamie could not succeed in towing her husband to Dr. Kelley until the following November. During the intervening seven months, probably sooner, the Secretary of State had acquired what Dr. Kelley's office records described as a clearly developed diabetic condition. He then prescribed a sugar-free diet with a much lower intake of carbohydrates. One may suspect that his patient was not particularly cooperative.

But it was drinking, not eating, that would next return the Bryans to international headlines. Their most important diplomatic gathering of the spring-summer season was a farewell luncheon honoring Britain's retiring ambassador, Lord Bryce, and his lady. The Bryans kept to their resolve to refrain from serving liquor. The Secretary had privately warned the Russian ambassador, who was apparently rated, however intense the competition, as the most advanced drunkard in the diplomatic corps. Mamie had cautioned the waiters not to serve until the Secretary had finished speaking. When the guests were seated, Bryan arose and explained that he and his wife had always been teetotalers, that their fathers were both teetotalers, that they could not depart from this tradition, and therefore hoped that their cherished guests would forgive their omitting wine.

Water tumblers were filled with a mixture of White Rock, grape juice, and water. Mamie observed that everyone at least *"seemed* contented." The Russian ambassador, who arrived duly fortified, appeared affably unconcerned. "In any case, we had broken the ice," Mamie summarized.

London papers guffawed, Paris papers resented the slur against wine, and many urban newspapers in the United States ridiculed the abstemious yokel Secretary. Smaller papers, particularly in the West and South, and most church publications joined in defending the Bryans. The upsurge of personal mail confirmed another boost for the new Secretary's popularity; from Lincoln, *The Commoner* proclaimed a "great moral victory."

Because America is America, the Secretary of State began finding his office and the nearby hallways cluttered with whole uninvited cases or sample packages of grape juice and dozens of other brands and concoctions of fruit drinks and bottled sodas, including—to Bryan's particular distaste—an Atlanta druggist's pop called Coca-Cola. He refrained from giving testimonials or personally accepting any of the wares. Bryan told Bill Savoy, his favorite messenger (a Negro) to give the deluge of samples to any department personnel wanting them. "Everybody's happy and sloshing," Savoy smilingly assured his boss.

Bryan confirmed in private a fact well-known to his immediate family: He never gave a whoop for grape juice, he never thought of ordering the stuff for his own use, and as a water lover he detested White Rock. Second only to water, buttermilk was still his favorite drink.

Bryan was busy trying to get on with the serious work of his office. He had begun with the devoted if somewhat vague hope that a first area of improvement could be in Pan-American relations. Bryan thought of the southern neighbors as good, lovable, God-fearing people. Only one week after his inauguration Woodrow Wilson had called a Cabinet meeting to review "Inter-American matters." Wilson had read a flowery essay about making the Americas more safe for Americanism.

Bryan apparently sought to adapt his techniques of manipulating political conventions to the Americas. He set about drafting what he pompously called a new Monroe Doctrine. Bryan's argument was that the objective of the original, which was concerned primarily with the protection of other American nations from literal conquest by alien powers, should be supplemented with "means and methods" for defending fellow American nations from citizen dictators or conspirators who were being, or might be, sustained and maneuvered by "alien exploiters." The style showed a distinct similarity to a Bryan-written party platform. The qualifier was to restrict U.S. military intervention to specific invitations or appeals from duly recognized governments then in power.

As he labored to make the facsimile of a Pan-American policy more convincing, the new Secretary of State bounded head on against reality. What are conveniently known as "international affairs" not only take annoyingly unpredictable tangents, but stated in Bryan's metaphor, plow at cross furrows to themselves.

Even while the new Secretary labored to shape a "Manifesto of Righteousness Regarding Inter-American Affairs" (this document eventually emerged as his Letter to the President of October 23, 1913), a vexing issue of sovereignty leered at him from the West. The California legislature was seriously considering a bill decreeing that Japanese residents of that state, as aliens ineligible for citizenship, would be denied the right to own farm or commercial garden lands or be subjected to severe limitations of such ownership. Thus, a state was openly usurping federal authority.

Bryan was sent to Sacramento with the President's orders to persuade the California legislature to cease and desist. He was permitted to address the body in a closed-door session, but the effort failed. The "anti-Jap" bill was enacted as law. Japan fervently protested California's violation of an existing treaty between two sovereign nations. To Bryan's intense chagrin, Secretary of War Lindley M. Garrison delivered at the next Cabinet meeting a tirade about a possible war with Japan and the need to protect U.S. shipping in the "Far Pacific." Bryan pointed out that the United States was not prepared for any show of force, that the need was to better the means of avoiding war, not waging wars.

With a labored smile of assurance, the Secretary of State told his good and longtime friend, Secretary of the Navy Josephus Daniels, that there would be no naval warfare while Will Bryan was Secretary of State.

He had hardly resettled himself to coping with smoldering and obviously deepening Mexican problems when, early in May 1913, the United States formally recognized the Republic of China. Bryan noted piously that "as other nations held back, our nation extended the hand of welcome." That hand held out in response revealed an imperative need for credit. Almost instantly an international banking lobby headed by Morgan partners moved on Washington to institute a six-power "loan arrangement" with China. This would pledge official U.S. support of U.S., British, French, German, Swiss, and Belgian banking interests then operative in China. The delegation called directly on the State Department to present its "conditions." These were that no additional American banking firms would be allowed to supply the Republic of China with credit, that all loans made by the six-power group would be secured by creditor control of all of China's official revenues, and that the lending group would expect the United States to enforce all debtors' obligations—with armed collections, as necessary. The lenders would also expect and require the "right" to renew the agreement without change of terms.

Scarcely trying to conceal his indignation, Bryan brought up what he called the "Wall Street piracy" at the next Cabinet meeting, where the unanimous "Nos" began with the President's. The Secretary of State took real and personal delight in carrying back the negative verdict. He anticipated surly protests and renewed tides of abuse from the Wall Street crowd, but nothing like that materialized. Actually, the financial community as a whole appeared to approve the rebuff. As one indication, barely a week later the Secretary of State was being photographed with big, burly James J. Hill on his left and foppish little Andrew Carnegie to his right. The next morning Secretary of the Interior Franklin K. Lane was seen smiling over his newspaper, "If Bryan finds poor Americans baffling, he must find rich ones absolutely bewildering."

As June began, another controversy burgeoned. The New York *Sun* opened the editorial uproar by revealing that Bryan was, as Secretary of State, again on the Chautauqua circuit.

With the deft assistance of Charles Horner, his booking agent, Bryan was accepting a few forthcoming (specifically four) speaking engagements for selected audiences. At least for the moment, *The Commoner* had no comment. Not so with the *Sun*. In a blistering editorial, the paper demanded to know why an official salary of twelve thousand dollars a year, then a handsome emolument, and "a very sizable personal fortune on the side" could not provide the Secretary of State with a life of Jeffersonian simplicity while attending to his sworn official duties. In Congress, Senator Breslow of Kansas introduced a resolution calling on the President to find out exactly what salary would cover the expenses of the Secretary of State to permit his attending to crucial duties.

Woodrow Wilson remained icily silent; with rationalizing naïveté, Bryan answered that in order to remain solvent he felt obliged to supplement his official salary. He could have noted that many other federal officials were also supplementing their salaries with lecture appearances, among them the redoubtable Champ Clark of Missouri, Henry Cabot Lodge of Massachusetts, and the dour but climbing Warren Gamaliel Harding of Ohio who had, so his fellow Chautauqua platform treader, Bryan, declared, "the most excellent speaking voice I have ever heard."

Had Bryan answered the *Sun* with total candor, he could have pointed out that he had already sacrificed some forty thousand dollars in available lecture earnings while helping to effect the election of Woodrow Wilson; that his personal expenditures incident to being Secretary of State were exceeding his income by well over fifteen hundred dollars per month; and that he honestly regarded the facing of living American audiences as an official duty prerogative. Speaking softly, *The Commoner* observed from distant Lincoln, Nebraska:

Among the masses the earning of a living is not a disgrace. Mingling with the multitude is not a cause of reproach. The forum is not below the level of official life. It is not stepping down to go from the desk to the platform.

In any event, attempts to rationalize or to castigate Bryan's recurring amours with the lecture platform solely or principally in monetary terms were hardly adequate. For better or worse, communion with living audiences was part of his fundamental evangelism, which in turn was of the Bryan genes and chromosomes.

While the Secretary of State was away on a binge of lecturing, Woodrow Wilson emphasized the determination of his Administration to stay imperialism and erase dollar diplomacy. He cited the humiliating bondage of Honduras to the Morgan Banks as a crying instance of noxious tyranny that could not and would not be endured. Bryan, of course, agreed. But on his belated return (his four lectures as contracted had somehow extended into fourteen), he could not find time to study the hurts and tribulations of Honduras. By then the Mexican crisis was on the verge of exploding into a shooting and killing war.

The chronicle of Victoriano Huerta was to pattern a long succession of imperiling fumblings and bumblings in U.S. foreign policy. Huerta was a professional soldier, an honor graduate of Mexico's Chapultepec Military Academy, an eminent younger general during the Presidency of Porfirio Diaz. Only a few weeks before Wilson's inauguration, General Huerta, on order of his then Commander-in-Chief, was assigned to suppress an insurrection. Instead Huerta, who had forced the resignation of Diaz, turned against Madero, and took over as provisional President of Mexico.

The outgoing Taft administration had deferred U.S. recognition of the Huerta regime; Wilson refused it on the grounds that Huerta was a "self-imposed dictator being kept in power by alien business interests," in greater part British and American oil companies. There was reasonable cause to believe that the strong man was not in power by the free choice of the people of Mexico. Bryan's appraisal, stated in a letter to Lester Markel of the New York *Times,* showed the discernible influence of a kind of catechism that he had composed all by himself:

> Let us not bother to discuss Huerta [personally] or the ways and means by which he seized office. His advocates assert that a Strong Man is necessary for preserving order in Mexico. They say that Huerta is the only Strong Man now in sight. If the United States recognizes him as President of Mexico, Huerta can get money, and with money he can put down any insurrection against him. . . .
>
> If, after thirty years of Mexican leadership, Diaz, with worldwide prestige and superb banking credit, could not maintain himself against Madero, but saw his government crushed like an egg shell, what reason have you to believe that Huerta, not only without prestige and credit, but guilty of high treason and blamed for the death of Madero, would be able to succeed where Diaz failed?

Once more Bryan found a catechism easier to state than to apply practically. The U.S. ambassador to Mexico continued to beseech recognition of the Huerta regime, even while the petroleum concessionaires meddled effectively in Mexican affairs. Much of the American press and too many members of Congress were urging aggressive intervention by the United States, conveniently overlooking the condition of the armed services, which were, as usual, deplorably weak, or, that aggressive intervention would obliterate the integrity of U.S. protestations of being friend and champion of "Pan-American sovereignty." In a belabored effort to overcome the Hearst argument that insofar as intervention was inevitable, the sooner the better, Bryan restated his personal devotion to anti-imperialism and the upbuilding of international peace agreements, beginning on the home continent. As Secretary of State he would, with the help of his President and his God, seek to use Mexico, the nearest American neighbor, as "a living pulpit for the perpetuation of peace and fraternal esteem."

More colloquially, the Secretary of State admitted that this would take some tall doing. Woodrow Wilson, meanwhile, was stating his fervent disapproval of foreign corporations that would try to manipulate Mexican affairs. Obviously W.W. was confident that what he said in Washington would carry to Downing Street in London. His move was temporarily effective. Like an accomplished wrestler who chooses to surrender an untenable hold, the British Foreign Office began encouraging British petroleum concerns to disassociate themselves from Huerta. A subsequent development was the report that German exporting firms were taking over as suppliers of war materiel and other goods for Huerta. As with diabetes, there seemed to be no certain cure.

19. The Ambiguous Peace Seeker

On the evening of July 13, 1914, a picnic materialized in the sylvan fringes of Washington's Rock Creek Park. The occasion was the fiftieth birthday of Secretary of the Interior Franklin K. Lane. Among those present were the Misses Smith and Bones of the White House staff, the Lanes, Mrs. McAdoo (the President's daughter), Secretary and Mrs. Bryan, and Senator and Mrs. Newlands of Nevada; among possible later arrivals were the Secretary of the Treasury and the President of the United States.

Bryan, smiling, so the President's daughter recalled, settled himself next to the birthday cake that the Newlands had brought. Miss Bones, while hanging the Bunsen lanterns, also observed that she had not seen Mr. Bryan looking so carefree in months. One reason for this emerged when he saw materializing out of the deepening shadows the slender shape of William Gibbs McAdoo. Bryan bounded toward the tallest and thinnest Cabinet member. "Guess what!" he shouted, "Huerta's out!"

Then, as one gathers, to the complete astonishment of

most or all of those present, the dignified McAdoo grasped Bryan's shoulders and they began to dance, first in solo efforts, then as partners, executing a sort of jig step. McAdoo rarely danced, and so far as anyone present knew, Bryan had never danced before, but look now! Next the two locked arms and began frolicking around the table, high-kicking and prancing like happy colts in a summer shower. Their wives may have gasped, but other onlookers began to applaud vigorously. The most surprised onlooker was the last to arrive. Woodrow Wilson came stalking through the settling darkness humming loudly and bearing a large towel that he evidently intended to use as a napkin. By then the other guests were improvising dances. The President did not join directly in the frolic, but after dinner he led an interval of group singing featuring a brief solo of his favorite song, "Shine On, Harvest Moon."

The cause for all the exuberance was evident. Huerta's exodus from his beleaguered status as Mexico's all-too-typical strong man was good news in foreign relations after dreary and withering months of bad news. One after another, inflammatory and avoidable mishaps had pushed U.S.-Mexican relations to the breaking point: the uncalled-for bullying by U. S. Navy brass of the Mexican port commander at Tampico, which Huerta had exploited so skillfully; the avaricious sales of war materiel by German and other nationals; the preposterous U. S. Navy bombardment of Vera Cruz—all had symptomized the relentless deterioration of U.S. relations with Latin America at large, and particularly the doorways to the *Americas del Sur.* "Unhappy Mexico" (the quote is Byran's) was the spotlight example, but the United States was getting into deepening mire in the Dominican Republic, in Cuba, and in much of Central America as well.

To ascertain which of the foreign-policy lapses or errors was most deplorable was almost impossible. Some observers held for the particularly odorous and shocking hoax of a "revolution" in Nicaragua. In effect this had already found the United States Government in conspiracy to defy and defile the sovereignty of an American nation at peace with the United States by supporting a wholly unlawful takeover of the Nicaraguan Government by means of collusion with U.S.-owned corporations and, for bad measure, effecting by duress the acquisition of a secondary canal route across Nicaragua without show of just compensation.

A complete listing of deplorable errors then current in U.S.-Latin American relations would have filled several volumes, and already more than a dozen painful mistakes were attributable to Bryan. Perhaps the most dourly delineative pertained to the deeply distressed Dominican nation. Like most of the rest, this appalling foul-up had begun long before the advent of the Wilson administration. During 1905 the United States Government had taken over the recipiency and management of Dominican customs collections. During the previous year that unhappy government had collapsed into literal bankruptcy, and alien creditors had swarmed in to collect by overt grabs or otherwise unlawful means. Following seven years of unwanted and wretched wardship, the U. S. Congress had granted by piecemeal authorizations permission to effect "military conversion" (via U. S. Marines) of Dominica to the status of a "supervised republic."

Not without some degree of cogency, Bryan had pointed out the primary need, as he stated it, of "first implanting a democratic government, even if less than perfect, being prerequisite to establishing a republic essential to Caribbean stability." But his moves to implement were hardly better than disastrous. In keeping with the most rancid patronage procedures, Bryan was in the hurtful process of confirming the appointment of a Tammany subchief as an overseer and "referee," presently, as minister-in-fact, to the proposed republic-by-mandate. Overlooking the facts that the oncoming sachem from Lower Manhattan admitted that he knew absolutely nothing about the Dominican problems and backgrounds, and that the local Banco Nacional, with more than local support, was already mastering and looting the tragic island nation, the "first free democratic election" was already being stacked. As Tammany appointee James M. Sullivan would shortly confirm, the imposed election of 1916 would not be either free or democratic or the first of its kind in the tragedy-ridden Caribbean. It would, however, provide the root bed for the most ruthless and long enduring dictatorship in the island's dark and bloody history.

Once more ignorance, past errors, and primitive patronage were comprising the ingredients for another deeply tragic mistake. The New York *Times* spoke out editorially:

> If all goes well we shall soon see the dawn of a "new era" in our Latin American relations due to the cheerful acceptance and amplification by the Wilson administration of the much condemned dollar diplomacy of its predecessors.

The picnic supper in Rock Creek Park marked the end of Bryan's 496th day as Secretary of State. Particularly during the most recent two hundred of those days, few evenings, or, for that matter, mornings or afternoons, had turned out to be even remotely appropriate for picnics. A prime reason was what the *Times* sarcastically listed as the "new era in our Latin American relations." It was not a new era; it was an old era getting to be ever farther out of hand and more conspicuously deplorable. The specific complications were proliferating like bitterweeds in a pasture. One close-to-hand reason for this outrageous sequence was the perennial and multilateral American lack of understanding of the "other Americas."

Bryan shared generously and more and more conspicuously in this ignorance. His unyielding befuddlement was, of course, enhanced by the fact that the United States had never devised or engendered so much as a reasonable facsimile of a workable Caribbean policy. In the realms of inter-American relations, vacuum continued to seek and all too often find its kind.

Bryan's pleasantly gabby and typically superficial tourist's acquaintance with a few of the nearer fringes of Latin America had mewled with kindly intentions. Any thinking commentator found it much easier to point out what Bryan didn't know about Latin America than what he did know.

Long before taking the first Cabinet post the Commoner had latched onto a seemingly indelible list of incorrect inferences. The first and perhaps the most pernicious was, of course, that all or practically all Latin Americans aspired to have governments and bodies politic exactly like or virtually identical to that of the United States. With closely rivaling gullibility, he had inferred, too, that all the Americas and Latin Americans are substantially like all others; at the very best, this befits the equation $2\times2=11$. In an auxiliary orgasm of erroneous assumptions, Bryan had apparently taken for granted that by dealing with a particular capital or principal town in Latin America one was dealing with an entire nation. In addition to being nearly the polaric opposite of the truth, this sort of assumption was at least doubly baffling in one who had based so much of his political career on the differentiations between city and country.

As a seasoned critic and flayer of big business and the soulless corporation, Bryan found himself in the unfortunate predicament of permitting business to serve and act in effect as an agent of the U. S. Department of State, and, at times, as the establisher of policy, such as it was. Individualist profit-seekers such as United Fruit, Morgan banks, Grace Industries, National Sugar, Rockefeller petroleum subsidiaries, and many others were going it on their own in the Caribbean and farther Latin America. Some of these "factors" repeatedly dealt with the *Americas del Sur* much like the oversize outlander who dropped into the sequestered country store, flipped a dollar on the counter, harrumphed at the proprietor, and with a meaningful clanking of six-shooters scooped up groceries and bolt goods. This, to his credit, was disturbing to the Secretary of State. But here again, Bryan was doing little to correct it. He lectured the erring exploiters much as a spinster lectures the sailor's parrot on the impropriety of swearing, and he attained as much real correction. None could deny that he was working hard. The work was made harder by the venality of U.S. business, particularly in the Caribbean, the persisting apathy toward and ignorance of hemispheric affairs that lingered in the Capitol and in the nation, his own acceptance of rapacious Jacksonian-style patronage (such as had already resulted so direly in the forthcoming Dominican "Republic"), and his almost unbelievable ineptness at heading an administrative office.

His big, red-carpeted, disheveled office in the War-State-Navy Building could not even boast a minimal filing system. His acting appointments secretary and his most effective assistant was still on the Department payroll as "Special Messenger Wm. Savoy (colored)." Unquestionably Will Savoy was a dedicated man, and his fixed expression of deep apologetic concern was well placed. His boss was chronically hexed and in trouble up to his big and balding pate. His mistakes were mutiplying almost as rapidly as his concerns.

By July 14, 1914, Bryan was uncomfortably aware that his Pan-American problems, painful and vexsome as they were, were no more than a front for far more imperiling developments. As he labored, his situation grew more and more like that of a parent who returns home and tries to quiet a prolonged and noxious family quarrel only to become aware that the entire household is at the verge of being razed by an onrushing flood.

Fifteen days before the picnic in Rock Creek Park, Archduke Francis Ferdinand, heir to the throne of Austria, had been assassinated by the Bosnian Serb terrorist, Gavrillo Prinzip. On the ensuing July 28, while Bryan was entraining for a speaking engagement in Milwaukee, Austria declared war on Serbia. As Bryan arrived in Chicago to speak in behalf of female suffrage, Germany declared war on Russia. On August 3, as Bryan entrained for Washington from Chicago, Germany declared war on France. Before he arrived at his office on August 4, the German invasion of Belgium was begun. By midnight he had received word of Britain's entry into the war against Germany.

Woodrow Wilson, the following morning, virtually gasped that his Administration was "standing neutral." Bryan hurried back to his Cabinet labors with fervency and a gust of long-dormant improvisation. He turned again to his proposed peace covenants, which the Senate Foreign Relations Committee had somewhat belatedly approved in principle. In a frenzy of work, he returned to seeking endorsement by leaders or high officials of both belligerents and peaceful states. By September 15, 1914, he had secured ranking signatures from two leading powers already at war, Great Britain and France, and by nonbelligerent Spain and the New Republic of China.

The wholly unprecedented enterprise moved along, yet so did the war. On August 23, Japan declared war on Germany in keeping with the Anglo-Japanese Treaty on the Far East. On October 12, Bulgaria declared war on Serbia; three days later Britain, France, and Italy declared war on Bulgaria. On November 23, Turkey joined Germany and the other Central Powers. By then Bryan had gained signatures for his "scheme" from thirty countries, including all the principal powers except Japan, Germany, and Austria-Hungary.

Surprising his political foes and friends alike, Bryan, the partisan pacifist, became Bryan the would-be neutralist. By September 1914, if not before, he was clearly aware that while Germany was winning militarily, Britain was winning the no less crucial war of propaganda. Himself no small potato as a propagandist, Bryan was profoundly impressed by Britain's deluge of propaganda and by her ruthless disregard of treaty documents and related interpower agreements.

More clearly than any other ranking member of the Wilson administration, too, he was cogently aware of trade factors. U.S. trade with belligerents was catapulting, and inevitably "war trade" was "war aid." And there was only one formally established classifier of war aid. That was the Declaration of London or the London Pact, an instrument of agreement subscribed to by sixteen powers.

Now Great Britain declined to abide even "extra-officially" by what it termed the "obsolescent text" of the London Pact. British spokesmen pointed out that the materiel of war inevitably change. For example, petroleum, which the pact did not even include, was now a primary military need. Accordingly, His Majesty's Government would add petroleum to the contraband list, and along with it some eight hundred other commodities formerly regarded as "nonmilitary."

Germany and her allies continued to profess willingness to abide by both the "moral principles" and the *ipso facto* terms of the pact. Britain's moves to establish sea blockades accentuated the issue; Germany's inevitable opening of a submarine blockade of Britain would shortly make it crucial. Refusing to deal with or through the State Department, British Ambassador Sir Cecil Spring-Rice went directly to the President. Shaken and angered, Bryan also found his interviews with the German ambassador most upsetting. Even as one of Bryan's best ambassador friends, Count von Bernstorff insisted that the Kaiser's War Ministry would have no choice other than to meet Britain's surface blockade with submarine warfare.

Bryan read multiplying reports of British violations of basic neutrality stipulations. British merchant ships were flying the Stars and Stripes: British port officials were illegally holding U.S. merchantmen in British ports while effecting the forcible purchase of desired cargoes. Bryan's protests were of no avail.

In London, Wilson's Colonel House and Ambassador Hay were busily negotiating without Bryan's knowledge, consent, or advice. Woodrow Wilson spoke of Britain and her allies as "standing with back to wall fighting wild beasts." When British naval craft began halting and searching the cargo ships of neutral nations, including the United States, the Anglophilic President remained oddly silent. But his Cabinet did not. Attorney General Thomas Gregory Wilson, for one, pointed out that the British actions, as they clearly emerged early in 1915, were close to being identical with those that had brought on the War of 1812. Bryan privately agreed. He protested when prominent city dailies branded him "pro-German" merely because in line of duty he continued to deal with official representatives of Germany, which at that point was at least demonstrating good faith regarding neutrality agreements.

In any case, as many saw it, at long last, Bryan was fully into his work as Secretary of State. It was remorselessly difficult. As 1914 neared its beclouded ending, German Ambassador von Bernstorff, as he had foreseen, was directed to point out that what Wilson had been calling "the American policy of strict accountability" was being applied only to Germany and her allies. When the President bristled, Bryan's unhappiness deepened. While granting that true neutrality is a "spiritual and moral attainment," he insisted that the United States could—and as a life-saving and soul-saving responsibility should—avoid participation in this most catastrophic of wars. On this basis Bryan worked as he had never worked before. Night after night he sat alone in his madly disordered office, with piles of papers spilling freely from his desk onto the worn red carpet. He had his favorite black sofa installed so that he could save the time otherwise required for going home and thereby "meeting himself coming back to work." He canceled most of his social engagements and rejected all speaking invitations. He bemoaned his wife's failing health without mentioning that his own was sagging. His daughter

Grace, a frequent visitor, observed that her father's hair seemed to be falling out by the handful and that every Sunday he looked a year older than he had the Sunday before.

On April 30, 1915, Woodrow Wilson dispatched to the Imperial German Government an especially angry letter protesting its "submarine offensive." On the same day a British-registered ship, the S.S. *Lusitania,* officially listed as an auxiliary cruiser of the Royal British Navy, sailed out of New York. The ship was carrying substantial quantities of ammunition and other war materiel. The German consul general in New York had posted warnings to passengers, crewmen, and others that the *Lusitania* was carrying contraband and accordingly was subject to submarine blockade action. On May 7 the *Lusitania* was torpedoed and sunk in the Irish Sea. The casualties included 124 passengers who were American citizens. As a whole the American press and news services reported the tragedy with much heat and few facts. From London, Special Presidential Assistant House, the peculiarly war-prone "peace emissary," predicted war between the United States and Germany within a month. British propaganda efforts were catapulted.

Bryan worked in a frenzy to mend the breakage. He cried out that House's statement was reckless, that American entry into the war was not inevitable. At the Cabinet meeting of May 9 he pleaded for forbearance and the shaping of a stand that would allow time for reasoning, and arbitration, preferably by a "high-level peace parley." The Cabinet listened tolerantly. The President again denounced the *Lusitania* "act."

Next, the German government asked for a clarification of Wilson's letter protesting the *Lusitania* sinking. The President replied with a virtual demand that Germany abandon submarine warfare, which was not counterbalanced with comparable demands on Britain and her allies. Again Bryan pointed out that the Wilson administration was violating its own definition of neutrality. At the next Cabinet meeting he pleaded even more heatedly for a "less partial view" of the belligerents; perhaps feverishly, he charged that "certain members" of the Cabinet were showing themselves to be unreasonably "pro-Allies." The President interrupted sharply: "Mr. Bryan, you are not warranted in making that assertion. We all doubtless have our own opinions in the matter, but there are none of us who can be justly accused of being unfair."

Bryan apologized, but his words implied his acceptance that the President and a majority of the Cabinet were against peace. Next, the President drafted a letter in the tones of an ultimatum to Berlin and dispatched it to Bryan for his signature. Bryan hesitated, then asked that the President redraft the letter to the end of making it more "moderate." Wilson flatly refused. Alone in his cluttered office, Bryan decided that he could not and would not sign the latest letter as it was written. Early the next morning, McAdoo called to make an appeal for "calmness." The President's son-in-law stated that he personally believed that for Bryan to "willfully drop out" (of the Cabinet) would be most unfortunate. But he could not hold out any promise that the President would "soften" the ultimatum.

The following Monday dawned hot and steamy in Washington. Bryan was feeling the heat and other discomforts. He had walked to his office early, but left by mid-afternoon. He made no explanation, but merely settled himself on the living room settee. Grace was again visiting her parents, concerned about them, particularly her father. The observant twenty-four-year-old had noted that Bryan stumbled on entering the living room, that his face was flushed, and that his eyes "looked feverish." She was certain that her father was not heeding his own health.

Less than a month before, Dr. Kelley had favored Mamie with another of his concise explanations of the condition called diabetes. He had repeated that for many adults, particularly those previously blessed with robust health, the onset of this disease of the pancreas system is frequently gradual. But unless it could be checked, even the strongest adult was not likely to endure it for more than ten years. Dr. Kelley had been reading of researches in Germany and Austria, and he was following Frederick Banting's more recent Canadian studies of the pancreal systems of animals. But the development of a pancreas "extract" suitable for treating human diabetes was not yet assured. Thus Dr. Kelley could only beseech that Bryan keep closely to his minimum-sugar, low-carbohydrate diet. He had repeated that Mrs. Bryan should not be unduly alarmed by commonplace emotional symptoms such as tenseness, despondency, and intermittent restlessness.

Although Grace tried to direct the conversation to more pleasant subjects, Bryan, still collapsed on the sofa, would speak only of his disagreement with the President. He was certain that Woodrow Wilson and he were at the parting of their ways. He repeated resignedly, "The President does not seem to realize that a great part of America lies on the other side of the Allegheny Mountains. . . ."

Grace Hargreaves saw in this a restatement of her father's belief that the best hope for keeping his country out of war also waited west of the Alleghenies. Bryan still held that the "sentiments" for peace were stronger outside of the industrialized East. She readily pieced together his resolve to quit the war-prone Cabinet and launch his own special peace crusade in what he regarded as his own homeland "so that Europe's tired earth might not be drenched with young American blood."

Later that afternoon Bryan wrote out a letter of resignation. Its gist was contained in a typically overlength sentence:

> Obedient to your sense of duty and activated by the highest motives, you have prepared for transmission to the German Government a note in which I cannot join without violating what I deem to be an obligation

27. Bryan's younger brother Charles, shown minding the store at *The Commoner* while WJB makes an extended speaking tour.

28. Bryan at the height of his career as Secretary of State in 1913.

29. The Bryan Peace Treaty being signed by its subscribers—Britain, France, China, and Spain—as the storm breaks in mid-September 1914.

30. Bryan at the angle of repose, on a train to Tillamook, Oregon, 1919.

31. From speaker to sermonizer: Bryan listens to a fundamentalist sermon of his being broadcast on the radio, 1922.

32. Remembrance of things past: Bryan and his wife at their last Democratic Convention, 1920.

33. July 1925—Darrow and Bryan; the famous Scopes Trial.

34. Bryan, two hours before his death, posed for a Dayton paper.

to my country, and the issue involved is of such moment that to remain a member of the Cabinet would be as unfair to you as it would be to the cause which is nearest to my heart, the prevention of war.

Bryan dated the letter the following day, but he did not revise the text. He showed the script to his wife. Mamie did not approve. Grace weighed her mother's reasons for being so deeply disturbed. Mamie Bryan was losing her health, her figure, and her easy smile, but she had not lost her ambition. She wished to remain the first lady of the State Department, and as a realist she knew that, however demanding the chores she had assumed, life could be harder out of "high office" than in. At the dinner table Bryan repeated that he had made his final decision. Mamie abruptly pushed back her chair.

Quietly leaving the dinner table, [Grace recorded], she went to her room and locking herself in, she refused admittance to everyone. For the only time in her life she gave way to loud hysterical sobbing.

But Bryan did not yield. Next morning he again walked alone to his office. At ten, the hour for the scheduled Cabinet meeting, he placed his letter of resignation in a plain white envelope and dispatched it by messenger to the President. He enclosed a scrawled memorandum that he would attend the meeting, his last, if asked to. Woodrow Wilson asked that he attend.

Bryan walked in and took his chair to the President's right. He was gray-pale and tired, and he said almost nothing. When the meeting adjourned, he invited fellow Cabinet members to join him for lunch at the University Club. In the dining room he peered thoughtfully at the six who chose to be his guests. They were Interior's Franklin K. Lane, Navy's Josephus Daniels, Postmaster General Albert

S. Burleson, War's Lindley M. Garrison, Labor's William B. Wilson, and Agriculture's David F. Houston. Speaking slowly, Bryan explained at length, and repetitiously, his reasons for resigning. At this very hour the President was drafting a reply to Bryan's letter.

> . . . I accept your resignation only because you insist on its acceptance. . . . I yield to your desire only because I must and wish to bid you God's-speed in the parting. We shall continue to work for the same causes even when we do not work in the same way . . .

With almost desperate attention to detail, Bryan completed his soliloquy. Josephus Daniels noted that in all his years he had never seen him so deeply moved. He reflected, too, that Bryan had entered the Cabinet a young fifty-three; he was leaving an old fifty-five. Franklin K. Lane was deeply touched. His voice faltered when he addressed his host: "You are the most real Christian I know." Tears rolled down Bryan's cheeks; his voice wavered. "I go out into the dark," he said. "The President has the prestige and power on his side. But I have many friends who would die for me."

At this point and perhaps without lapsing too far into what Bryan occasionally termed the "officious," one might be permitted to insert a brief, pondering, and, no doubt, oversimplified summation:

Bryan was for peace; throughout his conscious lifetime he had openly supported the fundamental conviction that peace is God's will and right, that war is ungodly and wrong. As a public official he had remained lacking specific, comprehensive answers for how peace is to be maintained. The Bryan "treaty" concept of sustaining peace by means of quasi-official good-faith agreements between sovereign nations had depended on the bona fide establishment and the cooperative enforcement of cooling-off periods for permitting arbitration or negotiations.

During his tenure as Secretary of State, fate and the prevailing temper of many nations, particularly those of Europe, had veered ever farther from the effective pragmatics of conciliation. The appalling European war had flared calamitously and, at least if adjudged superficially, with explosive abruptness. Meanwhile neither the Wilson Administration nor its predecessors nor any majority party had contributed effectively toward making the government of the United States truly competent to survive and serve as a peace-effecting neutral power.

Neutrality, of course, is a most exacting and sophisticated political and diplomatic science. Quite regardless of their intentions, in substantial part good, the American nation and government were not adequately educated and skilled in that science. Yet however valiantly, and personally, he had labored and pled for peace, Bryan had not succeeded in contributing adequately in terms of war preventives. Even as the first officer of the Cabinet he had neither adequately appraised nor sufficiently respected his nation's slate of reasons for moving into the war as one of the combatant Allies.

Granted, as one could hardly avoid doing, that the total of these motivations was almost as varied and contrasting as the United States itself, several were widely prevailing and outstanding. These included the lusty survival of the frontiersman's environment-prompted love of a big, rough, bloodying brawl and, close behind it, the greedy exploiter's lust for war profits, as already demonstrated by military-industrial complexes in Europe. There was also the persisting urge of the American to view himself, his government, and his country generally as the world's absolute and permanent best, and therefore deserving of being abjectly imitated by every other nation or body politic in existence. There were also the more noble motivations: Many, potentially a majority, of Americans were already on their way toward believing ever so sincerely that joining the Allies would be a move toward protecting the weak, saving democracy, and winning a war to end wars.

As a career advocate and exploiter of the great reality of American compassion, Bryan next elected to carry his own plea for peace *per se,* rather than the development of neutrality as an instrumentation for peace, directly to the American people. Even while he labored to clean up his office, Chautauqua manager and booking agent extraordinary Charles Horner arrived with the assurance that lecture fees totaling no less than $150,000 were awaiting him. Bryan answered that his primary interest was in facing the most influential audiences possible. He insisted that peace, not personal wealth, was his goal.

He opened his ambitious crusade with a one-night stand. On the evening of July 19 he was principal speaker for a "Labor Convene" at Carnegie Hall, New York. His address was an eloquent though rambling sermon stressing that the United States was in a God-given position to benefit all the world as keeper of the peace. He emphasized that war is profoundly hurtful to labor; it leads to the loss of legitimate jobs, the removal of prime workers to destructive military service, and subjugation to the cynical, ever-greedy merchants of death. The house was packed with union leaders; the sermon was received cordially.

His next effort, on June 25, found Madison Square Garden a sellout, with an estimated fifty thousand people turned away. The subject was "National Honor." Even the Bryan-critical New York *World* agreed that the Great Commoner was back in his old stride with "the flashing eye and passionate gestures and the ringing voice of Bryan of fifteen years ago." The "applause came in roars, deep chested and sincere."

From New York the crusader began working his way west to houses that were invariably full to overflowing. Before June ended, he had created a record traffic jam in downtown Lincoln, speaking from the balcony of the

Lindell Hotel. His little-changed theme was "The farmer's Interest in Peace." He reiterated that the grief of war would inevitably fall principally on the 80 percent of Americans who most emphatically did not want war. The United States was being herded toward slaughter by a minority of unscrupulous and self-guaranteed noncombatants. The American farmer, particularly the western farmer, knew ever so well that war means huge and undeserved wealth for the conscienceless few; and poverty, anguish, and death for the well-intentioned many.

William Jennings Bryan was no paragon of an internationalist; he was an American spokesman empowered only by listening American crowds. And, again, a fundamental believer who agreed that God meant what He said when He commanded: "Thou shalt not kill."

From Nebraska Bryan moved to the Pacific Coast. At the San Francisco International Exposition he attracted an audience reported as more than one hundred thousand. In downstate California he drew crowds of at least fifty thousand, and his campaign-style tour of Washington and Oregon was enormously successful. For his return to Lincoln he hired a platform car and delivered gratis speeches at train stops. From Lincoln he pushed on into the Middle West.

It was rough, hard trouping, but at least for the time being the crusader was regaining his health while extending his reach of popularity. Rumors spread that Bryan would shortly carry his one-man crusade for peace to England and quite possibly to Italy and Germany. Wilson's Colonel House was fearful that the maverick former Secretary would come swinging into the Court of St. James's. Without revealing long-range plans, Bryan continued playing to home audiences, moving on through sun, rain, and entangled train connections to evangelize the unfailing crowds. The Council of Churches of Christ in America urged him to carry his peace mission abroad. Others seconded. By November Henry Ford was urging the uncommon Commoner to join his widely publicized "Peace Ship." Bryan advised the industrialist that his more instant obligation was to oppose greedy schemes for launching a public-expense preparedness binge within the United States.

He called on the Congress to enact a law prohibiting ships of any belligerent nation from leaving American ports with American citizens as passengers. As the year neared its end, Woodrow Wilson renewed the ardor of his protests against submarine warfare, meanwhile seeking to muffle Bryan's contention that surprisingly few American lives had been lost at sea and that Germany was keeping her promise to refrain from sinking passenger liners without warning.

Bryan's exhortations for federal legislation to discourage Britain's use of U.S. citizens "as shields for the haulage of war materiel" were heard in Congress. Bills and resolutions to prohibit the issuing or visaing of U.S. passports for travel on any belligerent's ship reportedly caused the President deep concern; he confided that if permitted to continue, this kind of thing would presently find Bryan as a private citizen controlling the Congress from without.

When Wilson again blasted the Kaiser's War Ministry with a still more grim warning to abandon submarine warfare or face the ultimate severing of diplomatic relations with the United States, Bryan moved on Washington as a lobbyist. But for reasons of his own he turned about in midstride and made a week-long sixty-speech tour of Ohio to plead the cause of statewide prohibition there. An estimated quarter-million Ohioans crowded in to hear his arguments and to see and hear his experiment of converting his speaker's stands to open forums where listeners could state their own views. Then, back on the Chautauqua circuit, he turned his artillery on the growing urge to build up the Army and Navy. His thesis was that by its very nature "preparedness," which he derisively mispronounced "scaredness," provokes war.

Late in January 1916, the President set out on a trainside speaking tour from New York to Topeka. His theme was less than subtly an answer to Bryan's. He would stand for protecting the nation's honor by means of "peace with honor." Bryan responded. What accounted for the President's abrupt and mystifying change of position? With an old trouper's skill, he began crisscrossing the President's itinerary. When Wilson returned to Washington to face a distinctly aloof Congress, Bryan went west again and resumed his efforts with the farming populace. He kept on demanding to know if "militarism" was forsworn to "wholly devour" the American farm.

From all appearances Bryan was gambling that Wilson could not effect a preparedness program without the support of western congressmen. Confirmation was forthcoming when the President abruptly abandoned his intitial move to build up the Army. The retreat cost him the resignation of his Secretary of War, and Bryan, meanwhile, continued to point out that "preparedness" was already costing the nation almost as much as public education. He further flayed the Wall Street "conspiracy" to build up the Army to the end of using troops to break legitimate strikes.

As the long winter of words ended, the breath of war was nevertheless being felt throughout most of the nation. This accentuated the crusading effectiveness of William Jennings Bryan. Among farmers, laborers, shopkeepers, schoolteachers, and millions of other sons and daughters of everyday, the Bryan evangelism was unquestionably striking very deeply. By mid-March Bryan was back again to advocating prohibition. For this there were several discernible political motives. Back in Nebraska the primary elections were being stirred or, as some said, befouled by a statewide prohibition referendum. Bryan had already decided to enter the primary as a candidate for Nebraska's delegate-at-large to the Democratic national convention to be held in St. Louis the following June. While announcing his candidacy for public election as a convention delegate he opened a one-man crusade to "dry up" Nebraska without aid from the formally organized National Prohibition party.

Brother Charlie joined him as a candidate, for the Democratic nomination for the governorship. With his famous brother at his side, Charlie was assured an abundance of listeners. Nebraska voted "dry" the following November, but here in May the Bryan brothers lost. Democratic headquarters at Omaha, flush with patronage, fought them tooth and claw, branding the more famous brother a deserter of his party and President. Although the crusader again fared well in most of the central and western counties, he lost in Omaha and the other larger towns.

Without a pause, Bryan returned to his interstate campaign for peace. Again people gathered to listen, and once more the politicians in Washington heard.

John Dewey came forward from the academic shades to question Bryan's opposition to "force." In the language of the Vermonter, who was incubating a "new American philosophy," Dewey confronted Bryan's much-quoted arguments against war by differentiating, Vermont country-store style, between "force" and "violence." Force, so John pointed out, is "amoral"; of itself it is not an ethical phenomenon. Violence, on the other hand, is the destructive expenditure of force. War, in great part an institution of violence, therefore dissipates the necessary resource of force. Even so, mere squeamishness about the use of force is not really "idealism"; rather it is "moonstruck morals." And, therefore, war in support of "a constructive objective" is simply another employment of force and as such is not necessarily immoral. Bryan, with his own inexhaustible supply of semantics, could not have been less impressed.

Without the assistance of John Dewey, Dr. Lawrence Powell of Harvard and former President William Howard Taft became leaders in the founding in Philadelphia of what they called the League to Enforce Peace. True to its name, the League proposed the intelligent use of force for keeping peace instead of fighting wars. To that end it projected a "universal" league of nations with members pledged to submit disputes and grievances to arbitration or negotiation by a court of its own. It would use economic or military force as required to assure the compliance of any "uncooperative" member. Excepting only the latter proposal, this league was substantially a revival of the Bryan concept of an international agreement for inquiry into and arbitration of potential causes of war.

While saluting the Powell-Taft proposal, Bryan insisted that peace is essentially rooted in man's love and compassion for his fellows. He still could and did favor a worldwide league of nations, but he held that the special mission of the United States was to lead and inspire from a secure footing of national peace. He continued to insist that "peace" and "faith" are essentially the same.

Meanwhile, in a mood of happy homecoming, the crusader shifted back to his beloved Chautauqua circuit. His energy and platform presence never once faltered, even when, as on a night in Nebraska a chill autumn rain bellied down the tent top and broke a canvas seam. Barrelfuls of cold water came splashing down on the platform. Bryan paused only to mop his bespattered head and laughed heartily when his daughter Ruth, who was seated on the platform, said, "This is the first time Bryan ever spoke from a wet platform." And again, during a hot afternoon tent stand in Blue Water, Kansas, a straying steer made its way through the front entrance. Taken with alarm, the invader panicked and came charging loudly down the center aisle. Bryan looked up from an oratorical climax to welcome the newcomer: "As I live and breathe," he said, "my old friend, Theodore Roosevelt!"

If 1916 proved itself one of his most valiant and fame-building years, it was not among his happiest. His wife's worsening health was his heaviest concern. Now almost paralyzed by arthritis, "Mama" was no longer able to sit proudly among his listeners. She did cheer from afar, by mail.

Since Dr. Tom Kelley gave time in the Florida sun as the best prescription he could offer Mamie, Bryan found time to take her on a visiting tour of the Sunshine State, from Jacksonville to Miami. There the crusader paused long enough to yield to the persuasiveness of a team of real estate salesmen. Before he left he had purchased a home site and twenty acres of near-suburbs of Greater Miami. He also yielded once more to his cherished illusion of being an architect. The newest Bryan "estate" would be in the general shape of a shoebox, with three sun-porches, a gently sloping red tile roof, and a study, with fortresslike entrance arches built of cement. Mamie and Grace agreed that this was the least ugly of the Byran home designs as first incubated. They were less inclined to praise the name he chose, "Villa Serena"—there simply had to be a better designation than that. "We'll compromise," said the family head. They named it Villa Serena.

Shortly thereafter and in much the same compromising mood (since he was not even a delegate), Bryan turned to the oncoming national convention of his party. But the rumors that he would oppose the renomination of Woodrow Wilson were groundless. Bryan was well aware that the election would be perilously close even without changing the candidate, and that any additional splitting of the Democratic party would almost certainly give the victory to the Republicans, particularly with the engaging Charles Evans Hughes as the opposing nominee. When Bryan called on Wilson to run openly on a peace program, the President announced that he proposed to do exactly that.

When another June came, Bryan resumed his role as expert reporter of conventions. Still editor-in-chief of *The Commoner,* he described the Republican convention as a comedy, and the Progressive or Bull Moose convention as a tragedy. Meanwhile, he looked on alertly while the Democrats poured into St. Louis for the June 14 opening of what some ink-stained wretches were billing as the W.W. Admiration and Self-Advancement Society of Greater New

Jersey. But it would not be precisely that. The keynote speaker, former Governor Martin H. Glynn of New York, voluntarily cleared the text of his speech with Bryan.

The keynote address as readied began with a scholarly summation of previous American successes at keeping out of wars. As the keynoter in St. Louis was proclaiming that the convention that would renominate Wilson was for peace —not "preparedness," the President himself was leading a "preparedness" parade on Washington's Pennsylvania Avenue. When one of the President's handymen, Senator John Smith of Maryland, slipped to the platform and handed Glynn a note requesting that he insert, "but we are willing to fight if necessary," the New Yorker only smiled and resumed his slashing attack on warmongers. He climaxed with a Bryanlike gust: "Our policy will *not* please the fire eaters or the revellers in despair; but it will satisfy those who worship at the altar of a peace-commanding God. . . ."

Bryan joined lustily in the applause, quite certain that "the small still voices of the real people" were still being heard. Next day Chairman Ollie James of Kentucky delivered a party commitment that was no less Bryanlike. So many delegates and visitors recognized this that hundreds of voices began shouting, "Bryan, Bryan, Bryan!" The chairman introduced, to more applause, "a great world citizen and Democrat." Once more Bryan hurried to the platform, long-striding and smiling, to exhort his party to continue to lead the nation in peace, shrewdly indicating his awareness that the convention, though for Wilson, was *with* Bryan.

Within the month, Bryan was asked by the National Committee to serve as "key campaigner" for the entire West along with Pennsylvania, Kentucky, and Tennessee— twenty states in all. He accepted, knowing full well that fifteen of the twenty were listed as "Republican probables."

Bryan shaped his campaigning as a super-crusade for peace. Before September ended, western Democrats were pelting the National Committee with praise of his efforts; Democratic headquarters were listing him as indispensable to the chances for a Wilson victory, which most forecasters held would be razor-edge thin. Meanwhile, Bryan was making five public appearances daily, and according to on-the-scene correspondent David Lawrence, was drawing far bigger crowds and much more enthusiastic applause than either of the presidential candidates. When Woodrow Wilson openly stated his appreciation, Bryan responded with the forecast that Wilson would be re-elected by the West and South. Unexpectedly, the militantly anti-Bryan Chicago *Tribune* saw fit to agree. The largest Republican paper hailed Bryan as the "most powerful single individual in the United States. . . . He has permeated the West. His mood is the mood of the West. He is more responsible for President Wilson now than he was four years ago. . . ." On election day, fifteen of the twenty "probable Republican" states went Democratic.

Following a mankiller of a western finale, Bryan made his way back to Washington where an endless round of lunches and dinners waited him. Democratic congressmen were his principal hosts, and at the Lafayette Hotel he agreed to pose for newspaper photographers with his newest granddaughter. As the tripod cameras were set up, Bryan fed the baby from a bottle, then as the cameras clicked, the baby's smile changed to a mighty, milk-gushing burp.

When Congress reconvened on December 5, Bryan was on hand to receive a cordial honored-guest's welcome from the Speaker of the House. Within a week the Kaiser's desire for an armistice was reported responsibly from Berlin. Within another week (on December 18) Wilson dispatched letters to all the principal belligerents asking their respective terms or suggestions for ending hostilities. Bryan warmly congratulated the President. A month later Wilson appeared in person before the Senate to propose a "definite concert of powers" for guarding against future wars and, more immediately, the issuing of a call for a cessation of combat without a "finalized victory." Bryan listed that as Wilson's greatest "stroke."

On the side Bryan unquestionably began to make plans for organizing and leading his own peace mission to Europe. He wrote to the wealthy U.S. ambassador to Germany, James W. Girard, asking his good offices in setting up appointments with responsible officials of the German War Ministry and, if possible, with the Kaiser. Girard tattled to Wilson, who cooled abruptly and confided to his emissary, Colonel House, that he gathered "mischief was brewing Commonwards."

As usual, Bryan was persistent. He next appealed by letter to Britain's Prime Minister, David Lloyd George, for aid in seeking his government's consent to negotiations. Apparently Lloyd George did not answer, but other leaders of states did. By the year's end Bryan was prepared to resume his pleas for peace by seeking still larger and more opinion-molding American audiences. As an opener he received and accepted invitations to address the legislatures of Ohio, Indiana, Missouri, Tennessee, and North Carolina.

Then, for reasons he could only sense vaguely, he felt that the hopes for peace were beginning to dim. On arrival in New York for a February 3, 1917 address at Madison Square Garden, he saw headlines declaiming that Germany was renewing unrestricted submarine warfare. Quickly revising his text, the crusader delivered a ringing reminder that more than ever before the United States was responsible before God for exercise of Christian forbearance. He pleaded anew for an armistice by mediation. He then headed for Washington; on arriving at Union Station he saw new headlines: The United States had severed diplomatic relations with Germany. At the Senate Office Building a veteran Progressive agreed to join in a joint effort at renewed persuasion. Bryan would canvass the membership of the House; LaFollette, the Senate. Together they vowed that the nation would not be stampeded into war.

After a frenzied two weeks of man-to-congressman persuading, Bryan assembled and had published a brochure entitled, "An Appeal to the American People." It was an updated summation of all the Bryan peace proposals. The text included a fervent appeal for readers to write, telegraph, or, better still, call directly on their congressmen to remind them that the United States was being shoved into war and that Congress alone has authority to declare war.

As usual, the Bryan prose was far less effective than his spoken words. The public response was disappointing. For the most part the principal Eastern newspapers either overlooked the effort or commented unfavorably. The congressional responses ranged from ardently in favor to abusively opposed. In particular, Republican House members Augustus Gardner of Massachusetts and Clarence Miller of Minnesota joined in one of the most vituperative attacks ever recorded in the *Congressional Record,* branding Bryan a coward, a fraud, and a scoundrel.

But Bryan stood his ground, still confident that Congress would not vote the nation into war without an "overt act." After recovering from what he noted merely as a brief illness, he set out for Florida to spend a weekend with his wife. On February 27 he arrived in Jacksonville, where Mamie, accompanied by a nurse, waited at the railroad station. Mamie handed Will a late newspaper that told of Wilson's going earlier that day to Congress for authority to arm U.S. merchant ships and for, as the President put it, "instrumentalities or methods that may be necessary to protect our ships and our people." Without leaving the railroad station, Bryan began dispatching telegrams to the sixty-three members of the Congress he felt he could count on to oppose the President's move. That done, he said good-bye to his wife and returned to Washington, where the Wilson-dictated Armed Ship Bill was being introduced simultaneously in both Houses.

Outside the Capitol a group that called itself the Emergency Peace Federation waited to greet the tired and disheveled crusader. Among others, Bryan recognized Max

Eastman, Lillian Wald, Amos Pinchot, and Jane Addams. He greeted these unexpected cohorts warmly and returned to what he termed coat-lapel persuasion of congressmen. He was more grateful than surprised when Senators La Follette of Wisconsin and Norris of Nebraska teamed up to "question" the Armed Ship Bill on the Senate floor. When they finished, the "hot and angry" bill was neither hot nor angry; it was dead.

Immensely encouraged, Bryan again set forth as a peace-preaching circuit rider, returning directly to Carnegie Hall in New York, where he heard himself introduced as the American Tolstoy. Restored, he pushed on to Detroit, then Chicago, then hurriedly returned to Washington and first-hand lobbying. As March drew to a close, he wrote and dispatched a fervent and rather lengthy peace plea to each member of Congress. The open letter began with: "To you and only you is given the Constitutional authority to declare war." It reiterated the fact that the United States was not even remotely threatened with invsasion:

> . . . We are asked to go three thousand miles for a chance to fight. . . . I plead with you to use all honorable means to preserve peace before you take the responsibility of plunging our beloved land into this unprecedented struggle, begun without any sufficient cause.

With Washington as combat headquarters, Bryan resumed his rapid sorties at winning audiences. He reviewed his own position regarding peace and war; now, as a God-fearing believer in the fundamental rightness of peace, he was wholly certain that this war could be avoided by the United States. When April came again he returned to Miami for another reunion with his wife. As usual the couple could not be alone. Visitors were awaiting his arrival, and others kept dropping in. In his short time at home

Bryan decided to center his forthcoming appearances in the Deep South.

He was still in Miami on April 6 when word came that Congress had declared war against Germany. As he had done nineteen years before, Bryan promptly dispatched a telegram to the President of the United States, offering his services in any capacity desired:

> Believing it to be the duty of a citizen to bear his part of the burdens of war and his share of its perils, I hereby tender my services to the Government. Please enroll me as a private whenever I am needed and assign me to any work I can do. Until called to the colors, I shall through the Red Cross contribute to the comfort of the soldiers in the hospitals and, through the Y.M.C.A., aid in safeguarding the morals of the men in camp.

From Miami Bryan took the train for Auburn, Georgia, to fill a committed lecture engagement. There he told his audience that he would have gladly and thankfully given his life to save his country from entering the war, but now that his country was in the war he would most willingly give his life to aid it. The words were typically youthful, but the voice was tired and old.

20. The Patriot

At fifty-seven Bryan's chances for enlisting as a private were nil. None of the armed services could accept enlisted personnel of that age; the materializing draft legislation would name twenty-eight as the maximum age. Even the political maneuverings for the commissioning of officers rarely reached above forty-five. Apparently aware of this, Bryan followed his telegram to the President with a letter to the Secretary of the Navy, explaining that he was aware of being too old to "learn the art of war," but not too old to be helpful.

Josephus Daniels agreed cordially. At the White House the following week, Woodrow Wilson received his former Secretary of State, warmly by Wilsonian standards. As he walked out of the White House, Bryan assured a New York *Times* reporter that the nation now had no time or place for "dissension or division," and that in wartime the President "necessarily speaks for the country."

This and similar summations were well received by the press. The Washington *Post* observed that the War Department was receiving plenty of offers from self-confessed distinguished citizens who would condescend to accept commissions ranging from field marshal down to mere general, but only Bryan had shown willingness to enlist as a private. The Milwaukee *News* echoed that the nation breathlessly awaited the rush to recruiting stations by "jingo editors, war-shouting politicians, ultra-bellicose statesmen and other pseudo-patriots," adding, "Don't crowd, gentlemen!"

The President, of course, could have recommissioned his political benefactor an Army colonel or even a brigadier general on precedence of Spanish-American War service, or made him head of any one of the mushrooming multitudes of special boards and commissions. Instead, W.W. encouraged him to keep with his lecturing, writing, and publishing in support of the "war effort"; and, as Bryan reasonably assumed, of the peace effort to follow. Secretary of Agriculture Houston eagerly offered to enlist Bryan as a special advocate of that Department's already shaping drive to increase and conserve food supplies. Treasury Secretary McAdoo was delighted to welcome him as a master salesman extraordinary of the oncoming deluges of "Liberty bonds." Interior's Franklin K. Lane, whose affection for the Commoner had never diminished, volunteered, as he put it, to be his special welcomer home. Meanwhile, Charles Horner and the refurbished Redpath Lyceum and Chautauqua Bureau were brandishing dozens and presently hundreds of lecture offers.

The ensuing bookings ranged from a cow pasture tent stand in Blue Water, Kansas, to "grand solos" in New York's Madison Square Garden. The fan mail that followed reached a new highmark in laudation. A fairly typical response was written by H. M. Johnson of Shreveport, whose letterhead read "JUST AN HONEST WELL DIGGER."

> . . . Bryan was coming to town . . . and the heart of Shreveport began to rejoice. . . . The speaker's

platform had been erected in the beautiful courthouse square. . . . Bryan was worth looking at. . . . [and] There was a most enthusiastic demonstration when he came up on the stand. When he began to warm up in his argument, and his musical voice would ring out over the vast sea of upturned faces, I shall never forget the scene. . . .

I stood near a big, broad-shouldered, six-footer from Texas. . . . He stood as straight as an arrow and still as death. He seemed afraid to move, lest he should miss a word. He held his big derby in both hands on a level with his breast, the open part down. Just in front of him stood a smaller man, hat off and very intent on hearing all [Bryan] said.

Mr. Bryan had just reached one of his wonderful high points. He stood like an Apollo, with his right hand clinched and raised aloft. As he finished the sentence he brought down his fist like a sledgehammer. And that is when the Texan did likewise with his big derby, bringing it down on top of the little man completely covering him almost down to the shoulders.

When the Texan realized what he had done, he jerked his derby up, and said to the short gentleman, "O, friend, I'm sorry, I beg your pardon a thousand times. I didn't know what I was doing."

The small man smiled up and said, "That's all right, partner . . . I didn't know what I was doing either."

To one audience after the next, Bryan recited his own newly coined adage: The only way to get out of a war is to get through it. But the most exceptional platform attraction was in no mood to function as just another war-happy spellbinder. He approved the Selective Draft Act, but insisted that the government was no less duty bound to conscript private money and properties as well as and along with men. "Why place the dollar above the man?

Why authorize still another rich man's war and a poor
man's fight?" He struck out at war profiteers. Again and
again he stressed that the only good thing about a war is
the peace to follow. He avoided Wilson's vagary, "Make
the World Safe for Democracy," with his own "Make the
World Safe for the People Who Live in It, Including Our
Foes."

On platforms as in print, the crusader insisted that when
peace was won, America would be restored to her pristine
loveliness, her ails and evils erased by the return of the
glorious sunshine of peace. God and the good American
people, mostly Democrats, naturally, would see to that.

The United States was a belligerent in the First World
War for a total of 679 days. During this time Bryan delivered a total of 852 public speeches. His platform appearances were approximately doubled in number by impromptu speeches—at food or war-bond rallies, at Army
posts, in circus tents, wagonyards and, most frequently, in
crowded public squares or parks.

Throughout the grinding months Bryan's health held
strong. His dread of colds was his one nagging worry, a
phobia that he compressed in an especially dreadful cou-
plet:

> If I should take cold in my hands and my feet
> I'd take pneumonia and die *toots sweet*.

His ability to function without lambasting such irksome
wartime phenomena as glib war profiteers, hate-exploiting
movies, such as "The Kaiser: Beast of Berlin," and
hate-spilling evangelism such as Billy Sunday spewed
(". . . Thou knowest, O Lord, that no nation so infamous,
vile, greedy, sensuous and bloodthirsty [as Germany] ever
disgraced the pages of history") was noteworthy.

Bryan avoided much that was shocking and disgusting.
He failed utterly, however, to accept that when the war

ended, the United States, including Bryan himself, would not be able to saunter home to the good old days. Similarly, he was wholly unable to accept that the millrun American, while winning a war, was losing the wondrous and no doubt partly apocryphal American resource of innocence.

But he was not blind to political expediencies. Among these was the advancement of the cause of national prohibition. When the United States formally entered the war, the dry forces were gaining conspicuously in at least thirty states. Other war talkers, including the unquenchable Theodore Roosevelt and the Administration's Food Administrator, Herbert C. Hoover, chorused the advocacy of prohibition as a boon to conserving grain supplies and improving military discipline and effectiveness. Bryan seized the opportunity to exhort that the Hoover-urged weekly wheatless and meatless days be supplemented by seven liquorless, wineless, and beerless days per week.

There was evidence on every side that, regardless of party in power or war in progress, a federal dry law and a Constitutional amendment sustaining it were forming; many were predicting that both would win enactment by 1920, if not before. The come-uppance of female suffrage was no less evident. Both issues were substantially bipartisan; by 1917, certainly, both were definable as grass-roots developments. Bryan neither denied nor openly affirmed this. On a personal basis, at least, he found both quite easy to take. Most of his life he had been surrounded by strong-willed women who frequently made decisions without formality of franchise. His view of liquor was hardly less fortuitous. As one raised among nondrinkers who piously viewed imbibing as a sin of the flesh, Bryan could and did bypass liquor with the greatest ease. He had never required tippling as a device for winning friends, or as a sedative or emotional stimulant; the applause and admiration of crowds were consistently adequate as lift-providers. He freely used the liquor issue as a political drum, and he blandly took credit that he did not deserve for the attention given to it.

This tranquil expediency was climaxed by his definitely bovine acceptance of the honorary presidency of a rough-and-ready amalgamation of twenty-eight antiliquor groups into the National Dry Federation. Certainly he was not surprised when the Armistice of November 11, 1918, turned out to be only sixty-nine days behind the final ratification of the Eighteenth (dry) Amendment to the U. S. Constitution.

Ten months before the Armistice, Bryan was hinting strongly for a presidential appointment to the peace commission that was so certainly forthcoming. When 1918 was barely a week old, Bryan wrote President Wilson:

> . . . Acting on the theory that I may be honored by a place on the peace commission . . . I am devoting all my time this winter to a study of European politics and the important treaties of the past century. . . .

That, of course, was a whopper of an exaggeration. Bryan was devoting most of that winter to speaking appearances, well above twenty per week. By April and the first anniversary of his country's formal entry into the war, Bryan was openly seeking the good offices of mutual friends of the President, including Secretaries Burleson and Daniels, and Senator Ollie May James of Kentucky, then chairman of the National Democratic Committee. None was of avail. Already the President had passed to his individualist assistant, Joseph Tumulty, Bryan's direct application for appointment to the peace commission; on it he had scrawled the notation:

> What *do* you think of this and what possible answer can I make, for, of course, the assumption he is acting on will never be realized. . . .

In a note marked "Personal and Confidential," the President similarly assured Josephus Daniels, who had strongly urged Bryan's appointment as a "crowning ambition and a well-earned reward," that though he, Wilson, felt cordially toward the Commoner, he could not grant his wish "because it would be unjustly taken for granted that he would be too easy and that he would pursue some Utopian [sic] scheme. . . ." Bryan, meanwhile, did not repress the confidence that he would rather be a successful peace maker than President.

When the Armistice of November 11, 1918, ignited celebrations throughout most of the areas of the inhabited earth, and practically all of the United States, Bryan took sanctuary in Miami. In a letter to his son he freely admitted feeling conscience-stricken about having been so long absent from his invalid wife. He also mentioned that he was waiting for an invitation to serve on the peace commission. He repeated that he would accept "even an advisory assignment," but he hoped that the President would see fit to provide him with a more effective "station."

An entire week passed without word from the White House. Meanwhile, the President had made known that he would attend an oncoming peace conference in Paris. On November 17 the White House announced that the liner *George Washington* had been chosen as official "peace ship," and would sail from New York the following December 4. In distress, Bryan renewed his quest of a place on the commission. Again Josephus Daniels was on the receiving end. The Secretary of Navy went directly to the President, reminding him that the incumbent Congress was strongly Republican, that preludes of "isolationism" were already audible in both Houses, and that Bryan was unquestionably in a position to favorably affect the indispensable Senate ratification of what Wilson had already named "the lasting peace covenant." The President took a new tack of negativeness. He said that his peace commission was already topheavy with Democrats; if he appointed Bryan he would be obliged to drop either House or Lansing, and he would not drop either.

Bryan continued to hope. Surely the President, this on-and-off student of treaties, would see the light. Up until the moment of the *George Washington*'s sailing, Bryan believed he would be included in the official manifest.

At noonday on December 4, the *George Washington*, loaded to her gunnels and bar rails with a rather multitudinous "presidential party," weighed anchor and yielded to tug. The passengers included an impressively long list of petty functionaries and favored henchmen, but no Bryan.

The most widely heeded American "authority" on treaties and agreements did not cry out. Instead, and taking pains to avoid public notice, he traveled back to Lincoln for a brief visit with his brother and *The Commoner*. Charlie expressed astonishment when Bryan arrived wearing a heavy, ankle-length overcoat with a fur comforter inside. Granting that the Nebraska winter was settling in, this just wasn't like Will, who used to prowl out in zero weather without benefit of a topcoat, or even so much as a suit jacket. Was something wrong? Was Will losing his built-in heating equipment? When the homecomer repeated candidly that he was in terror of pneumonia, Charlie expressed his doubt that the overweight horse blanket of an overcoat was helping. Charlie found himself wondering if this seemingly neurotic dread were in some way connected with his brother Will's diabetic condition.

On the second day of his visit Will received a telegram from his daughter that caused him to jump on a train for Baltimore. Mamie had taken a turn for the worse, and Grace and her husband had practically carried her to Johns Hopkins Hospital. When Bryan arrived he was gasping and wheezing with a heavy cold. Mamie, not without cause, was more concerned about his illness than her own. She insisted that he go immediately to Washington to see Dr. Kelley. For a change Bryan accepted her entreaty. He arrived at the capital, went to Dr. Kelley's office, then decided to stay at the home of his old friend, "Cotton" Bride.

As usual, Bride was delighted. "Honestly, it was very near to having God as my house guest," he declared, adding that he proposed to do his utmost to help his hero get well again. Bryan was seriously and painfully ill. Dr. Kelley saw no indication of pneumonia, but was concerned about the worsening of the diabetes. He made additional urine tests and prescribed a more restricted diet.

Two days later Bryan wrote his wife a baffling letter. He reported that he had had "an anxious night" because he was again panic-stricken by the belief that he had pneumonia. Was this a hypochrondriacal imagining? Or could it have been a pathological aftermath of what was almost certainly the deepest disappointment of his life—Wilson's refusal to let him attend the peace parley? Again Dr. Kelley found no trace of pneumonia, but he noted even more virulent symptoms. These included a skin inflammation of the face and neck, which Dr. Kelley diagnosed as facial erysipelas and listed as "neuro-systemic." He also noted intensive swelling of the feet and ankles, with gangrenelike discolorations. The physician continued to follow the extraction or other derivation of pancreas fluid from sheep and related research reported by Dr. Frederick Banting and colleagues in Montreal. Although there was still no immediate prospect of an insulin, Dr. Kelley was convinced that the Banting research was revealing many heretofore unknown facts or, as he said, correlations of and about diabetes. He was confident that more accurate dietary treatment would tend to relieve the erysipelas and the swelling of the feet and ankles.

Bryan endured almost unbearable pain, for the most part quite stoically. He welcomed his host's offer to read him the news of the peace conference. Unfortunately, excepting the almost delirious welcome of the American head of state, that news was far from encouraging. When Wilson announced that the Covenant of the League of Nations would be written into the text of the treaty document, the responses from Washington, particularly the U. S. Senate, were dour, and for the seriously ailing Bryan and many others, downright distressing.

The alleged "throat-ramming" tactics of the American President were adding to the already ominous Senate opposition. The astute opposition of Massachusetts' Henry Cabot Lodge was swiftly developing. The aristocrat of Greater Boston had already mustered a bloc of thirty-five opposing signatures; if tenable, this Round Robin alone could thwart the two-thirds majority required for the Senate ratification of the combined treaty and covenant.

David Lawrence, newly returned from Paris, called on Bryan and favored him with an on-the-scene account; Lawrence believed that with some fairly minor and surely attainable improvements the League Covenant could win Senate acceptance. With obvious difficulty Bryan wrote his brother, mentioning that he was "almost too weak to think," but nevertheless deeply concerned about the Wilson stumbles, as well as the distressingly extensive American opposition to the League of Nations; ". . . But I must wait till God gives me strength before I undertake anything in the way of leadership. . . ." He closed with, "Be patient with me. I have never felt so helpless before. . . ."

Charlie, who had never been other than patient with his brother, answered that he hoped and prayed that Will could regain and use his strength; "A Will Bryan push could very well get this wagon to rolling." Evidently, Will agreed. Before he could stand alone he released a statement strongly favoring the proposed League of Nations, which he defined as "a heroic step toward a just and lasting peace." The statement won wide press acceptance. Though still bedridden, Bryan promptly began planning a nationwide crusade in behalf of the League.

From that point on, his recovery was almost miraculous. The painful and purplish rash faded from his face and neck; the swelling and discoloration of his ankles and feet vanished. On April 3, as he set out for his "Pennsylvania crusade," photographs at a trainside press conference showed that he was almost thin. His hairline had retreated even further; his eyes seemed much larger than before and the extensive mouth seemed more determinedly diagonal. He stood less erect than before. Bryan lacked and would never entirely regain his long, strong stride, but his features seemed to have acquired a quality of gentleness. At fifty-nine he looked recognizably like his mother had looked at about that age.

Throughout April he followed speaking circuits in Pennsylvania, Michigan, and Missouri—three known centers of opposition to the League of Nations. Once more, large crowds turned out, though nobody could say how many came to learn of the League and how many for the thrill of hearing Bryan. But by the tens of thousands the people came and heard his exhortations for their support of the League and his bold forecast that the Senate would approve because the majority of Americans had already approved. Back in Washington he continued to recommend expedient changes in the League Covenant that could be made *after* ratification of the basic document. In May, when he rejoined Mamie in Florida, he brought the glad tidings that the original draft of the Covenant was being revised and, as he saw it, greatly bettered. He had not yet learned the dangerous truth that the President was beginning to refuse all subsequent suggestions for compromise of the League text.

As Bryan's health improved during his weeks of platform crusading, Mamie's grew worse. Again she was unable to dress herself and required around-the-clock nursing. Bryan tore himself away from the crowded Chautauqua circuit and took her for a recuperation tour of summer resorts in the North Carolina mountains. While they tarried on what Bryan called a real honeymoon thirty-five years delayed, Woodrow Wilson undertook his ill-fated trip across the nation to carry the League of Nations issue to the people.

The valiant play extended as far as Wichita, where the President was stricken with an illness that was not immediately described and would never be remedied.

When October came, the Bryans traveled together back to Nebraska, where both reveled in the prairie autumn. As the beautiful month ended, Bryan took Mamie to Miami, employed another nurse, and returned to Washington to resume persuasion of Democrats in the Senate. His best efforts were not good enough. On November 19 the United States Senate voted down both the Covenant and the total text of the League of Nations.

Bryan went forth again. This was not the time to give up, not that such an idea was conceivable in the canon of the Commoner.

21. The Classical Corn

As another decade and his sixtieth birthday came in view, Bryan was in the fight of his life. A stubborn man, he was fighting both with and against other stubborn men. But struggle as he would, hopes for United States membership in the League were slowly but surely dimming.

The gravely ailing President remained at loggerheads with the Henry Cabot Lodge "revisionists" in the Senate. As a frequently close onlooker, Bryan was all but awed by Lodge's depth of stubbornness and heights of competence as a parliamentarian. And the Commoner was deeply disturbed by Wilson's pronouncement that the election of 1920 would be a "great and solemn referendum" that would see the American people accept membership in the League of Nations. Bryan did not see this as inevitable. He favored carrying the crusade to the "common people" but more immediately he favored supplementing that enterprise with more direct efforts in the portals and lobbies of the U. S. Senate.

He was honored by the Oldine Club of New York with

a prestigious first place on its speakers list. In New York his agent, Charles Horner, was waiting with a portfolio of engagements. Horner had set up the next lecture tour in New England.

Bryan's opener on Harvard Square was more of heat than light. He began with a ringing attack on the Senate "conspiracy" "to slaughter in cold blood" the infant League of Nations, the one bright hope for a just world peace. He deplored the rule that Congress can declare war with a majority of only one vote in each House while a two-thirds majority of the Senate is required to approve a peace treaty.

His ensuing speeches were more cogent; there in the chill bluish ending of a New England winter the crusader grew cerebral. To his own amazement he found himself liking this "Yankee country" that he had so often lambasted from afar. He was deeply impressed by the villages, including their church spires that rise like carved pointed gems to symbolize what he now sensed as the invincible soul of New England. He was delighted, indeed astonished, to find his Yankee audiences excellent listeners, attentive, slow smiling, yet exceptionally alert.

It followed that Bryan, in the main speaking impromptu, began thinking aloud with more than usual effectiveness and trying out many ideas and recommendations both revived and newly invented. As an opener and with bubbly confidence, he pointed out that one of the more regrettable shortcomings of New England, the "garden land of American thought," was its deplorable shortage of trustworthy newspapers.

To ease this painful lack he strongly recommended establishment of a weekly "national bulletin" to be provided for all periodicals and to all private citizens who might wish to subscribe. The bulletin would be managed by a bipartisan editorial board selected by Congress and the President; it would provide space in which all political parties would be permitted to state their policies and beliefs

and offer and answer criticisms of rivals. He added that
as matters stood, the Republicans controlled most of the
prinicpal news media, and his own party lacked suitable
means for reaching the public in most sections; in New
England it had no real medium or voice.

Apparently, too, something in the chilly New England
air prompted him to revive his advocacy of government
ownership and operation of railroads. He vowed that as
of 1920 the bona fide private "proprietorship" of railroads
was completely impossible—because of the cynical domi-
nation by trusts, combines, bankers' conspiracies, and their
overpowering legislative lobbies.

Bryan also proposed the creation and development of
a nationwide federal and state highway system (very similar to what now prevails). He recommended the creation
or extension of the powers of federal and state trade commissions (along the lines of the present Federal Communications Commission). He recited a self-devised plan for
government-administered insurance for bank deposits (that
was virtually a blueprint for the now highly successful
Federal Depositors Insurance Corporation). Intertwined
with pleas for the acceptance of membership in the League
of Nations were various other recommendations: Repeal
of all statutes that contribute to restriction of free speech
or a free press; law-making by means of initiative and
referendum; federal ownership of the merchant marine and
of all telephone and telegraph facilities. He stated rather
superfluously that he had not come begging Democratic
votes; rather he had come to gain awareness that New
England had been and remains the nation's first and best
schoolyard, and by way of its town meetings the great
source spring of American democracy.

Bryan headed west again. At Lincoln, where he visited
his brother, the customarily untidy premises of *The Commoner* were cluttered with still another surge of fan mail.
"I want to live to see Mr. Bryan President," was a typical
refrain. But Mr. Bryan himself expressed no such wish.

What he wanted began with his country's acceptance of membership in the League of Nations. He chose to remain in what he now called "creative politics."

On the last night of March, Bryan spoke in Denver, then moved along to Santa Fe, working toward San Francisco, where the 1920 national Democratic convention would be taking form. At the New Mexico capital he took time for a sightseeing tour of nearby Indian pueblos. His taxi broke down near Taos Village, and Bryan walked to the pueblo, where he viewed the oldest apartment houses in the nation with considerable awe. He was impressed by the adobe structures with their outside stair ladders, the shelves of sun-drying beef and mutton, and the dusty strands of last year's pepper pods. Most of the Indians spoke their own language or Spanish, or both, and Bryan did not speak either, but he located an elderly tribesman who spoke English and who invited him into his apartment. Bryan settled before the bucket-size corner fireplace, where he noticed two thin ears of water-soaked dried corn roasting on spits. He had never before seen corn prepared so temptingly. When the aroma grew even more enticing, Bryan inquired of his host if he might buy the extra ear of corn, offering a dollar for it.

Politely but firmly, the Taos man declined. He explained that he did not sell his food; his corn was in short supply and he had only a few ears left that were suitable for roasting. Besides, he was very hungry himself. "But you could use my money to buy other food," Bryan pointed out. The Indian answered that he already had a dollar, but that roasted ear corn was his kind of fare. "I keep to my way, you keep to yours," he admonished.

Bryan went his way, struck by the presence of an aboriginal American who declined to be influenced by the offer of a dollar. "That Indian was right as rain," Bryan told his son, who had journeyed to Phoenix for a visit with his itinerant father. "I get the feeling that he is a more real fundamentalist than I am. His whole life is a living religion. I only strive for that. There are people who say I am unable to find the twentieth century. Well, my friend at Taos isn't obliged to, and I have a distinct feeling he is a more right and righteous American than I am."

At San Francisco, where the convention was already beginning to simmer, Bryan girded himself. A reconnaissance led him into yet another burst of activity. His effectiveness in the oncoming convention would be augmented or perhaps finally decided by his ability to gain a place on the platform committee. That, of course, required that he be a delegate. Nebraska's Democratic primary, scheduled for the final Tuesday in April, was already brewing. Bryan decided to again seek election as delegate-at-large. If he could win this he was confident that he could also regain his leadership of the state's delegation. That, in turn, would be of nationwide interest and possibly of decisive consequence to the platform and its paragraphs on the League.

From Lincoln on April 7 Bryan blandly announced his candidacy for the post of Democratic delegate-at-large. He was well aware that the patronage-enriched state Democratic organization was against him. Newspapers in Omaha and Lincoln said that Bryan's humiliating defeat of 1916 could be repeated, and several showed willingness to do their parts in assuring that it would be. Bryan, meanwhile, expressed his determination to roast and eat his own ear of corn in his own way. He put on his wrinkled alpaca suit, his frayed white shirt, his black string tie, and battered gray hat and set out in a Ford touring car with his brother behind the wheel. The statewide canvass continued for two busy weeks. Once more the prophet spoke from any available platform, from courthouse steps to wagon beds. Once more he aired his own "hatful of Democratic dreams." Once more he centered on a fairer deal for the farmers and laborers.

The so-called Administration Democrats struck back hard, trumpeting warnings that if Bryan ever got to San

Francisco as a delegate he would wreck the convention. But the primary vote count saw him San Francisco-bound with a winning majority of 44,103. News commentators were disposed to list it as a "personal triumph." The Administration forces were obviously concerned. Woodrow Wilson babbled that if Bryan should bolt it would "besmear the reputation of the party." Wilson apparently deemed it possible that Bryan might maneuver to split the party. As Democratic national chairman, Homer Cummings admitted that Bryan held as many as 125 delegate votes; the New York *World* guessed 200. Postmaster General Burleson saw the likelihood that the Commoner would proceed to shape the "regular party platform" pretty much to his own liking, but would stop short of trying to effect an open break. During May the *Literary Digest* poll of "voter preferences" gave McAdoo 102,719, Wilson 67,588, Bryan 46,488, and James M. Cox, the eventual nominee, 32,343.

The crusader meanwhile was in a tartly critical mood. When Cummings of Connecticut was announced as the convention's keynote speaker, Bryan observed in print that if the Democratic party were to be wrapped up in a wet shroud, locked in a Wall Street safe, and buried at sea, Cummings was just the man to officiate. In the same style he slapped at the emergence of James M. Cox, the petty Ohio newspaper publisher whom Bryan openly appraised as a deplorable little stooge for the liquor interests.

Once more the Nebraska delegate-at-large invested in a generous supply of pencils which, as usual, he sharpened with his pocket knife. For a tidy twelve thousand dollars he maneuvered an assignment to report both major conventions for the Newspaper Enterprise Association, a respected newspaper syndicate headquartered in Cleveland.

Bryan had described the Republican convention, in Chicago, as the most reactionary livestock pen he had seen or smelled in many years. Certainly the Commoner had never been more vehemently anti-Republican. On its sixth day, when he saw and heard his sad-featured, one-time Chautauqua colleague, Warren G. Harding of Ohio, receive the Republican nomination, he noted that the candidate fitted the platform. All this, of course, was of the Bryan journalistic prelude to the Democratic convention.

On arriving in San Francisco, two days before the June 28 opening, the Nebraska delegate-at-large went to work on the Committee on Platform and Resolutions. In four overlong days he got nowhere at all. Woodrow Wilson's man controlled the convention's most important committee, and one after another Bryan's spirited lunges to advance ratification of the League of Nations, support compulsory investigation of labor disputes, improve prohibition enforcement, and institute a national news bulletin were barred from the platform text.

The sick President was now even more anti-Bryan than he had been a year earlier. As a bedridden near-paralytic, Woodrow Wilson was groping to hold party leadership by way of loyal emissaries. At San Francisco these had joined in producing a bumblingly loquacious platform that sought to lure the support of the big city "organizations," middle-class town voters, and the discouraged farm vote, all with the same spread of verbiage.

Bryan, meanwhile, made ready to carry his battle to the convention floor. "If you are on the side of a righteous cause, you never know what you can do until you try—." He seemed almost boyish as he chatted with a gathering of women delegates and delegates' wives, but when he took his place on the littered floor of the Civic Auditorium he looked old. One reason, perhaps, was his profound annoyance with the loudly squawking amplifiers that towered above the speaker's platform. They were part of the first loudspeaker system ever used in a national convention. James Byrnes, a perceptive young delegate and amateur violinist from South Carolina, noted that with this rather horrible accouterment the poorest voices could carry al-

most as well as the finest—the latter, of course, being
Bryan's.

After Resolutions Chairman Carter Glass of Virginia
had put in two hours at reading the platform text, Bryan
came forward to propose amendments and additions. The
listeners had anticipated his proposal of more aggressive
enforcement of the Eighteenth Amendment, but certainly
not all were expecting his "plank" to prohibit compulsory
military training in peacetime, or his move to commit the
party to support the establishment of a "national bulletin"
for dispensing "fairly balanced" news of government. All
three would-be amendments were rejected. But the old-
timer would not be repressed or discouraged. He next
moved for a recommendation in the platform of the statutory limitation of profits on all basic commodities, the
verified publication of the costs and selling prices of all
"essential products" in interstate trade, and the use of
federal licensing and drastic reduction in the number of
wholesalers, commission merchants, and other "middle-
men."

The huge crowd continued to cheer, and the voice,
though repeatedly garbled and counter-echoed by the loudspeaker system, gained clarity. He recognized the sons and
daughters of delegates from other years. He could see and
hear that they were cheering him. But they were not voting
for his proposals.

Even so, he would not be quelled. He returned to the
platform to deliver what many would long remember as
his valedictory. He spoke of the League and the Versailles
Treaty, pointing out that ratification without revisions or
reservations was by then completely impossible, that the
document would have to be "tailored." He added that if
the treaty were defeated the Democratic party would have
to bear the blame. As the crusader stepped back from the
podium he seemed for a moment to fade into an almost
crushing silence.

Then, like a delayed crash of thunder, the applause arose. Delegates and gallery listeners alike began getting to their feet and shouting and moving forward as if to push down the platform.

Bryan wept unashamedly. He stumbled as he moved toward the edge of the platform, but regained his balance when a fellow Nebraskan thrust a Nebraska banner into his hand. Still weeping, the oldest member of his delegation began waving the banner. The crowd's uproar continued to grow, an en masse tribute to a prophet who now stood above defeat or error.

Chairman and U.S. senator from Arkansas Joseph Taylor Robinson permitted the uproar to continue for almost half an hour. Brash and husky Joe Robinson was not the kind one expected to show emotion in public, but even as he used one hand to wield his gavel, he used the other to hold a large handkerchief into which he pretended to blow his nose. Years later, while interviewing the then senior senator from Arkansas, the writer reminded his subject of the Bryan hour at San Francisco. Mr. Joe winked while trying to deny that he had wept. "A lot of damned tommyrot, Sonny. The fact is that the last time I let tears was when I was five years old in England, Arkansas, with a chamber pot stuck on my head. Well, so maybe I was a *little* misty eyed when Colonel Bryan finished off his speech, but . . ."

During the second muddled week in San Francisco the choice of nominees eventually narrowed to McAdoo and Cox, the latter aggressively supported by urban Democratic organizations, including Tammany and others of what were dubbed the liquor interests. Bryan kept with the darkest horse, Senator Robert L. Owen of Oklahoma, holding most of the Nebraska delegation with him. Then, on the forty-fourth ballot, the unimpressive James Cox of Ohio won the nomination.

Bryan shuddered. The subsequent nomination of handsome young Franklin Delano Roosevelt as vice-presidential candidate did not assuage his anguish. From San Francisco he once more promised his wife by letter that he would take a rest. He assured his brother, who had remained close at his side, that he would visit a clinic in Denver. The following week he wrote Charlie that he was "resting" in Norris, Montana.

Beginning on July 21, Lincoln, Nebraska, was the scene of the fifth national convention of the Prohibition party, which was frantically seeking a presidential nominee. On receipt of a second overture, Bryan telegraphed Clinton Howard, the convention chairman, that he could not accept and that his brother would explain in detail. When Howard conveyed the message to his fellow prohibitionists, the convention responded by nominating Bryan by a tumultuous voice vote. Again Charlie passed along the message, and again Will declined, repeating that his advocacy of reforms other than prohibition demanded his time and efforts.

He would remain a Democrat, but he would not support candidate Cox. The Democrats were still the "party of the common people," but under prevailing circumstances the common people were being betrayed. "My heart is in the grave with our cause," he cried out, "I must pause until it comes back to me."

In September, when Cox came to Lincoln to personally solicit his aid, Bryan was adamant. When he returned to the Redpath Chautauqua circuit, he struck out at both major parties for their spineless platforms and their wholly inadequate nominees. He urged his listeners to vote for a Republican dry in preference to a Democratic wet, or a Republican "progressive" in preference to a Democratic reactionary.

He spent most of October with his ailing wife, and then the heavy-hearted crusader returned to Nebraska to vote as a Democrat. While in Lincoln he confided to his brother his determination to begin anew as a true prophet of the American people. Once again, he gained reassurance from an unexpected source, the militantly Republican Chicago *Tribune:*

. . . [Bryan] will be a leader as long as he lives because he is the expression of the normal habit, taste, moral thought, custom and life of the average American.

Our subject, who usually avoided the word "normal," and never applied it to himself, took time for an interval of self-appraisal. He reiterated that his "place in history" would be decided by what he did for the American people, *not* by what the people did for him. As a devotee of reform, he had already seen dozens of Bryan-promoted reforms become statutes; two, prohibition and female suffrage, had emerged (the latter was materializing) as Constitutional amendments. He was sincerely grateful for this, but he continued to term himself a "child of fortune"—more good than bad because everyday Americans remained his sustainers and redeemers.

Directly after his sixty-first birthday he had drawn up a list of ten books or writings in what he considered the order of their influence on his life, thought, and conduct: (1) the Bible; (2) writings of Thomas Jefferson; (3) essays of Tolstoy; (4) *The Fact of Christ* (by Carnegie Simpson); (5) William Cullen Bryant's poetry; (6) Plutarch's *Lives;* (7) the works of Shakespeare; (8) Demosthenes' *Orations on the Crown;* (9) Homer's *The Iliad* and *The Odyssey;* and (10) the novels of Charles Dickens.*

* Bryan was, indeed, an exceptionally able Bible scholar. I do not believe he was either an objective or thorough student of Thomas Jefferson, and I doubt the competency of his knowledge of Shakespeare. He was certainly an admiring friend of Tolstoy; I doubt that he was capably acquainted with Tolstoy's writings. *The Fact of Christ,* although a once revered if less than scholarly sermon guide, was soon to be relegated to guidebook limbo. His fondness for Bryant's poems, particularly "Ode to a Waterfowl," was evident.

In his own appraisal of himself at sixty-two, Bryan reiterated that his best attainments were and would no doubt remain rooted in the "rights of majority rule." He insisted, too, that the "virtuous masses," given the fullest attainable participation in democracy, would in time free themselves of such deplorable faults as the persecution of minorities. His comment applied to the multiplication of the Ku Klux Klan and its proclivities for Jew baiting. Late in 1920 a Jewish educator, Dr. Willis Spargo, sought to establish at his "retreat" near Bennington, Vermont, a defensive headquarters for shielding Jewry from defamation by the Klan and similar hate groups.

Without confrontation in person, Spargo sought Bryan's support and promptly received it. The support included a personal gift, reportedly of two thousand dollars (I cannot confirm this), and vigorous support from Chautauqua and other lecture platforms. "Our national character is very strongly indebted to Jewish sources, to the Rabbis who are traditional great judges as well as ministers. We are morally obligated to champion our Jewish friends by way of our ballot boxes well used," Bryan solemnly recited.

But the close of 1920 found Bryan openly admitting and, so far as this writer knows, for the first time, that not all that comes out of ballot boxes is good. The motivation was unquestionably related to the fact that the vacuous

---

But there was little to indicate that he was well acquainted with Plutarch's *Lives,* and only a few indirect and generally vague gleanings to show that he had succumbed to Dickens' influence. During his college years he had studied *The Iliad* and *The Odyssey* and the *Orations on the Crown,* but I find little evidence of their influence on his speeches or writings.

I cannot see Bryan as convincingly Jeffersonian. He heeded and trusted the common people, the virtuous masses, far more completely than did the philosopher of Albemarle. Jefferson never contended that the everyday people are invariably or even usually right. Bryan held insistently that common people are the best expression of God's will to be found on earth, and are therefore the indispensable sustainers of democracy.

Mr. Cox had lost to the pitiable Mr. Harding by some seven million popular votes and 377 electoral votes. But Bryan's greater hurt was his belief that his, the Democratic party, had betrayed its people; in particular, it had sinned before God and man by botching what could very well be the last real hope for attaining U.S. membership in the League of Nations.

Accordingly, and with a somewhat bewildering blend of humility and punitive anger, Bryan resolved to direct his next crusade toward "purifying" the Democratic party. Using both *The Commoner* and open letters to the New York *Times* as paddles, he set about vigorously spanking its National Committee. Between whacks he warned that if the Democratic leadership were not improved, the party was surely and properly doomed.

With the help of his brother, he set about drafting the recommended groundwork of legislative policies for all true Democrats. Then the Bryan brothers compiled a list of Democrats whom they deemed worthy of serving on the National Committee. Next, with the help of another well-to-do Nebraska Democrat, Judge R. C. Roper, they proceeded to set up a Bryan Center in the Endicott Hotel in New York: its primary mission, to educate true Democrats by distributing Bryan's *Statements of Principles* and related publications. The branch headquarters also undertook to promote a series of special conventions for Bryan followers and a list of Bryan birthday parties for the oncoming March 19.

The propaganda shop did not work out. Bryan closed the Endicott center and with his brother launched a drive to increase *The Commoner*'s circulation from a modest but loyal 120,000 or thereabouts to at least half a million. This venture also failed; the prevailing circulation and advertising held firm.

Bryan refused to be diverted from his role of nurturing national conscience. During the previous December he had accepted an unpublicized invitation to visit the President-

elect at the latter's home in Marion, Ohio. Shortly before
his Inauguration Warren G. Harding and Mrs. Harding
had called on the Bryans in Miami. Inquiring reporters had
wondered whether the Commoner was polishing oranges
for the President-elect or leading him into a trap.

Even before Inauguration Day Bryan had again baffled
his inquisitors by praising Harding's choice of Charles
Evans Hughes as Secretary of State and deploring his
choice of Andrew W. Mellon as Secretary of the Treasury.
Subsequently he flayed Mellon's efforts to reduce taxes on
large incomes—even though for 1921 Bryan reported his
own net income as $106,773.34. Next, he denounced the
Harding administration's "sneak play" of paying out half
a billion dollars to guarantee railroad dividends while evading a war veterans' bonus bill. He further decried the Federal Reserve Bank as a tool of Wall Street and warned
emphatically of the worsening plight of the American farmers, particularly in the grain-growing Great Plains and
the cotton-growing South.

By contrast, in his magazine writing for *The Century,*
The Outlook, and *World's Work,* as well as for *The Commoner,* the master of Villa Serena downrated the prevailing
alarm about the "red" menace, insisting that the more
serious danger came from the pernicious lunatic fringe of
conservatives here at home—whether on Wall Street or at
Ku Klux Klan cross burnings. He granted, however, that
unless "true progressivism remained on the march," the
insurgence of Marxists and other "unstable extremists" was
inevitable.

His climaxing journalistic feat of 1921 was his publication by way of The Commoner Press of the *Bryan National
Legislative Program.* The contents covered most of his
frustrated recommendations for the 1920 Democratic party
platform and a number of other heretofore undisclosed
proposals. Among the latter were appeals for limiting future presidential terms to one term of six years, nationwide
primaries open to all voters, a U.S.-sponsored world dis-

armament conference, federal legislation prohibiting the gambling in futures of essential commodities, and federal ownership of all water power resources. He further urged the individual states to inaugurate "public-good enterprises," such as cooperative fuel yards (along lines already shaped and proved by his brother in Lincoln), state-owned slaughterhouses, and nonprofit, state-owned filling stations. He pounded away at monopolies, taking as his special target Rockefeller's Standard Oil Company. He reiterated the special role of towns and cities in effecting public-good benefits, citing Mayor John F. Hylan's plan for New York City's ownership and operation of its own transit system as an admirable example of municipal progressivism.

The Bryan program included minimum wage laws at the state levels, rigorous control of work hours, and state and federal legislation to enforce the proper inspection of food, sanitation, and housing conditions; also a specific plan for ascertaining monthly changes in the price level of staple foods and other necessities for the purpose of adjusting wages to fit the actual cost of living.

His stand for labor included the federally assured right to organize and accredit unions, the practice of collective bargaining, and the establishment of federal and state commissions authorized to investigate labor disputes. However, he denied the right of labor to use violence or "concerted force" (which would apparently include militant picket lines), or to strike against public employment essential to public safety. With like zeal he urged the acceptance of railroad workers' plea for a nationwide minimum wage and urged that Congress establish minimum or "floor" prices for the premier farm crops.

Meanwhile, the Commoner resumed his role as unofficial international peace maker.

He bombarded the President with his recommendations to call a major-powers conference to reduce armaments. In Chicago he helped sponsor a national conclave of the privately sustained Congress on Reduction of Armaments. Bryan set forth to persuade the General Assembly of Presbyterian Churches to join the cause, and having met with considerable success at the annual conference, he helped organize and lead a series of somewhat noisy peace rallies.

Early the following November the unhappy President proceeded to invite major powers to participate in a Washington conference to discuss world disarmament. Having warmly congratulated Harding on his move, Bryan maneuvered a United Press assignment to report the conference. As an opener he praised rapturously Secretary Hughes' opening address and the conference itself, which undeniably served as a prelude for the Four Power Disarmament Treaty. Bryan's ardor for the peace moves continued in conspicuous contrast to his angry castigation of federal, state, and local laxity in enforcement of prohibition laws.

For better or worse, 1922 continued to be the year of Bryan-invented or Bryan-recommended reforms.

In a follow-up of eloquent righteousness, he also exhorted that all materials related to gambling be excluded from the U.S. mails; further, that criminal statutes be revised to abide a single standard of morality, applying particularly to the equalizing of guilt of prostitutes and their customers as well as their accomplices. All the foregoing, along with the Teapot Dome and other materializing scandals of the scoundrels-fringed Harding administration, provided grist for Bryan's Chautauqua sermons. They also motivated his concentration of lecture appearances in the West, which seemed more amicable to reform than the South or East.

There were other motivations for the westward shift of the still formidable Bryan energies; these included Charlie Bryan's fervent and well-planned candidacy for the governorship of Nebraska. Having demonstrated his exceptional competence at mule farming, law practice, and managing street railways and coalyard cooperatives as well as family magazine publishing, the younger Bryan had now set his sights first on winning the Democratic nomination, and election as chief executive of his adopted state.

Bryan was confident that he could best help his brother by trouping in the general area and blowing his blessings, so to speak, from nearby and influencing areas. Not incidentally, he would also be boosting the candidacies of other western Democrats whom he saw as good Democrats.

Charlie's well-earned victory did not surprise the elder brother. Neither did his confidential announcement that following his induction as governor he could not continue to ride herd on *The Commoner,* even though the latter by then had been reduced to monthly status. Regretfully, Will agreed that it would be best to suspend publication as soon as the already accepted or committed material could be published.

By then Bryan was well aware that he had an abundance of more effective outlets for his writing. Financially he had no need for the scant, occasional profits from the family publication. His total income, including profits on real estate, totaled about $175,000 for 1922. Indeed, and less than rationally, Bryan continued to find his possession of money far more upsetting than he had earlier found the lack of it. Again, he reacted angrily to reports that the poor people's champion was now a rich man. Again he wrote testily in *The Commoner* that if frugal living and painstaking investment of one's earnings are to be regarded as hallmarks of wickedness, he had no choice other than to stand condemned as a wicked man.

"I've known Will to be a happy poor man," the governor-elect repeated. "I dang sure don't savvy why he has to keep in such a mad sweat about being a rich man."

Charlie brought the matter up with his brother, using Junior as backup man. "Why don't you take off a spell, and spend some time at home with your wife?"

Both Charlie and Junior were surprised when Will agreed that he should, adding that he wished to make another "self-invoice," and also to get in some reading. "I've almost stopped reading books," he admitted. "All I've been doing is to turn through a few, picking up a thought here and there."

As Bryan rounded out his sixty-second year, those who knew him best were aware that along with picking up a thought here and there he continued to rack up a contrasting array of successes and failures. His crusade in behalf of the League of Nations was wholly quagmired; his longtime dream of a new and better epoch of international peace agreements had faded like a summer rainbow at twilight. His labors to refurbish and uplift the Democratic party were engulfed in doubt.

The same held for his status as a family man. He had dozens of kinfolk with whom he had lost all real contact, even though, on occasions, particularly at Christmastime, he showered them with stuffily ornate greeting cards. With the exception of his daughter Grace, Bryan had not remained close to his own children. Ruth, now a busy young matron with political aspirations of her own, was virtually out of his orbit. Junior, an attorney and special prosecutor for the U. S. Justice Department, had chosen frontier Arizona as his bailiwick. Though their relations were cordial, the father and son rarely met more frequently than every second year. The separation had effectively begun when Junior was shipped off to a military academy.

As for Mamie, his very deep affection persisted, and for the usually absent husband, very deep concern. He stated, "My wife is entirely helpless, unable to stand or walk or dress or undress herself." Grace and he were uncomfortably aware that in her recurrent distress Mamie on occasions was patronizing faith healers. Bryan returned home from prolonged trips to find his wife in tears because she "had no family left to mind."

This, from all appearances, contributed to Bryan's somewhat wavery resolve to enter Florida politics. He had declined to make a try for the post of U.S. senator from the Sunshine State in 1922, openly doubting his ability to win even the Democratic primary there.

After the passing of another almost fantastically busy year Bryan returned at least temporarily to Villa Serena, as he explained, to do some courting of Mamie Baird and some explaining of her Will. Grace Hargreaves, with her usual perceptiveness, noted that her father's primary loves remained God, people at large, and the unceasing stimulation of crowds. He could still express himself to crowds and in so doing gain ego massage and thereby restore his sometimes sagging self-confidence.

Offsetting the anchorage of his fundamentalism were lacks and shortcomings that the daughter knew surely and the father did not deny. Bryan had never been a lover of the fine arts. He got little out of music. "Poetry," as he continued to define it, "means the clothing of a pleasing idea with beautiful words." Art he saw and felt as a "receptacle for ideas which cannot be effectively expressed in the spoken word." His "favorite" art was Biblical art. He confided that the Madonna and Child is the "superior art subject" and mentioned those of Raphael and Bodenhausen as among those that "touch the heart most deeply."

As Grace appraised her father's health, she was aware that his recuperative powers were still good, but felt certain that his hardiness was not invincible. In the course of her occasional visits with Dr. Tom Kelley in Washington, Grace had gathered that her father was not quite so bad a patient as some believed. To her positive knowledge, during January 1923, Bryan had agreed to "go on insulin," at least for a trial period of six to eight weeks, when it was ready, though for his own reasons he insisted that he would administer his own injections of the new radical "drug."

However, Junior was somewhat less confident of his father's ability to "nurse" his own diabetes. "Father had mentioned to me that he found great difficulty in keeping with his prescribed diet when traveling," Junior told this writer. "I am quite certain he slipped now and then, particularly when exposed to his favorite sweets such as fruit cobblers, chocolate cake, and custard and pumpkin pies. I recall that when I visited him in 1922 he had given up such favorite items as corned beef and spiced sausages. He was still losing weight intermittently and suffering from diabetic thirst."

By 1922 insulin had been finally isolated and classified as an analyzable hormone secreted by blood cells of the pancreas system. From the McLeod Laboratory in Montreal, the brilliant pioneering work of Drs. Frederick Banting and Charles Best was beginning to gain medical accreditation in many countries. By April 1922, the case for therapeutic insulin gained a memorable advancement when one of Dr. Banting's associates, chemist J. B. Collif, developed an insulin-alcohol compound suitable for direct injection by subcutaneous needle. Bryan's physician, Dr. Kelley, was among the throngs of intently interested onlookers.

By autumn 1922, Dr. Kelley was ready and waiting to try insulin on William Jennings Bryan. All he had to do was lay hands on his extremely mobile patient.

22. The Believer

Early in January 1923, the Bryans returned by way of
Washington from a trip to Mexico City. Mamie's severe
flare of arthritis was the immediate cause for their call at
Dr. Kelley's office. The physician persuaded Mrs. Bryan to
return to Johns Hopkins Hospital for a week or so of
observation.

His greater concern was with Mr. Bryan. This became
even more marked when his hard-to-corner patient with
ninth-year diabetes revealed his decision to place himself
on a diet of gluten bread, recommended to him by a baker
friend as the industry's very special gift to diabetics. Bryan
eagerly explained that the flour had been washed free of
starch prior to the breadmaking. Without further explanation of how the remarkable chemistry was effected, he took
from his jacket pocket a sample of the bread. The physician
nibbled and found it utterly abominable. Dr. Kelley then
brought up the improving outlook for insulin. Unenthusi-
astically, Bryan agreed to return to Washington and permit
his physician to observe reactions after a week of injections.

Dr. J. Thomas Kelley speculated that putting Bryan on insulin might be like loading him aboard a train going, say, eighty miles an hour. But eventually it might work out.

Though the initial results of the first week of test injections showed promise, they were far from definitive. Even so, Dr. Kelley succeeded in exacting his patient's promise to follow the insulin treatment at least through February.

The writer does not know whether Bryan kept his promise. I do know that early that March, Junior received from his father a rambling and disturbing letter that noted that he was feeling badly, that he was discouraged about the "Banting concoction," and still found "gluten bread his best prospect and stayer against his disease." Bryan also confided that he had regretfully postponed his usual spring-summer Chautauqua tour until he "found his health again."

In his next letter, which was not dated, Bryan gave indications of suffering from what his son had heard called diabetic clouding of the mind. One such indication was an apparent and total lapse regarding already confirmed plans for discontinuing *The Commoner*. Bryan now suggested that his son take over as editor-manager of the family magazine, which had long since officially announced its closing with the upcoming May issue. Another puzzling entry was Bryan's request that his son, as his executor, insert in his will a provision that all his worldy goods be held intact for the exclusive use of his wife during the remainder of her lifetime. Some three years earlier Bryan had personally written that provision in his original draft of his will.

During March 1923, Bryan's enterprises took still another turn, if not for the better certainly for the more bewildering. Although his already proffered lecture fees totaled above fifty thousand dollars, he had abruptly entered in agreement with the Miami Chamber of Commerce and Real Estate Board whereby for a fee of $250 per lecture he would extol the virtues and charms of that growing community with a succession of lectures entitled "What Miami, Florida, Means to William Jennings Bryan." Nobody could argue that the meaning and/or opinions were in any way derogatory of Greater Miami, or obnoxious to Florida Rotary or other luncheon clubs. There seemed, however, no explainable difference between the health hazards incident to speaking at far separated club luncheons and the better integrated Chautauqua bookings, and certainly no financial advantages. As one would expect, the public reaction was not of total approval. Several newspapers, including one in Jacksonville, pointed out that a revered social prophet and a well-heeled defender of the poor had no proper business exploiting his talent and fame as a dispenser of Chamber of Commerce hokum regarding, of all places, Miami.

Again, Bryan's answers, principally by way of letters to editors, tended to be waspish. He reiterated that "untruthful reports" of his wealth were causing him more distress than any other adversity except his wife's illness. His protests did not mention that even while accepting modest fees for blurbing Miami, he was carrying forward a much more extensive and strenuous effort without the request or prospect of any fees at all. This was his effort to win badly needed financial aid for the deplorably neglected University of Florida, then a down-at-the-heels men's academy lost in the pine woods and grass bogs at Gainesville. In any case, the don't-dare-call-me-rich letters seemed to reflect diabetes-aggravated tensions.

Shifting easily and frequently from the third to the first person, the master of Villa Serena pointed out that although the world at large persisted in regarding him as a moralist, he was not. Rather he was an unwavering fundamentalist, who would weigh right and wrong only in terms of total belief in a fundamental, all-powerful God.

In a renewed exchange of letters with Adolphus Talbot, his first law partner, Bryan reflected that he had always been more interested in religion than in government. After all, he began speaking in church when he was twelve; he did not take to the political stump until he was substantially older, and before all, his first remembered belief was in God, not in moral theories or principles. He observed again that since the Holy Bible holds the one true moral code directly of and from Almighty God, morality must be born of faith before it can be expressed in statutes or by way of governments. Good politics, too, must necessarily be an institution and demonstration of a living faith and must embody a living church—"duly aroused and warned." Accordingly, Bryan insisted there can be no conflict between good politics and good religion. Both are divinely obligated to join forces and devotions in serving "the zone which separates that which can be *legally ordained* from that which is *morally necessary.*"

By late April, when he outlined his oncoming series of Chautauqua sermons, he stressed his awareness of the paramount need for a nationwide revival of fundamental faith or "Divine believing." He deplored the fact that the nation was being imperiled by unbelieving and vacuous "modernists." In an article published in the July 1923 issue of *The Forum,* he proclaimed:

> Give the "modernist" three of his favorite words— "allegorical," "poetical," and "symbolical," and he can suck the meaning out of every vital Christian doctrine and every passage in the Bible which he chooses to erase. . . . The presentment of "evolution" is being used as an anesthetic to deaden pain while the Christian religion is being removed. . . .

While rededicating himself to his self-defined duties and responsibilities as a Christian statesman, Bryan also announced his intention of giving attention to "church politics." Late in May the annual general assembly of Presbyterian Churches of America would be convening at

Indianapolis. Bryan resolved to seek election as a lay moderator of "Presbyterianism," and from that vantage to espouse the cause of fundamentalism in his own expansive family of churches.

As the convention of 878 churchmen got under way in the Indiana capital, two of the four announced candidates for the moderatorship dropped out of contention. But Charles F. Wishart, a longtime pastor who had moved on to the presidency of Wooster Presbyterian College, held to his stand as a "faithful liberal" and stalwartly opposed Bryan's "platform of fundamental faith." Following a lengthy platform debate, the assembly chose Wishart as moderator by an impressively close vote of 451 to 427.

Pleased with his strong following, which was larger than he had expected, Bryan returned with a resolution that would withhold financial support from any Presbyterian school that permitted the teaching of "Darwinism" as a proven fact. When that move failed, the eloquent layman retreated briefly but returned again with a winning resolution to uphold the "viewpoint of fundamentalism." Flushed with that dealing of victory and just possibly by excessive blood sugar, Bryan next struck out at the scriptural laxity of Presbyterian preaching, choosing the rather well-publicized ministry of a youthful and emphatic New York pastor, Harry Emerson Fosdick, as a deplorable example. The move succeeded to the extent of causing Fosdick to receive a mild reprimand that appeared to perk him up quite a lot.

Layman Bryan, too, seemed to be having a good time. He left Indianapolis explaining solemnly, "My real goal was simply to write out that all the fundamentalist truly seeks is the rights of all in terms of religious belief."

Back at Villa Serena, with growing evidence of the wrath of diabetes, he set about taking a closer bead on the false prophets of "modernism," which would be the theme of his next lecture series. Bryan turned to the works of another from whom he had also lifted ideas here and there but never very studiously.

Charles Robert Darwin had departed this life back in 1882, while Bryan was working his rather lonely way through the Union College of Law of Chicago. Darwin, of course, had been personally spared the ordeal of clerking his way through a poor man's law school in frontier Chicago, along with another ordeal that Bryan had found next to impossible, viz., adaptation to the twentieth century.

That Bryan had picked Darwin as a deplorable example of "modernism" might well have seemed extremely baffling. In great part the contemporary generation of scientists was finding Darwin's works still interesting but in some respects distinctly obsolescent. Yet for his own purposes, which were to epitomize what he deplored as modernism under a commonly recognized name, Darwin served Bryan exceptionally well. He could share his lack of real knowledge with tens of millions of his fellow Americans.

The Origin of Species, first published during the year prior to Bryan's birth, and *The Descent of Man,* published during his eleventh year, had been "discussed" in Bryan's presence during Dr. Hiram Jones' evening forums. Quite probably other Darwin works, such as *Power and Movement in Plants* and *Different Forms of Flowers in Plants of the Same Species,* had not been so honored. But the fact held that although Bryan insisted he "owned" all of Darwin's works, he soon demonstrated that he had not read them all. In a typical venture at challenging Darwin, he questioned his projection of the beginning of animal legs: "But why did man stop at two legs while the centipede kept on until it got a hundred?," later adding, "How can one support a linking of rose to onion, eagle to mosquito, the mocking bird to the rattlesnake, the wolf to the lamb and man to all . . . ?"

As a rule, factual answers to rhetorical questions do not come easily—a fact of life and semantics that in their own ways and times both Darwin and Bryan had exploited ably. Darwin and Bryan actually had a great deal in common. Both began life in uncontrollable oceans of religious conformity. Both had sternly pious fathers, both had been blessed with more than the going average of intelligence, and both had moved or been led into the folds of at one time comparatively liberal sectarian groups; Darwin had been able to effect a first mutation from severe Calvinism to the somewhat compromising if paunchy Church of England creed, while Bryan had eased from exposure to hard Baptist to a puberal acceptance of relatively soft Cumberland Presbyterian.

Both had acquired liberation from moderate poverty, and both had gained comparatively early maturity. More significantly, just as Darwin was not literally antireligion, Bryan was not really antiscience. A more primary difference was in the fact that whereas Darwin was a moralist and Bryan a fundamentalist, Bryan may have misconstrued Darwin's twittings of the rather hilarious pomposity of the Church of England, which he came to know from wedlock to the daughter of Josiah Wedgwood, Britain's pottery magnate.

In any case, by choosing Darwin as his particular Devil's henchman (granting as he did that Darwin's works do not directly contradict the *fact* of God, but they do impede man's appreciation of the need of God), Bryan was keeping with the great American tradition of saying much and knowing little about what one says. Our subject's sequel, that "Darwinism" serves to discourage man's love ("fear") of God and thereby diminish his respect for his fellow men (the children of God) was rather clearly a Bryan (in my own opinion a sick Bryan) *non sequitur*.

The point of immediate consequence here was that Bryan in sickness or health and otherwise for better or worse was being inducted—certainly not wholly by his own choice or planning—as unofficial leader of what was widely labeled the Fundamentalist Movement of the 1920s. To a degree Bryan had joined the movement; to a much greater degree the movement was joining Bryan, and on that basis hoisting him to its leadership.

Diabetic brain-clouding or no, Bryan seemed aware of this. As an irrepressible politician he knew the political implications, particularly in the West, Border South, and South, wherein all the dependable and vote-qualified Bryan followers almost certainly numbered five million; enough, certainly, to decide the outcome of comparatively close elections. In a letter to his longtime friend Edward Keating of the Washington *Post,* Bryan commented:

> I have a larger majority on my side than in any previous controversy, and I have more intolerant opponents than I ever had in politics. . . .

Certainly by 1923 Bryan was disturbed by the fringers and taggers-along. These included various extreme or fanatic "religionists," "reversionists" from major sectarian groups, and literally hundreds of self-described "leagues," "federations," "congresses," and "foundations," most of which would advance only their own credos or taglines. The fringers also included the Ku Klux Klan. More than any other fanatic group, the Klan epitomized, at least to Bryan, the fearful difficulties of keeping fanatic zeal from miscegenating with catastrophic intolerance.

But with God directing and his diabetes permitting, William Jennings Bryan was resolved to try. He sought to indicate this in his expanded pamphlet, "Orthodox Christianity versus Modernism," which the respected religious publisher, Fleming H. Revell, would bring out successfully early in 1924. He stated his case still more effectively in his speaking later in 1923. These efforts, painstakingly centered in smaller towns and countrysides, saw the Bryan following divided into two groups: those who "figured" that his best speeches were sermons, and those who "figured" that all his speeches were sermons.

For himself, Bryan persisted in seeing the American countryside as an enchanted land; his view of it gained first as a fence-breaking toddler continued to thrive. But his disapproval of American urban life had revived. Quite possibly intensified by the sinister progress of his disease, he pointed to the American city as the ever-growing supplier of the ever-contaminating rivers of disbelief.

His repeated expressions of concern regarding the cities and their overly numerous but duty-evading churches were not without repercussions. One source of evidence was by way of his syndicated and tightly capsuled "Bible Talks," which he continued to produce while traveling from one speaking engagement to the next. Reader mail regarding these usually pious tidbits was growing increasingly querulous. Newspaper editors wrote to urge that they be made more timely or "newsworthy"; Bryan's stock answer was that nothing could ever be more newsworthy or timely than the Word of God.

Despite his diabetes, the crusader kept on carrying his unbelievable work load and from time to time expanding it. After sweating through his late summer-early autumn tour, he returned to Miami, where he found Mamie feeling somewhat better. He resumed two projects that he found particularly challenging. One was his interdenominational "out in the open Sunday school class," the other his voluntary fund raising for the University of Florida. He was successful in both these undertakings; he won friends for Florida as well as aid for the university, and his class continued to grow and gain popularity among a highly diverse group of urban or quasi-urban males.

For these and no doubt other reasons, Bryan's health seemed to improve. His brother was among those who expressed particular joy in this, and as early as May 19, 1923, the governor of Nebraska wrote Bryan urging him to consider seeking the presidential nomination in 1924. "It's looking like the right time for W.J.B. to reach for the big biscuit again," he insisted. Charlie pointed out that by then Will had personal wealth, improving health, preassurance of the dry vote, the women's vote, poor folks' vote, a share of the labor vote, and the following of the "moral element."

In that and subsequent letters Charlie pointed out that the Democratic party was grievously short of talent, and was reactionary prone. Will had what was needed, including invaluable experience as a convention handler and an incomparable campaigner. One tends to suspect that Charlie was also indulging in the therapy of encouragement. Will seemed to harbor the same appreciative suspicion. He confirmed that he certainly planned to take part in the next convention and to "serve the party's cause." He also urged that a concerted effort be made to take the convention out of the "wet conspiracies" of New York and put it in dry, and more wholesome, Miami.

But Bryan stated categorically that he could not see himself as a "restorable" nominee and that the possibility of being drafted involved so many ifs that it "is not worthwhile to build any calculation on it." He definitely stated his plans to seek election as a convention delegate in the oncoming Florida primary, and he agreed that the scarcity of acceptable Democratic presidential candidates was appalling. Such officious hopefuls as Oscar Underwood, the reactionary senator from Alabama, and John W. Davis, the Morgan bootlicking lawyer, made him sick. He himself had some prospects to recommend. He would shortly reveal, somewhat deliriously, his choice of prospects including such "names" as Governor Pat Neff, the duck-hunter governor of Texas, and A. A. Murphree, the controversial president of the University of Florida, who was forbidden entry into any political activity by Florida law.

Charlie interpreted these suggestions as symptoms of another flareup of diabetic poisoning. This foreboding was partially confirmed when Grace reported that following his return from another Chautauqua circuit, her father was "quite ill." On October 4, Jacksonville newspapers noted that Bryan had canceled a local appearance because of illness. Directly thereafter he was in Washington for a visit with Dr. Kelley.

Back at Miami for Armistice Day, Bryan successively revealed that he was "giving study" to a Democratic platform for 1924, and completing arrangements to "canvass" Florida during the oncoming Democratic primary in quest of election as Democratic delegate-at-large. More significantly, and less openly, he had revealed to a local newspaper-publisher friend, R. L. Dean, of the Sanford (Florida) *Herald,* that he was seriously considering seeking election in 1926 as U.S. senator from Florida. He felt confident that in that office he could bring southern and western Democrats together. Also, he said that he had responsible medical assurance that he had a good chance of living at least through 1932.

Dr. Tom Kelley was not the provider of that assurance. He had confided to Grace Hargreaves his diagnosis that "Mr. Bryan's diabetes was keeping ahead of Mr. Bryan." He granted, however, that his patient was more a man of unusual spirit than usual pathologies.

Bryan made the winter of 1923–24 one of the most sociable of his life, and that season his lengthy guest list included the charming young owner of the modified yacht, the *Laroco,* Franklin Delano Roosevelt, who was borne ashore for a "nice talk with Mr. Bryan."

During March Bryan yielded to his first purchase of an automobile. Within a few days, and without instruction, he taught himself to drive, much to Mamie's amazement and alarm. Beginning early in April, he began a series of overnight stands that extended to every county in Florida. After the sultry primary he found that he had carried 85,462 votes against barely 40,000 for the next runner-up. "I've taken Florida like Grant took Richmond, except a lot more happily," he exultantly informed his younger daughter.

May was his month of preparation for what he saw as certainly the most difficult convention and possibly the most

challenging one since 1896. The challenge was of his own
inferring. Following a brief scouting trip, Charlie had hurried back to gubernatorial duties with the certain knowledge that Tammany's Alfred Emanuel Smith, with that
friendly-appearing Franklin Delano Roosevelt as an especially nefarious henchman, had, in Charlie's own words,
"pretty well degutted the Donkey."

Brother Will would not be dismayed. He completed a
Bryan-written platform; made a series of junkets to Washington to confer with senators and other congressmen,
particularly the Westerners; and impetuously contributed
seventy-five hundred dollars to help reduce the party's perennial deficit.

The Bryan brothers arrived in New York on June 18,
four days before the scheduled convention opening. Charlie
was already placed on the Qualifications and Rules Committees, Will on the Platform and Resolutions Committee.
From Pennsylvania Station Will taxied to the Waldorf for
a meeting with McAdoo, his announced first choice of a
nominee.

Reporters and news photographers who trailed along
noted that the older Bryan was thinner, indeed, than his
once lanky brother and more suntanned. Also that he was
wearing a well-tailored white Palm Beach suit, white shoes,
a rakish Panama hat and, as the ultimate touch of super-
fluity, a lapel name card. His black string tie and round
palmleaf fan were his only standard trappings.

The progress of the platform drafting, behind closed
doors, though prolonged and loudly argumentative, seemed
to be going Bryan's way. Certainly the book-length text
was in a familiar style. Many of its pages ran with such
telltale advocacies as federal aid for schools, relinquishment
of congressional rights to declare war except when supported by public referendum, Democratic support of the
League of Nations, including a national referendum in its
behalf, increased federal aid for highways, stronger antitrust laws, and so on and on.

There were omissions that implied Bryan failures to convince his fellow committeemen. The child-labor plank, which Eleanor Roosevelt helped write, failed to gain acceptance. The anti-Ku Klux Klan stand came out warped and feeble. Bryan had sought to compromise between the southern conservatives who vowed that antagonizing the Klan would cost the party a million or more votes, and the liberals, mostly Westerners, who vowed that failure to smite the Klan would cost the party the election. Bryan had taken the lead in shaping a "moderation plank," which apparently satisfied no one, certainly not Bryan. The topic of illegal disfranchisement of blacks came thundering into the discussion; Bryan hedged, by declaiming that the "oversight" could be solved only by time and the godly enlightenment of the majority of the American public. It was far from being a good show, but worse ones were in the immediate offing.

By official opening time, noonday, June 24, Madison Square Garden was uncomfortably crowded with about sixteen hundred delegates and alternates, and considerably more than ten times that number of spectators, with God only knew how many more seeking admission. At first Bryan seemed enraptured by the pageantry of opening. His brother, at least momentarily, seemed lost on a vigilant tour of the galleries.

Charlie was frowning when he picked his way back to the Florida delegation. "It's a stacked house," he said darkly. "I've been watching those Tammany goons handing out the passes. . . . Seems a lot of their gorillas don't speak English. They've also posted instruction signs in Italian, Spanish, and German."

When the sergeant-at-arms assured him that the objective was to permit new citizens and young people to gain acquaintance with a "distinguished American institution," the governor of Nebraska was unimpressed. He had observed that most of the pass holders were not especially young, and already great numbers were jarring their tonsils whooping for Al Smith, days ahead of the nominations.

Will was not too deeply disturbed by what Charlie reported. He had learned long before that Tammany-staged jamborees come salty, wet, and loud. His concern of the moment was with the intrusion of electrical technology. The platform was spiderwebbed with elaborate wiring and blobs of amplifiers that already boomed and squawked and roused outrageous echoes. Worse, the convention was being broadcast by radio, which Bryan doubly detested.

The gross confusion of opening sprawled through two loud and long days. Bryan did not take the platform until well along into the evening of the twenty-sixth, when he was granted three-quarters of an hour to "open consideration of the platform." He made a favorable impression with his plea for party unity. Then, annoyed by the loudspeaker system, he began intermixing pauses with his improvised text. At that point he noted the odd-looking eccentrics who were crouching back of microphone stands and intermittently making peculiar clutching motions. Bryan had been hearing about "sound engineers." Now he was observing their remarkable antics at close range. He was also beginning to hear some loud noises not related to electronics; these were boos and jeers from the galleries.

He managed to make himself heard until he began an explanation of the "moderation stand" against the Ku Klux Klan. Almost instantly the downpouring of catcalls and hisses increased. He ably restated the party's respect for and appreciation of minorities, including Catholics and Jews. Yet even then he was unhappily aware that the volume of boos was growing. When he pled again for a moderate stand against the Klan, pointing out that temperate disapproval was preferable to severe castigation that served to bestir public sympathy for the "martyrdom" of the sheet wearers, he was treated to a confusing mixture of moderate applause and louder boos. The latter kept gaining until the once-revered voice was drowned out.

Grimly, Bryan clung to the podium and completed his speech. Then, in tired loneliness, the apparently unwanted master of conventions left. As he walked to his hotel he assured himself that he was forever finished with conventions. He stumbled into bed, having taken time to remove only his shoes. At around three the next morning Charlie awakened him to report that the Bryan anti-Klan plank had won acceptance by a majority of one vote of the 1083%₀ cast. "It's God's work," Bryan murmured. "I'd never have risked that small a margin."

Next day the defender put on his black alpaca suit and returned to the convention. The nominations were upcoming. With revived persuasiveness, he succeeded in uniting the delegations of Florida and Nebraska as a nucleus of support for William Gibbs McAdoo. From the first, the fusion was blocked and harassed by Al Smith and his vociferous New York delegation. The deadlock held inexorably through two days and thirty-eight ballots. Bryan, aware that his candidate's chances were bleeding away, gained recognition to "clarify" his support of McAdoo. But this time most of the thirty minutes were virtually erased by the gallery uproar of epithets, which merged into an uproarious chanting of "Give us Al Smith!"

As he pushed his way to his seat, Bryan heard no applause, faced no stampede of cheering admirers. Where were the Bryan people? Where in the oversize carnival were the divine believers? And where was his century, the nineteenth century, the century of the American?

On the 103rd ballot the bankers' flunky John W. Davis ("anyhow he *looks* like a President") won the nomination. Charlie Bryan shambled to the side of his distressed brother in the Florida delegation. Charlie's long arm settled over Will's sagging shoulders. "I sorrow for our party, likewise for the poor sap Pretty Boy tags to be his Vice President."

Late the following afternoon the brothers met again at Schein's Restaurant, where Will took only a glass of water.

"Guess what," Charlie glowered. "Davis and his gang have picked *me* for his Vice President. A western dry to serve up with an eastern wet; a western progressive to garnish a Wall Street puppet. Or maybe it could be to guarantee that the Bryans won't split the party. Acting like a loyal Democrat and feeling like a complete idiot, I'll accept and run."*

Will did not answer. He seemed unable to believe what he heard. The benumbing and unreal dream kept with him throughout his ensuing sashays as a crowd-winning campaigner in still another election-losing campaign. His words and moves were sown with politicians' contradictions. At intervals he predicted victory, repeated that the Democrats refused to go backward whereas the Republicans could not go forward. He listened resignedly to the outcome: Calvin Coolidge victorious in thirty-nine of the forty-eight states.

Bryan's grievous lament was that no more than 51 percent of the nation's voters had voted. The week after the election, while briefly visiting his home on Antelope Creek, Bryan was seen weeping. The following day he smiled determinedly while confiding to his son that he proposed to shift from the politics of ballot boxes to the politics of saving souls.

* According to Silas Bryan II, Charlie's son, this is approximately what Charlie said.

23. Thy People—My People

Bryan resumed his correspondence with Dolph Talbot. He mentioned again that although his health was somewhat less than robust, he was more and more aware of a continued strengthening of his faith.

This particular blessing, he observed, also served to stimulate his range of activity. His lifelong interest in law endured by way of his touch-and-go relationship with the Washington law firm of Douglas, O'Bear, and Douglas, which specialized in practice related to inter-American affairs. Though listed on the letterheads as a member of the firm, Bryan explained that he had remained an extremely silent partner. He may have planned to participate more actively in the firm at a later date, but that is inferential or hypothetical; Bryan had confided to his first law partner that his first devotion would relate to the "American politics of faith."

When Dolph Talbot inquired more insistently of his friend's health, Bryan returned to his practice of affable evasion. He discussed Mamie's health at length, noting that although she still could not be assured of a pain-free day as long as she lived, she was well enough to be of real help and inspiration.

In helping defend her husband from the bodily disease that could destroy him and the swarmings of religious extremists and charlatans who could frustrate his foremost devotion, Mamie was also striving to keep the immediate family more closely together. William Jennings Bryan, Jr., had resigned from his Department of Justice post and was resettling himself, his wife, and three young daughters in Los Angeles, where he was setting up a private law practice.

During December 1924, Junior had managed to visit his parents in Miami at length. He noted with concern his father's occasional mention of intensive seizures of "head roars" and insomnia. He found that his father was using insulin only intermittently and continued to experiment with his own prescription of diet; for the time he was subsisting principally on milk toast and water. Although Bryan insisted he was thriving on the diet, Mamie and Grace held with the general estimate that Papa was fooling himself, not his diabetes.

A short time before, his old friend "Cotton" Bride had offered unintentional confirmation. Late that November Bryan had again spent several days in Washington as house guest of his former boardinghouse keeper. In a letter to his own daughter, Bride mentioned again that every time Bryan visited his home he "glorified" it. On this occasion he vowed that his guest room was pervaded by the fragrance of lilac blossoms—in late November. When Grace, who had heard this somewhat bizarre revelation secondhand, mentioned it to Dr. Kelley, he told her that the exudation of a lilac-like fragrance is a recognized symptom of bodies afflicted by far-advanced *Diabetes mellitus*. He showed her the exposition about the disease in the redoubtable *Encyclopædia Britannica*.

Junior made no headway with urging that his father

keep in closer touch with Dr. Kelley. "I'm very fond of Dr. Tom," his father assured him, "but I have other medical authorities who are a lot more encouraging." Again without mentioning names, Bryan returned to a lengthy discussion of his "climaxing crusade in behalf of Divine believing." When Junior mentioned that he himself was being offered or at least overtured with the presidency of the Anti-Evolution League in California, Bryan urged him to take it. (Soon thereafter Junior complied.)

Bryan assured his son that he had finally decided to take over as "first servant for the defenders of the faith." He would keep Villa Serena as his national headquarters, and he would pay particular attention to "anti-Bible and pro-Bible approaches in the public schools."

He pointed out that his ever-increasing volume of mail indicated the need of this "positioning," also that the fundamentalist movement was clearly progressing on its own power. The littering stacks of letters sustained the point, but somewhat less than literately. Even the letters from state legislators were rife with fanaticism as well as misspellings and grammatical errors. There were pencil-scribbled notes from preachers who signed themselves "revrent" or "paster" and failed to capitalize "God," who wrote "in violet" for "inviolate," and so on. A succession of letters came in from William Marr, a Nashville lawyer who sought to compile an authentic listing of Bryan's public statements or published views on the subject of religious teaching. Marr had opened by republishing the text of one of his hero's frequently repeated Chautauqua lectures, "Is the Bible True?" and mailing copies to all members of the Tennessee legislature.

Bryan responded with a sampling of his own "explanatory statements." The gist was that insofar as an undeniable majority of U.S. citizens "still believe in God and help sustain the Christian religion," they are justly entitled "to have their belief accommodated by the public schools they support." This "God-revering majority" would not willfully seek to deprive others of their right to learn, rather it would protect with moderation and due process of law its "fundamental rights of faith." Insofar as the believers in evolution could claim no prior or superior rights, why should those who chose to "worship brute ancestry" not be willing to found and finance their own schools for teaching the same to their own children?

Bryan pointed out that throughout his "public career" he had stood consistently for more and better public education, but always with the belief that in any schooling the development of the "good heart" is more to be sought after than the development of the "trained mind." Both were attainable and compatible, but if faced with an "enforced choice," he would surely take the good heart.

He reiterated that insofar as science, per se, has no morality, it cannot properly be accorded unrestrained freedom in any classroom; science, too, must submit to the discipline and priority of "a morality born of belief in God." Through his adult lifetime Bryan had insisted that the "directional mechanism" of public schooling is best managed by the local school board duly elected by local voters. Accordingly, the local school board, or the academy or college board of trustees or regents, is undeniably the "most proper supervisory authority."

As the flapping 1920s became more conspicuously marked by cleavages between the "free thinkers" and the "orthodoxists," a number of state legislatures got into the controversy. By January 1925, at least eight were considering additional bills to prohibit or restrict the teaching of evolution in their public schools. Bryan's adopted state was fairly typical of those, at the time seven, that had laws overtly prohibiting the teaching of evolution theory. During May 1923, the Florida legislature, by way of its Concurrent Resolution No. T, had established that for any teacher in any state-supported school to "teach as true any theory that would link man to any other life form" would be "improper and subversive."

Bryan particularly favored the Florida resolution because it kept with his "conviction" that no specific punishment should be stipulated for the violation; the resolution was simply a policy directive. As he neared his sixty-fifth birthday and the beginning of his eleventh year of unarrested diabetes, Bryan's accentuation of the "noncompulsion feature" was showing some indication of wavering. Mamie revealed her dread that Will was in danger of yielding too much to the extremists.

From the governor's office at Lincoln, where folding chairs were once more being substituted for cabinet files, Charles Weyland Bryan expressed a like concern. He also warned his brother against trying to exert undue outside influence on state legislatures. Charlie did not believe that faith could ever be legislated, or superior teaching enacted by law. He reminded Will that state legislatures are littered with traps; if Will failed to exercise care he could very well find himself in the horrible plight of a rabbit caught in a box trap and left there just to mellow away.

Late in January John A. Shelton, a member of the Tennessee Senate, had come up with a bill to discourage the teaching of "the evolutionary descent of man." As a longtime admirer of Bryan, Shelton had sought and heeded his counsel in drafting his proposed law, which did not stipulate the punishment of teachers found in violation, but sought to provide what its author called an authoritative directive for local school boards and other school officials. One can surmise, indeed, that the Shelton bill was substantially what Bryan favored. ("The special thing I want to suggest is that it is better *not* to have a penalty." Bryan repeated.) But the Shelton attempt died quietly in the judiciary committee.

Soon hereafter and without Bryan's advice or knowledge, another anti-evolution bill emerged from the lower house of the same legislature. George Washington Butler, a farmer and lay preacher from backwoods Macon County, took pains to recount that his bill, which would make the teaching of "any theory that denies the Story of Divine creation as taught in the Bible" unlawful and directly punishable, was wholly of God's will as revealed to himself. The Butler Bill sped to easy passage, 71 to 5 in the House and 24 to 6 in the Senate with its "stinger," fines of one hundred dollars to five hundred dollars for convictions, intact.

Governor Austin Peay of Tennessee, who had apparently disapproved of the bill but assumed it could easily override his veto, signed it with the rationalizing observation:

> . . . Something is shaking the fundamentals of the country both in religion and in morals. It is the opinion of many that an abandonment of the old-fashioned faith and belief in the Bible is our trouble in a large degree. . . .

Bryan responded to the news with a conspicuous flurry of befuddlement. He telegraphed congratulations to the governor, wrote an open letter to the New York *Times* describing the Butler Act as a profound victory for the cause of fundamentalism, and dispatched another letter to State Senator Shelton, deploring that the Act included a "punishment feature." He then trumpeted via the Associated Press that the Butler Act proved that the South was leading the nation in "Bible Christianity," and that other states would unquestionably follow the example of Tennessee.

From Lincoln, Governor Bryan was "real upset" by his brother's inconsistencies. Their youngest sister, Mary Elizabeth Bryan Allen, the dutiful keeper of the family scrap book, told this writer twenty-five years later: "At about that time Charles and I were noticing many things that suggested how Will's illness was hurting his ability to remember and speak consistently. . . ."

Junior was advised by his Aunt Mary that she expected

the "whole thing to blow over." She regularly read and clipped about twenty principal newspapers, and she adjudged that "this monkey bill wasn't being taken too seriously even in Tennessee."

However, there were reports that the constitutionality of the act would be challenged; the American Civil Liberties Union had reportedly indicated its willingness to serve as challenger. Several publications for teachers bitterly condemned the legislation, while greater numbers of church papers, particularly in Protestant folds, lauded it. Both the New York *Times* and the *Christian Science Monitor* deplored the "monkey law" and branded it an historic impediment to the progress of public education.

Bryan evidenced little or no interest in the legalities. At the time he was enormously busy with a mass of chores relating to his Believing Leadership Program. To nobody's surprise he was making plans for another lecture tour. Bookings were centered in Michigan, Missouri, and Pennsylvania, with a week-long "windup stand" in the Pittsburgh area. Agent Horner had gone along with Bryan's suggestion that the usual Chautauqua tour be deferred.

In a hurriedly scribbled letter to his son postmarked April 3, Bryan reported that he was feeling "more fit," adding that he would be carrying along several bagfuls of letters for answering, as well as peering out of Pullman windows at the spring landscapes and other people's gardening. "The whole country has gotten to be my own garden," he reflected, "but like the other gardens, mine has to be tended and worked. That is"—the scribbling ended there without signature.

In a casual gathering in Robinson's Drug Store of Dayton, Tennessee, the proprietor, F. E. Robinson, who doubled as chairman of the county school board, was chatting with George Rappelyea, a local mining engineer, and a young substitute and temporary teacher, the then twenty-four-year-old John Thomas Scopes. The conversation got around to the Butler Act. Rappelyea asked the teacher: "Can you teach biology without teaching evolution?"

Scopes replied that according to his own understanding he could not. The state-approved textbook, Hunter's *Civic Biology,* accepted the theory of evolution. Robinson pointed out that by then such a presentation was in violation of state law. Scopes answered that if it were, most biology teachers throughout the state were in violation. Rappelyea repeated that the matter deserved a court test. He subsequently wrote the Civil Liberties Union that the ingredients for a definitive test trial were at hand; all the Union had to do was to get the show on the road.

From that point on the exact developments became blurry. The Civil Liberties Union, through Arthur Garfield Hays, its senior counsel, accepted the challenge and began seeking out suitable (and publicity-assuring) defense counsels. Reported overtures to Charles Evans Hughes and Charles W. Davis were apparently ineffectual. Scopes, meanwhile, had expressed his willingness to accept the proffered services of a respected local attorney, John Randolph Neal.

Clarence Darrow of Chicago, the defender of the youthful Chicago thrill slayers, Loeb and Leopold, came striding into the picture as a volunteer and pivot member of the voluntary defense staff. Though slightly splattered by an effective grand jury indictment for jury tampering, Darrow was waxing liberal.

Another less than daisy-shy defense volunteer was Dudley Field Malone, then best known as a Manhattan socialite divorce lawyer. Although attorney and rhetorician Malone had served as a special counselor for the State Department while Bryan was Secretary, the Defender of the Faith did not seem to remember him. Meanwhile, A. T. Stewart, the attorney general of Tennessee, was shopping about for eminent assistants for the prosecution.

On May 5, Scopes submitted to arrest. Five days later Bryan received a telegram from L. M. Aldridge, the executive director of the World Christian Fundamental Association, requesting that he aid in the prosecution of the young teacher in Tennessee. Bryan accepted at once, assuring the officious stranger that he would gladly contribute his services gratis—"provided the Law Department of Tennessee is agreeable." Apparently he gave no heed to the fact that the largely on-paper World Christian Fundamental Association had no official or otherwise convincing authority for making the request, which was worded more as a regal command. Apparently, too, Bryan had wholly overlooked his repeated objection to what he had listed as the "punishment feature" of the Butler Act.

Next, and one gathers wholly coincidental to the Aldridge request, he received from a Mrs. Susan Hicks a telegram stating that the prosecution staff would be honored to have Bryan as "an honorary member." Again Bryan accepted, without having identified the personnel of the prosecution staff, the date of the trial, or the content of the indictment. Without dependable confirmation, he began to discuss the "fact and meaning" of the forthcoming trial in the texts of his lectures. He repeatedly asserted from public platforms that the State of Tennessee would surely win, and that "a tremendous reaction of public confidence" would ensue.

On or about May 15, William Jennings Bryan, Jr., received from his father an undated letter, postmarked Pittsburgh, urging Junior to join him in the prosecution of "that young Tennessee teacher whose name I keep forgetting." He gave the place as Nashville instead of Dayton. Junior, who excelled at understatement, recalled that he was a "trifle confused. . . . At the time I had practically no experience as a trial lawyer. I had no way of preparing in advance my proposed part in the case, and, as you know, I never was worth a whoop or more than a whisper as a public speaker. But more as a son than a lawyer, I accepted that Father was sick, in peril, and needed help.

Naturally Darrow had me worried. So I set about trying to steal the time."

On or about May 25, Bryan went briefly into seclusion in a hotel at Mechanicsburg, Pennsylvania, where he wrote his wife that he had been obliged to "rest and recuperate." Presumably the recuperation was rapid, for by May 31 he had returned to Miami and was busily preparing for the local *Herald* the "Bryan Plan for Religious Exercises in the Public Schools."

This effusion resulted in another change of plans. He next appeared at the annual General Assembly of Presbyterians, where he exhorted the "drastic expansion" of Bible teaching in all schools. He again discoursed on the "Tennessee Test Trial," by then scheduled for July 10, pointing out that it "demanded a clearly defined and unmistakable victory," adding that the test could not be a "success for fundamentalism" unless it "surely and finally put an end to all controversy and doubt." He would personally and gladly pay the young teacher's fine and court costs, if that were needed.

On June 10 he wrote Wallace Haggard, chief prosecutor, that the "unbelievers are definitely uneasy." Yet on the following day, apparently forgetful of the specific request of Tennessee Attorney General Stewart that no more voluntary prosecutors be invited, Bryan opened or resumed diligent but unsuccessful attempts to enlist the help (as fellow prosecutors) of Samuel Untermeyer, a renowned Jewish attorney of New York, and two eminent Catholics, U. S. Senators Thomas Walsh of Montana and David Walsh of Massachusetts. During the same week Bryan had journeyed to Atlanta to meet with the prosecuting staff but arrived there too ill to be effective.

During the final week of June the defense counsels assembled in Dayton for what Darrow termed a strategy meeting. The town was markedly friendly; the Progressive Club honored the distinguished visitors with a banquet. Wallace Haggard wrote Bryan that quite regardless of Darrow's brilliance and aggressiveness, he doubted that the Chicagoan would "fit in" with any locally chosen jury. Bryan replied that whatever else was attained, the trial should be objective and permit the "entire American public to fully understand both sides of the issue."

His son agreed in principle, but felt discomforting doubts as to how the upcoming test trial could effect this. In any case, Junior managed to join his father in Miami on June 30. The master of Villa Serena was preoccupied with stacks and boxes of mail, which all but canopied his two big writing desks and the study floor. Bryan still had no full-time secretary; from time to time, girls and young men from the local business colleges called by to "report for work." Except for Mamie, who was limping noticeably and intermittently in discernible pain, nobody was actually helping. Bryan appeared to be answering in longhand what he regarded as the most important letters. From time to time he strolled among the mounds of papers, pausing to trade pleasantries with two young male business college students who appeared to be eating almost constantly.

He heard with admiration his mother's announcement that regardless of her arthritis she was going to Dayton, Tennessee, to look after her Will. He noted that his father now lacked his ability to take brief naps by day or to sleep soundly at night. The cook reported that Bryan insisted on preparing his own meals, and that with the exception of an occasional bowl of milk toast he seemed to have gone back to gluten bread and water. Except when "important" guests were present he insisted on eating alone.

Bryan reiterated that he had "responsible medical assurance" that he could "count on being around for many years." But again he failed to give the source of this information. Junior noticed also that his father seemed to be suffering even more than ordinarily with the heat; his sweating was almost alarming.

Yet even though he had not faced a jury in almost a

third of a century, Bryan seemed confident that he could contribute to winning the case. "We have God, a righteous cause, and a good prosecution staff on our side. Darrow's the one to be worried." Junior was able to locate only one evidence of preparation for the oncoming court contest— an incomplete transcript of Darrow's defense of Leopold and Loeb. When he suggested that they leave for Dayton the following Sunday evening in order to gain an extra day for conferring with the prosecution, his parents agreed but vetoed his suggestion that they take along a nurse. Junior was hard put to persuade them to take along a secretary.

After boarding the train Bryan surprised Junior by suggesting that the prosecution's first emphasis should be the blocking of the defense from gaining a dismissal. Junior was confident that was one thing the publicity-loving Darrow did not wish. Throughout the dinner hour Bryan remained in his Pullman compartment, studying the Leopold-Loeb transcript and nibbling gluten bread.

Next morning, when the train pulled into Dayton, the depot and platform were crowded with several hundred townspeople who clapped and cheered when the party made its way down the coach steps. Bryan had already shed his black alpaca jacket; except for the inevitable black string tie, he was tastefully clad in white. His one surprising item of apparel was a white pith helmet that looked somewhat like a watermelon half, scooped out and whitewashed. Smiling, he joined his son in helping Mrs. Bryan into the open car, which moved out to head a parade from the depot to the courthouse. After sitting through luncheon where he nibbled, he set out afoot, as he said, to learn the town.

Junior recalled that the afternoon was killingly hot, the sidewalks fit to fry eggs on. Mamie was worried, but Bryan ignored her protests. Instead he seemed to find Dayton, Tennessee, the ultimate American El Dorado. He went among the everyday people, returning greetings, listening intently to the small talk as if every word were spoken by an oracle. Fortunately, learning Dayton did not require extensive walking. The census was only slightly more than three thousand; the thirteen stores, seven churches, and two office buildings were conveniently scattered along the stubby streets, which easily faded into poorland fields. Even so, the balding and freely sweating visitor was being led, at times virtually shoved, into welcoming shops, offices, and one after another of the heat-poxed churches, including the Methodist, where he had agreed to be guest pastor the following Sunday.

Next day, which was also blisteringly hot, the "banquet" of the Progressive Club took place. During the dinner the elder Bryan smiled almost continuously, glanced benevolently at his fellow diners, but refrained from eating. He spoke more slowly than usual, repeatedly pausing for breath. He opened by stating that the contest between "ev-o-lu-tion" and Christ-i-an-ity" is a duel to the death; that the two simply cannot "co-ex-ist." He defined the forthcoming court trial as a "con-front-a-tion" within the "larg-er duel." He said that the "foes of "Christ-i-an-ity" were already assembled and "con-fi-dent" that if "ev-o-lu-tion" won the case, belief in the Divine in these United States was surely doomed.

Next day, the Associated Press and the United Press were on hand in strength, and Western Union technicians were busily installing additional service wires. An estimated two hundred reporters had already arrived and most of them seemed to be searching for a room—any kind of a room. The overflow was being directed to nearby resort hotels. News cameramen were on hand and "setting up." The town was being besieged by miscellaneous transients, including a clan of Holy Rollers, and competing groups of Jehovah's Witnesses and Primitive Baptists; all had lately held brush arbor services in the immediate area. "Prophets" with beards and wind-blown hair had arrived with banners and signs exhorting all to Repent and Prepare to Meet Thy

God. Peddlers were hawking the streets with a variety of goods, including toy balloons lettered "Jesus Saves."

That night, Bryan addressed an audience on the grounds of the Morgan Spring Hotel, an old-fashioned mountainside resort overlooking a stretch of the Tennessee Valley seven miles out of Dayton. Supper finished (to the chagrin of Mamie, Bryan had made bold to sample the pepper-fried chicken), he was escorted to the front veranda, where an audience of several hundred villagers and farm people had assembled on the open lawn and porch edges. A rising wind pressed through the oak forests below as a summer night thunder squall began taking form farther down the valley. But the waiting crowd seemed to show no dread of rain and no urge to find places to sit.

Bryan stood on the veranda, his left hand clutching the railing, his right hand raised in a gesture of supplication. Two cripples had been placed directly beside him: an old man in a wheelchair, and an elderly woman who, supporting herself on crutches, listened as if in hypnosis. There was no light except what filtered through the windows, but the Bryan voice was everywhere, well-modulated, reassuring, musical. He preached of the faith and the right and duty of all to sustain faith, of the "great earth-cleansing tidal wave of Divine belief" then arising in the South. When he finished almost two hours had passed, yet no listener seemed to have moved more than a step or two. There was almost no applause, but the silence seemed to be reverent and adoring.

The following day, cruelly hot, had been chosen for completing trial preparations. Junior was favorably impressed by the work of Haggard and Stewart in putting together the plans for the prosecution. Haggard asked him to "give a hand" with the questioning of prospective jurors; he felt that Junior's "objectivity as an outsider" would be to the prosecution's advantage. The attorney general stated, "We want to leave your father as free as possible to use his talents and energy as he sees fit."

Bryan arrived at the conference late and looking ill. The son noted that his father walked uncertainly; also that his temple veins were bulging and pulsating, and that one of his eyes—as he recalled, the left—showed a small but recently formed blood clot.

Bryan seemed unable to hear well. Instead of sitting, he paced aimlessly. He confided to Wallace Haggard that he had stayed up very late "putting together a summation of my views and purposes for living." When Junior remarked that the endeavor would require a lot of time and thought, his father informed him that the news services, certainly the Associated Press and United Press, and possibly even the Hearst-owned International News Service, would carry his "final summation" as a "special feature." He avoided his son's inquiry as to why he deemed such a summation in order at precisely this time with the smiling comment that not everybody is invited to write his own obituary, at least not in such generous length. He added that he would be drafting the document as his time permitted during the course of the trial.

"You'll be having a mighty busy week or two," Stewart smiled.

"All my weeks are busy."

Bryan excused himself from the meeting. When Junior next noticed his father he was on the courthouse lawn surrounded by reporters to whom he was reciting plans for improving Bible teaching in schools. He advocated creating a National Bible Scholarship Committee to include one member from each church or sectarian group. The committee in turn would recommend sequences of Bible reading and reference works to the education departments of all the states. The restive reporters seemed grateful for any printable material.

The trial's opening was humdrum. News photographers crowded about Bryan; local lawyers and other courthouse followers clamored to be photographed in his company. Without need for excessive persuasion, also without shedding his deep frown, Darrow presently posed with his best-known adversary. But the actual convening of the trial in the dreary courthouse seemed dimly if at all related to either the cause of freedom in American education or the enlightening presentation of the case for fundamentalists. It was beginning as a publicity field day for the Messrs. Bryan and Darrow, with a Farmers' Grange-style kangaroo court in the immediate background.

Circuit Judge John T. Raulston, a fundamentalist-minded native of nearby Buzzard Creek, was aware of all this. He fidgeted, stretching his tall form in the shapes of X's and Y's, and advised the crowding audience that this was a court of law and a trial of justice—not a the-ater.

The selection of jurors followed conventional procedures; in part it featured the whispery drawl of William Jennings Bryan, Jr., in losing competition with the faulty acoustics. When court was adjourned until ten the following morning, prosecutor Haggard observed that it looked like a long trial. The obviously ailing Bryan inserted, "But we will easily win it and prove our point."

His confidence held through a typical Bryan weekend. At Saturday noon he spoke to a gathering of townspeople for an hour on the everyday citizen's right to worship without impediments or prejudice of what he called "alien beliefs." His afternoon address dealt with the "moral and cultural progress of the South." There were listeners who noted that the voice seemed unusually tired and at intervals gave indications of the return of a slight lisp. Next morning, in the role of guest pastor of the local Methodist church, the crusader seemed in better voice and spirits, although he was obliged to struggle at times in order to make himself heard by the outer folds of his overflow audience. In an afternoon billed as "A Special Address to Country Neighbors and Other Visitors," Bryan was obviously tired and afflicted with muddled and repetitive sentences. But at least his text was clear; it dealt with the rights and obligations of parents to safeguard the religious welfare of their children. The crowd was immensely friendly. For about an hour Bryan stood in the sun, shaking hands and, one could guess, listening to small talk and confidences. Here particularly he was an aging and ailing American believing with and speaking for a preponderance of his listeners.

Next morning the reopening of the trial proved to be without merit either as a court case or a public forum. Bryan looked on resignedly, intermittently wagging his palmleaf fan, but not speaking. Indeed, he seemed oddly disinterested. While his soft-spoken son succeeded in establishing by witnesses that John Scopes had "acceded" to the teaching of "Darwinian principles," the father seemed preoccupied with defending himself against invading houseflies.

The following day brought out what some of the hard-scrambling press called the "conflicting philosophies." Darrow's opening statement, though certainly not relevant to the direct progress of the trial, stressed that the cause of education admits no compromise with repression, including fundamentalism; that the banning of legitimate teaching by statutes can only set legitimate believers against other legitimate believers, using the body politic as a "weapon of arbitrary enforcement." The attorney general of Tennessee answered that if the defense won, the next step would deprive the Christian American of his right to believe in the Divine conception and the resurrection of his Savior, and "ultimate destruction of the Scriptures on which our civilization is built." From time to time Bryan's lips moved, but he did not speak. Instead, he poured and drank successive glassfuls of water and made hurried exits to the men's room.

Next day the exhibition began to fall apart, at least as a trial, when the defense announced that it would introduce as "special witnesses" a succession of fifteen scientists and theologians who would establish that there is no implicit conflict between the Biblical and scientific interpretations of "creation." Bryan peered intently while Darrow

summoned the defense's first "scientific witness," Maynard
F. Metcalf, a zoology teacher from Johns Hopkins.
Promptly and loudly, Attorney General Stewart challenged
the admissibility of this evidence. The judge, disturbed,
withheld decision and adjourned court until the following
morning.

Next day found Bryan even more restless and flushed
than before. He stood up, pulled open his collar, and
stripped off his tie. While returning to his chair he dropped
his palmleaf fan, and for the first time in his son's recollection he did not bother to recover it. Then without
rising, also most unusual for Bryan, he asked for and
received the court's permission to speak. He got to his feet
shakily and for a moment leaned heavily against a table.
His right arm trembled when he sought to raise it.

He moved uncertainly toward the jury box, first glancing
toward the bench, as if seeking reassurance. When he began speaking, supposedly to the jury, he seemed to be arguing with himself, intermittently gazing at the ceiling as
if listening to voices from above. He repeated that the so-
called experts could not properly be permitted to reinter-
pret the law, that this trial was not a forum for arguing
about whether the Butler Bill should have been made law.
Having agreed with himself, he shuffled toward a nearby
table and snatched up a Hunter's *Civic Biology*. With ro-
bot motions, he began to display various pages without
giving the audience time to view them or to make certain
that the pages were right side up. Then without looking
directly at the book he opened it to a marked full-page
illustration. He pointed out that the diagram represented
some thirty-five hundred species of animal lives, but listed
man as only one entry among the multitude. As the enter-
tainment-hungry crowd began to smile and presently applaud, Bryan braced himself for a declamation. But he did
not look directly at the audience. His expansive lips
shaped words that somehow failed to fit together.

"So *there* is the book . . . *here* is the book . . . the

book they were teaching your children . . . teaching your children that man is a mammal and so indistinguishable among mammals that they leave him there with other mammals. Including elephants! . . . Shall we be detached from the throne of God and be compelled to link our ancestors with the jungle . . . ?"

He took from the table Darwin's *The Descent of Man,* tried fumblingly to quote from memory, then began to read random and flagrantly disconnected excerpts. He complained about the "big words," milked laughs by noting that Darwin told how man is descended, not from honest, forthright American monkeys, but from cynical, degraded Old World monkeys. Again reverting to a kind of grumbling sleep talk, he shifted to the philosophy of Friedrich Wilhelm Nietzsche, which he linked with Darrow's defense of Leopold and Loeb, correctly stating that Darrow had successfully contended that the University of Chicago "professors" who had taught the Nietzsche credo to the afflicted Leopold were collaterally responsible for the slaying of the Franks child.

Darrow loudly denied that his defense arguments had followed the course being alleged. Bryan was able to refute with the court records, which he had studied, though clearly neither he nor Darrow was well qualified as a student of Nietzsche.

For a time the Chicagoan's angry contradictions seemed to prod Bryan toward a return to a more recognizable continuity of argument, but the wrathful exchange caused both men to shed stature. Darrow's embittered improvisions seemed to comprise particularly obnoxious exit lines from illustrious legal performance as one of America's most gifted defenders in the courts; Clarence Darrow, the premier labor-defense lawyer of the 1890s; the great defender of Eugene V. Debs in 1894; the heroic advocate of the Miners' Strike case of 1902; the illustrious defender of the McNamara Brothers case of 1911, and so on and so valiantly, now seemed to be casting himself away.

Bryan, too, one could say was being decimated—cut to a tenth part—in greatest part by his own ill-chosen devices. Never a legitimately or spontaneously motivated court action, the so-called Monkey Trial was changing to a deplorable, seemingly uncontrollable hoax. The dozen jurors looked depressingly like escapees from a convicts' road gang, and they mugged for the cameras and leered as if rehearsing for a Hal Roach comedy. Judge Raulston continued to scowl and writhe as if in terminal anguish and unbearable humiliation. John Scopes, the pompous young defendant, appeared wholly uninterested in anything even remotely related to his temporary trade of teaching. He blinked and solemnly ogled the burgeoning conclave of reporters and their cameras, seeming to delight in the contrived publicity that would make his an historic name.

For several more minutes the Bryan-Darrow slander bout continued. Then as if by supernatural intervention, Bryan managed to resume his address and to regain at least a semblance of lucidity. With pained effort he restated what he termed the fundamental right of a sovereign state to enact and enforce its own laws without alien imposition of "unreasonable pressure, propaganda, or derision."

Bryan spent the ensuing weekend in a dogged but unsuccessful struggle to endure the heat, keep in close range of the bathroom facilities of the Hicks home, and complete the drafting of what he had recaptioned, "Final Message of William Jennings Bryan." The latter document, still in untidy pen-and-ink draft, continued to cause his breeches pockets to bulge and his lace-canopied bed to look like a waste heap. Amiably but emphatically, he declined all offers of help.

The resumption of the trial on Monday brought a renewal of the crass showmanship of the previous week. With weary forbearance, Judge Raulston permitted the visiting scientists to continue their rehearsed routines, but declined to allow some of their antics to stand as "jury material." With cause he decided to divert the show from the extremely crowded courtroom to the relative safety of the courthouse yardway. Outside, the onlookers and principals could still sweat themselves to death, but the peril of being violently terminated by collapse of the ramshackle courthouse was diminished.

Later that day there was a lift of interest when Arthur Garfield Hays "invited" Bryan to take the witness stand. The State protested the move as irregular. Attorney General Stewart and some of his colleagues sensed a trap. They were fairly responsibly informed that Darrow and his colleagues, including the imported "scientists and educators," had been rehearsing, using, so onlookers vowed, Kirkley Mather, a Harvard faculty man, as a dummy for Bryan.

But there was no real need of a trap. Bryan, stumbling, took the witness stand. Many reporters, not excepting the wide-staring H. L. Mencken and towering Heywood Broun, both vehemently anti-Bryan, joined in describing Darrow's ensuing and hyperbole-infested "questioning" as cruel.

Speaking heavily and with an unusual quality of breathlessness, Bryan answered that he did, indeed, believe that Adam and Eve, created by God, were the first people. He believed that the flood really occurred and that the whale swallowed Jonah; he at least indicated that had the Bible said so he would have believed that Jonah swallowed the whale. In the progressive garroting Bryan granted that the six days of creation as stipulated in Genesis may have included great numbers of calendar years, and that Joshua's feat of causing the sun to stand still may have been a Biblical "adaptation" of the limited knowledge then prevailing. But he repeated his absolute acceptance that Eve was the first woman, and that she was literally made out of Adam's rib. Did Mr. Bryan know where Cain got his wife? No, sir, he would let the agnostics hunt for her. How did Mr. Bryan think the snake moved *before* God commanded it to crawl on its belly?

Bryan began to show anger. He called out that the tormentor's real purpose was to "slur the Bible," using for that purpose "this honorable court of Tennessee." Darrow strode toward his victim with raised fist. ". . . I am examining you on your fool ideas that no intelligent Christian on earth believes," he shouted. The judge banged angrily for order, and no less angrily adjourned the court until the following day. Bryan asserted that he was prepared to ask Darrow to take the witness chair. No longer in a permissive mood, Attorney General Stewart flatly refused his permission. When court reconvened, Judge Raulston ordered the previous testimony stricken from the trial records, and directed the defense to complete its case. The completion was most unimpressive. There was no closing argument. "Of course we could have exonerated Scopes," Darrow later told this writer, "but that wasn't what we were after. We were there to expose bigotry and show up Bryan."

Among the many who were disposed to disagree with Clarence Darrow were the twelve men who comprised the jury. They required only eight minutes to find the defendant guilty as charged. The judge took nine minutes to impose the minimum penalty, a fine of one hundred dollars and court costs.

Legalistically the prosecution had won. As contributors to a valid clarification of the issues, neither the prosecution nor the defense had scored a victory. If the Dayton trial were a way marker to the responsibilities and liberalization of public education in the United States, it was certainly not a cogent or definitive one. As Bryan's son had anticipated many weeks in advance of the trial, the so-called test case had not clearly revealed any side of the issue; the pathetic little court of Dayton, Tennessee had not even supplied a valid forum. While contributing insubstantially to winning the state's case, Bryan, a sick man who would not yield to his sickness, had dealt fumbling but irreparable hurt to his own cause. When he left the courthouse premises of Dayton, Tennessee on that sultry July 24, 1925, he was no longer the prophet beyond error, no longer the high-hearted fence breaker with the talent for finding his way home again.

While resuming his prodigiously busy way, Bryan seemed unaware of the catastrophe of anticlimax in which he was the principal victim. When he congratulated his son on his "lawyerlike conduct," he seemed entirely unaware of the younger man's expression of extreme discomfort.

But Mamie was watching her son, deeply concerned. She whispered to him, "Your father is a very sick man."

Junior nodded. "But he will have to get well in his own way."

In the back seat of the Haggard automobile, Mamie spent several minutes pleading once more with her husband to be wary of those untrustable fanatics who waited to mislead their chosen leader. "I have seen a great many of them here in Dayton," she continued. "If you let them do it they can and will destroy you and your cause."

Bryan smiled easily and said again, "Well, Mama, I haven't made that mistake, have I?"

He spent the dinner hour strolling the streets, as he later told his wife, "visiting with new friends." He seemed wholly unaware that the eight days actually devoted to the Dayton trial had certainly begotten for him more scorn and more derision than all his previous and controversial years of public life. Throughout the following two days (Wednesday and Thursday) Bryan worked closely on "my big apology." He told both his wife and his son that he proposed to cancel or defer all outstanding speaking engagements in order to complete his memoirs and, late in the year, to lead a "kind of pilgrimage to the Holy Lands." He did not mention his health, but repeated his confidence that "God will give me several more years of life."

By Friday morning Bryan seemed satisfied with his "big apology," which by then he had retitled, "The Final

Message." When he confided to his wife that he hoped that his "speech" would be published and distributed nationally, Mamie insisted that judging by the few pages he had shown her, the work required painstaking editing. Bryan replied that he had already made an arrangement with an editor-printer friend, George Milton of Chattanooga, who had agreed to edit the manuscript and set it directly in type. He insisted on making the short train trip to Chattanooga alone and immediately.

By then Junior had learned that his ailing but irrepressible father had accepted an invitation to spend Saturday in the nearby village of Winchester as guest of Judge Raulston and Attorney General Stewart, who were residents of that village. Another Bryan rally was being arranged, and the much-fatigued guest of honor had agreed to favor them with another address.

Early Saturday the younger Bryan, who freely admitted his dislike of auto driving but believed his own somewhat less perilous than his father's, awaited Bryan's return to Dayton, drove him to Winchester and spent an extremely busy day as his aide and escort. The ensuing speech was rife with repetitions, memory lapses, and other evidences of great weariness.

Instead of resting, as his son begged him to do, Bryan insisted on returning by train to Chattanooga, where Milton had proofs of "The Final Message" ready for reading.

Back in Dayton on Sunday morning, Bryan happily greeted his son, who waited to drive him to the Haggard home and presently to church. Letters from the first grandson and Junior's two elder daughters markedly pleased the grandfather. When he had read the rest of his mail he asked his son to take him and Mamie to "that nice little church where I preached my first Sunday here in—by the way, what is the name of this town?"

At the pastor's insistence Bryan offered the closing prayer. The Bryans were guests of the Wallace Haggards at lunch, and Bryan joined in a pleasantly spirited conversation but again refrained from eating. After leaving the table he settled himself at the telephone and began making reservations for a brief vacation trip to the Great Smokies.

He then told his wife, "Mama, from now on *I* am taking care of *you*." A few minutes later he confided that he was feeling drowsy. "I could use a bit of a nap." He followed his host to an upstairs guest room, remarking on the way that as he grew older his work load kept growing bigger. Bryan turned to confide to his son: "Seems there's hardly time enough for resting . . . none at all for dying."

The hour was near three in the afternoon. At about four, Mamie, who had picked her way upstairs with considerable difficulty, glanced in to make sure her Will was all right.

Will, eyes closed and lips shaping an engaging smile, was dead.

W. S. Gregg, M.D., gave his opinion that a massive cerebral hemorrhage was the cause of death. The Associated Press reported it as an apoplectic stroke; The New York *Times,* as apoplexy. From Washington, Dr. J. Thomas Kelley, in a long and carefully detailed letter to Grace Bryan Hargreaves, concluded thoughtfully:

> . . . Mr. Bryan died of Diabetes Mellitus, the immediate cause being the fatigue incident to the heat and the extraordinary exertions due to the Scopes trial. . . .

In any case, Bryan was dead. The exceptional prophet of the poor and the believing, the most exceptional defender of their faith and his own, had somehow found time to meet his Maker, in Whom he believed so invincibly.

Mamie Bryan was quite certain that the bit of a nap that her Will had felt for had been extended and somewhat transformed by the processes of Divine believing and the wondrous powers thereof. She was wholly convinced that he was and would ever remain within arm's length and voice's reach of his beloved America and his people; that his soul waits, as she said, "just beyond our mortal vision."

Tens of millions of Americans were disposed to agree. Throughout the United States and in many other nations, pulpits and press marked Bryan's passing with uncountable millions of words, thousands of prayers, and thousands of columns of type. Anticlimactic and deplorable as the Scopes trial had been and despite the subject's procession of failures, this American had been widely and deeply eulogized.

Certainly no other American has been remembered by such an array of appellations: Bryan, the People's Man; the Boy Orator from Nebraska; the Silver-Voiced Orator of the River Platte; the No Cross of Gold Man; the Praying Colonel; the Great Voice of the Small Voices; the Peerless Leader; the American Conscience; the American Prophet (some said Joshua, some Jeremiah, still others, Moses); the Man of the American Century (the nineteenth century); the Defender of the Faith.

Few noted that the champion of the American poor had died a millionaire (his estate was evaluated at $1,160,-000). Not many noted that by most standards Bryan had been an exceptionally unsuccessful office seeker; two terms in the Congress and slightly more than two years as Secretary of State could not, in view of his effort and following, be considered success in the quest of public office.

But by or before July 25, 1925, many millions had personally heard Bryan speak, had listened directly to the musical deluges of his words, his gesticulating, spellbinding, rhythmic and frequently ringing sermons, most of them outside of churches.

Bryan's spoken words would live; directly or indirectly, a great many of his words and ideas would live as enduring components of American life, government, and faith.

But, on this sultry July Sunday afternoon, in the ugly

little town where his final and most misguided try as a crusader had fallen into spittle and dust, the remarkable Commoner was dead. His burial services began in Dayton, recurred in Nashville and Chattanooga, where the body lay briefly in state, and ended in Washington and across the bridge in Arlington National Cemetery.

Fittingly, his final journey was by train, a five-coach funeral train pulled by a noisy camel-back locomotive puffing along through a sleepy succession of summer-slow countrysides. The train made many stops, including more than thirty impromptu waits at small depots and rural junctions where crowds, mostly of country people, were assembled to pay farewell to a crusader, their own crusader who was for once quiet, who was of America, its air and sky, its unconquerable dreams.

Bryan was their man.

Appendix

Cross of Gold Speech

Delivered on July 8, 1896 before the Democratic National Convention, in closing the Debate on the Adoption of the Platform.

I would be presumptuous indeed to present myself against the distinguished gentleman to whom you have listened if this were a mere measuring of abilities; but this is not a contest between persons. The humblest citizen in all the land when clad in the armor of a righteous cause, is stronger than all the hosts of error. I come to speak to you in defense of a cause as holy as the cause of liberty—the cause of humanity.

When this debate is concluded, a motion will be made to lay on the table the resolution offered in commendation of the Administration, and also the resolution offered in condemnation of the Administration. We object to bringing this question down to the level of persons. The individual is but an atom; he is born, he acts, he dies; but principles are eternal, and this has been a contest over a principle.

Never before in the history of this country has there been witnessed such a contest as that through which we have just now passed. Never before in the history of American politics has a great issue been fought out as this issue has been, by the voters of a great party. On the fourth of March, 1895, a few Democrats, most of them members of Congress, issued an address to the Democrats of the nation, asserting that the money question was the paramount issue of the hour; declaring that a majority of the Democratic party had the right to control the action of the party on this paramount issue; and concluding with the request that the believers in the free coinage of silver in the Democratic party should organize, take charge of, and control the policy of the Democratic party. Three months later, at Memphis, an organization was perfected and the silver Democrats went forth openly and courageously proclaiming their belief, and declaring that, if successful, they would crystallize into a platform the declaration which they had made.

Then began the conflict. With a zeal approaching the zeal of Peter the Hermit, our Silver Democrats went forth from victory into victory until they are now assembled not to discuss, not to debate, but to enter upon the judgment already entered by the plain people of this country. In this contest brother has been arrayed against brother, father against son. The warmest ties of love, acquaintance, and association have been disregarded; old leaders have been cast aside when they refused to give expression to the sentiments of those whom they would lead, and new leaders have sprung up to give direction to this cause of truth. Thus has the contest been waged, and we have assembled here under as binding and solemn instructions as were ever imposed upon the representatives of the people.

We do not come as individuals. As individuals we might have been glad to compliment the gentleman from New York [Mr. Hill], but we know that the people for whom we speak would never be willing to put him in a position where he could thwart the will of the Democratic party. I say it is not a question of persons; it is a question of principle, and it is not with gladness, my friends, that we find ourselves brought into conflict with those who are now arrayed on the other side.

The gentleman who preceded me [ex-Governor Russell] spoke of the State of Massachusetts; let me assure him that not one present in all this convention entertains the least hostility to the people of the State of Massachusetts, but we stand here representing people who are the equals, before the law, of the greatest citizens in the State of Massachusetts. When you [turning to the gold delegates] come before us and tell us that we are about to disturb your business interests, we reply that you have disturbed our business interest by your course.

We say to you that you have made the definition of a businessman too limited in its application. The man who is employed for wages is as much a businessman as his employer; the attorney in a country town is as much a businessman as the corporation counsel in a great metropolis; the merchant in a crossroads store is as much a businessman as the merchant of New York; the farmer who goes forth in the morning and toils all day—who begins in the spring and toils all summer—and who by the application of brain and muscle to the natural resources of the country creates wealth, is as much a businessman as the man who goes upon the board of trade and bets upon the price of grain; the miners who go down a thousand feet into the earth, or climb two thousand feet upon the cliffs, and bring forth from their hiding places the precious metals to be poured into the channels of trade, are as much businessmen as the few financial magnates who, in a back room, corner the money of the world. We come to speak for the broader class of businessmen.

Ah, my friends, we say not one word against those who live on the Atlantic Coast, but the hardy pioneers who have traveled all the dangers of the wilderness, who have made the desert to blossom like a rose—the pioneer away out there [pointing to the West], who rear their children near to Nature's heart, where they can mingle their voices with the voices of the birds—out there where they have erected schoolhouses for the education of their young, churches where they praise their Creator, and cemeteries where rest the ashes of their dead—these people, we say, are as deserving of the consideration of our party as any people in the country. It is for these that we speak. We do not come as aggressors. Our war is not a war of conquest; we are fighting in the defense of our homes, our families, and posterity. We have petitioned, and our petitions have been scorned; we have entreated, and our entreaties have been disregarded; we have begged, and they have evaded us when our calamity came. We beg no longer; we entreat no more; we petition no more. We defy them.

The gentleman from Wisconsin [Senator Vilas] has said that he fears a Robespierre. My friends, in this land of the free you need not fear that a tyrant will spring up from among the people. What we need is an Andrew Jackson to stand, as Jackson stood, against the encroachment of organized wealth.

They tell us that this platform was made to catch votes. We reply to them that changing conditions make new issues; that the principles upon which Democracy rests are as everlasting as the hills, but that they must be applied to new conditions as they arise. Conditions have arisen and we are here to meet those conditions.

They tell us that the income tax ought not to be brought in here; that it is a new idea. They criticize us for our criticism of the Supreme Court of the United States. My friends, we have not criticized; we have simply called attention to what you already know. If you want criticisms, read the dissenting opinions of the Court. There you will find criticisms. They say that we passed an unconstitutional law; we deny it. The income tax was not unconstitutional when it was passed; it was not unconstitutional when it went before the Supreme Court for the first time; it did not become unconstitutional until one of the judges changed his mind, and we cannot be expected to know when a judge will change his mind. The income tax is just. It simply intends to put the burden of government justly upon the backs of the people. I am in favor of an income tax. When I find a man not willing to bear his share of the government that protects him, I find a man who is unworthy to enjoy the blessings of a government like ours.

They say that we are opposing national bank currency; it is true. If you will read what Thomas Benton said, you will find he said that, in searching history, he could find but one parallel to Andrew Jackson; that was Cicero, who destroyed the conspiracy of Cataline and saved Rome. Benton said that Cicero only did for Rome what Jackson did for us when he destroyed the bank conspiracy and saved America. We say in our platform that we believe that the right to coin and issue money is a function of government. We believe it. We believe that it is a part of sovereignty, and can no more with safety be delegated to private individuals than we can afford to delegate to private individuals the power to make penal statutes or levy taxes. Mr. Jefferson, who was once regarded as a good Democratic authority, seemed to have differed in opinion from the gentleman who has addressed us on the part of the minority. Those who are opposed to this proposition tell us that the issue of paper money is a function of the bank, and that the government ought to go out of the banking business. I stand with Jefferson rather than with *them,* and tell them, as he did, that the issue of money is a function of government, and that banks ought to go out of the governing business.

They complain about the plank which declares against life tenure in office. They have tried to strain it to mean what it does not mean. What we oppose by that plank is the life tenure that is being built up in Washington, and which excludes from the participation in official benefits the humbler members of society.

Let me call your attention to two or three important things. The gentleman from New York says that he will propose an amendment to the platform providing that the proposed change in our monetary system shall not affect contracts already made. Let me remind you that there is no intention of affecting those contracts which according to the present laws are made payable in gold; but if he means to say that we cannot change our monetary system without protecting those who have loaned money before the change was made, I desire to ask him where, in law or in morals, he can find justification for *not* protecting the debtors when the act of 1873 was passed, if he now insists that we must protect the creditors.

He says he will also propose an amendment which will provide for the suspension of free coinage if we fail to maintain the parity within a year. We reply that when we advocate a policy which we believe will be successful, we are not compelled to raise a doubt as to our own sincerity by suggesting what we shall do if we fail. I ask him, if he would apply his logic to us, why he does not apply it to himself. He says he wants this country to secure an international agreement. Why does he not tell us what he is going to do if he fails to secure an international agreement? There is more reason for him to do that than there is for us to provide against the failure to maintain parity. Our opponents have tried for twenty years to secure an international agreement, and those are waiting for it most patiently who do not want it at all.

And now, my friends, let me come to the paramount issue. If they ask us why it is that we say more on the money question than we say upon the tariff question, I reply that, if protection has slain its thousands, the gold standard has slain its tens of thousands. If they ask us why we do not embody in our platform all the things that we believe in, we reply that when we have restored the money of the Constitution all other necessary reforms will be possible; but until this is done there is no other reform that can be accomplished.

Why is it that within three months such a change has come over the country? Three months ago, when it was confidently asserted that those who believe in the gold standard would frame our platform and nominate our candidates, even the advocates of the gold standard did not think that we could elect a President. And they had good reason for their doubt, because there is scarcely a state here today asking for the gold standard which is not in the absolute control of the Republican party.

But note the change. Mr. McKinley was nominated at St. Louis before a platform which declared for the maintenance of the gold standard until it can be changed to bimetallism by international agreement. Mr. McKinley was the most popular man among the Republicans, and three months ago everybody in the Republican party prophesied his election. How is it today? Why, the man who was once pleased to think that he looked like Napoleon—that man shudders when he remembers that he was nominated on the anniversary of the Battle of Waterloo. Not only that, but as he listens he can hear with ever-increasing distinctness the sound of the waves as they beat upon the lonely shores of St. Helena.

Why this change? Ah, my friends, is not the reason for the change evident to anyone who will look at the matter? No private character, however pure, no personal popularity, however great, can protect from the avenging wrath of an indignant people a man who will declare that he is in favor of fastening the gold standard upon this country, or who is willing to surrender the right of self-government and place the legislative control of our affairs in the hands of foreign potentates and powers.

We go forth confident that we shall win. Why? Because on the paramount issue of this campaign there is not a spot of ground upon which the enemy will dare to challenge battle. If they tell us that the gold standard is a good thing, we shall point to their platform and tell them that their platform pledges the party to get rid of the gold standard and substitute bimetallism. *If the gold standard is a good thing, why try to get rid of it?*

I call your attention to the fact that some of the very people who are in this convention today and who tell us that we ought to declare in favor of bimetallism—thereby declaring the gold standard is wrong and that the principle of bimetallism is better—these very people four months ago were open and avowed advocates of the gold standard, and were then telling us that we could not legislate two metals together, even with the aid of the world. If the gold standard is a good thing, we ought to declare in favor of retention and not in favor of abandoning it; and if the gold standard is a bad thing, why should we wait until other nations are willing to help us to let go? Here is the line of battle, and we care not upon which issue they force us to fight; we are prepared to meet them on either issue or on both. If they tell us that the gold standard is the standard of civilization, we reply to them that this, the most enlightened of all nations of the earth, has never declared for a gold standard and that both the great parties this year are declaring against it. If the gold standard is the standard of civilization, why, my friends, should we not have it? If they come to meet us on that issue we can present the history of our nation. More than that; we can tell them that they will search the pages of history in vain to find an instance where the common people of any land have ever declared themselves in favor of the gold standard. They can find where the holders of fixed investments have declared for a gold standard, but not where the masses have.

Mr. Carlisle said in 1878 that this was a struggle between "the idle holders of idle capital" and "the struggling masses, who produce the wealth and pay the taxes of the country"; and, my friends, the question we are to decide is: Upon which side are we, [the side of] "the idle holders of idle capital" or upon the side of "the struggling masses"? This is the question which the party must answer first, and then it must be answered by each individual hereafter. The sympathies of the Democratic party, as shown by the platform, are on the side of the struggling masses, who have ever been the foundation of the Democratic party. There are two ideas of government. There are those who believe that, if you will only legislate to make the well-to-do prosperous, their prosperity will leak through on those below. The Democratic idea, however, has been that if you legislate to make the masses prosperous, their prosperity will find its way up through every class that rests upon them.

You come to us and tell us that the great cities are in favor of the gold standard; we reply that the great cities rest upon our broad and fertile prairies. Burn down your cities and leave our farms, and your cities will spring up again as if by magic; but destroy our farms, and the grass will grow in the streets of every city in the country.

My friends, we declare that this nation is able to legislate for its own people on every question, without waiting for the aid or consent of any other nation on earth; and upon this issue we expect to carry every state in the Union. I shall not slander the inhabitants of the fair State of Massachusetts nor the inhabitants of the State of New York by saying that, when they are confronted with this proposition, they will declare that this nation is not able to attend to its own business. It is the issue of 1776 over again.

Our ancestors, when but three million in number, had the courage to declare their political independence of every other nation; shall we, their descendants, when we have grown to seventy millions, declare that we are less independent than our forefathers? No, my friends, that will never be the verdict of our people. Therefore, we care not upon what lines the battle is fought. If they say bimetallism is good, but that we cannot have it until other nations help us, we reply that, instead of having a gold standard because England has, we will restore bimetallism, then let England have bimetallism because the United States has it. If they dare come out in the open field and defend the gold standard as a good thing, we will fight them to the uttermost. Having behind us the producing masses of this nation and the world, supported by the commercial interests, and the toilers everywhere, we will answer their demand for a gold standard by saying to them: You shall not press down upon the brow of labor the crown of thorns, you shall not crucify mankind upon a cross of gold.

Notable Published Speeches of

William Jennings Bryan

"The Money of the People," Chicago, 1895; C. H. Sergel Company, Chicago, 1895.

"Republic or Empire? The Philippines Question," Chicago, 1899; The Independent Company, Chicago, 1899.

"Life and Speeches of William Jennings Bryan"; R. H. Woodward, Baltimore, 1900.

"Speeches Delivered in Tokyo," 1905; Japanese Society of New York, 1905.

"British Rule in India," 1906; British Committee of the Indian National Congress, Westminster, England, 1906.

"Bryan's Silver and Gold Speeches," 1907; BiMetalism Association of America, New York, 1907.

"Bryan's Speech at the Brooklyn Democratic Club," April 1907; Brooklyn Democratic Club Record, 1907.

"The Coming of the University," June 1908; University of Indiana Bulletin, Vol. VI, Bloomington, 1908.

"Thou Shall Not Steal"; Civic Forum, New York, September 1908.

"Speeches of W. B. Cochran and W. J. Bryan, delivered at the Chicago Congress on Trusts"; Civic Federation of Chicago, 1910.

"Address to the Puerto Rico Association of San Juan," April 9, 1910; San Juan Press, 1910.

"Bryan on Imperialism," Chicago, 1910; Bentley and Company, Chicago, 1910.

"Speeches of William Jennings Bryan, Revised and Rearranged by Himself"; Funk & Wagnalls Company, New York, 1912.

"Remarks of Secretary of State William Jennings Bryan before the California Legislature of 1913"; Sacramento, 1913.

"The Causeless War and Its Lessons for Us," August 1915; *The Commoner,* Lincoln, 1915.

"Citizenship in a Republic," February 1916; National Education Association, Washington, D.C., 1916.

"America and the European War," Madison Square Garden, February 1917; Emergency Peace Federation, New York, 1917.

"Heart to Heart Appeals, Speeches Delivered 1890–1916"; Fleming H. Revell, New York, 1917.

"Heart to Heart Appeals"; Speeches Delivered 1910–1916; Fleming H. Revell, New York, 1917.

Chapter Source Notes

Chapter 1. *THE FENCE BREAKER*

Baldridge, Chloe, *The Bryans and Jennings of Illinois*. Privately published, Jacksonville, Illinois, 1896.

Bryan, William Jennings and M.E., *Memoirs of William Jennings Bryan*. John C. Winston Co., Philadelphia, 1925.

Coletta, Paolo E., "The Youth of William Jennings Bryan." *Nebraska History*, Vol. XXI, No. 1, pp. 147–163, Lincoln, 1953.

Daughters of the American Revolution, *The Bryan Family*. File 694, Atlanta, 1907.

McKeever, P., *History of Marion County, Illinois*. Privately published, Salem, 1890.

Minutes of the Illinois Constitutional Convention, 1870–71. Springfield, Illinois, 1871.

Murdock, T. B., *History and People of Marion County, Illinois*. Standard, Chicago, 1888.

Records Third and Fourth Judiciary Districts, Illinois. State of Illinois, Springfield, 1881.

Sienes, J. R., *Portraits and Biographical Records of Clinton, Washington, Marion and Jefferson Counties* (Illinois). Privately published, St. Louis, 1904.

Vandalia, Illinois *Journal*, November 5, 1870.

UNPUBLISHED

Journal notes by Bryan's eldest daughter, Ruth Bryan Owen Rohde.
Scrapbook and interviews with Bryan's youngest sister, Mary Elizabeth Bryan Allen of Lincoln, Nebraska, 1959–62.
Letter collection of Silas Bryan, II of Lincoln (Bryan's nephew and the son of Charles W. Bryan). Document Collections of the Bryan Museum at Salem, Illinois; the Grace Bryan Hargreaves Collection, now part of the Bryan Collection, Library of Congress; and the Occidental College (Los Angeles) Bryan Collection.

CHAPTER 2. *THE BOY BELIEVER*

Bartholomew, H. E., *Bryan Unveiled*. Privately published, Chicago, 1908.
Bryan, Williams Jennings and M. E., *Memoirs of William Jennings Bryan*. John C. Winston Co., Philadelphia, 1925.
Cole, Arthur C., "The Illinois Era of the Civil War." *Contemporary History of Illinois*. Illinois Historical Society, Springfield, 1913.
Coletta, Paolo E., *William Jennings Bryan*. University of Nebraska Press, Lincoln, Nebraska, 1964.
Glad, Paul W., *The Trumpet Soundeth*. University of Nebraska Press, Lincoln, Nebraska, 1960.
Hibben, Paxton, *The Peerless Leader*. Farrar & Rinehart, Inc., New York, 1929.
Smith, T. U., *Youth of William Jennings Bryan*. Privately published, Utica, New York, 1901.
Williams, Wayne C., *William Jennings Bryan; A Study in Political Vindication*. Revell, New York, 1923.

UNPUBLISHED

Boell, Jesse E., "William Jennings Bryan Before 1896." A thesis, University of Nebraska, 1929.
Scrapbook, Mary Elizabeth Bryan Allen, Lincoln, Nebraska.
Letters: Mariah Bryan to Mrs. J. Antwerps, 1863–1870 (Bryan Museum, Salem); The George R. Poague Papers (Silas Bryan, II Collection).

CHAPTER 3. *WELLS OF LEARNING*

Anderson, Paul R., "Hiram K. Jones and Philosophy at Jacksonville." *Journal of the Illinois State Historical Society*, Vol. XXXIII, pp. 478–520, Springfield, 1949.

Bryan, William Jennings, *Speeches.* Funk & Wagnalls Co., New York, 1909.

———— and Bryan, M. E., *Memoirs of William Jennings Bryan.* John C. Winston Co., Philadelphia, 1925.

Donahue, Jeremiah, "Bryan at College." Illinois College *Rambler,* Jacksonville, October 1896.

Illinois College *Rambler,* Jacksonville, October 1879; November 1880.

Jacksonville Female Academy Catalogue and Register, 1881, 1882.

New York *Sun,* July 14, 1913.

Poague, George R., "College Career of William Jennings Bryan." *Journal of the Missouri Valley Historical Society,* Vol. XV, pp. 172–77, March 1941.

Whipple's Academy, Jacksonville, Illinois, 1876–77.

UNPUBLISHED

Scrapbook, Mary Elizabeth Bryan Allen, Lincoln, Nebraska.

Interviews, William Jennings Bryan, Jr., 1964, 1965.

Letters: George R. Poague to L. A. Trent, July 3, 1896; to Kansas City *Star,* July 18, 23, and 24, 1896; William B. Slater Journal, Jacksonville, 1900; Mariah Bryan and J. Van Antwerps Correspondence, 1878–1880 (Silas Bryan, II Collection).

CHAPTER 4. *THE SEEKER*

Bryan, William Jennings and M. E., *Memoirs of William Jennings Bryan.* John C. Winston Co., Philadelphia, 1925.

Coletta, Paolo E., "The Courtship of William Jennings Bryan and Mary Elizabeth Baird." *Journal of the Illinois State Historical Society,* Vol. L, No. 3, Springfield, Autumn 1951.

———— *William Jennings Bryan,* University of Nebraska Press, Lincoln, 1964.

Herrick, G. F. and J., *Life of William Jennings Bryan.* John R. Stanton Co., Chicago, 1925.

Hibben, Paxton, *The Peerless Leader.* Farrar & Rinehart, Inc., New York, 1929.

Jackson, Illinois *Journal,* May 6, 1880.

Marion County (Salem, Illinois) *Herald,* April 23, 1880; July 17, 1881.

UNPUBLISHED

Minutes Book, Sigma Phi Fraternity, Jackson College, 1880–81.

Interviews: Mary Elizabeth Bryan Allen, Lincoln, Nebraska; John H. Reed, Jacksonville, Illinois; S. L. Kagy, Chicago.

Letters: Bryan and Mary E. Baird Letters (Ruth Bryan Rohde Collection), May 1880; Mariah J. Bryan to Dr. H. K. Jones, June 4, 1880; John Kendrick to John Reed, July 25, 1901; S. L. Kagy to John Reed, July 21, 1896; William P. Staten to George R. Poague, September 3, 1896; (Occidental College Collection).

CHAPTER 5. *THE LAWYER*

Bryan, William Jennings, "The Spirit of Brotherhood." *The Viewer,* Vol. IX, Chicago, 1911.
———— and Bryan, M. E., *Memoirs of William Jennings Bryan.* John C. Winston Co., Philadelphia, 1925.
Catalogs, Union College of Law, Chicago, 1880–88.
Debs, Eugene V., *The Truth of the Railway Wage Struggle.* Union of American Railroad Workers, Chicago, 1884.
Illinois College *Rambler,* Jacksonville, October 1881.
Jacksonville, Illinois *Journal,* July 5, and August 3 and 22, 1884.
Trumbull, Lyman, *Papers and Remembrances.* Privately published, Chicago, 1891.
White, Horace, *Life of Lyman Trumbull.* Houghton Mifflin Co., Boston, 1913.
Wilson, George H., *Centennial Celebration of the Founding of Illinois College,* Jacksonville, 1929.

UNPUBLISHED

Scrapbook, Mary Elizabeth Bryan Allen, Lincoln, Nebraska.
Letters: Bryan and Mary E. Baird letters (Ruth Bryan Rohde Collection) 1880; Mariah J. Bryan and H. K. Jones, 1880–86; John Kendrick and John Reed, July 21, 1896, July 27, 1901, and miscellaneous; Bryan to Charles W. Bryan, November 1885; to Mariah J. Bryan, June 1883 and November 8, 1884; W. B. Slater Papers (Occidental College Collection); Edward A. McDonald to author, September 3, 1965 and September 15 and October 16, 1966.

CHAPTER 6. *LINCOLN, NEBRASKA*

Billingsly, L. W. and R. J. Green, *Revised Ordinances, City of Lincoln, Nebraska, 1890–1895.* Lincoln, Nebraska, 1895.
Board of Trade *Report,* Lincoln, Nebraska, 1888.
Bryan, William Jennings and M. E., *Memoirs of William Jennings Bryan.* John C. Winston Co., Philadelphia, 1925.

Dick, Everett N., "Problems of the Post Frontier City as Portrayed by Lincoln, Nebraska, 1880–1890." *Nebraska History,* pp. 41–55, Vol. XXVIII, No. 2, Lincoln, 1947.

Lincoln, Nebraska *Call,* July 7, 1884 and June 4, 1888.

Minutes of the City Council, Lincoln, Nebraska, 1888.

Porterfield, T. E., "A Reporter at Large." *Munsey's Magazine,* Vol. XXIV, No. 3, New York, 1901.

Union Pacific Railroad, Brochure No. 21, Omaha, 1881.

UNPUBLISHED

Scrapbook, Mary Elizabeth Bryan Allen, Lincoln, Nebraska.

Letters: A. Talbot to C. W. Bryan, July 1, 1889; to T. K. Reynolds, September 7, 1889; to T. S. Allen, November 1, 1890; to B. A. Schultz, January 3 and February 27, 1888 (Silas Bryan, II Collection).

CHAPTER 7. *THE UNCOMMON COMMONER*

Abstract of the Eleventh U. S. Census, Department of Commerce, Washington, 1892.

Arbor Lodge, Nebraska *Journal,* May 5 and June 10, 1888.

Boggs, Allen, *Money at Interest.* McConkey, Chicago, 1911.

Bryan, William Jennings and M. E., *Memoirs of William Jennings Bryan.* John C. Winston Co., Philadelphia, 1925.

Carey, Fred, *Mayor Jim: The Life of James C. Dahlman.* Omaha Printing Co., Omaha, 1930.

Chicago *Daily News,* April 15, 1888.

Dawes, Charles G., *Journal of the McKinley Years.* P. Tower, La Grange, Illinois, 1950.

Fall City, Nebraska *Broadax,* August 1 and 19, 1888.

Forum, "The New West," Vol. X, Feb., 1135–1201, New York, 1888.

Lincoln, Nebraska *Call,* May 3, 1888 and October 13, 1899.

Long, J. C., *Bryan, The Great Commoner.* D. Appleton-Century Company, Inc., New York, 1928.

Mullen, Arthur Francis, *The Western Democrat.* Funk & Wagnalls Company, New York, 1940.

Omaha, Nebraska *Bee* (*Bee-News*), May 3, 1888 and February 4, 1889.

Omaha, Nebraska *World* (*World-Herald*), May 8 and 29, August 15, and December 8, 1888.

Pound, Louise, "Old Nebraska Customs." *Nebraska History,* Vol. XXVIII, No. 2, Lincoln, 1942.

UNPUBLISHED

Scrapbook, Mary Elizabeth Bryan Allen, Lincoln, Nebraska.
Grace Bryan Hargreaves Manuscripts, Bryan Papers (Library of Congress).
Bryan's Office Journals, 1888–1891.
Letters: A. Talbot to B. O. McKinney, June 7, 1888; to W. O. Springer, April 5, 1888; Morton to Bryan, August 10, 1888 (Silas Bryan, II Collection).

CHAPTER 8. *THE LOSER AS WINNER*

Barr, Mary Elizabeth, *History of Kansas.* Vol. II, Pioneer, Emporia, 1929.
Brooks, Sydney, "Mr. Bryan." *The Nineteenth Century: A Monthly Review,* Vol. LXXXXXVI, New York, July 1915.
Bryan, William Jennings and M. E., *Memoirs of William Jennings Bryan.* John C. Winston Co., Philadelphia, 1925.
Dunn, Arthur Wallace, *How Presidents Are Made.* Funk & Wagnalls Company, New York, 1920.
Glad, Paul W., *The Trumpet Soundeth.* University of Nebraska Press, Lincoln, 1960.
Hicks, John D. *The Populist Revolt.* University of Minnesota Press, Minneapolis, 1931.

UNPUBLISHED

Scrapbook, Mary Elizabeth Bryan Allen, Lincoln, Nebraska.
Letters: Bryan to Mary B. Bryan, November 9, 1888; to Grover Cleveland, December 1, 1888; to Charles W. Bryan, December 19, 1889; to Walter H. Page, August 16, 1889; to Charles G. Dawes, August 6, 1901; to T. S. Allen, undated (Bryan Papers, Library of Congress).

CHAPTER 9. *GOD AND THE TARIFF*

Beard, Charles A., *Contemporary American History.* Macmillan Co., New York, 1914.
Boeckel, Richard, *Labor's Money.* Harcourt, Brace & Co., New York, 1923.
Bryan, William Jennings, *Speeches.* Funk & Wagnalls Co., New York, 1909.
———— and Bryan, M. E., *Memoirs of William Jennings Bryan.* John C. Winston Co., Philadelphia, 1925.
Lincoln, Nebraska *Call,* July 31 and November 1, 1890.

Lincoln, Nebraska *State Journal,* June 18, July 8 and 31, October 10 and 13, and December 7, 1890.

Omaha, Nebraska *Bee-News,* June 21, October 1, and November 6, 1890.

Omaha, Nebraska *World-Herald,* July 31, August 2, September 3, 9, 12, 21 and 30, October 13, and November 6 and 11, 1890.

St. Louis *Post-Dispatch,* December 12, 1890.

UNPUBLISHED

Interviews: Mary Elizabeth Bryan Allen and William Allen White.

Letters: A. Talbot to Thomas Calfer, August 9, 1890; J. S. Morton to Bryan, October 2, 1889 and November 8, 1890; Mariah J. Bryan to Bryan, November 10, 1890.

CHAPTER 10. *"O'BRIEN" GREETS TAMMANY*

Anti-Nicotine Society of America, *The Evils of Cigarettes.* Chicago, 1894.

Associated Press, "Bryan." J. P. Clark, March 16, 1892.

Bryan, William Jennings and M. E., *Memoirs of William Jennings Bryan.* John C. Winston Co., Philadelphia, 1925.

Elizabeth, Kentucky *News,* March 17, 1892.

Gale, A. L. and G. W. Kline, *Bryan the Man.* Thompson Publishing Co., New York, 1908.

Kramer, Dale, *Wild Jackasses.* Hastings House, New York, 1956.

Nebraska *State Journal,* Lincoln, September 6, 1892 and January 9, 1894.

New York *Sun,* July 4, 1894.

New York *Times,* March 17, 1892 and February 2, 1894.

New York *World,* March 16 and 17, 1892 and January 13 and 14, 1894.

Omaha, Nebraska *Bee-News,* January 27, 1892.

Omaha, Nebraska *World-Herald,* November 1, 1894.

Washington *Post,* March 16 and 20, 1892; January 13, March 13, and August 16 and 18, 1894; and March 12, 1895.

Washington *Star,* March 5, 1892.

UNPUBLISHED

Scrapbook, Mary Elizabeth Bryan Allen, Lincoln, Nebraska.

Letters: Bryan to A. Talbot, January 26, 1892; to Charles W. Bryan, February 11, 1892; to C. E. Thompkins, March 19, 1892 (Silas Bryan, II Collection, Omaha).

CHAPTER 11. *THE "SECOND DECLARATION OF INDEPEND-ENCE"*

Associated Press, "Bryan of Nebraska." Washington, May 14, 1894.

Beard, Charles A. and Mary, *The Rise of American Civilization.* Macmillan Company, New York, 1927.

Bryan, William Jennings, *Speeches.* Funk & Wagnalls Co., New York, 1909.

——— and Bryan, M. E., *Memoirs of William Jennings Bryan.* John C. Winston Co., Philadelphia, 1925.

Davis, Hayne, editor, *Among the World's Peacemakers: Epitome of Interparliamentary Union.* Progressive Publishers, New York, 1907.

Griffith, Will, *The Great Commoner: William Jennings Bryan.* Privately published, Carbondale, Illinois, 1908.

Hibben, Paxton, *The Peerless Leader.* Farrar & Rinehart, Inc., New York, 1929.

New York *Times,* July 1, 1896.

Omaha, Nebraska *Bee-News,* June 27, 1894.

Omaha, Nebraska *World-Herald,* May 17, and June 14 and 27, 1894; July 16, 1895.

St. Louis *Post-Dispatch,* July 2, 1896.

UNPUBLISHED

Interviews: Mary Elizabeth Bryan Allen, 1960; William Allen White, 1938; William Jennings Bryan, Jr., 1965.

CHAPTER 12. *THE LONG ODDS*

Bryan, William Jennings, *Speeches.* Funk & Wagnalls Co., New York, 1909.

——— and Bryan, M. E., *Memoirs of William Jennings Bryan.* John C. Winston Co., Philadelphia, 1925.

Griffith, Will, *The Great Commoner: William Jennings Bryan.* Privately published, Carbondale, Illinois, 1908.

Hibben, Paxton, *The Peerless Leader.* Farrar & Rinehart, Inc., New York, 1929.

New York *Times,* July 1, 3, and 21, 1896.

CHAPTER 13. *CROSS OF GOLD*

Bishop, Joseph B., *Presidential Nominations and Elections.* Charles Scribner's Sons, New York, 1916.

Bryan, William Jennings, *A Tale of Two Conventions.* Funk & Wagnalls Company, New York, 1902.

———— and Bryan, M. E., *Memoirs of William Jennings Bryan.* John C. Winston Co., Philadelphia, 1925.

Chicago *Chronicle,* July 25, 1896.

Kansas City *Star,* July 19, 1896.

Lincoln, Nebraska *Call,* August 8, 1896.

Louisville *Courier-Journal,* July 16, 1896.

Masters, Edgar Lee, "The Christian Statesman." *American Mercury,* New York, December 1924.

New York *Sun,* September 29, 1896.

Pearce, Eugene L., *Statesmen and Gadflies.* Privately published, Clearwater, Florida, 1930.

St. Louis *Post-Dispatch,* September 30, 1896.

Whichen, George F., *William Jennings Bryan and the Campaign of 1896.* McNaught, New York, 1897.

UNPUBLISHED

Samuel P. Martin's adventure in eavesdropping on the telegraphed dispatch of the "Cross of Gold" speech is recounted by Dr. Samuel P. Martin, III, formerly provost for medicine, University of Florida, and currently a member of the faculty of Harvard Medical School, Boston.

Interviews: William Jennings Bryan, Jr., 1965; Mary Elizabeth Bryan Allen, 1959; William Allen White, 1938; Lemuel Parton, 1949.

Letters: Grace Bryan Hargreaves Manuscripts, Bryan Collection, Library of Congress, and the two significant letters owned by the late William Allen White—Edgar Lee Masters to White, September 1, 1920 and Bryan to White, June 1, 1923.

CHAPTER 14. *REMEMBER THE* MAINE!

Associated Press, "Bryan the Soldier." Jacksonville, Florida, August 11, 1898.

Bryan, William Jennings and M. E., *Memoirs of William Jennings Bryan.* John C. Winston Co., Philadelphia, 1925.

Freidel, Frank B., *The Splendid Little War.* Little, Brown & Co., Boston, 1958.

Jane, Fred T., *All The World's Fighting Ships.* Harper, New York, 1901.

Lee, Fitzhugh, *Under the Flag and In the Open.* Privately published, Omaha, 1903.

Lincoln, Nebraska *Call,* July 5, 1898.

Lincoln, Nebraska *Evening News,* June 3 and 13, 1898.

Lincoln, Nebraska *State Journal,* July 2 and December 14 and 26, 1898.

Little Rock, Arkansas *Gazette,* "Bryan and the Silver Regiment," September 3, 1898.

New York *Times,* June 3, July 4 and 5, and August 19, 1898.

Omaha, Nebraska *Bee-News,* May 31 and July 2, 1898.

Omaha, Nebraska, *World-Herald,* February 11, May 1, and July 2, 1898.

Pershing, John Joseph, *Under Fire with the Tenth Cavalry.* Rand-McNally, Chicago, 1902.

Roosevelt, Theodore, *The Rough Riders.* Charles Scribner's Sons, New York, 1902.

Scarborough, F. C., "Bryan the Soldier." Kansas City *Star,* January 4, 1917.

Senn, Nicholas, M.D., "Disease in the Military Establishment." *Journal of the American Medical Association,* Chicago, October 1898.

UNPUBLISHED

Scrapbook, Mary Elizabeth Bryan Allen, Lincoln, Nebraska.

Letters: F. C. Swartz, "Journal of the Silver Regiment"; Bryan-Talbot correspondence, 1898 (Bryan Papers, Library of Congress).

CHAPTER 15. *HURRAH FOR TOMORROW*

Bryan, William Jennings, *Bryan on Imperialism.* Chicago, 1900.

———— *The Philippines Question (Independence).* Chicago, April, 1899.

———— *Republic or Empire.* Chicago, 1899.

———— *Second Battle, Or the New Declaration of Independence.* McConkey, Chicago, 1900.

———— and Bryan, M. E., *Memoirs of William Jennings Bryan.* John C. Winston Co., Philadelphia, 1925.

Lincoln, Nebraska *State Journal,* January 2 and 18, February 19, and July 1–24, 1900.

St. Louis *Post-Dispatch,* July 1–November 6, 1900.

Sedgwick, Ellery, "Bryan." *Atlantic Monthly,* Vol. CX, No. 3, pp. 803–14, Boston, Mass. (also issue of September 1912).

Thompson, Charles Willis, *Presidents I've Known and Two Near Presidents.* Bobbs-Merrill Company, Indianapolis, 1929.

Webster's Collegiate Dictionary, 1900 Edition, Springfield, Mass.

White, William Allen, "Bryan the Progressive." *McClure's Magazine,* Vol. XV, No. 3, New York, July 1900.

UNPUBLISHED

Letters: Bryan to A. Talbot, October 3, 1900 (Silas Bryan, II Collection). William Allen White to author, August 6 and October 20, 1939.

CHAPTER 16. *FAIR VIEW*

Barnes, Harry Elmer, *Genesis of the World War.* Alfred A. Knopf, Inc., New York, 1927.

Bishop, Joseph B., *Theodore Roosevelt and His Time shown in his own letters.* Charles Scribner's Sons, New York, 1920.

Bryan, William Jennings, "British Rule in India." An Address published by the Indian National Congress, Westminster, England, 1906.

────── *Bryan on Japan.* Japan Society, New York, 1909.

────── "The Coming of the University." University of Indiana Bulletin VI, Bloomington, 1908.

────── "Thou Shall Not Steal." An Address, Civic Forum, New York, 1908.

────── and Bryan, M. E., *Memoirs of William Jennings Bryan.* John C. Winston Co., Philadelphia, 1925.

Causy, J. L., *The London Correspondent.* Macmillan, New York, 1909.

The Commoner, Vol. 1, Lincoln, Nebraska, 1901.

Guthrie, Oklahoma *Daily Leader,* June 26 and July 18 and 20, 1895.

New York *Times,* December 23, 1907.

New York *Sun,* August 30, 1906.

Rosser, Charles McDaniel, *The Crusading Commoner.* Mathis, Van Nort & Co., Dallas, 1937.

Tuttle, C. R., *The New Democracy and Bryan Its Prophet.* McConkey, Chicago, 1900.

Willey, Malcolm and Stuart A. Rice, *William Jennings Bryan as a Social Force.* Crowell, New York, 1924.

UNPUBLISHED

Papers and Reminiscences of Alfred M. Wilson, executive officer, Governors Commission, Oklahoma and Indian Territories, 1877–1900.

CHAPTER 17. *THE CHALLENGER AND THE CHALLENGED*

Bartholomew, H. E., *Bryan Unveiled.* Privately published, Chicago, 1908.

Bryan, William Jennings, "The Old World and Its Ways." *The Commoner,* Lincoln, Nebraska, 1907.

―――― *World Peace: A Written Debate Between William Jennings Bryan and William Howard Taft.* Forum Press, New York, 1917.

―――― and Bryan, M. E., *Memoirs of William Jennings Bryan.* John C. Winston Co., Philadelphia, 1925.

The Commoner, Lincoln, Nebraska, issues of April, May, and June 1908 and January 1911.

Daniels, Josephus, "Behind the Scenes with William Jennings Bryan." Daniels Papers, 1921, Library of Congress.

New York *Herald,* July 30, 1908.

New York *Sun,* July 30, 1908.

New York *Times,* February 16, 1908.

Washington *Star,* March 8, 1911.

Werner, Morris Robert, *Bryan.* Harcourt, Brace & Co., New York, 1927.

UNPUBLISHED

Interviews: William Jennings Bryan, Jr., 1965.

Seven letters: William Allen White to author, 1936.

CHAPTER 18. *THE SECRETARY OF STATE*

Bryan, William Jennings, "America and the European War." Emergency Peace Federation, New York, 1917.

―――― "The Causeless War and Its Lesson for Us." Commoner Press, Lincoln, 1915.

―――― "Citizenship in a Republic." An Address, National Educational Association, Washington, 1916.

―――― *Heart to Heart Appeals: Speeches Delivered 1890–1916.* Revell, New York, 1917.

―――― "Remarks of Secretary of State William Jennings Bryan Before the California Legislature of 1913." Sacramento, 1913.

―――― and Bryan, M. E., Memoirs of William Jennings Bryan. John C. Winston Co., Philadelphia, 1925.

The Commoner, Lincoln, Nebraska, issues of May, June, July, August, and September 1913.

Dunn, Arthur Wallace, *How Presidents Are Made.* Funk & Wagnalls Company, New York, 1920.

House, Edward Mandell, *Intimate Papers;* arranged as a narrative by Charles Seymour. Houghton Mifflin Company, Boston, 1926.

Houston, David F., *Eight Years with Wilson's Cabinet, 1913–1920.* Doubleday, Doran & Company, Inc., Garden City, New York, 1926.

Literary Digest, July 26, 1913.

New York *Times,* July 21, 1913 and October 3, 1914.

St. Louis *Post-Dispatch,* August 6, 1914.

Washington *Post,* March 4 and 5 and May 3, 1913.

UNPUBLISHED

Interviews: Mary Elizabeth Bryan Allen, Senator Joseph T. Robinson, William Allen White.

Letters: Wilson to Bryan, Wilson Papers, Box 356, IV, National Archives, including Bryan to Wilson, October 13, 1913; Bryan to Wilson, July 11, 1914 (Silas Bryan, II Collection), including D. Bride to B. E. Burleson, undated.

CHAPTER 19. *THE AMBIGUOUS PEACE SEEKER*

Baker, R. S., *Woodrow Wilson and the World Settlement.* Vol. V, Doubleday, Page & Co., Garden City, New York, 1922.

Barnes, Harry Elmer, *Genesis of the World War.* Alfred A. Knopf, Inc., New York, 1927.

Bernstorff, Johann H. A. H. A., graf von, *My Three Years in America.* Charles Scribner's Sons, New York, 1920.

Bryan, William Jennings and M. E., *Memoirs of William Jennings Bryan.* John C. Winston Co., Philadelphia, 1925.

Chicago *Tribune,* August 3, 1916.

Clark, Champ (James Beauchamp), *My Quarter Century of American Politics.* Harper & Brothers, New York, 1920.

Daniels, Josephus, "Wilson and Bryan." *The Saturday Evening Post,* Vol. CXCVIII, pp. 34–38+, Philadelphia, September 5, 1925.

Horner Charles F., *Strike the Tents.* Doran, Philadelphia, 1938.

Houston, David F., *Eight Years with Wilson's Cabinet, 1913–1920.* Doubleday, Doran & Company, Inc., Garden City, New York, 1926.

Kent, Frank R., *The Democratic Party.* D. Appleton-Century Company, Inc., New York, 1928.

Levine, Lawrence W., *Defender of the Faith: William Jennings Bryan; The Last Decade, 1915–1925.* Oxford University Press, New York, 1965.

Lincoln, Nebraska *State Journal,* July 1, 1915; November 6, 1916; and February 4 and 23 and March 10, 1917.

London *Express,* May 8, 1915.

Long, J. C., *Bryan, The Great Commoner.* D. Appleton-Century Company, Inc., New York, 1928.

McAdoo, William Gibbs, *Crowded Years.* Houghton Mifflin Company, Boston, 1931.

Millis, Walter, *Road to War: America, 1914–1917.* Houghton Mifflin Company, Boston, 1935.

New York *Times,* April 21, 1915; August 23, 1916; and April 7, 1917.

New York *World,* June 10, 1915.

White, Morton G., *Social Thought in America.* Beacon Press, Inc., Boston, 1957.

UNPUBLISHED

Interviews: William Hope Harvey, October 1926; Charles F. Horner, June 1960.

Letters: Bryan to Wilson, April 19, 1915 and May 12, 1915, Vol. IX, National Archives, Washington; Wilson to Bryan, June 8, 1915; Wilson to House, December 3, 1916, Wilson Papers, Box 491, National Archives.

CHAPTER 20. *THE PATRIOT*

Arkansas *Gazette,* Little Rock, December 18, 1916.

Bryan, William Jennings, "Why I Am a Prohibitionist." *The Independent,* Vol. LXXXXVII, No. 11, pp. 9–11, New York, July 17, 1916.

—— and Bryan, M. E., *Memoirs of William Jennings Bryan.* John C. Winston Co., Philadelphia, 1925.

The Commoner, Lincoln, Nebraska, issues of June and July 1916 and August and December 1917.

Krout, John Allen, *Origins of Prohibition.* Alfred A. Knopf, New York, 1925.

Levine, Lawrence W., *Defender of the Faith: William Jennings Bryan; The Last Decade, 1915–1925.* Oxford University Press, New York, 1965.

Milwaukee *Journal,* April 21, 1914.

New York *Sun,* December 17, 1917.

New York *Times,* April 17, 1917; February 27 and April 14, 1918; and March 12, 1919.

New York *World,* November 1, 1918.

Sullivan, Mark, *Our Times; the United States, 1900–1925*. Vol. V, Charles Scribner's Sons, New York, 1929.
Washington *Post*, New York, 1929.

UNPUBLISHED

Letters: Bryan to Mary B. Bryan, February 27, 1919; to Richard Hargreaves, March 1, 1919; to Charles W. Bryan, March 7, 1919; Bride to Charles W. Bryan, March 1, 1919 (Silas Bryan, II Collection); Wilson to J. Tumulty, January 15, 1918, File VI, Box 491, Wilson Papers.

CHAPTER 21. *THE CLASSICAL CORN*

Bryan, William Jennings and M. E., *Memoirs of William Jennings Bryan*. John C. Winston Co., Philadelphia, 1925.
Chicago *Tribune*, January 8, 1920.
Cleveland *Plain Dealer*, March 14, 1917.
The Commoner, Lincoln, Nebraska, issues of July and October 1920, March 1921, and November 1922.
Lansing, Robert, *The Lansing Diaries*. Bobbs-Merrill Company, Indianapolis, 1935.
Lincoln, Nebraska *State Journal*, August 9, 1920.
Link, Arthur S., "What Happened to the Progressive Movement of the 1920s?" *Journal of the American Historical Society*, July 1959.
Literary Digest, January 31 and June 12, 1920.
New York *Times*, March 17 and July 1 and 6, 1920.
New York *World*, June 27, 1920.

UNPUBLISHED

Letters: Bryan to Wilson, January 15, 1918, Box 191, File 6, Wilson Papers; Bryan to McAdoo, December 29, 1917, Box 491, File VI, Wilson Papers; Bryan to McAdoo, June 27, 1916, Box 161, McAdoo Papers, Library of Congress; Bryan to Charles W. Bryan, July 22, 1922; to E. D. Lambeth, April 20, 1923; to A. Talbot, November 5, 1923, Silas Bryan, II Collection; Bryan's "Defense of Jewry" Letters, Bailey Library, University of Vermont, 1920–21.

CHAPTER 22. *THE BELIEVER*

Bryan, William Jennings, "Bryan's Letter of Faith." *Christian Science Monitor*, Boston, May 3, 1924.
———— "The Fundamentalists." *Forum*, July 23, 1924.

———— *In His Image* (James Sprunt Lectures, 10th Series). Revell, New York, 1922.

———— "Is the Bible True?" An open letter, New York *Times,* April 25, 1925.

———— "Mr. Bryan's Nominating Speech." New York *Times,* June 23, 1924.

"Bryan: Delegate-at-Large." *Official Tabulations of the Florida Primary Election,* Tallahassee, 1924.

Frank, Glenn, "William Jennings Bryan: A Mind Divided Against Itself." *Century* Magazine, New York, pp. 109–117, September 1923.

Freidel, Frank B., *Franklin D. Roosevelt.* Little, Brown & Co., Boston, 1954.

Levine, Lawrence W., *Defender of the Faith: William Jennings Bryan; The Last Decade, 1915–1925.* Oxford University Press, New York, 1965.

New York *American,* June 23, 1924.

New York *Times,* March 22, 1923 and March 11, 1924.

White, William Allen, *Politics, The Citizen's Business.* Macmillan Company, New York, 1924.

UNPUBLISHED

Interviews: William Allen White, Emporia, Kansas, 1936; Senator Joseph T. Robinson, Washington, 1937; Mary Elizabeth Bryan Allen, Lincoln, 1959; William Jennings Bryan, Jr., Laguna Beach, California, 1965.

Letters: Bryan to R. L. Dean, March 11, 1925; to George Wyman, November 24, 1924; to G. D. Huddleston, March 30, 1923 (Occidental College Collection, Los Angeles); McAdoo to Gaven McNab, June 5, 1924 (McAdoo Papers, Box 305, Library of Congress); Dr. Kelley to Charles W. Bryan, February 15, 1924; Charles W. Bryan to J. P. Class, May 13, 1924; Charles W. Bryan to Bryan, May 19, 1924 (Silas Bryan, II Collection, Lincoln).

CHAPTER 23. *THY PEOPLE—MY PEOPLE*

Allen, Leslie Henri, ed. and comp., *Bryan and Darrow at Dayton.* A. Lee & Company, New York, 1925.

Bailey, Kenneth M., "The Enactment of the Tennessee Anti-Evolutionary Law." *Journal of Southern History,* Vol. XVI, Nashville Tenn., November, 1950.

Bryan, William Jennings, "The Layman's Faith." An Address,

Transcript of the Ecumenical Christian Conference, Edinburgh, May 11, 1912.

―――― *The Last Message of William Jennings Bryan.* Associated Press, June 26–27, New York, 1925.

―――― Bryan Memorial Association, *Minutes of Dedication,* a Brochure. Washington, 1934.

Chattanooga *Daily Times,* July 18, 1925.

Coletta, Paolo E., *William Jennings Bryan.* University of Nebraska Press, Lincoln, Nebraska, 1964.

Darrow, Clarence Seward, *Story of My Life.* Charles Scribner's Sons, New York, 1932.

Ginger, Ray, *Six Days or Forever? Tenn. vs. John Thomas Scopes.* Houghton Mifflin Company, Boston, 1925.

Hays, Arthur Garfield, *Let Freedom Ring.* Liveright Publishing Corp., New York, 1928.

Kemler, Edgar, *Irreverent Mr. Mencken* (Atlantic Monthly Press Book). Little, Brown & Company, Boston, 1950.

Krutch, Joseph Wood, "Tennessee, Where Cowards Rule." The *Nation,* pp. 134–37, Vol. CXXI, No. 8, July 15, 1925.

Levine, Lawrence W., *Defender of the Faith: William Jennings Bryan; The Last Decade, 1915–1925.* Oxford University Press, New York, 1965.

Mencken, Henry Louis, *Happy Day 1880–1892.* Alfred A. Knopf, Inc., New York, 1940.

Noteworthy Books Relating to

William Jennings Bryan

Adams, C. F., *An Autobiography, 1835–1915*. Boston, 1919.

Allen, Leslie H., *Bryan and Darrow at Dayton*. New York, 1925.

Barnes, Harry Elmer, *Genesis of the World War*. New York, 1929.

Barr, Mary E., *Kansas and Kansans*, Vol. II. Emporia, 1917.

Bartholomew, Harry E., *Bryan Unveiled*. Chicago, 1908.

Beard, Charles and Mary, *The Rise of American Civilization*. New York, 1927.

Beard, Charles A., *Contemporary American History*. New York, 1914.

Bernstorff, Count Johann von, *My Three Years in America*. New York, 1920.

Bishop, Joseph B., *Presidential Nominations and Elections*. New York, 1916.

——, *Theodore Roosevelt and His Times*. New York, 1920.

Boechel, Richard, *Labor's Money*. New York, 1922.

Brown, John H., *Bryan, Sewell and Honest Money Will Bring Prosperity*. New York, 1896.

Chadwick, F. E., *The Relations of the United States and Spain*. New York, 1911.

Coletta, Paola E., *William Jennings Bryan*. University of Nebraska Press, 1966.

Clark, Champ, *My Quarter Century in American Politics*. New York, 1921.

Cole, Arthur C., "The Era of the Civil War." *Contemporary History of Illinois*, Vol. III, pp. 171–79. 1919, Springfield.

Croly, Herbert, *Marcus Alonzo Hanna*. New York, 1919.

Davis, Hayne, *Bryan Among the Peace Makers*. New York, 1906.

Dunn, Arthur Wallace, *How Presidents Are Made*. New York, 1920.

Glad, Paul W., *The Trumpet Soundeth, William Jennings Bryan and His Democracy*. Lincoln, Nebraska, 1964.

Griffith, Will, *The Great Commoner, William Jennings Bryan*. Carbondale, Illinois, 1908.

Harvey, William Hope, *Coin's Financial School*. Chicago, 1894.

Hayes, A. B. and S. D. Cox, *History of Lincoln, Nebraska*. Lincoln, 1890.

Hays, Arthur Garfield, *Let Freedom Ring*. New York, 1928.

Herrick, Genevieve and John, *Life of William Jennings Bryan*. Chicago, 1925.

Hibben, Paxton, *The Peerless Leader*. New York, 1929.

Hicks, John D., *The Populist Revolt*. Minneapolis, 1931.

House, Edward M., *Intimate Papers of Edward M. House*, edited by Charles M. Seymour. Boston, 1926.

Houston, David F., *Eight Years with the Wilson Cabinet*. Garden City, 1926.

Kent, Frank Richardson, *The Democratic Party*. New York, 1928.

Levine, Lawrence W., *Defender of the Faith: William Jennings Bryan; The Last Decade, 1915–1925*. New York, 1965.

Long, J. C., *Bryan, the Great Commoner*. New York, 1928.

Mahon, John C., *Answer to Bryan on Evolution*. New York, 1922.

Merriam, Charles Edward, *Four American Leaders*. New York, 1926.

Osborn, Henry Fairfield, *The Earth Speaks to Bryan*. New York, 1925.

———, *Evolution and Religion in Education*. New York, 1926.

Pearce, Eugene L., *Statesmen and Gadflies*. New York, 1930.

Rosser, Charles McDaniel, *The Crusading Commoner*. Dallas, 1957.

Smith, T. V., *Basis of Bryanism*. Utica, 1933.

Stoddard, H. L., *As I Knew Them: Presidents and Politicians from Grant to Coolidge*. New York, 1927.

Sullivan, Mark, *Our Times*. New York, 1927.

Thompson, Charles Willis, *Presidents I've Known and Two Near Presidents*. Indianapolis, 1929.

Tuttle, C. R., *The New Democracy and Bryan, Its Prophet.* Chicago, 1896.

Warren, S., *The Pathology of Diabetes Mellitus.* Philadelphia, 1958.

Whedon, Charles O., *Mr. Bryan and His Platform.* Lincoln, Nebraska, 1900.

Whicher, George Frisbie, *William Jennings Bryan and the Campaign of 1896.* Boston, 1953.

Willey, Malcolm and Stuart A. Rice, *William Jennings Bryan as a Social Force.* New York, 1924.

Williams, Wayne Cutter, *William Jennings Bryan: A Study in Vindication.* New York, 1923.

———, *William Jennings Bryan.* New York, 1934.

INDEX